WRITING FOR THE BROADCAST MEDIA

WRITING FOR
THE BROADCAST MEDIA

PETER E. MAYEUX

The University of Nebraska–Lincoln

ALLYN AND BACON, INC.
Boston   London   Sydney   Toronto

Managing Editor: Bill Barke
Production Administrator: Jane Schulman
Editorial-Production Services: Harkavy Publishing Service
Interior Design: Harkavy Publishing Service/Chris Simon
Cover Coordinator: Christy Rosso
Cover Design: Graphics Plus

Library of Congress Cataloging in Publication Data

Mayeux, Peter E.
    Writing for the broadcast media.

    Includes bibliographies and index.
    1. Broadcasting—Authorship. I. Title.
PN1990.9.A88M39 1985   808′.066791   85-1358

ISBN: 0-205-08343-9

Printed in the United States of America.

10 9 8 7 6 5 4 3 2 1 90 89 88 87 86 85

808.02

77351

This book is dedicated to the many writers who strive to improve the quality of the broadcast media and who continually seek an increased measure of professional satisfaction. It is hoped that this book serves as a useful guide for the development of sound standards of professionalism and craftsmanship, a renewed sense of ethics and responsibility, and an enhanced spirit of creativity, inquisitiveness, and determination to serve better the challenging demands of today's broadcast audiences.

P.M.

CONTENTS

PREFACE

The importance and influence of the broadcast media continue to grow in today's society. Because of their accelerating level of sophistication, today's viewer and listener demand more from mass media outlets. This creates new challenges for those who design, create, and produce the program material available to millions.

From networks to local stations, major studios to small corporate production units, commercial copywriters to news reporters, dramatists to editorialists, effective and professional writing skills form one of the bases of the growing telecommunications media. Clear, concise, positive writing skills contribute noticeably to the overall efforts of virtually every facet of the industry.

This book is intended to be a concise but thorough introduction to the basic approaches and techniques for the principal forms of writing for the broadcast media. Before this book was written, several objectives were formulated to better identify its scope and focus. The principal objectives of this book are: to provide a basic study of the scripting forms, approaches, and techniques used to write effective broadcast script material; to instill an awareness of the role and responsibility of the writer, with emphasis on the audience, content and impact of the broadcast media; to apply the production and business principles of the broadcasting industry to the design and preparation of effective script material; and to emphasize and describe the process involved in writing for the broadcast media.

There are several noteworthy features about this book: special chapters and chapter sections have been included to examine topics and material not fully explored or illustrated in similar books (e.g., mini-documentaries, promotional announcements, industrial and corporate presentations, nationally syndicated programs, made-for-television movies and writer-related production techniques and terminology); script material has been integrated into the chapters in full and complete form to supplement basic descriptions and to better illustrate writing styles and techniques in a meaningful and stimulating manner; professional broadcast writing processes and practices are illustrated by a varied selection of script material from professionals within the broadcasting industry, from networks, local stations, production companies, advertising agencies, newsrooms, and national program syndicators; and at the end of each chapter, suggested exercises, projects, assignments, and additional readings related to the topics discussed provide additional writing practice and information.

The first three chapters of this book provide essential, introductory information about broadcast writing and serve as a foundation for the chapters that follow. For example, standard broadcast scripting formats are illustrated in one place, in Chapter 3, to help the reader understand basic scripting forms and to serve as a reference when various types of writing situations are examined in later chapters.

This book is designed for use in a one-semester course or in a two-semester course sequence. If used in a two-semester course sequence, the introductory chapters and the shorter writing forms (e.g., commercials and announcements, talk programs, music and variety programs, news and sports copy, and editorials and commentaries) could be examined in the first course. The longer and more intricate broadcast writing forms (e.g., documentaries and investigative reports, dramas and comedies, and instructional/educational/industrial/corporate presentations) could be studied in the second course sequence.

Several chapters in this book would be appropriate for specialized instruction and course work. Portions of this book may be used without the need for continual or direct classroom supervision.

This book can be used by writers from divergent backgrounds, possessing different levels of writing proficiency. Certainly, fundamental English grammar and composition skills are needed. And it would be helpful, but not required, to have some background or prior experience in mass media work, basic broadcast production, or print journalism.

Both for those pursuing careers as broadcast writers and for those wanting to expand their writing capabilities and secure more extensive job mobility, this book offers the opportunity to acquire the basic and necessary skills to accomplish such goals. Both the veteran and novice broadcast writer can use this book to sharpen and refine skills and techniques to broaden their job potential within the industry. Those who have written for other media, especially newspapers and magazines, will find that this book provides the basics for this specialized form of writing.

ACKNOWLEDGMENTS

A special note of gratitude is extended to Lew Hunter for his helpful advice, suggestions and encouragement. For their tireless efforts in obtaining script material, the author thanks Todd G. Smith (KIRO TV, Seattle), J. D. Hansen (NBC Sports), Donald E. Browers (KMTV, Omaha) and Frank Hyland (CNN Radio).

The author wishes to thank the following individuals and organizations for their assistance in obtaining script material and providing information for use in this book: Deb Kneip McDermott, Ron Hull, Sean McManus, Linda Jonsson, John Dixon, Jack Hurley, Robin Hughes, John Burns, Rich Adams, Marjorie M. Arons-Barron, Burt Reinhardt, CBS News, Bill Moyers, NBC News and Entertainment, John Chancellor, Richard P. Gitter, Kay Henderson, Carl Trunk, Jenét Dechary, the Mutual Broadcasting System, Tom O'Brien, The Public Broadcasting Service, Michael E. Hobbs, Harry Harding and Dick Gage of the National Broadcast Editorial Association, Jeff Hanson, Steve M. Meyers, Pat Ryan, Bill Danch, Bob Furman, Jacques Chevron and Chuck Werle of Leo Burnett Company, Inc., J. Alexander Strautman of Mutual of Omaha, Gary C. Grahnquist of Neiman-Marcus, Fred Bergendorff, Paul Nichols, Tony Novia, Dale Baglo, Ted Pound, Bob Casazza, Susie Whetstone, Lucy Antek Johnson, Noreen Friend, Francine Bergman, Bob Stewart, Dan Enright, Mark Goodson, Betsy Haney, Bob Concie, Kenny Bosak, Marty Pasetta, Rick Alloway, Chuck Stevens, Jay Rodriguez, Peter Calabrese, Danny Arnold, Bruce Davis, Rod Bates, Richard H. James, Chris Carmody, Randall Haag, David L. White, Ron Tillery, Kayte Kuch, Gene Fogel, Cliff Chase, Rubin Reibel, Eleanor Riger, Dale Holt, Shimon Wincelberg, W. W. Lewis, Linda Gottlieb, Burt Metcalfe, Arlene Sherman, Jeffrey M. Goldstein, Mike McCann, Sandra Walker, Tom Walch, Mike Feduk, Sandra Cowley, Gene Thomas, Richard Friedenberg, Marshall Jamison, A. Thomas Spann, Steven L. Carter, Patricia Lehecka, Lana Crockett Weldon, Gloria Jatczak, Suzie Sybouts, Julie Snyder, International Television Association, and Great Plains National Instructional Television Library. Other contributors of script material are indicated throughout the chapters of this book.

All of these individuals and organizations will not necessarily agree with everything contained in this book. And, obviously, none of them is responsible for errors, omissions or opinions expressed by the author.

The author thanks the following for the advice and assistance provided in reviewing and preparing the manuscript for publication: Bill Barke (Senior Editor) and Jane J. Schulman (Production Administrator) of Allyn and Bacon, Inc.; Madelaine Cooke and Maria Chiarino (Managing Editors) and Donn Teal (Copy Chief) of Harkavy Publishing Service; W. Joseph Oliver, Department of Communications, Stephen F. Austin State University; and ElDean Bennett, Department of Mass Communications, Arizona State University.

A special thanks is extended to my wife, Sue and my son, Ben for their patience during this extended project.

WRITING FOR
THE BROADCAST MEDIA

Chapter One

INTRODUCTION TO WRITING
FOR THE BROADCAST MEDIA

A professional broadcast writer is a skilled craftsman shaping ideas and concepts into words and sentences that eventually will be shared by an immense audience. It is a challenging profession that requires a special kind of person and a unique set of writing skills. For such a writer, there is nothing that matches the satisfaction and exhilaration experienced when ideas come together on paper and, eventually, are transformed into a broadcast that touches thousands of lives directly. That is the challenge offered to the novice broadcast writer—to develop the insights, skills and techniques needed to write effective broadcast script material. And that is the intent of this book—to provide basic information about how to write various kinds of script material for the broadcast media. It is hoped that mastering these skills and techniques will invigorate your writing experience.

This first chapter will help you understand and appreciate the role, responsibility and activities of the broadcast writer in today's media. The essential qualifications needed to become a broadcast writer are discussed so that you can assess your abilities and interests as a writer. Next, the role and function of the writer are examined to emphasize the impact a broadcast writer can have. Then, the resources needed to function as a broadcast writer are outlined. Finally, laws, regulations, and concerns which affect the work of the broadcast writer are examined to stress the need to develop a deep, professional sense of ethics and responsibility and to help avoid common legal and ethical problems. The principal purpose of this chapter is to help the reader understand and appreciate the work and concerns of the professional broadcast writer. The books, as well as the suggested exercises and projects listed at the end of this chapter and all other chapters, expand upon the information provided here.

QUALIFICATIONS OF THE WRITER

Formal training or education to understand and develop effective broadcast writing skills is not necessarily a prerequisite for success; however, such an undertaking is recommended. Interests that you may have acquired earlier in life can be developed with supervision and direction using established criteria and forms to sharpen the necessary skills and techniques. Such training or formal instruction may not necessarily create a passion for writing, but could develop and expand your talent.

Diversified experience in the telecommunications media as well as in life provides a solid basis for the aspiring writer. Internship or part-time experience in a broadcast facility usually provides an interesting perspective on the internal workings of the mass media. Your life experiences—part-time jobs in school, the loss of a close friend or relative, your hopes and disappointments, the first time you drove a car, your first date—all combine to provide you with a unique perspective from which to write. The more you know about various life experiences, the better your writing will be.

A good writer is a lover of words—their meanings, innuendos, emotional impact, nuances. Examine carefully the use of words in great literature. Experience the satisfaction that comes from finding the right combination of words to inform clearly, entertain creatively, and to influence with purpose and emotion the attitudes and behavior of others.

The writer is a conscious observer. Develop a sense of curiosity, inquisitiveness, and sensitivity to people and events outside your own world. Develop the ability to project yourself into the lives of those around you. Learn to observe, retain, and then use the gestures, mannerisms, and language habits of those around you so that you can write in the personal, conversational style expected of the broadcast writer. Never stop seeing, listening, feeling, questioning, and probing to explore the wonders and intricacies of the human experience in your writing. This insatiable desire to know, understand, and experience the human spirit is a lifelong learning commitment and adventure.

The writer must be creative. There must be continual development of the ability to communicate—visually, aurally, as well as on paper. The creative person must attempt to reexperience human emotions and situations with clarity and inventiveness. In short, the writer must cultivate a creative spirit that enriches reality with imagination and presents it in an especially effective manner.

The writer must also be realistic and practical. Although it is admirable to reach for lofty, creative goals, this must be tempered with the reality and practicality of the situation. Understand and appreciate the constraints of budgets, deadlines, and technical limitations and know how they influence the writer's work.

An effective broadcast writer knows the intricacies and requirements of the media. A thorough sense of what is acceptable now and what might be possible in the future is essential. Critically evaluate the current product of the media for form, style, conceptualization, visualization, communicative effectiveness, use of language.

Writing is work. Good writing is hard work. An unidentified wise man, certainly an experienced writer, once said: "The art of writing is the art of applying the seat of the pants to the seat of the chair." A writer does not suddenly create material because of a flash of inspiration. A good writer works at it, writing something every day. This applies to broadcast writing as well as to writing in general. Establish a routine or schedule for your writing. Discipline your mind and body to the rigors of writing.

Deadlines for broadcast writers are demanding, exacting. Program material is consumed by radio, television, and motion picture audiences more quickly and with less regard than perhaps by other media. To meet unforgiving deadlines with quality material requires rigorous discipline by the writer. You must be creative and imaginative every hour of every day that you work. And if you are a good writer, your work never stops. It becomes an inseparable part of your life.

A good writer displays flexibility in attitudes, work habits, and writing skills. Many effective writers for the broadcast media began their writing careers in other media—poetry, playwriting, newspapers, magazines. The basics of effective writing are essential and applicable to all media. The demands of the broadcasting industry often require a commercial copywriter, for example, to create an award-winning announcement in less than thirty minutes. The outline for an interview with an important governmental official may have to be written at 6 A.M. on a Monday for use on an early-morning broadcast. Often, the best writing is done under pressure, something the broadcasting industry has accepted as reality.

Good writing requires commitment—to yourself and to your unseen audience. You must want to write. The urgent need to express yourself through writing must already be in place. The desire and willingness to share and express, in a meaningful way, your knowledge, observations, feelings, and discoveries must be important to you and to those for whom you write. Without this total commitment and the resultant discipline, your measure of success and satisfaction as a writer will be limited.

You must have confidence in your ability to write. You must be determined to succeed despite the likelihood of criticism and rejection of your work. Others will criticize your writing, some with malice and others in a sincere effort to make your creative work even better. The amount and degree of criticism and rejection that you receive often hinge on what you expect of yourself. Give yourself and your unseen audience only the best that you have, now and in the future.

The writer must establish goals and objectives. Establish a "game plan." What kind of writing work do you want to be doing three years from now? Five years from now? And then, how will you get there from here? What path of professional development will you follow? Without a specific career goal, you cannot develop a sense of direction and purpose and cannot measure your success and progress. Since so much of your success as a writer depends on your own efforts, realistic and challenging goals (both personal and professional) become essential.

The writer must be organized. It is often necessary to create order out of chaos, to take a large volume of information and condense it into a short, informative, effective announcement or program. A sense of orderliness about life-style, goals, and ambitions helps the writer to produce quality work and to remain alert for the business aspects of the writing profession.

The work of the broadcast writer requires a strong commitment and desire to communicate and to share human experiences with others. This commitment—coupled with some measure of talent, a fascination for words, discipline, persistence, flexibility, knowledge of the media, maturity, integrity, energy, and unshakable confidence in the ability to touch other lives in a special, interesting, and meaningful way—combines to provide a unique, challenging, and rewarding life.

ROLE AND FUNCTION OF THE BROADCAST WRITER

Perhaps the words of an unidentified writer spoken some time ago best express the nature of writing:

> I'm only a writer . . . I deal in the politics of words . . . of human experiences . . . of dreams . . . of sadness. When I am at my best my pages laugh and sing and they also cry. When I'm at my worst my pages wait impatiently for me to make them come alive . . . to add layers of texture and shading until my pages become dimensional . . . I'm a painter. I'm a composer. I'm a rabble rouser . . . a provocateur. I'm a patriot. I'm the enemy. I wave the flag. And sometimes I hide from it. I'm a tender lover . . . I'm a hard bargainer. I'm sweet and innocent. I'm hardened and brutal.
>
> I'm a writer. This is my world. Welcome to it. It's a world filled with the unpredictable . . . with blind spots and dead ends . . . with straight lines which out of nowhere, it seems, suddenly change direction. It's a world of ethics and erotica . . . pathos and pleasure . . . and the writer sits in the middle of all this confusion like a sponge being soaked and squeezed . . . and if you really want to write you face a constant dilemma of values . . . yours and everyone else's.
>
> This is the writer's world . . . this is our world.

The writer is a prime mover. An effective radio or television program or announcement begins with the writer—thinking, dreaming, imagining, creating. While many processes and priorities interplay to mount and present a broadcast program or announcement, it is the writer who first generates an idea and then prepares material in a form which can be used by many others.

Maintaining standards of excellence should be important to the writer. Pride in your work means caring—what you do and how you do it. The pursuit and attainment of excellence bring with them the confidence and reassurance necessary to accept new challenges. Pressure to compromise standards, which often confronts the writer, can best be resolved from a position of strength, confidence, and quality.

Good writing has an impact—on the writer and on the audience. You should grow and develop as a writer and as a person each time you write. Writing can and should be a source of personal satisfaction as well as a contribution to the improvement of your world. If done well, your writing can have a significant impact upon the daily attitudes, habits and behavior of the audience. It can make them more aware of the world around them, establish or support social values and trends, perhaps even help standardize the use of language. Writing is a powerful tool that, when used ethically, professionally, and responsibly through the influential broadcast media, can inform, influence, and persuade large numbers of people.

RESOURCES OF THE BROADCAST WRITER

It is important to know the tools or resources available to the broadcast writer. They are a necessary part of the job. There will be a brief review of language and writing aids available to refine your expressiveness. The importance and benefits of membership in professional organizations will be discussed. Periodicals which enhance your writing ability and understanding of the broadcast media will be evaluated. And two essential resources, research and interviewing, will be examined since they both help the writer obtain information.

Language and Writing Aids

Two primary language aids which should be beside the writer at all times are a dictionary and a thesaurus. The dictionary will help you with the spelling and meaning of words. The thesaurus will help you find a synonym for a word you have used several times in the same script or if you get stuck and cannot think of a specific word to express yourself. An excellent dictionary is *Webster's Third New International Dictionary*. The latest edition of *Roget's Thesaurus of the English Language* is recommended.

Another item which should be added to your writing library is a reference book on English grammar and writing style. Although there are several excellent general reference works, three are recommended: *A Manual of Style*, 12th ed. (Chicago: The University of Chicago Press, 1969); John E. Warriner and Francis Griffith's *English Grammar and Composition* (New York: Harcourt, Brace and Company, 1957); and William Strunk, Jr., and E. B. White's *The Elements of Style*, 3rd ed. (New York: Macmillan Publishing Company, 1979). While there are specific writing styles and formats unique to broadcasting, which will be described in Chapter 3, this type of reference work will provide basic information on correct use of language in any medium.

A few tabletop items should be kept nearby: scratch pads, index cards, and inexpensive newsprint paper, or a similar item for making quick notes to yourself as you write and formulate your writing strategy. Ballpoint pens and sharpened pencils (heavy lead) complete your tabletop accessories, except as personal preference dictates.

It is essential to have access to a typewriter or a word processor. Although you may sketch out your thoughts or outline your ideas with a pencil and pad as you begin the creative process, your final product must be in typewritten form. It is an accepted, industry-wide requirement. If you cannot type or if you use the tedious "hunt-and-peck" method, your work as a serious, professional broadcast writer is limited. Clean, typewritten scripts are a mark of your professionalism. Your scripts represent you to those who read them. The typewriter most often used in professional scriptwriting is the IBM Selectric, which features a wide carriage and the Courier 72, 10 pitch element (10 characters per inch). Although this is the ideal typewriter to use, a sturdy and reliable manual or electric, tabletop or portable machine would be fine. It is important to use a good typewriter. Your typewriter is your lifeblood. Without it, you cannot hope to become or to remain a professional broadcast writer.

Microcomputers or word processors, customized for the special needs of the mass media, can be used instead of a typewriter to generate script material. Word processors do not help your creativity. That is still up to the writer. Writers who have used such systems, however, find that word processing expedites the writing, revision, and copying of scripts, increases the writer's efficiency, and cuts costs. An alternative to purchasing such a system is to lease a unit or to pay for word processing time at a central location.

Professional Associations and Related Periodicals

Professionals normally associate with other professionals, both in and out of their field. Such associations keep them in tune with the current attitudes and developments of those with similar interests and concerns. It enhances their skills and provides perspective on constantly changing situations affecting all professionals in that field. Often, it is a means of formulating specific positions on issues and events.

One way to formalize this professional attitude is to participate in the activities of professional associations or organizations that relate directly to your work. Often these groups publish material periodically that serves both as an internal organ for the membership and as a means of fulfilling some of the objectives indicated earlier. Many professional writers find the benefits and services provided by such memberships far outweigh any costs and inconveniences that may be involved.

Because the broadcasting industry changes and adjusts so rapidly to contemporary demands, many professional writers find it essential to subscribe to one or more periodicals that keep them informed about developments. These subscriptions would be in addition to those provided as part of membership in a professional organization. A broadcast writer must also be a reader of industry news and the trade press. It is part of the job. Often, it becomes the source for a writing assignment.

Appendix A provides a selected list of professional associations that relate to writing for the broadcast media. Appendix B is a selected list of media periodicals. Your review. and use of both lists is encouraged. They provide a measurement of your commitment to professionalism as a writer for the broadcast media.

Research

There are several reference works that provide a more comprehensive and standardized discussion of formal research procedures and techniques. This brief discussion stresses the importance of research and outlines the primary methods used to gather information to complete broadcast writing assignments.

Research is vital to good writing. Without research, the writer cannot present information that is accurate and applicable to the audience being addressed. Research helps the writer know more about a particular subject. It helps uncover information that can provide depth and texture as well as fuel for inspiration and creativity.

It is important to let the kind of information you need determine the nature and scope of your research. For example, if you are preparing a television drama about an older widow who faces the problems of making ends meet, you certainly would want to read material on that topic; but you would also want to talk to people in that situation, observe their habits and mannerisms, listen to their concerns, and then formulate a gripping plot that features lifelike characters in realistic situations, facing problems you now know and share intimately. The effectiveness of the script will hinge on the way you have used the information you gathered.

There are several ways or methods for the broadcast writer to gather information. These include the following:

* *Reading.* This involves finding, digesting, organizing, and retaining information from written sources such as books, magazines, catalogs, and collections. It is important to know how to find such information and how to collect and organize it once you have found it. Take a course in basic research methods or seek the help or advice of a research librarian.
* *Interviewing.* In a face-to-face situation (if not, then by letter or by telephone) an expert or resource person can respond to questions. These responses provide the information needed. How the writer handles such interviews for research purposes is discussed in the next section of this chapter.
* *Observing.* A keen sense of observation is an important tool for the writer. You can learn a great deal about people by consciously watching and listening to what they say and do. The method(s) used to gather the necessary information will depend upon the preferences of the writer, the topic(s) involved, and the particular writing assignment.

Several recommendations can be made about gathering information for use as a broadcast writer. Organize your efforts to make the results worthwhile. Each fact or piece of information gathered should lead the inquisitive writer to successive ideas, facts, and sources. The more you know, the more you should want to know. Search out all possible leads. If necessary, ask a knowledgeable librarian for help. Learn how to use the basic as well as special supplementary services of a good library. Get to know the services available that could be helpful for current as well as future writing projects. Careful reading and clipping of a reputable daily newspaper or a weekly news magazine is an excellent source for ideas and information for many broadcast writers. Remember to date and file these clippings in a way that helps to organize the material for future use. You should do enough research on a subject so you can write accurately and intelligently.

Research Interviews

Interviewing an expert or a resource person is one of the primary ways or methods used by the writer to gather information for use in various kinds of broadcast scripts. Several suggestions are offered to help make this kind of interview situation more productive.

1. *Get the interview.* Write or call to make a specific appointment. Indicate clearly who you are, what you hope to accomplish, and why the comments of the person you want to interview are important. Then get a personal interview if at all possible.
2. *Prepare.* Gather enough information to know and understand the general subject area, but let your resource person provide new ideas and dimensions. Find out as much as possible about your resource person (credentials, background, career, accomplishments).
3. *Prepare an outline or list of questions.* An outline or list should be prepared before the interview takes place, but after your preliminary research on the topic and the person you will interview.
4. *Ask to record the interview.* Your effectiveness as an interviewer will be enhanced if you persuade the resource person to allow you to record the interview on audiocassette. If you explain that the purpose of the recording is not to use it on the air, but to ensure accuracy and for later reference, then what has become an established procedure for most print journalists should be acceptable to your expert or resource person.
5. *Listen.* Listen attentively to your source's responses. Hear what he or she has to say. React to what is said. Ask follow-up questions not prepared in advance.
6. *Converse.* Talk with your resource person, from his or her point of view. Do not interrogate or cross-examine.
7. *Be yourself.* Be natural. There is no reason to pretend to be someone other than who you are—a person interested in obtaining information. Be relaxed and confident.
8. *Do not interrupt unnecessarily.* Let your source talk freely and openly about the topic. Just as in an interesting conversation with a friend an occasional pause is not distracting—it may even be welcomed—so it may be in your interview.
9. *Determine immediate concerns.* What most bothers, interests, concerns, bores, disturbs, bewilders, confuses the person whom you are interviewing?
10. *Probe.* Delve into the attitudes, positions, beliefs, and convictions of this individual. Get to the heart of this person. Find out who and what he or she really is. Determine how these findings relate to the topic being examined.
11. *Be tenacious.* Diplomatically, keep probing with your questions until it is obvious that you are not going to obtain any substantial additional information. You may need to make your respondent formulate or commit to a point of view or to a feeling. Carefully guide your source through this process.
12. *Maintain control of the interview.* Avoid letting minor concerns or distractions

dominate your interview time. Stay on course. The quality of your preparation, plus your own tenacity, will determine your success.

13. *Handle legal concerns carefully.* Questions concerning invasion of privacy, personal attack, libel, and slander must be considered carefully and judicially. Requests to make off-the-record comments during your interview must be decided quickly and with sound judgment. Be prepared for such situations.

14. *Thank the interview guest.* Express your appreciation for the time and effort given. It would be best to contact your resource person after the interview, repeat your appreciation, and provide a brief progress report on the project for which help was received.

REGULATIONS, RESTRAINTS, AND RESPONSIBILITIES

Misuse or fear of misuse of the power of the mass media often results in regulations and restraints being placed upon the media by the government, by other organizations, and by the media directly. To some, regulation is only a distasteful restriction on their activities. To others, regulation is a welcome protection of basic rights and responsibilities.

Broadcasting is a heavily regulated industry. It has been since the earliest days of the crystal radio sets and continues today in the era of satellite communications, expanding cable systems, and burgeoning home video entertainment centers. It is important to recognize and understand that regulations and pressures placed upon the broadcasting industry filter down to the work of the broadcast writer. The writer needs to know, even on a basic level, the rights, privileges and responsibilities associated with writing material for use in this closely monitored and regulated industry.

This is not intended to be a comprehensive discussion of regulations and restraints that affect the broadcasting industry. Rather, it is a summary of major restrictions and concerns that have an impact on the responsibility of writing for the broadcast media. Specific legal questions should be directed to appropriate legal counsel. It is hoped that by presenting this information in one place in the first chapter of this book, the reader will be able to consult this information as needed in other chapters and will begin to formulate specific personal and professional attitudes toward key issues that affect the work of the broadcast writer.

Censorship

Section 326 of the Communications Act of 1934 prohibits the FCC (Federal Communications Commission) from censoring programs and from promulgating rules that interfere with the right of free speech. The FCC does have an affirmative obligation to take appropriate action against a station that does not follow regulations, but only after the fact. However, unofficial censorship of program content does exist because of biases of networks, stations, and production companies that produce the programs and sponsors with vested interests and prejudices.

Those who are responsible for producing programs for mass audiences prefer to work with established writers, themes, and topics. Often, fear of controversy or adverse audience reaction to a character, theme, or setting will compel program producers to discard experimentation and exploration of contemporary issues. It is becoming more difficult for new writers to sell their work and for established writers to provide new, perhaps controversial, perspectives on contemporary themes and topics.

Sponsors tend to disassociate themselves from programs that they believe will alienate even a portion of potential customers for their products and services or that run counter to entrenched corporate image and sales policies. The sponsor's objective is to become identified with quality programming that meshes with overall sales and corporate philosophy and that impresses a large audience who then purchases or utilizes the sponsor's products or services.

Program producers and sponsors generally do not want to offend anyone at any time. This philosophy often results in mediocre, self-serving, and safe scripts and programs that lack sparkle and durable quality.

Offensive Material

Radio and television signals enter the home or workplace as a trusted friend. The programs that are seen and heard provide entertainment, information, and inspiration to all ages, races, and social classes. Because of this expectation, those who write for the broadcast media need to exercise restraint and display a responsible attitude toward their work.

The FCC continues to affirm that the airwaves belong to the people. Service to the people has been an established principle of broadcasting in the United States since its earliest years. The flick of a switch brings numerous programs which shape opinions and mold life-styles. The intrusive nature of the broadcast media creates additional responsibility for the broadcaster. This responsibility is not necessarily shared or embraced by those in the printed media, where the material to be read is consciously purchased for consumption and can be more readily controlled. Since language in its broadest interpretation (both words and pictures) is the primary vehicle for any broadcast writer, it is important to know what is allowed under the law and to make an informed evaluation of ethical concerns.

Obscenity. The FCC is authorized under provisions of the Communications Act to revoke a broadcast license or to impose a fine upon the licensee for violation of Section 1464 of the U.S. Criminal Code. This section prohibits the utterance of "any obscene, indecent or profane language by means of radio communications [the term has been interpreted to include television]."

The current standard for determining obscenity was established by the United States Supreme Court in 1973 in the case of *Miller* v. *California* (413 U.S. 15). The Court's test is

> whether the average person, applying contemporary community standards, would find that the work, taken as a whole, appeals to the prurient interest; whether the work

depicts or describes in a patently offensive way, sexual conduct specifically defined by the applicable state law; and whether the work taken as a whole, lacks serious literary, artistic, political or scientific value.

The Court has not ruled directly whether the terms "indecent" and "obscene" are synonymous. The FCC attempted to define "indecent language" with a declaratory Order issued in 1975 (Pacifica Foundation, 56 FCC 2d 94), but the Court held that the Commission's Order violated Section 326 of the Communications Act and was unconstitutionally vague. Instead, the Court said the FCC should continue to trust the licensee to exercise judgment, responsibility and sensitivity to the community's needs, interests and tastes.

Program and Advertising Material. Many observers of the broadcast media have noted with alarm a growing promiscuity and lack of sensitivity towards traditional human values. Many listeners and viewers are offended by the flippant treatment of such themes as drugs, divorce, and unfettered sexual relationships in the programs and commercials now on the air. They are disturbed by the increasing number of adult scenes, situations, and subjects now shown when impressionable young minds are near the set. For some, titillation of the viewer has become an accepted practice.

Sponsors and program producers contend that this technique is a viable means of competing with other media, that today's sophisticated broadcast audience demands more programming choices than ever before, and that to capture the available audience certain calculated decisions and compromises must be made. Most advertisers and program producers will agree that quality content and a recognition of significant responsibility are important, but they would also admit that the economic realities of the media marketplace often prevent this pursuit of excellence. The writer, working in this environment, must make a difficult, but necessary, personal and professional decision based on ethical and legal concerns.

The Violence Issue

The amount and effect of violence seen on television in the United States have been perennial concerns for parents, educators and other interested parties. Active citizens and consumer organizations (e.g., National Citizens Committee for Broadcasting, National Coalition on Television Violence, Action for Children's Television, and the national and local groups of the PTA) continue to monitor and record the amount of violent behavior seen on television and report their findings in hopes of encouraging alternatives to what they regard as a deteriorating situation.

Some observers note that the mass media simply reflect society and the values it displays, that reality in broadcast programming is essential for audience acceptance. Others counter that the media have a responsibility to enhance and to reinforce worthwhile social values and to present such values in an attractive, effective manner for potential audience acceptance. The dramatic writer, for example, uses conflict as a cornerstone for effective drama. Conflict often leads to violence. So the issue of violence is not easy to resolve, for the writer or for the audience.

Children's Television Programming

Despite concern for the effects of obscene, offensive, and violent programming on children who maintain a steady diet of television viewing, the FCC continues its trust in the broadcasting industry and the adherence to voluntary codes of ethics. The FCC has continued to reject proposals by citizen groups demanding higher-quality children's programming and elimination of commercials from shows intended primarily for children. Generally, it is believed that eliminating commercials from such programs would not encourage commercial broadcasters to develop more creative and wholesome programming.

Political Broadcasts

Broadcasters have a number of special obligations and responsibilities with regard to political broadcasts. These requirements stem from certain sections of the Communications and Federal Election Campaign acts, the Fairness Doctrine in general, and various FCC rulings on the subject.[1] Writers preparing news copy, documentaries, investigative reports, editorials, and commentaries must be aware of these regulations since they affect those who write such material. The importance and complexity of these regulations for those involved in writing certain kinds of broadcast material cannot be overemphasized.[2]

Broadcasts by Candidates. Section 315(a) of the Communications Act indicates that

> no station licensee is required to permit the use of its facilities by any legally qualified candidate for public office [except for federal elective office], but if any licensee shall permit any such candidate to use its facilities, it shall afford equal opportunities to all other candidates for that office to use such facilities. Such licensee shall have no power of censorship over the material broadcast by any such candidate. Appearance by a legally qualified candidate on any (i) bona fide newscast, (ii) bona fide news interview, (iii) bona fide news documentary (if the appearance of the candidate is incidental to the presentation of the subject covered by the news documentary), or (iv) on-the-spot coverage of bona fide news events (including, but not limited to political conventions and activities incidental thereto) shall not be deemed to be use of a broadcast station.

Political Editorials. Section 73.123(c) of the Commission's Rules requires that when a station editorial endorses or opposes a political candidate, the licensee (station owner) is required to notify the other candidate(s) for that office within twenty-four hours, give the date and time of the editorial, and offer *free* time (not necessarily *equal* time) for the candidate(s) or a spokesperson to respond. If the editorial is broadcast within seventy-two hours of election day, sufficient notice must be provided to prepare and present a response in timely fashion.

Even when a station editorial makes no direct reference to an election but takes a partisan position on a politically significant issue, clearly and readily identified with a legally qualified candidate, the FCC has ruled that this gives rise to the affirmative obligations noted above.[3]

The Fairness Doctrine

Any writer working on programming involving potentially controversial issues, for example, in talk programs, dramas, editorials, must grapple with the complexities of the Fairness Doctrine. Failure to understand and to apply these regulations can have serious consequences for the writer and the writer's employer.

General. Under the FCC's Fairness Doctrine, a licensee has a responsibility to devote a reasonable amount of programming time to the presentation of controversial issues of public importance and to offer a reasonable opportunity for the presentation of contrasting points of view. The FCC has suggested that issues which could have a significant impact on the community served by the station be considered potential controversial issues of public importance. There is room for considerably more discretion on the part of the licensee under the Fairness Doctrine than under the equal opportunities requirements of Section 315.

It should be noted that the Fairness Doctrine *does* apply to paid institutional broadcast advertising that contains commentary on controversial issues of public importance. For example, an announcement prepared and sponsored by an organization opposed to legalizing abortion can present a particular position on this controversial issue of public importance. But the Fairness Doctrine would apply in this situation. Other institutional announcements that do not involve debate on public issues are *not* covered under provisions of the Fairness Doctrine.

Personal Attack. This is part of the Fairness Doctrine, but does not provide the wide discretion allowed under general application of the Doctrine. If an attack is made against "the honesty, character, integrity or like personal qualities of an identified person or group" during the discussion of a controversial issue of public importance, under Section 73.123(a) of the Commission's Rules, the licensee is required, within one week of the broadcast, to inform the individual or group of the time of the broadcast, provide a script or a tape of the broadcast, and allow an opportunity to respond. This requirement applies to all personal attacks broadcast over a station whether done by station personnel or in programs supplied by network or syndicated services.

Excluded from this regulation are personal attacks made during bona fide newscasts (including commentaries used during regularly scheduled newscasts), news interviews, and on-the-spot coverage of bona fide news events, attacks on foreign groups or foreign public figures, and attacks by candidates on other candidates or their associates.

Libel and Slander

Libel is one of the oldest regulations affecting both print and electronic media. A number of cases have been prosecuted on the basis of inaccurate use of names in news stories or a striking resemblance between a real-life person or situation and a purportedly fictional character or situation in a play, story, broadcast, or novel.

Basically, *libel is anything written, brought to the attention of a third party, that tends to accuse someone of unlawful, ridiculous or disgraceful acts. Slander* essentially is spoken libel. Technically, broadcasters would be subject to slander restrictions, but since very few states have slander laws, libel laws generally apply.

Four conditions are necessary for libel to occur:

• *Identification*. All that is necessary is for a third person to recognize that a libelous statement has been made against someone whom they know or can identify.
• *Defamation*. Statements made by someone must *tend* to do harm.
• *Publication*. This is technically interpreted as the moment a third person is exposed to the libelous material.
• *Malice*. The person making the damaging statement must intend to commit, without just cause or reason, an unlawful act that will result in injury to others.

If you should become embroiled in a libel suit because of your writing efforts, you would be advised to consult an attorney. You should know the basic defenses used in libel actions and the damages awarded by the courts in such cases.

Broadcast of Telephone Conversations

Writers working in a broadcast newsroom preparing routine newscasts, special documentaries, or news-related features should be aware of Section 73.1206 of the FCC Rules.

> *Before* recording a telephone conversation for broadcast, or broadcasting such a conversation simultaneously with its occurrence, a licensee shall inform any party to the call of the licensee's intention to broadcast the conversation, except where such party is aware, or may be presumed to be aware from the circumstances of the conversation, that it is being or likely will be broadcast. Such awareness is presumed to exist only when the other party to the call is associated with the station (such as an employee or part-time reporter), or where the other party originates the call and it is obvious that it is in connection with a program in which the station customarily broadcasts telephone conversations.

The Commission has ruled that a conversation begins whenever a party answers the telephone. The prior notification requirement is strictly enforced. Giving such notice to a caller during or after the time a conversation is recorded from the telephone, even before any part of it is used on the air, is not allowed under this regulation. Use of beep tones while recording telephone conversations does not eliminate the requirement that you give specific *prior* notice to a party on the telephone that you are recording or broadcasting the conversation, depending upon the circumstances.

Invasion of Privacy and Release Forms[4]

Although the particulars of invasion of privacy laws vary greatly from state to state, it is possible to say that invasion of privacy most often occurs when you use someone for commercial purposes, such as a product endorsement in a commercial, or when you use someone's name or picture in such a manner as to cause them embarrassment (as in a documentary or investigative report). These uses may be considered invasion of privacy only if a person has not consented to your use of his name, or face, or performance. In legal terms, such consent is called a release or, more specifically, a talent consent release form.

When you want a producer or other prospective employer to review material that you have written on speculation, most often you will be asked to sign a program material release form. The signing of this document should precede a full and formal writing contract offer from the individual responsible for developing such properties. As you can see in the sample provided in figure 1-1, the form protects the parties to the contract from potential legal entanglements.

Copyright

The current copyright law, in effect since January 1, 1978, protects artistic and literary efforts, recognizes ownership, and grants to the creator of a work all rights, benefits, and privileges that ownership entails. The copyright owner has exclusive rights to print, duplicate, distribute, adapt (i.e., allow "derivative works"), perform, record, sell or display literary, dramatic or musical works publicly. To be valid, transfer or assignment of these rights must be in writing and must be made voluntarily by the owner of the copyrighted material. Invasion of any of these rights is termed infringement, the remedies for which include actions for damages and injunctions.

Whether published or unpublished, works fixed in tangible form (e.g., a script, record, videotape, film, photograph) are provided statutory protection from the moment of creation. This protection lasts through the life of the author plus fifty years after his or her death. Exceptions are made-for-hire works (which includes work done as a regular employee of a company such as a broadcast outlet) and anonymous and pseudonymous (fictional) works whose copyright protection lasts from seventy-five to one hundred years after creation of the work.

As a broadcast writer, the use of copyrighted material confronts you often. You may need a particular photograph for the opening shot in a television program or you may want to suggest the use of a specific piece of music in a commercial announcement or a dramatic script. All of these situations require a review of copyright regulations

_____, 19_____

Title and/or Theme of Material Submitted Hereunder:

_____

_____

I am submitting to you today certain program material, the title and/or theme of which is indicated above (which material is herein after referred to as the program material), upon the following express understanding and conditions.

1. I acknowledge that I have requested permission to disclose to you and to carry on certain discussions and negotiations with you in connection with such program material.

2. I agree that I am voluntarily disclosing such program material to you at my request. I understand that you shall have no obligation to me in any respect whatsoever with regard to such material until each of us has executed a written agreement which by its terms and provisions, will be the only contract between us.

3. I agree that any discussions we may have with respect to such program material shall not constitute any agreement expressed or implied as to the purchase or use of such program material which I am hereby disclosing to you either orally or in writing.

Figure 1-1 Sample television program material release form.

and proper application of procedures to obtain permission to use the copyrighted material.

Previously released material can be used in any of three situations:

1. If the material is in the public domain. This means that the material either was never protected by copyright or that copyright protection has expired. For a fee, the copyright office will determine the copyright status of any previously released or published work.[5]
2. If you have obtained written permission to use copyrighted material from the copyright owner who may be the creator of the work, a publisher, a television producer, or any number of people.
3. If the legal doctrine of fair use can be applied even though the material is copyrighted—in which case prior permission is not required. This is a complex, intricate legal alternative. Essentially, you need to determine the amount of the

4. If such material submitted hereunder is not new or novel, or was not originated by me, or has not been reduced to concrete form, or if because other persons including your employees have heretofore submitted or hereafter submit similar or identical program material which you have the right to use, then I agree that you shall not be liable to me for the use of such program material and you shall not be obligated in any respect whatsoever to compensate me for such use by you.

5. I further agree that if you hereafter produce or distribute a television program or programs based upon the same general idea, theme or situation and/or having the same setting or background and/or taking place in the same geographical area or period of history as the said program material, then unless you have substantially copied the expression and development of such idea, theme or situation, including the characters and story line thereof, as herewith or hereafter submitted to you by me in writing, you shall have no obligation or liability to me of any kind or character by reason of the production or distribution of such program(s), nor shall you be obligated to compensate me in connection therewith.

I acknowledge that but for my agreement to the above terms and conditions, you would not accede to my request to receive and consider the said program material which I am submitting to you herewith.

_____

(signature)

Fig. 1-1 *(Continued)*

---

original copyrighted material you will use, its importance, and the impact your use of this copyrighted material will have on the original copyrighted work.

Pressure Groups

There are several types of organizations or groups that demand the attention of the broadcasting industry and ultimately the attention and response of the broadcast writer. These pressure groups may be labeled as activists, advocates, lobbyists, or by some other designation.

They operate upon two basic assumptions: (1) that broadcasting stations or the electronic media are primary "shapers" of one's personality next to one's immediate family; and (2) that those who attend movies, watch television, and listen to radio should help determine the kinds of programs which exert such a powerful influence on all of our lives.

These groups continue to try to influence the kinds of material presented on radio and television and the types of films shown in movie theaters. Their active campaigns against what they perceive as the violence and obscenity seen on television, for example, have been noticed by network and station executives. While it is difficult to point to these pressure groups as the sole reason, there appears to be a noticeable trend toward better, perhaps more conscientious, children's television programming. Also, programs featuring minorities, women, and special interest groups are receiving more attention from these groups as well as from program executives.

The broadcast writer needs to be aware that such pressure groups exist, understand the kinds of concerns and priorities each group represents, and be prepared to respond to the pressure exerted. The writer may not have to deal directly with such groups, but will be expected to respond to their concerns when preparing script material for the broadcast media.

Self-Regulation Efforts

The broadcasting industry, like many other industries, has made an effort to regulate itself over the years. Perhaps because of government regulations or pressures from special interest groups, but one hopes because of a continuing sense of responsibility, these self-regulation efforts have received mixed reactions.

Supporters of such efforts contend that self-regulation in such areas as programming and advertising becomes essential if broadcasters are to maintain control over what they make available to their audience. Supporters add that self-regulation efforts help anticipate problems, issues, and concerns which ultimately might require lengthy and potentially severe regulations and restraints.

Opponents counter that such efforts are of little value and impact, probably call attention to issues and concerns unnoticed by the FCC and other regulatory agencies, and generally produce vague minimal standards for the diverse subscribers to such codes or standards of good practice. Since enforcement of and adherence to these codes or standards are questionable, one could legitimately speculate about their effectiveness.

Although the standards and practices codes of the National Association of Broadcasters (NAB) no longer exist as industry self-regulatory controls, broadcasting networks, individual stations, and professional broadcasting associations have formulated, and attempt to adhere to, ethical guidelines and policies to meet the exacting demands of individual circumstances. Appendix C contains the codes of ethics of two national news-related professional organizations (the Radio Television News Directors Association and the Society of Professional Journalists, Sigma Delta Chi) and a portion of the program standards and practices of two major broadcasting networks.

Effects of Regulations and Restraints

After reviewing major regulations and restraints that affect the work of the broadcast writer, one might conclude that the situation appears hopeless. However, a more optimistic viewpoint realizes things could be worse and have been worse in the past. While some controls have been removed, others continue to challenge the broadcast writer and others involved in the media.

To avoid controversy and to achieve higher ratings that result in increased profits, networks and stations have maintained a safe middle ground. This philosophy in turn has produced programming which often lacks innovation, responsiveness, and sparkle. The imitation of successful formats and styles continues. Selection of "the least objectionable program" becomes a nightly chore for the regular television viewer.

The cumulative effect of these regulations and restraints has been to make writers and broadcast executives more responsive to audience demands and tastes. The law requires some of this responsiveness, but a large share of it should be attributed to the desire to provide better programs which eventually result in higher ratings and more profits. Since broadcasting is a profit-motivated industry, it will most likely continue to aim to please as much of the audience as possible.

Certain types of program material no longer are automatically rejected or discarded. For example, in television dramas, sensitive contemporary themes and situations (child abuse, homosexuality, abortion, drug use, child pornography) are presented in an effort to attract a large audience concerned with these issues and problems.

The criteria of acceptability and appropriateness evolve constantly to match the capabilities of the media and the demands of the audience. The challenge for the broadcast writer is to provide quality work that addresses contemporary needs within the realistic framework of established restraints and regulations both from within and outside the broadcasting industry.

CONCLUSION

This chapter has focused on the work and concerns of the broadcast writer. The section devoted to examining the qualifications as well as the role and function of the broadcast writer should enable you to assess your goals and interests as a writer. The impact and influence of the broadcast media should motivate you to cultivate a personal and professional sense of pride, ethics, and responsibility toward your work and the audience for whom you write. It is important to know how to use the resources available (especially research tools such as interviews) to write effective broadcast script material. As a broadcast writer, you must also be aware of the various laws, regulations, and concerns that influence such writing and take steps to avoid ethical and legal problems as they develop during the creative writing process.

Once you have assessed the work of broadcast writing, developed an appreciation for the impact of such writing, and the pressures that influence the final product, you will be in a position to determine your place in this challenging field and take the steps necessary to acquire the skills and insights to become the best broadcast writer that you can be.

SUGGESTED EXERCISES AND PROJECTS

1. Using as a basis the characteristics listed in this chapter, take a personal inventory of yourself to determine your qualifications and interests as a writer.
2. Schedule a personal or group visit to a nearby broadcast facility. Determine the organizational structure and management system used within the facility and the role of the writer within the facility.
3. At a nearby library, look up the research aids available for future writing assignments. While there, locate one of the periodicals listed in Appendix B, read one of the major articles in one issue of the publication and then provide a brief summary of the article.
4. Discuss the impact of current broadcast programming trends, policies, and strategies on the work, role, and function of the broadcast writer.
5. Observe a particular event (e.g., people in the park, a busy street corner, a checkout stand at a supermarket). Report your observations and indicate the possible future use of these observations in a broadcast writing situation.
6. Using one of the reference works on English grammar and writing style listed in this chapter, review basic usage rules.
7. For another class project or perhaps for a publication, interview someone using the suggestions offered in this chapter.
8. Discuss the impact of censorship and pressure groups on the work of the broadcast writer.
9. Discuss your observations of violence and offensive material in today's broadcast media. What is the impact of these developments on broadcast media writing and programming efforts?
10. Describe a recent situation in which a local broadcast station was faced with the exigencies of complying with the requirements of Section 315 of the 1934 Communications Act, the Fairness Doctrine, or libel/slander regulations.

NOTES

1. National Association of Broadcasters, *Legal Guide to FCC Broadcast Rules, Regulations and Policies* (Washington, D.C.: National Association of Broadcasters, 1977), p. II–15.
2. A detailed study of rules regarding broadcasts by candidates for federal and non-federal public office is available in the FCC public notice of July 20, 1978, "The Law of Political Broadcasting and Cablecasting." Copies of this public notice may be obtained upon request to the FCC in Washington, D.C. Another publication, which provides a comprehensive treatment of this subject as well as the Fairness Doctrine, is the latest edition of *Political Broadcast Catechism and the Fairness Doctrine* available from the National Association of Broadcasters, 1771 N Street, N.W., Washington, DC 20036.
3. National Association of Broadcasters, *Legal Guide to FCC Broadcast Rules, Regulations and Policies* (Washington, D.C.: National Association of Broadcasters, 1977), p. II–18.

4. Summarized from Legal Department, National Association of Broadcasters, "A Broadcaster's Guide to Releases," L-910, June, 1979.

5. The Copyright Office, Library of Congress, Washington, DC 20559 can provide an information kit on several copyright-related topics: Registration Procedures (Circular R1D), Radio and TV Programs (Circular 47e), and How to Investigate Copyright Status of a Work (Circular R 22).

ADDITIONAL READING

Adler, Richard P., ed. *Understanding Television: Essays on Television as a Social and Cultural Force*. New York: Praeger, 1981.

Baldwin, Thomas F., and McVoy, D. Stevens. *Cable Communication*. Englewood Cliffs, N.J.: Prentice-Hall, 1983.

Blakely, Robert J. *To Serve the Public Interest: Educational Broadcasting in the United States*. Syracuse, N.Y.: Syracuse University Press, 1979.

Brady, John. *The Craft of Interviewing*. Cincinnati: Writer's Digest Books, 1975.

Brohaugh, William, ed. *The Writer's Resource Guide*. Cincinnati: Writer's Digest Books, 1979.

Cantor, Muriel G. *Prime-Time Television: Content and Control*. Beverly Hills: Sage, 1980.

Coleman, Howard W. *Case Studies in Broadcast Management: Radio and Television*. 2d ed. New York: Hastings House, 1978.

Eastman, Susan Tyler, Head, Sidney W., and Klein, Lewis. *Broadcast/Cable Programming: Strategies and Practices*. 2d ed. Belmont, Calif.: Wadsworth, 1984.

Franklin, Marc A. and Ruth K. *The First Amendment and the Fourth Estate*. Mineola, N.Y.: The Foundation Press, 1977.

Hamburg, Morton I. *All About Cable: Legal and Business Aspects of Cable and Pay Television*. 2d ed. New York: Law Journal Seminars Press, 1981.

Head, Sydney W., with Sterling, Christopher H. *Broadcasting in America: A Survey of Television, Radio, and New Technologies*. 4th ed. Boston: Houghton Mifflin Company, 1982.

Johnston, Donald F. *Copyright Handbook*. New York: R. R. Bowker, 1978.

Kahn, Frank J. *Documents of American Broadcasting*. 4th ed. Englewood Cliffs, N.J.: Prentice-Hall, 1984.

National Association of Broadcasters. Legal Department. *Legal Guide to FCC Broadcast Rules, Regulations and Policies*. Supplements. Washington, D.C.: NAB, 1977.

———. *Political Broadcast Catechism*. 9th ed. Washington, D.C.: NAB, 1980.

Quaal, Ward L., and Brown, James A. *Broadcast Management: Radio-Television*. 2d ed. New York: Hastings House, 1976.

Rivers, William L. *Finding Facts: Interviewing, Observing, Using Reference Sources*. Englewood Cliffs, N.J.: Prentice-Hall, 1975.

Rivers, William L., and others. *Responsibility in Mass Communication*. 3d ed. New York: Harper & Row, 1980.

Roper Organization. *Evolving Public Attitudes Toward Television and Other Mass Media 1959–1980*. New York: Television Information Office, 1981.

Rowan, Ford. *Broadcast Fairness: Doctrine Practice, Prospects*. New York: Longman, 1984.

Sterling, Christopher H., and Kittross, John M. *Stay Tuned: A Concise History of American Broadcasting*. Belmont, Calif.: Wadsworth, 1978.

Chapter Two

BASIC BROADCAST
PRODUCTION TECHNIQUES

A broadcast writer needs to know about broadcast production. It is a necessary part of the job. It is important to know the technical potential and limits of broadcast production tools so that when you write a script you will know what is possible and what is not. Also, the writer needs to use standard production terms in broadcast scripts to communicate creatively with production personnel.

This chapter provides basic broadcast production information needed by the broadcast writer. The qualities of each medium will be examined to help the writer understand and use the creative and technical capabilities available. There will be a description of the basic procedures and techniques used by the production team so that the writer understands what happens when the script is transformed into the finished product. For both radio and television, there will be a description of the basic production tools used as well as the production terms and abbreviations found most often in broadcast scripts. Motion picture production is examined briefly.

SELECTING THE MEDIUM

As you formulate ideas as a writer, consider the medium in which you intend to display your work. Your thought process, writing style and technique, and manner of presentation will differ if you are working on a biographical novel rather than a teleplay for national distribution. As a writer, you function differently if preparing a television commercial than if designing an instructional television program series. You will need to analyze the capabilities of the medium to be used.

Usually, because of employment requirements and constraints, the writer must create a particular type of message for a specific medium (e.g., a commercial for radio).

Sometimes, for specific kinds of projects, the seasoned writer can select the medium to be used to reach a target audience most effectively with a particular kind of program or announcement.

Each available medium should be analyzed on two bases: (1) the suitability of the medium to present a particular kind of message effectively and (2) the capability of the medium to deliver the right kind of audience.

Shared Attributes

Several attributes are common to the broadcast media:

• *Universality*. They are readily available throughout the country and are enjoyed by a large number of people on a regular basis.
• *Diversity*. They offer a variety of program material appealing to a wide range of audiences.
• *Immediacy*. They can present material which is topical and contemporary for audience needs.
• *Reusability*. Material can be recorded, edited and duplicated for multiple playbacks.
• *Impermanence*. They are but fleeting, perishable images and sounds in the audience's mind.
• *Researched*. They are being studied and evaluated continually by companies providing analysis of specific audience tastes and characteristics.

Attributes of Radio

Principal characteristics of radio include the following:

• a "theater of the mind" can be created for the listener, using only sound
• it is generally regarded as a friendly, personal medium
• it is not conducive to presentation of detailed information (e.g., prices at a food store in a radio commercial)
• messages must be presented often to reach radio's fragmented audiences
• radio must compete with the listener's inattention and distractions caused by the way in which the medium is consumed
• it is not particularly suitable for reaching young children in the audience because of current programming
• it is a portable, mobile medium going where the listener goes
• the profile and density of the radio audience are relatively stable
• production costs are less than in most other media

Attributes of Television

Principal characteristics of television include the following:

•the potential for the combination of sight, sound, motion, and color offers exciting creative possibilities
•the audience is not as fragmented as in radio (although it may be in the future)
•nationally, more time is spent with television than other media
•production costs almost always are higher than for radio

Attributes of Film

Some of the program material seen on television is produced on film. Motion picture films share many of the characteristics just listed for television. Films offer several production advantages and disadvantages:

•special effects (e.g., animation, slow motion, picture enlargement or reduction, freeze frames, or "frozen action") are accomplished effectively using motion picture film
•a specific audience will see the finished motion picture because of the G, PG, PG-13, and R ratings placed on practically all films released in the United States today and because the theme, situation, or characters displayed in a particular film will attract an identifiable target group
•subject matter presented is not as restricted as in open-circuit broadcasting; closed-circuit alternatives, through cable systems, are available for presenting sensitive, controversial and stylized material to appropriate audiences
•the length of a film presentation can vary according to the topic to be covered and its target audience; for example, a presentation tracing the history of the nation's Capitol may be any length appropriate to the subject and to those who will view the final product
•production of theatrical motion pictures generally requires more time and money than for similar kinds of radio and television programs
•it is difficult to transfer effectively the large-screen cinematic experience of the darkened movie theater to the bright, small-screen format required to reach the television viewer
•many of the primary advantages once offered by motion picture production (e.g., special effects, precision editing, image sharpness, equipment portability) are now incorporated in the growing sophistication of television equipment, facilities, and personnel.

RADIO PRODUCTION

The writer is only one member of a team of individuals working together to produce program material for radio. The responsibilities and scope of the work done by each individual may be limited or expansive depending upon the project to be produced and the size and operating philosophy of the production facility. Networks and large production companies have larger staffs with more specialized production responsibilities than smaller radio operations in which one person may be assigned several production jobs. For practical purposes, the radio production team will be outlined for the typical small- to medium-size radio station.

The major components involved in producing various types of radio program material are as follows:

• *Music and sound effects*. This part of the production process involves having access to the list or catalog of music and sound effects available for commercials, promotional announcements, introductions to news and sports programs as well as talk shows, documentaries, and the music played regularly on the station. Radio stations may designate a music librarian or music director for this work.

• *Writing*. Generally, the writing for certain types of radio program material is done after the sales staff sells air time to clients (e.g., commercials) or after the news director decides on the opening, closing, and format for a regularly scheduled talk program series. Often, the writer works with other station personnel to develop script ideas and research to meld the elements of the finished, on-the-air program. Some stations complete the writing and production phases as part of other responsibilities. For example, news department personnel generally write their own copy for newscasts as well as many of the public affairs programs. The station manager may work with a committee within the station to develop effective editorials and then assign someone to write the editorials read by the manager on the air. The continuity or copywriting personnel in the station are responsible for the regular writing assignments within the facility, usually spot announcements.

• *Announcing*. At small and medium-size radio stations, announcers are assigned to a regular on-the-air shift and, in addition, announce or voice the other kinds of program material needed for the station. In most cases, this consists of reading the copy written by the continuity writer and merging the various elements to produce an effective commercial announcement. Announcers at most stations, however, are expected to perform many other announcing functions (e.g., special events such as parades or sports play-by-play broadcasts) depending upon the demands and programming format of the station.

• *Engineering*. In non-union markets and production facilities, the announcer performs the necessary technical functions of mixing voice, music, and sound effects to produce the finished announcement or program. With a unionized engineering staff, the announcer only reads the copy and an engineer operates the audio console. Separation of this production responsibility permits careful attention to specific production details.

Production Tools

The primary tools available to produce radio or audio program material include the following:

Control Board or Console. Located in the control room or central control point, the control board or console processes the voices and sounds during recording, editing, and dubbing.

Microphone. There are several types of microphones with pickup pattern characteristics designed to meet various recording requirements and situations.

Turntable. The turntable picks up information prerecorded on a disc or record and sends this information to the control board for amplification, mixing, processing, and integration with other sound elements.

Audiotape. Sounds can be recorded in the studio or in the field onto audiotape at standard speeds. Quarter-inch audiotape is used, except in portable audiocassette recorders. The audiotape may be in the form of continuous loop cartridges or carts with inaudible stop tones or cues placed between the various segments, or the material may be recorded on standard reel-to-reel audiotape machines and later edited.

Music and Sound Effects. Both may be produced and recorded on audiotape in the studio or on location. Both may also be prerecorded on disc or audiotape and integrated into the program material using the control board or console.

Audio Terminology

In broadcast production, certain terms and abbreviations become accepted methods of shorthand allowing all those involved to quickly understand precisely what is meant and what is needed. Precise use of terms and abbreviations will ensure that your script is produced almost exactly as you have envisioned. Imprecise or careless use of terminology, undoubtedly, will lead to confusion, frustration, and ineffective production value.

Voice Terms. The writer can indicate the voice to be heard by use of some easily understood designation (e.g., Voice 1 or Billy or Announcer #2, etc.).

Several terms describe the placement and quality of voices used in radio or audio production. Unless otherwise specified in your script, a voice or character is heard at a normal distance from a microphone—that is, the voice is "on mike" (or "on mic"). If you want the voice to be heard as though speaking from the back of the room or from a distance, you would indicate "off mike." If the voice needs to sound as though it is approaching the center of action in the mind's eye of the listener, then write "fading on" or "fades on." The reverse process, where the voice starts at a normal distance from the microphone and then slowly moves away, could be noted by writing "fading off" or "fades off." To create suspense or to heighten a mysterious mood, you might want the voice to be heard with a slight echo or reverberation; after the talent's designation, you would note "reverb," indicating the need for a slight or controlled use of echo. To create the illusion of a telephone conversation, the notations "filtered" or "behind barrier" can be used, or simply write "as heard through a telephone." Terms used to describe the quality and placement of the voices heard are written immediately after the name of the specific talent affected.

Music and Sound Effects Terms. The writer can choose from several terms to denote the manner in which to use music and sound effects. As chapter 3 will illustrate, music and sound effect notations are written as separate lines in the script. Although the word *music* could be used, often the abbreviation "ET" (electrical transcription) alerts everyone involved that music is to be used at a particular point in the script. Some writers use ET to denote both music and sound effects. However, the common abbreviation for sound effects is "SFX."

It is not enough simply to indicate that music or sound effects will be used in a script. It is necessary to note *how* each is to be used. You might want music or a sound effect to "fade in" (or "up") at the beginning of a program or announcement. You could note that it "fades out" at the end of a program segment. Various notations indicate that the music or sound effect should be heard at full volume and the volume then brought down so another production element (e.g., a voice or another piece of music) can be heard more prominently. Generally, these terms are interchangeable: "up full and then under"; "feature (establish) briefly and then under"; "up for (number of) seconds and then under." If you wish to have either music or sound effects begin under a voice, for example, you could note either "music (or SFX) under" or "sneak under." The last term is used when the music or sound effect is heard in the "background" ("b.g.") and then is heard at full volume after a character finishes a particular word.

The transition between two pieces of music or sound effects may be accomplished by writing "segue" (pronounced seg-way), in which one selection ends and the next selection begins immediately, or "cross-fade," in which one selection gradually fades out and the next selection gradually comes in to replace it. Be as specific as possible in writing music and sound effect notations to ensure that your script is produced in the manner you have envisioned.

Other Terms. Other terms often used in radio scripts include: "ad lib," which allows characters or voices momentarily to create their own words, but always in keeping with the general tone, mood, and purpose of the script (e.g., spectators in a crowd at a football game or patrons seated at nearby tables in a restaurant); "bridge," which is a general term applied to a transition between sound elements (e.g., "Music: up full and then bridge to SFX of frog under Voice #3"); "Anncr" or "Ann" which are common abbreviations for the designation announcer. Be certain to add a number or letter after this designation or after the other common term, "Voice," if multiple use of either term is anticipated (e.g., Anncr #1, Anncr #2, etc., or Voice A, Voice B, etc.).

TELEVISION PRODUCTION

Essentially, coordinating the audio portion of a television production makes use of the same components as outlined for radio. As in radio, the responsibilities and scope of the work done by television production personnel can be isolated into designated job descriptions. Such variables, however, as personnel capabilities, budget, type of production, organizational structure, and philosophy of the production facility may cause two or more jobs to be assigned to one individual or may require an adjustment in production responsibilities. Generally, the larger the television production facility, the more delineated the job descriptions and responsibilities. For practical considerations, only the essential television production components in the typical small to medium- size facility will be outlined.

Producer. The producer assumes responsibility for the entire television production (single program or series), which includes such essentials as planning, budgeting, scripting, production coordination, scheduling, and editing. Depending upon the type of production and the facility involved, these responsibilities often are combined with those of the director, the writer, or both.

Director. He or she coordinates the efforts of the technical crew members and the performance of the television talent. The director must execute creatively the production designed by the producer, conceptualized by the writer, and envisioned by other creative personnel.

Writer. It is difficult to describe the precise role the writer plays in the television production process. Often, the writer works in close cooperation and shares some responsibilities with the producer and/or the director. The type of program or announcement affects the kind of work and amount of participation by the writer. Basically, the writer must conceptualize and formulate the essential television elements into proper script form to accomplish specific objectives.

Technical Personnel. The technical director operates the equipment used to make video changes during the production. The audio engineer supervises all audio components. The engineering staff is crucial for the proper installation, maintenance, and operation of all of the television production equipment. The floor manager (sometimes called the stage manager) coordinates the director's commands to the talent and production personnel. The floor manager supervises the floor crew who position the sets, lighting instruments, and cameras used in the production.

Talent. During production, the director and producer supervise the efforts of the on-camera talent—announcers, narrators, and performers who read the words and perform the actions required.

Special production situations or larger, more expansive production facilities may require more specialized production personnel. For example, an executive producer may be designated to coordinate the efforts of several producers and directors working on individual programs in a multi-part series. A unit manager may be hired to handle budgeting, equipment, and scheduling details. An art director or scenic designer may be required to plan the physical setting. A graphic artist may be needed to prepare artwork and graphics. A lighting director may be designated to plan the lighting needed. Perhaps assistance is needed for the makeup, wardrobe, or music to be used. In smaller production facilities, these special responsibilities are handled by the technical personnel already mentioned.

Production Tools

All of the tools used to produce radio or audio program material are also used in television production. Just as in radio, the television control room serves as the central control point where the many production elements are combined to produce the finished program or announcement.

Besides those already listed for radio, the primary production tools available to produce television program material include:

Video Switcher. The video switcher allows the operator to select a picture or a combination of pictures from various live and recorded sources. The manner of selecting and changing the visual elements determines the pace, tempo, and look of the program, announcement, or segment.

Cameras. Studio or field (outdoor) cameras capture pictures for later processing into the finished program or announcement.

Lights. Various types of lighting instruments provide illumination for studio and field production. Specialized lighting techniques and equipment make it possible to produce some special effects.

Videotape. This magnetic material permits the recording of sound and picture for later editing and processing or rebroadcast.

Motion Picture Film. The standard film gauge or size used in practically all local station applications is 16mm. Networks and large production houses do use 35mm, the theatrical film gauge, for specialized applications.

Slides. Illustrations, graphics, sketches, and pictures may be photographed on 35mm slide film, placed in slide mounts, and then inserted into the television production as needed. Rather than slides, many production facilities use a frame storage system that electronically captures and retrieves single video images.

Studio or Flip Cards. An alternative to 35mm slides is the use of in-studio cards which are made of stiff-backed material. The television camera captures the picture of the card or graphic at the studio location.

Character Generators. Except for photographs, most of the graphic material needed for television production can be attained with the use of a character generator. These typewriter/television screen systems make it possible to load, store and retrieve various types and sizes of letters and printed characters.

TV/Film Terminology

The writer can use the audio terms described earlier to write the audio portion of television and motion picture scripts. The video terms that will be described for use in both television and motion picture scripts are more complex because of the nature of video production.

Precise use of production terminology in broadcast scripts ensures precise application in the resultant production. The writer needs to provide enough production information in a video script to indicate to production personnel what is to be seen and heard. Production personnel, however, must have an opportunity to contribute their skills and creative talents to the finished production. Thus, the broadcast writer needs to know how to use essential video terms in scripts to permit the writer a full and creative experience, but be prepared to curtail the extensive use of such terms as circumstances dictate. Do not plan to use all of the terms described in every video script you write. Find out how precise you need to be and then provide only that amount of production detail in the script. The amount of detail needed depends upon program, production, personnel, and contractual demands and preferences.

The essential video terms and abbreviations needed for the broadcast writer to function in a full and creative manner have been grouped into four categories: composition, camera adjustment, visual transition, and other useful terms. Script examples in chapter 3 will illustrate how writers use video terms in broadcast scripts to creatively communicate with production personnel.

Composition Terms. Several terms describe what is seen by the camera. Essentially, these terms denote the composition of each shot. The principal composition terms are as follows:

• *Cover shot (CS)/full shot (FS)/establishing shot (ES).* The major area of action is to be seen. These interchangeable terms can be used at the beginning of a dramatic scene or at the beginning or ending of a studio production. This type of shot helps establish or reestablish the setting for the viewer.
• *Long shot (LS).* The widest possible view of the scene is to be shown. This general term is often imprecise; for example, if your script indicated the use of a LS of a building, when the scene was produced, production personnel could interpret the LS of the building to include all of the building and its surroundings. Despite its imprecision, LS is used often in video scripts.
• *Medium shot (MS).* A smaller portion of the scene is to be shown than might be in a LS. In effect, a long shot comprises several medium shots.
• *Close-up (CU) tight shot (TS).* A smaller portion of the scene is to be shown than might be in a MS. Several close-ups make up a medium shot.

Some hybrid television composition terms indicate intermediate designations. Common examples are "medium-long shot" (MLS), a camera shot showing more than a MS but less than a LS; "medium-close up" (MCU), a camera shot showing more than a CU but less than a MS; and "extreme-close-up" (ECU or XCU), a camera shot showing only a very limited or small portion of an object or talent (e.g., the face of a clock or the eyes of a villain).

If the script specifies a LS of a building, then a MS of the same building would show perhaps a few windows or one side of the building. A CU of that same building would then become one window on one side of the building. Because the terms LS, MS, and CU often lead to imprecise interpretations, it would be better to indicate exactly what is to be seen. For example, instead of writing "MS of building," it would be better to write "MS of building (a few windows)." Even this is not precise enough, but it is better than using only LS, MS or CU. The interpretation of such terms as LS, MS, CU, and so forth is generally left up to the director of the show, although the writer is certainly free to make some suggestions as to what should be shown.

There are other terms available which help add precision to video composition notations in broadcast scripts:

• *Anatomical designations.* These describe the portion of a person to be shown on camera. These types of descriptions indicate that a person is to be shown from the head to the anatomical part listed. For example, you could write "FS of Bill," which would indicate that the camera would show Bill from his head to his feet. Other common designations of this type are: "knee-shot" (from the knee to the head of the person); "waist-shot" (WS); and "head-and-shoulder shot" (H&S). Use of these terms will ensure precision when describing how much of one talent to show on camera.
• *Grouping designations.* By indicating how many of each are shown in a particular shot, these terms describe how groups of individuals or items are to be shown. For example, a "two-shot" indicates that two people or items are shown; a "three-shot" would include three people or items, and so on. Grouping designations could be combined with anatomical designations to produce more precise visual descriptions in scripts. For example, it is common to write "two-shot of Bill and Mary." It would be more precise to write "two-shot of Bill and Mary (WS)." Now the camera operator can be instructed to take a shot of Bill and Mary together, showing both from the waist up.
• *Perspective designations.* These describe the relationship between the subject and the viewer. If the viewer is simply to observe what is happening in a detached, non-involved manner, *objective* camera terms are used. The video terms described so far generally are considered objective camera terms. However, to offer the viewer a specific viewpoint (usually from the talent or character's perspective), *subjective* camera terms can be used.

Here are some of the common subjective camera terms used in broadcast scripts:

• *POV (point-of-view)*. Here the camera shows the viewer the scene from the subject's viewpoint. For example, write "POV" when you want the viewer to see out of a car window, from the driver's perspective.

• *Over-the-shoulder (OS)*. Here the camera is placed over the shoulder of one of the characters to show what that character sees. For example, the use of OS is effective during an interview or dramatic scene as one character talks to another.

• *High angle/low angle*. Here size and dimension can be emphasized. The camera could look down (high angle) on a child to stress his or her diminutive size; you could write "high angle on Bobby," which would show Bobby looking up into the camera lens, emphasizing his short stature. The low angle notation could be used when showing an adult talking to a child; thus "low angle on John" would indicate that John would be shown from a low angle, emphasizing his size and height (as a child would see him).

• *Canted shot*. If the camera shows a scene or character out of the normal horizontal and vertical orientations, this could emphasize unreality, distortion, or disorientation; the canted shot can illustrate the effects of drunkenness, drug use, or a severe head injury.

The writer may want to indicate that a change is needed in the composition of a camera shot, but may not wish to be specific, allowing production personnel more leeway. One term that can be used in this instance is "angle on," most often used in dramatic scripts to indicate that the character should be shown from a slightly different perspective than in earlier shots. The new camera angle would be selected by the director at the time of production.

Camera Adjustment Terms. Often, it is desirable to remain with the shot seen from a particular camera, but to adjust the picture composition to make a transition to another shot. This permits the viewer to see more than the camera is showing at present, provides subtle visual emphases and perspectives, or controls and directs the viewer's attention to a particular aspect of the character or setting. Each camera adjustment specified in a script must be used purposefully and with proper motivation for a specific desired effect. The principal camera adjustment terms are as follows:

• *Follow*. The camera can be instructed to follow the character's actions while maintaining approximately the same image size and perspective.

• *Zoom in/out*. Use of a standard Zoomar lens permits the camera to present shots ranging from a CU to a LS and any designation in between. The camera mount remains stationary while the lens performs the visual transition.

• *Dolly in/out*. A similar effect can be achieved by having the entire camera move toward (dolly in) or away from (dolly out) the character or scene. Technically, a dolly is more difficult to execute than a zoom shot and produces essentially the same results. A fast zoom or dolly shot produces a much different effect than a slow zoom or dolly shot. If you think it is appropriate, note how fast the perspective should change and at what point the zoom or dolly should stop.

• *Pan right/left.* The panorama of the scene can be shown by having the camera mount remain stationary, but pointing the lens of the camera to cover the scene. "Pan right" would indicate that the camera is to cover or show the scene beginning at the left and continuing to the right. "Pan left" provides the opposite perspective.

• *Tilt up/down.* The camera can show a setting or a character going from a low to a high angle and vice versa. For example, if you wrote "tilt up to the top of the stairs," the viewer would see a continuous shot from the bottom to the top of the stairs. "Tilt down" provides the opposite perspective.

• *Truck right/left.* To follow the action, but to maintain the same distance between camera and subject, the term "truck" is used. Examples of this technique would be showing a character walking down a busy street or items placed on a display table, but always keeping the same distance between camera and subjects.

• *Arc right/left.* An "arc" shot is a combination of a dolly and a truck shot. To illustrate the dimension, size, and beauty of an automobile, for example, the camera could arc either right or left around the automobile.

• *Pedestal/boom/crane up/down.* The camera can show the scene or character from an extremely high or low angle to provide extra visual perspectives for the viewer. The camera shot would be continuous from a normal angle to an unusually high or low angle.

Visual Transition Terms. It is necessary for the writer to use other terms to describe the visual changes or adjustments between each carefully composed shot. As with camera adjustments, the broadcast writer must select visual transitions to help the viewer move easily from one shot to another with appropriate motivation and a predetermined effect.

The principal visual transition terms are as follows:

• *Fade in/out.* At the beginning of a scene, for example, you would write "Fade in to _____." The viewer would see a blank screen and then gradually the first picture would come into view. "Fade out" would be used at the end of a scene, act, or major division of a production.

• *Cut.* Because this is the most common type of transition made between individual shots, "cut" is not written in the script. It is understood that an instantaneous change is to be made from one shot to another shot unless otherwise specified in the script.

• *Dissolve (diss. or dis.).* In a dissolve, one shot gradually fades out as another gradually fades in to take its place. The two images overlap momentarily. The writer can specify a "quick dissolve" or a "slow dissolve" to indicate the speed of the transition between shots. There are special kinds of dissolves: a "matched dissolve" is one made from one shot to another that is closely related in picture size and appearance (e.g., a matched dissolve from a CU of a clock face to a CU of a tire wheel); and a "ripple dissolve," in which a standard dissolve is achieved, but the picture "ripples" or wavers as the shots change.

• *Super (superimposition).* If one image is superimposed upon another, "super" is used.

Essentially, a super is produced by stopping a dissolve midway so that both images overlap and are seen simultaneously. The clarity and intensity of each image are diminished because of this overlap.

• *Key.* The special effects equipment available on most video switchers makes it possible to electronically "key," or place one image into another background picture. Often, the graphics used in "keys" can be colored to produce a more pleasing effect and to blend with other production elements.

• *Defocus/refocus.* One alternative to the use of a dissolve or fade to make a transition between scenes or segments in a production is to have the camera operator turn the focus knob on the camera so the shot gradually goes out of focus ("defocus"). After changing to another camera location, the shot can begin out of focus and the camera operator can be instructed to focus (or "refocus") the new shot.

• *Rack focus.* Various camera lens controls can be adjusted so only a small portion of the scene is in focus. This characteristic of the camera lens allows the camera operator and the writer to better control the viewer's attention within a shot. A common application of this technique occurs in commercials in which the character is demonstrating the use of a particular product. At the end of the commercial, when the brand name is to be displayed, the camera will "rack focus" to the box, can, or bag in the foreground so only the product is in sharp focus while the background and other parts of the screen are slightly out of focus, thus directing the viewers' attention one last time to the product advertised.

• *Wipe.* A "wipe" is a visual transition made by gradually replacing entire portions of one picture with the corresponding portions of a new picture.

• *Split screen.* When two shots occupy approximately the same amount of screen space simultaneously, it is considered a "split screen." If four images are seen simultaneously in approximately equal portions of the screen, it is considered a "quad split."

• *Whip or swish pan.* An extremely quick pan by the camera appears as a momentary blur on the screen. This technique can be used, for example, to move the viewer rapidly from one location to another and then instantly into the new setting.

Other Useful Visual Terms and Abbreviations. Other terms available to the broadcast writer to describe a desired effect more exactly or to enhance a particular production include the following:

• *B.G./F.G.* The abbreviations B.G. and F.G. indicate a specific visual element in the background (B.G.) or foreground (F.G.) of a particular shot.

• *VO.* This stands for "voice-over," indicating that the words provided are to be read by an unseen character while various images, pictures, or shots are shown.

• *B-Roll.* "B-Roll" indicates a film or videotape segment is to be inserted into the main program. The B-Roll material can contain only picture, only sound, or both picture and sound. For example, during a live broadcast of a parade, the script can indicate that a B-Roll be shown at one point. This B-Roll may show the floats being prepared or perhaps one particular float in various stages of preparation. The talent for this broadcast then ad-libs or perhaps reads from a prepared full script information that matches what is seen on the preproduced and edited B-Roll segment.

•*Stock shot.* When it is not convenient for production personnel to record a particular shot, "stock shots" or footage may be used. For example, this can include shots of a busy downtown street or an aerial view of a forested area. Before this term can be included in a script, the writer must know what stock footage is available in the production facility's library.

•*Freeze frame.* The term "freeze-frame" indicates the action or motion of a shot is stopped or frozen suddenly.

•*Montage.* A "montage" is a rapid series of shots used to produce a particular mood or image to heighten the tempo of the production.

•*Reverse motion.* "Reverse motion" indicates that the sequence of images is seen in reverse of the normal order.

•*Slow/fast motion.* "Slow motion" or "fast motion" indicates that the images appear at a reduced or an accelerated pace.

FILM PRODUCTION

The use of motion picture film in television production is diminishing and is being replaced by more sophisticated videotape systems. Still, many television commercials as well as dramatic and comedy programs are produced on film. Of course, motion picture film can be used to produce presentations, if not for television then for theaters, schools, hospitals, and businesses. This trend away from film production for television applications is likely to continue as more versatile videotape systems are designed to provide the same kinds of visual effects once offered only through film production. Other factors have contributed to an escalated use of videotape, such as improved videotape picture quality, increased portability of camera and recording gear, reasonable set-up and maintenance costs, and the growing acceptability of videotape production within the broadcasting industry. The writer should continue to monitor this shift in emphasis in production methods because of its impact upon the kinds of scripts written.

Generally, the information provided for television production (tools, terminology, procedures, and techniques) applies to motion picture production as well. Some differences, however, should be noted; for example, in motion picture production there is no control room, no video switcher, no videotape, and no character generator used. Practically all of the other television production terms can be used in motion picture scripts; if anything, a limited number of terms and descriptive phrases are used in most motion picture scripts. There is no technical director (T.D.), but there are other, more specialized, personnel involved in film production.

Large-budget motion picture production makes use of 35mm film stock using traditional film-style, one-camera production techniques rather than the in-studio, three-camera process that is common in videotape television production. The single-camera process is used, even in videotape production, when out-of-doors or location shooting is involved.

A large production crew, with diverse production specialties, working in a studio or on location, will spend a long time with a single film project. The film may be a theatrical release, a made-for-TV movie, or perhaps the pilot program for a prospective television series. Careful planning and coordination are needed to produce a quality product on time and within the specified budget.

CONCLUSION

This chapter has examined basic production information needed by the broadcast writer. You should explore the creative potential offered by each medium. Remember that the writer is but one member of a team of people collectively and creatively working together. Know the tools of production that help bring a script to life as it moves from the typewriter or word processor to the radio or television set. Remember to use production terminology in your scripts to clarify what is seen or heard, but not so much that it distracts the reader of a script or interferes with the creative participation of production personnel.

Knowledge of these basic production tools, terms, and techniques should help the writer anticipate technical limits and expand creative potential. Such knowledge should be an integral part of the broadcast writer's work. It will lead the writer to a more satisfying sense of participation in the creative process of broadcast writing and production.

SUGGESTED EXERCISES AND PROJECTS

1. Compare and contrast the advantages and disadvantages of various mass media (radio, television, motion pictures) from the writer's viewpoint. What kinds of writing challenges do the characteristics of each medium offer?
2. Watch a 30-minute television program. Chart the length of each major program segment. Note the use of the various camera composition designations, visual transitions, special effects, camera positions, and so on. Report on the production value of the program and the effectiveness of the visual elements included.
3. Schedule a personal or group visit to a broadcast production facility. Determine production procedures and processes and how these affect the role of the broadcast writer.
4. Record a radio commercial. Note the use of voices, music, and sound effects. List the production terms (described in this chapter) needed to accomplish these audio effects.
5. Watch (and if possible record) a television commercial. Note the use of sound and

picture. List the production terms (described in this chapter) needed to accomplish these audio and video effects.

6. Do the same as in exercise 5 but for a current motion picture film. Comment on the effectiveness of the production elements used and how they interrelate with the work of the writer for the film.

ADDITIONAL READING

Alten, Stanley R. *Audio in Media*. Belmont, CA: Wadsworth, 1981.

Burrows, Thomas D., and Wood, Donald N. *Television Production: Disciplines and Techniques*. Dubuque, Iowa: Wm. C. Brown Co., 1978.

Happe, Bernard. *Basic Motion Picture Technology*. 2d ed. New York: Hastings House, 1975.

McLeish, Robert. *The Technique of Radio Production: A Manual for Local Broadcasters*. London: Focal Press, 1978.

Nisbett, Alec. *The Technique of the Sound Studio: For Radio, Recording Studio, Television and Film*. 4th ed. London: Focal Press, 1979.

Oringel, Robert S. *Audio Control Handbook*. 5th ed. New York: Hastings House, 1983.

Wurtzel, Alan. *Television Production*. 2d ed. New York: McGraw-Hill, 1983.

Zettl, Herbert. *Television Production Handbook*. 4th ed. Belmont, Calif.: Wadsworth, 1984.

Chapter Three

BASIC BROADCAST WRITING STYLES, TECHNIQUES, AND FORMS

The broadcast writer must prepare written material in proper script form to ensure that the work will not be rejected outright because of improper presentation. Use of the proper format will permit the writer to communicate essential scripting information clearly and succinctly. Once the writer has mastered the mechanics of putting script material on the page properly, the various standard presentation forms can be used to express ideas and concepts easily and effectively.

The purpose of this chapter is twofold: (1) to present basic concepts for writing effective aural and visual script material; and (2) to present basic scripting formats to help the writer provide script material in a standard and effective manner. There will be a discussion of essential aural writing styles and techniques. This will include how to select words, organize sentences and creatively incorporate music and sound effects in a script. The discussion of visual writing styles and techniques will indicate how to select and use various visual elements creatively. The rest of the chapter will be an explanation of standard broadcast scripting styles and formats to show how aural and visual script material is presented on paper by the professional broadcast writer. This discussion will cover such writing mechanics as use of punctuation, abbreviations, timing considerations, and the standard scripting formats used for material in various stages of development. Full-scripts will receive more attention because of their complexity and constant use in many writing situations and applications.

The broadcast scripting styles and formats presented in this chapter reflect those used throughout the broadcasting industry. This does not imply that all broadcasting facilities will use these styles or formats exactly as presented here. There are variations. It is important to master these basic script forms to acquire the insight and flexibility necessary to adjust to such writing presentation requirements in the future.

All basic script formats will be presented in this chapter to show the progression of forms available and to serve as a reference for the discussions in later chapters.

Several kinds of script material are presented to help the writer understand how to apply the various script forms in practical writing situations. In this chapter, you should focus on the *form,* not necessarily on the specific content, of the script examples used.

(However, it is important to note that margin and spacing adjustments have been made in the material presented. Book design considerations have made these adjustments necessary.)

AURAL WRITING STYLES AND TECHNIQUES

The use of sound in broadcast scripts is an important technique for the broadcast writer. The use of sound is important in television presentations even though visual elements tend to dominate. Sound is the entire means of communication in radio.

Sounds have the unique capability of creating an environment for the listener or viewer. Sounds help create and enhance many mental images. Creating an environment or setting is important for the writer since often this determines the acceptability of future messages and the ultimate success of the communication process.

Imagination is the only limit imposed upon the writer's ability to create environment effectively—the imagination of the writer and the imagination of the audience which is willingly stretched to accept altered or enhanced reality. The success of aural messages hinges on this tenuous, although important, human characteristic. Imagination is the key to creating an effective environment through sound.

Radio's often-criticized disadvantage of no pictures actually becomes its greatest advantage since the absence of tangible pictures provides no visual or mental restraints on the imagination of the writer and, ultimately, the listener. Through the creative use of various writing and production techniques, entire worlds can be created in the human mind. Actions, emotions, characters and even words take on new dimensions when they are presented effectively by the writer and accepted by the audience. Persons and objects can project uncharacteristic or unreal qualities. The writer's creative sensitivities and appreciation for the beauty and functional cohesiveness among the various elements of sound are important determinants to the effectiveness and acceptability of sound in broadcast messages.

There are many techniques available to create an environment with sound. The major techniques available to the broadcast writer are: language (words and sentences), music, and sound effects. Each will be examined to provide insight into creative potential for the broadcast writer.

Language Usage

The primary goal of language is to communicate ideas and information to be easily understood. Only after a message has been understood can a writer hope to entertain, inspire, or persuade the audience.

A writer needs a solid foundation in the basic use of language, especially in the selection and use of words and the combining of words into meaningful sentences. This discussion can touch on only a few of the elements necessary for the broadcast writer to use the English language effectively. A solid foundation in English grammar is highly recommended. Each time you learn something new about the use of language, you bring that knowledge to all future writing assignments. In effect, you become a better writer.

Words. Words are the primary tool of the writer for the expression of thoughts, ideas, and emotions regardless of the medium. Words have power and meaning. They are capable of expressing the most complicated reality and the subtlest emotions. Do not waste words. Choose them carefully and precisely to express a specific thought. Calculate the impact or result of the words you write.

When selecting and using words, it is important to remember the audience—their interests, preferences, likes, and dislikes. Use words which are familiar, touch the lives of your audience directly, create immediate and lasting attention, and have strong, personal impact.

The broadcast audience is most familiar with reality. The broadcast writer can reflect reality by using simple, common words which are easy to listen to and understand. Informal, rather than formal, language or word choices is preferred. There is no second chance for the audience to reread what is heard, so words must be chosen carefully. Remember to write for the ear, not the eye, of the audience. Be sensitive to how individual words sound when spoken and heard only one time with no opportunity to hear that word again. Think about the wide range of meanings and nuances possible through careful selection of words. One way to learn how to reflect reality in broadcast scripts is to listen to various kinds of people talk and to capture the informal, conversational style you hear. The more you observe and retain about language habits, the more realistic your word choices will be.

Avoid using complex, technical terms unless absolutely necessary. When such terms are used in a broadcast script, explain the terms in straightforward, common language, easily understood by the average listener or viewer. Your extra efforts will be rewarded when you realize that the audience better understands and appreciates the subject matter.

The broadcast writer should avoid the use of clichés, a combination of words used too often to have significant continued impact on the audience. Repeated exposure to clichés leads to a lessening of impact. The use of clichés shows the writer's lack of creativity and willingness to struggle to find and use words in a fresh, original way. Clichés make writing sound boring, trite and unintelligent. Good writing is simple writing. Simple writing does not imply the use of clichés.

The broadcast writer must know the basic units of language and word usage. Nouns designate a person, place, or thing; they attach a label to something; they provide a specific perspective which influences the audience. Adjectives are used for description; they add dimension and color to the language and should be chosen carefully. Verbs provide the power or action in a sentence; they should be chosen carefully, accurately, and with a desired effect; verb tenses should vary to better match what is communicated. Adverbs modify or complement verbs and adjectives; they provide an extra dimension or description to verbs or action words; they can tell how much, how fast, how tall, and so on.

Sentences. Sentences are the principal units of organized thought. The way in which carefully selected words are arranged or put together to form phrases and sentences extends the creative potential for the writer. While it is important that each word in a broadcast script be chosen carefully, it is crucial that those individual words be combined into sentences which lead to the understanding of a message by the audience. This initial goal of understanding forms the basis for further writing objectives—inspiration, information, persuasion, entertainment. The keys to constructing effective sentences for broadcast scripts are: informality, clarity, simplicity, and conciseness.

Incomplete sentences (i.e., those that do not display the usual subject-verb-object arrangement) are acceptable in broadcast scripts. This kind of sentence construction reflects contemporary usage, saves words, and adds vigor and variety to language and sentence structure.

Clear, simple sentences are attractive to a broadcast audience. They make your message distinctive, and help it stand apart from the barrage of words and images inundating your audience daily. Do not separate the subject from the verb in a sentence; these two sentence units form a logical arrangement. Avoid interjections or explanatory clauses, especially in the middle of a sentence; these clauses are confusing and do not reflect a conversational language style. Clear writing does not have to mean sterile writing. It is possible to write strong, meaningful, expressive sentences with clarity and simplicity.

Concise writing is "lean" writing. Use only the words necessary to express an idea or emotion. Critically examine each sentence you write. Discard words that do not help move forward the idea that you want to express. Express only one idea in each sentence. It would be better to use a few short sentences than one complex sentence. Longer sentences are acceptable if appropriate pauses are marked in the script and if the reader or performer follows such directions and punctuation notations. Vary sentence length. Too many short sentences sound disjointed and "choppy" and disturb the normal flow of a conversational style.

The best way to test the effectiveness of your use of language is to read each sentence aloud. Your choice of words and sentence construction may look fine on paper, but until you *hear* how the words *sound* when they are combined into a sentence, and how each sentence works with the previous sentence, the sentence which follows, the one after that, and so on, you have not tested the effectiveness of your writing. You must *hear* the sounds of the words, the meanings they convey, the emotions they evoke, the impact they have.

Music and Sound Effects

Uses. Both music and sound effects can be used in broadcast scripts to produce the following effects:

•attract and hold the attention of the audience
•enhance but not overpower the script by adding reality and authenticity
•create a mood or atmosphere
•establish locale or setting by visualizing the scene
•direct attention to a specific portion of the setting (e.g., a character, an action, or an object) by emphasizing that particular element with a short music excerpt or sound effect
•make transitions between program segments or to bridge between time, place, locale, or mood changes
•move the action of the script forward
•heighten or punctuate a climactic moment in a script
•enliven something that is normally silent (e.g., providing a musical or sound effect identification for an automobile)
•counterpoint the mood or tone of the words heard (e.g., a sound effect of a noisy jet plane or a street scene used as counterpoint to a quiet, narrative delivery style)

As a separate element, music can be used as the principal program content (e.g., in a radio music program), as the theme or identification for many types of programs and entertainment personalities (e.g., the theme songs associated with such personalities as Bob Hope, Johnny Carson, Danny Thomas), or as a substitute for a sound effect (e.g., a musical instrument or phrase used to characterize a specific person, character, animal, or event).

Suggestions. When inserting either music or sound effects into a broadcast script you should do the following:

1. Relate the music or sound effect used to your overall script goal or purpose.
2. Make certain either or both elements integrate well with the other script elements in style and content, tone and quality, and that there is an effective blend of audio elements.
3. Find the relevant, prominent, representative, or key sound effect or music to create mood, atmosphere, locale, or setting. For example, to create a restaurant locale, do not specify in the script all of the possible sounds heard in a restaurant. Instead, select the one or two key sounds that will suggest the locale to the listener. The rest of the picture will be created in the mind and imagination of the audience.
4. Be specific in your music or sound effects notations. Always identify the exact sound effect or type or title of music to be used. Indicate how each is to be heard (up full, under announcer, up and then under, etc.) and how each is to be disposed of (fades out, under and then out, etc.).
5. Be certain to note that the music or sound effect is "under" or "in the background" when a voice is to be heard over either audio element. Suggest the use of an instrumental version of a particular musical selection when a voice is to be heard over the music. Song lyrics tend to distract the audience from such narration or dialogue.

6. Be cautious in the use of familiar music for production purposes; such music may provide connotations and images for the listener that you do not intend.

VISUAL WRITING STYLES AND TECHNIQUES

When writing for the primarily visual media of television and motion pictures, the writer must be able to envision images that convey the mood, the purpose, and the direction of the situation. It is necessary to envision the *development* of the script—shot by shot, scene by scene, sequence by sequence. The writer must use imagination to see and hear all of the elements in the script—objects, people, action, dialogue, continuity—before words can be written on paper. Thinking must precede writing. Idea and image must develop side by side so that one reinforces and strengthens the impact of the other. The usual script development pattern is thinking, then seeing, and finally writing. Visualization and sequencing are the processes which assist the writer in selecting and using appropriate visual elements to reinforce the audio portion of the script.

Visualization

Visualization is the process of translating concepts and ideas into individual images or pictures. The writer imagines individual, perfectly composed images of scenes, backgrounds, locales, settings, and characters which best portray what is to be communicated.

Objectives. When the writer uses visualization for nondramatic presentations, the objective should be to show objects, performers, and actions as clearly as possible. This is the objective for such programs as newscasts, talk and informational programs, game shows, instructional and documentary programs.

When using visualization for dramatic presentations, however, the writer should attempt to show objects, settings, locales, and performers in such a way as to convey a particular meaning, idea, or perspective. The next time you watch a television or film drama, notice how the position of the camera relates to the performers and the objects in the picture. A change in camera or performer positions can alter the viewer's perspective and interpretation of a particular scene or sequence, or change the reaction to a particular character.

Limitations. There are several factors which influence the visualization process:

1. Television is an intimate medium because of screen size. Thus, more close shots should be used to show material in more detail.
2. The vertical and horizontal dimensions of the television screen are in a ratio of approximately 3 to 4. The shape of the medium must be part of visualizing set-

tings and planning sequences so that most of the shots are horizontally rather than vertically oriented. Motion picture screens are also horizontally oriented.
3. Television and motion picture screens are two-dimensional. Thus, to create an illusion of depth, the writer should suggest the use and emphasis of foregrounds and backgrounds in the composition of individual shots.
4. Objects, performers, and cameras are constantly moving, yet to the viewer they may appear static because the screen itself does not move. This, of course, is not the case when the writer and director visualize characters and settings for a stage presentation, for example. The writer must keep in mind the audience's visual perceptions of each medium.
5. Because of the severe time limitations involved in television and motion picture production, the writer has to limit the number of sets or shooting locations as well as the diversity and difficulty of shots suggested in a script.

Whoever ultimately directs the acting and production personnel using your completed script will have to make crucial decisions about visualization and will be most concerned with the best techniques for accomplishing your visual scripting goals. If you know some of the considerations involved in determining the staging and framing of individual shots, however, you can improve the quality of your visualization process and ultimately the script from which the director will work.

Visualization, then, is the first major step toward completing the writing process for the visually oriented media of television and motion pictures. If the writer's visualization process is done conscientiously, competently, and with some foresight, the process of visual sequencing will follow naturally and provide the final step for the visual portion of the writing process.

Sequencing

Sequencing is the process of placing individual images or pictures in a certain order or sequence to convey a specific message or meaning. A specific idea or perspective can be communicated by changing the order of these individual images and by using continuous motion to bridge the gap between individual shots. Sequencing is the process of creating a *succession* of images formulated or structured through the process of visualization.

Storyboards and similar visual representations help the writer and others involved in the project plot effective sequencing. Such representations serve as a link between the words written in the script and the ultimate visual motion displayed on the screen. Each frame in a storyboard illustrates the camera's view of the essential shots in a sequence and shows the correlation between the sounds and pictures. The visual portion of each storyboard frame illustrates optical effects and camera angles. The audio portion (written under each appropriate frame) indicates the music, sound effects, and dialogue to be heard. Storyboards may be useful in highly visual presentations. Motion pictures such as *Star Wars* and *Raiders of the Lost Ark* have benefited from elaborate storyboard displays, although the technique is used most often in planning broadcast commercials and announcements.

Visual sequencing can be accomplished by using one technique or a combination of several techniques: movement of performers in front of the camera, camera adjustments, and visual transitions between shots. Each technique, when used carefully and purposefully, will help produce an effective succession of images.

For the broadcast writer, the processes of visualization and sequencing are perhaps the most difficult to master. At first glance, the terminology and specific justifications for use of certain techniques and procedures may seem bewildering and unimportant. Skillful use of these processes, however, will determine the acceptability, production value, and ultimate success of the script. Without creative application of the principles of visualization and sequencing, the broadcast writer cannot hope to prepare effective, meaningful, visually stimulating script material.

MECHANICS OF BROADCAST WRITING STYLE

Several important broadcast writing style considerations apply equally to radio and television writing. It is important to master these before trying to use this information in later scripting format and writing style applications. The script examples in this chapter illustrate many of the considerations that will be described.

How to Prepare Broadcast Script Pages

Longer scripting presentations (e.g., drama and comedy scripts and program series proposals) require a cover page. A cover page contains the title of the series or program, complete information about the writer (name, address, telephone number), the date the script was submitted, and the sections of the script (designated by acts and scenes) along with the appropriate page numbers for each section. Cover pages are not used for shorter scripts (e.g., commercials, talk program show formats, interview outlines).

For shorter scripts or for segments within longer programs, writers provide identification information at the top left corner of each page: program series or client (for commercials), program or script number (assigned by the production company, advertising agency or station), program or announcement title (a phrase which illuminates the central theme or concept used), estimated length, the date and the writer's name. This information readily identifies your work and provides an efficient means of processing the script material. Here are two typical script presentations: the one on the left for a commercial; the one on the right for a talk program.

```
        First National Bank          In Perspective
        "We've Got Your Interest"     Mayoral Candidates
```

```
FNB 4182-A              IP -- #43
30-second Film          30-Minutes
Jones  9/20             Jones  10/4  5 P.M.
```

There are several routine broadcast copy preparation items which should be remembered:

1. Use a typewriter with pica type. In some situations, it is helpful to use extra large pica type (great primer, executive size, or orator), particularly when a script is to be used directly by on-camera television talent from a through-the-camera-lens prompting device. Keep the type clean and change the ribbon frequently. Dark black ribbons are always preferred.
2. Leave approximately a 1¼-inch border around all edges of each script page. This provides space for content and production notations.
3. Type on standard size sheets of paper (8½ by 11 inches). Use a soft grade of quality bond paper. If the script is to be used or seen on the air, select paper that will not reflect television studio lights and that will make a minimum of sound when handled near a microphone. A special continuous paper roll is used for through-the-camera-lens prompting situations.
4. Type on one side of the paper only.
5. Double-space all script material. There are situations when triple-spacing may be required. Never single-space broadcast script material.
6. Determine marginal settings for each writing situation.
7. Do not hyphenate any word at the end of a line in a script. In an on-air situation, breaking a word at the end of a line makes it difficult to read the script smoothly. It is much better to correct this simple mechanical deficiency earlier in the scripting stage rather than allowing this distraction to cause unnecessary production problems.
8. Conclude each page with a complete sentence. The on-air reader or performer will not have to flip to the next page in the middle of a sentence and disrupt the flow of the script.
9. If it is necessary to provide more than one page to complete a particular writing assignment, one of several scripting techniques may be used: number each page in the script consecutively (e.g., p. 2, p. 3, etc. or 2-2-2, 3-3-3); indicate the total length of the script as well as the specific page number (e.g., p. 2 of 8, p. 3 of 8, etc.); place the notation "add 1," "add 2," and so on at the top of consecutive pages; or draw a conspicuous, heavy black arrow (⟶) in the lower right-hand corner of each page except the last. This last technique is required only in news-related work.
10. If at all possible, retype scripts which contain marginal notations, numerous corrections and errors. Remember that your scripts represent your ideas, concepts, and standards of professionalism to others.

Spelling

It may not seem important to spell words correctly, but consistent misspellings detract from the overall quality of the script, distract on-air readers or performers, and serve as another measure of the writer's grasp of the basics of effective writing. Efficient and frequent use of a standard dictionary is an essential tool of an effective broadcast writer. The thirty seconds required to look up a word in the dictionary pays dividends by producing a more readable broadcast script. Spelling correctly is mandatory at all times!

Pronunciation

Since broadcast scripts often are read live, on-the-air, it is necessary to provide pronunciation assistance for the presenter or reader. This is done to avoid embarrassment and to provide a smoother flow for the script. This pronunciation assistance is provided for difficult-to-pronounce names, places, and objects, especially those available locally. If in doubt, it is better to include pronunciation assistance in the script.

Although the International Phonetic Alphabet (IPA) is the most precise and universal system for transcribing speech sounds, it is not widely used by media professionals. The most useful method for communicating pronunciation is a common sense approach using capitalization to indicate syllables to be stressed. Enclose the phonetic spelling in parentheses immediately next to or just above the difficult-to-pronounce word.

> Our guest today is Harry Schizas (SHY-suss), candidate for Mayor.
>
> Be sure to shop at Finkleheimers (FINKLE-high-murrs) Department Store in the Roca (ROW-ka) Mall.

Abbreviations

Eliminate most abbreviations from broadcast scripts. Scripts will be read more smoothly without on-air hesitations, if words are written in full exactly as they are to be read. It is acceptable to abbreviate commonly recognized titles of personal address—Mr., Mrs., Ms., Dr.—rather than create odd phonetic spellings such as "mister" and "missus."

Use abbreviations or alphabetical designations that are to be read as such if the general audience is quite familiar with them. It is acceptable, for example, to write "C-I-O" instead of "Congress of Industrial Organizations," and to write "Y-M-C-A" instead of "Young Men's Christian Association." Hyphens are used to separate the letters to be read individually. Use the full name the first time it appears in the script if there is reason to believe that the audience will not understand the abbreviation. Thereafter, when the audience has adjusted mentally to the name of the organization in full, it is permissible to use the abbreviation.

Well-known acronyms such as NATO, UNICEF, and OPEC should not be hyphenated or spelled out when placed in a script. The letters are not meant to be read individually.

Do not use symbols in lieu of words. For example, do not write "&" for "and"; or "#" for "number"; or "%" for "percent." Shorthand now will cause confusion later.

Capitalization

Unless otherwise instructed, use standard capitalization in broadcast scripts. FULL CAPS (i.e., uppercase letters) are reserved to note character designations, video and audio production details, and special production and interpretation information. Use of this system helps differentiate between the words spoken by the talent and all other script information.

Numbers

Good judgment and consistency must be used when handling numerals in broadcast scripts. Eliminate as much statistical information as possible. Generalize and simplify intelligently. But in the interest of accurate and complete communication, do not omit or distort highly important numerical information (as in a documentary or broadcast news story).

Use numbers sparingly. When spoken aloud, numbers are often difficult for the talent to read, difficult for the listener or viewer to understand and, more important, to remember. Even numerical information displayed on a television screen may become difficult to understand and absorb as the numbers flash on and off the screen quickly.

It is best to convert figures, especially large ones, into round numbers whenever feasible. "1,605" may be rounded to "16-hundred" and "227,523" may be expressed as "a quarter-million." Identify rounded numbers with such general terms as "about," "almost," "nearly," or "approximately." Strive for as much variation as possible. To avoid repetition and to facilitate understanding, translate trends or changes expressed in figures into such terminology as "doubled," "cut in half," "dropped 50 percent," or "dipped sharply."

Spell out numbers under eleven—"three," "six," "ten" . . . Use numerals for numbers from 11 to 999—"85," "118," "865" . . . Years can be written as numerals—"1986," "1492," "1776," and so on.

Spell out ordinal numbers under eleven—"first," "eighth," "tenth," and so on. Use "st," "rd," "th," and "nd" after dates, addresses, streets numbered over 11—"February 13th," "22nd and 43rd Avenue". . .

Use a hyphenated combination of numerals and words to express large numbers—"17-million," "15-hundred." Express fractions in words, not numerals. Hyphenate the words in a fraction—"three-fourths," "one-half of one percent."

Avoid use of the dollar sign and the cent sign. Write "ten dollars" and not "$10." Write "75-cents" and not "75¢." This same guideline applies to other terms or symbols—inches, feet, miles, seconds, minutes, hours, and all metric terms (e.g., write "85 kilometers" instead of "85 km").

When writing license numbers, telephone numbers, addresses, and similar series of numerals, use a hyphen to break the numbers as they ordinarily would be read most effectively—"H-14-21," "Emerson 2-17-76," "6-21 Lake View Road," and so on.

Punctuation

Appropriate use of standard punctuation marks in broadcast scriptwriting applications is essential if the writer hopes to make full use of available language tools. Only with systematic use of punctuation will the writer ensure that a specific feeling or idea is communicated correctly.

The use of short sentences of simple construction removes the need for much punctuation. Still there is a need to assist the performer or talent in phrasing or reading the script more intelligently and to communicate an idea more clearly. In most instances, traditional punctuation rules can be followed. The punctuation marks described are not used in every scriptwriting situation. Exercise good judgment and common sense when using punctuation marks in your scripts.

Period. The period indicates the end of a complete thought. Broadcast scripts often are not written in grammatically complete sentence form since a conversational style is stressed. In conversation, most people do not speak in complete sentences (subject–verb–predicate). Even then a period is used to indicate the end of an idea. The period also indicates that a slight pause should be inserted when the script is read aloud. As in most conversation, we pause at the end of a thought. The period signals both the end of a single thought and the need for a pause, the length of which is determined by the nature of the script and the pacing or rhythm desired.

Comma. Commas have many uses in broadcast writing situations. Most often they are used to separate words, phrases, or clauses which are part of a single thought unit or sentence (e.g., "trains, rain, and body sprains. Only some of the features on tonight's ten o'clock magazine report"). Commas are used for parenthetical phrases inserted in a sentence (e.g., "The full impact of unemployment, on the other hand, remains unknown"). This punctuation mark is also used for short interjections or for naming directly a particular person (e.g., "Ah, Sarah, how well you look today"). A comma is used to emphasize a particular phrase or to avoid ambiguity (e.g., "To Harry, Leo was someone special, really special"). Just as the period indicates a pause, the comma suggests a slight pause in the reading. In broadcast scriptwriting, use a comma when it helps group words and phrases together to produce a more effective and understandable presentation. This guideline does not coincide with conventional punctuation rules for use of commas.

Dash. This punctuation mark (--) suggests a more exaggerated response than other related punctuation marks. For example, if you write

The Vietnam veteran returned home -- to an unknown future.

the dash would indicate that a longer pause was needed at that point in the sentence. Use of a comma instead of a dash would shorten the length of the pause. Although this is a fine point of punctuation, careful consideration must be given to each punctuation mark since each provides a specific direction for interpretation of the words in each sentence. The dash is also used to indicate a break in a sentence or portion of dialogue. For example, if you wrote

> FRED: Now is the time to --
> BILL: Shop at Petersen's.

the dash would be used to note that one character interrupts the other to complete the sentence or thought. The dash is often used after a series of words or phrases to bridge into a summary statement. For example,

> Balance, strength, and determination -- all are needed for athletic success.

Ellipsis. Some writers use the dash and ellipsis interchangeably; however, each should suggest a subtle difference in interpretation. An ellipsis (...) can be used to add an extra thought or to clarify an idea; for example,

> He went back home...to start a new life.

This punctuation mark could be used to intensify a dramatic effect; for example,

> He stepped into the car, touched the starter, and...a blinding flash!

While the only technical grammatical function of an ellipsis is to indicate that words or phrases have been omitted from a direct quotation, the broadcast writer can use this same punctuation mark to clarify and intensify scripts and to provide a new shading of meaning. (For broadcast writing purposes, the ellipsis generally has its "dots" set tight, not spaced out as in a more general type of writing.) Although officially the ellipsis has only three "dots," the longer we make the elipsis—e.g., ... —the longer the pause.

Hyphen. Use the hyphen to connect closely related letters, numerals or words ("A-F-of-L," "125-thousand," "president-elect"). Hyphens may be used as unspoken substitutes for the words "(up) to and including" or simply "to" ("The years 1970-78 were crucial to the company's development" and "The New York-Chicago train was delayed").

Emphasis. There are two ways to indicate that a key word or phrase is to be stressed in a sentence—underlining or writing the word(s) in FULL CAPS. Either method produces the desired effect. Indicating those words or phrases to be stressed or emphasized in your scripts will ensure a better interpretation of your work. Notice the difference in emphasis and meaning between these two sentences, each with a different word stressed:

> <u>Now</u> is the time to act.
> Now is the time to <u>act</u>.

Apostrophe. Use an apostrophe (') to indicate possession (e.g., "Frank's car" or "Neil Diamond's songs"); to form contractions to enhance the conversational style used in broadcast writing (e.g., "couldn't," "that's"); and to form plurals of letters, numbers, and words (e.g., "He has trouble with his r's, 8's and the's.").

Colon. Use a colon (:) to separate the name of a character or a music and sound effect notation from the description to follow. For example,

> MARY: Now is the time to buy that new car you've always wanted.
> MUSIC: <u>(UP FOR 2 SECONDS AND THEN UNDER)</u>
> MARY: Yes, they're selling them as fast as they come in....

Parentheses. The broadcast writer uses parentheses ( ) to suggest the manner or style of delivery and presentation as well as to note any necessary technical instructions.

> MAN: (PLEADING) I <u>know</u> it's my turn to drive today.
> WOMAN: (CRYING) I told you I'd drive.

Other Punctuation Marks. There are several other punctuation marks available which are not commonly used by broadcast writers: brackets [ ], quotation marks (" "), and the semicolon (;). The grammatical purposes for each of these can be accomplished with the punctuation marks already described.

An informed use of the few punctuation marks widely accepted in broadcast writing situations is essential. Since the words you write are meant to be read aloud, proper and effective use of these notations provide yet another means of indicating variations in meaning, emphasis, tone, pauses, and interpretation. Correct use of punctuation marks avoids ambiguity and adds clarity to your writing.

Broadcast Editing Marks

Only in emergency situations (e.g., news or public affairs programs produced under extreme deadlines) should standard broadcast editing marks be used. They should be used sparingly and only as time constraints and common sense dictate. When these marks are used, they should be used boldly, but neatly, so that they are clearly understood. They should never deter the performer or on-air talent from making interpretation marks on the script or from reading the script smoothly and accurately.

Even if proper broadcast editing marks are used, if there are too many of them, the script will not be acceptable. In most cases, it is best to retype the entire page and avoid using any script editing marks.

Most of the more complicated copyreading symbols used in the print media should never be used in broadcast scripts. Here are the basic broadcast editing marks:

1. To separate words run together, use a single slanted line, or virgule:

   The decade was of great/concern to the American people.

2. To close up space between letters in the same word, use curved lines both above and below the gap:

   The de͡cade was of great concern to the American people.

3. To delete a word or phrase that is not needed, black out the unwanted material completely and bridge the gap with a *single* line above the connecting words in the sentence:

   The decade was of great ~~most~~ concern to the American people.

4. To insert a word or phrase, print it boldly or type it clearly above the line and funnel it into the proper place in the sentence:

             great
   The decade was of concern to the American people.

5. To correct a misspelled word, black it out *completely* and then print boldly or type clearly the correct version above the line and funnel the correction into the proper place in the sentence:

             concern
   The decade was of great ~~conncern~~ to the American people.

6. To close up space when a word, a phrase, or an entire sentence is deleted, use a curved line to connect the two parts of the finished sentence:

   The decade was of great ~~significance to politicians~~
   ~~and of course~~ of concern to the American people.

7. To insert a missing punctuation mark, simply provide the missing notation neatly but conspicuously at the proper place in the script:

   The decade was of great concern to the American people .

8. To insert script material at the beginning of a paragraph, use an extended indentation mark:

> The decade was of great concern to the American people.

Timing Considerations

The precise timing of complete programs, program segments and announcements is essential in broadcast writing. Unfortunately, highly dramatic and effective scripts have had to be trimmed because of poor judgment used by the writer when estimating the amount of time needed to present the script.

There are several variables which prevent precise word and time equivalencies: the broadcast script format used (for instance, a one-page semi-script could provide the same amount of program time as several pages of a full-script for the same program); the number and duration of elements other than spoken words (music bridges, sound effects inserts, bits of dramatic "business" by performers, etc.); and the inconsistent delivery style and speed of the reader or performer.

With the basic tools of a studio clock (to time an entire program) and a stop watch (to time particular segments and entire announcements), the writer can design scripts for longer programs using the front timing approach or the back timing approach. When using front timing, each segment of the presentation is timed as it is to be broadcast, starting from 0 seconds to the end. When using back timing, the last 2 to 4 minutes of the program are timed. Back timing allows the director and talent to pace the show to the end by timing the material needed to complete the crucial last segment of the program. When this point is reached during a live broadcast, the pre-timed final segment is begun, allowing the show to leave the air on time.

The best way to approximate the length or running time of each page of a broadcast script is to have the reader or performer who will deliver it read the script aloud and walk through the actions required. After some experience writing material for the same acting and production situations, the writer can better judge how much playing time each page of a script will occupy. It is helpful to have the reader or performer actually vocalize or read the words out loud several times to fine tune the timing of the script.

BROADCAST SCRIPTING FORMATS, APPROACHES, AND TECHNIQUES

Several basic scripting formats can be used to write material for broadcast use. Later chapters will illustrate the application of these basic formats in specific kinds of writing situations.

While the information presented here reflects acceptable industry standards, it must be understood that each scripting format and approach can be modified to meet specific requirements for a given writing project. Find out the standard scripting format needed in each scripting situation and incorporate the format modifications preferred by your employer in your writing.

Proposals

Before writing a script, it is often necessary to provide a proposal for the development of the project. Sometimes, this document is called a premise or a concept. Whatever the label attached to this preliminary scripting document, the same kind of information is supplied for review, authorization, and funding by the appropriate officer or executive of the funding organization or company.

Proposals for regular program series generally are six to ten pages long. The first page indicates the series title, program length, name and address of the series creator, and the writer's agent (if there is one). The second page is a brief description of the series and what makes it unique and saleable. The third page is a more detailed description of the series—the situations, locales, and settings. The fourth and subsequent pages are concise one-paragraph descriptions of principal characters. The last few pages are short, one-page story summaries or premise statements for three or four episodes in the prospective series. Proposals for special scripting projects (e.g., made-for-TV movies, miniseries, and anthologies) are in the form of a treatment or step outline.

Most proposals are presented orally in a "pitch" rather than in written form. A written proposal either is never done or is prepared as a matter of contract after initial approval has been received for the project. There are many reasons given for this practice—the collaborative nature of television and motion picture production, the desire to remain flexible in expressing preferences for script development, the fear of outright rejection without another chance to sell an idea, and the constraints of time which preclude reading, rather than hearing, about an idea. Whatever the reasons, the determined writer must be prepared to pitch ideas. It has nothing really to do with writing, but it is an essential step in the survival of a creative writer in major production centers. (See chapter 13).

Treatments

Essentially, a treatment is a short story or narrative written in the present tense which describes the progressive development of a program or story idea from the beginning to the last segment. This document can be sometimes as few as four, but often as many as fifty pages long.

It is best to prepare a treatment when the various developmental stages of a scripting project must be reviewed and approved by several individuals or groups. It is easier to make adjustments at the treatment stage than after a full-script has been written. Also, generating a treatment makes the writer critically examine the progression of key segments or portions of a presentation before the full-script is written. A carefully prepared treatment makes the scriptwriting task even more creatively fulfilling.

The treatment should indicate a tentative point of view which will be explored and adjusted later by the writer and the production staff. Additionally, it should describe the style, mood, emphasis, and shape of the presentation—whether dialogue, commentary, narration, or music will be used, whether the presentation style will be factual, dramatized, or stylized, serious or light, and so on. In the treatment, there needs to be a preliminary indication of the length of the final presentation and the content of each major sequence.

Depending upon the type of program ultimately to be written, the treatment could supply essential information about program objectives, the main and supporting characters, locations, themes, and the action anticipated. Some treatments include information about crucial camera shots or graphics or short pieces of narration or dialogue to be used. Some treatments also include a tentative development budget, production timetable, and a description of how the finished program could be used beyond the initial broadcast.

To help write the treatment, many writers place information on index cards or slips of paper and then adjust the contents and shuffle the order to devise the most effective program structure. The process used to write the treatment is left to the discretion of the writer, who should devise a planning system that works best for the kind of writing project underway.

Some of the many ways to structure or present the treatment document are: a simulated magazine or newspaper article; an outline of the program segments with only brief phrases to indicate the continuity and flow of ideas; a condensed script in which the opening and closing segments are fully scripted and the rest of the presentation is only outlined; and a complete storyboard of major sequences. The writer may use a combination of approaches. The treatment structure used must present the writer's ideas in a style that enables others to understand and experience the content, characters, situations, and settings as the audience will.

Once the treatment has been written, it is reviewed and modified (either by written or oral exchanges between the writer and employer) until the project is approved and funded or abandoned. Once the treatment document has been accepted, the writer can then begin to prepare the appropriate type of script for the program or presentation.

Developing a treatment requires hard work, thought, imagination, ingenuity, and creative energy. But in the process of evolving new ideas, revising, testing, discarding, and restructuring them, the writer experiences a creative "high" unmatched by anything else as the pieces of the scripting puzzle begin to lock into place.

KGO Television of San Francisco and Co-Producers Dave Garrison and Steve Skomp received a National Association of Television Program Executives (NATPE) Iris Award for children's programming and an Action for Children's Television (ACT) Achievement in Children's Television Award for the series *Dudley's Diner*. Figure 3-1 is the treatment document for this imaginative, locally produced children's television series. The treatment illustrates the presentation style, format and content description used most often in this kind of document. Notice that the treatment indicates the interesting use of a series within a series, "The Adventures of Ace Reporter Benjamin."

Show Formats

The show format script provides only a skeletal outline of a program. There are two types of show formats.

The rundown or fact sheet indicates only the order and length of each program segment (fig. 3-2).

The routine sheet incorporates rundown sheet information but also supplies additional program content and some of the exact wording to be used in a few segments of the program (e.g., transitions between program segments, cue-aways to commercials, etc. (fig. 3-3).

The show format is a "bare bones" script form. It is written to be used for most regularly scheduled programs. Since these types of programs are produced often and since the nature and length of the segments remain fairly constant, a more detailed script form is not necessary.

Semi-Scripts

The semi-script is a more complete scripting format than the show format. In a semi-script, opening and closing segments, transitions between program segments, and commercial cue-aways are fully scripted, but the rest of the program is indicated only in outline form (e.g., interview questions or topics, demonstration segment rundown, etc.) (fig. 3-4).

Full-Scripts

The full-script is the most complete and exacting scripting format. It contains every word to be spoken, together with specific audio and/or video instructions. A full-script ensures precise pacing, sequencing, and development from both a writing and a production standpoint.

This scripting format is used often and is the most intricate of the formats available. It requires more explanation.

BASIC FULL-SCRIPT FORMATS

A full-script provides an exact blueprint, the ultimate guideline or framework for a program or presentation. It is important that each element in a full-script be clearly identified, properly positioned, and carefully punctuated to permit skilled professionals to interpret and to act upon the information provided.

The scripting style for both radio and television full-scripts will be described and then illustrated. Efforts have been made to provide a *complete* discussion of each scripting format without unnecessary repetition between format descriptions. It is recommended that you read carefully the detailed description of each scripting format with pencil, paper, ruler, and typewriter nearby. As each format is described, mark the paper for margin settings, make notes about directions for the actors or readers, the spacing needed between items, and so on. Construct your own personal reference guide for each format. Then, examine the script example provided for each format to recheck your notes. Measure the margins. Notice how punctuation marks and capitalization

"Dudley's Diner" - a one-half hour puppet comedy that presents problems and possible solutions to young people.

Produced by: Steve Skomp and Dave Garrison

TREATMENT

"Dudley's Diner" uses a situation comedy type format to present its messages to its 8-12 aged intended audience. The show is set in a San Francisco fast food restaurant and features a cast of likeable puppet characters. Waiter Dudley and his school pals Regina, Ernie and Clyde are joined by cook Wally and patrons Jangles, Woofer and Mrs. Gumms. Each "Dudley's Diner" episode focuses on one issue that a child might face on the rough road to adulthood. Show topics range from managing money, manners and water safety to more complicated problems such as vandalism, divorce and the special problems of handicapped people. Each subject is carefully researched and the problems and their widely accepted solutions become the basis for the humorous story lines on "Dudley's Diner." There is emphasis on positive self image, sex-roles and moral development.

Young People and Alcohol: Dudley's pals Clyde and Ernie find a bottle of whiskey. They talk Dudley into joining them for a drink. Dudley gets a headache, Ernie gets sick and Clyde passes out. From their sick bed, they receive a stern lecture from wise old diner cook Wally on the bad mix of small bodies and powerful drink.

How to Study: Dudley is a contestant on a TV game show, "The Big Money Question." We follow Dudley's efforts to become an expert on bees so that he can win big money. A multitude of study tips are presented that kids can use with their school work.

Bullies: Dudley is paying "protection" money to the school bully. When hiding and fast talk don't work, Dudley stands up to the bully and tells him he won't pay and he won't fight.

Figure 3-1 Treatment for *Dudley's Diner* series. *(Courtesy of KGO Television, San Francisco, and Co-Producers Dave Garrison and Steve Skomp)*

---

are used. Finally, type a clean copy of your notes for each format and keep these scripting format reference guides handy for future writing situations.

The references that will be given for tab settings on standard typewriters can be easily converted for use on word processing systems. The keyboards for these units generally have a control key which, when pressed in tandem with standard alphabetical keys that have been designated for special margin settings, allows the writer to move script information to the proper place on the page. While it will require careful study of your word processor manual and a little time to set these standard margins, once this task has been accomplished the writer can focus on writing and not margin set-

<u>Sex Roles</u>: Dudley's friend Regina is entered in the Soap Box Derby. Dudley believes this is man's work. Dudley also finds himself babysitting on the day of the race. Dudley learns that people should do what they like to do and do best and not try to fit into anyone else's mold.

<u>Pet Care</u>: Dudley's pet toad Winston isn't feeling well and Ernie's puppy pal Woofer ends up locked in the dog pound. The boys learn that different pets have different special needs which are the responsibility of the pet owner.

Included in each show is a dialogue concerning the show's events by Dave and his other half, ventriloquist Dave Garrison. This humorous review serves to condense the educational points of the show. A similar regular segment on each show is Dudley's visit to Steve Skomp at Steve's magic and gap shop. Here the teaching tool is magic, a sure hook for the 8-12 audience. Also included in each show is an invitation for Dudley's audience to submit story ideas. In this way, a child can take an active part in deciding what he wants to see on television.

"The Adventures of Ace Reporter Benjamin" is a series within a series on "Dudley's Diner." Benjamin is a puppet reporter for his school newspaper. Each show finds Benjamin tracking down a story of interest to his readers. Some of the segments deal with history and culture, others with exceptional children who have gained an expertise in their chosen hobby and still others present adults from all walks of life who have something special to share with kids. Benjamin's stories have featured hot air ballooning, hang-gliding, the wheel-chair Olympics, a child gymnast, the Golden Gate Bridge, a kid skateboard whiz, Fisherman's Wharf and a kid fencer; to name a few.

The puppets, ventriloquism, magic and interviews combine to make "Dudley's Diner" a unique vehicle for reaching pre-teens. Topics that might not catch a child's attention in another format become intriguing through the adventures of Dudley and his friends.

Fig. 3-1 *(Continued)*

---

tings when it is time to create a script. Each word processing program has its own system for customizing or configuring the keyboard for margin settings as well as other writing and script filing functions. If your word processor does not have this kind of feature, there are several utility programs available which will allow you to perform this customization.

These basic guidelines for radio and television full-scripts are presented with the understanding that adjustments will be made to match more closely specific writing and production situations as well as the preferences and practices of future employers. The examples shown for all radio and TV full-scripts (and later semi-scripts) do not coincide with typewritten margins and spacings of the original materials; design con-

Length of Selection	Selection Title	Artist	Record Label	Music Licensee[1]
3:16	1. Sister Golden Hair	America	W.B.	A
3:46	2. For the Good Times	Ray Price	Columbia	B
2:50	3. This Will Be	Natalie Cole	Capitol	A
4:47	4. Wildfire	Michael Murphey	Epic	B
2:35	5. I'd Really Like to See You Tonight	England Dan/John Ford Coley	Casablanca	B
2:41	6. It Don't Matter to Me	Bread	Elektra	B
2:54	7. My Cherie Amour	Stevie Wonder	Tamla	B/A
3:00	8. Best of Both Worlds	Lulu	Epic	A
4:43	9. Slip Slidin' Away	Paul Simon	Columbia	A
3:27	10. Autobahn	Kraftwerk	Vertigo	B
3:10	11. Daytime Friends	Kenny Rogers	U.A.	A
3:33	12. Eres Tu (Touch the Wind)	Mocedades	Tara	B
4:41	13. Hello It's Me	Todd Rundgren	Bearsville	B
3:38	14. We're All Alone	Rita Coolidge	A&M	A
3:10	15. Daybreak	Barry Manilow	Arista	B
3:40	16. The Long and Winding Road	Beatles	Apple	B
3:15	17. Changes in Lattitudes, Changes in Attitudes	Jimmy Buffett	ABC	B
2:37	18. House at Pooh Corner	Nitty Gritty Dirt Band	U.A.	B
4:45	19. Me and Mrs. Jones	Billy Paul	Phil Intl.	B
3:28	20. Have You Never Been Mellow	Olivia Newton John	MCA	B
3:45	21. Garden Party	Rick Nelson	Decca	B
3:54	22. The Way I Feel Tonight	Bay City Rollers	Arista	B
2:20	23. Mr. Tambourine Man	Byrds	Columbia	A
3:30	24. Don't Give Up on Us	David Soul	Private St.	A
3:28	25. Once a Fool	Kiki Dee	Rocket	B
2:51	26. Sentimental Lady	Bob Welch	Capitol	A
2:58	27. To Love Somebody	Bee Gees	RSO	B

[1] A = ASCAP; B = BMI. Individual subscribing stations pay these music licensing fees.

Figure 3-2 A rundown or fact sheet show format for a syndicated music tape service. (*Courtesy of Broadcast Programming International, Inc.*)

60

MUTUAL NEWS ON-THE-HOUR

:00:00   Opening Theme

:00:04   News Content

:00:55   Commercial cue - "This is news from Mutual Radio...

.........I'm_____."

:01:00   STATION POSITION (Network fills with commercial position
#1 :60)

:02:01   News Content

:03:28   Commercial cue - "You're listening to Mutual News."

:03:30   STATION POSITION (Network fills with commercial position
#2 :60)

:04:31   News Content

:04:57   Sign off - "This is_____, Mutual News."

:05:00   End of program

Figure 3-3   A routine sheet show format for a regularly scheduled network radio newscast.
(Courtesy of the Mutual Broadcasting System)

---

siderations have precluded this. Not every scripting guideline presented is meant to be used in every broadcast writing situation. The better you understand and remember these basic guidelines and the more experience you acquire using them on a regular basis, the more secure and flexible you will be when scripting format adjustments are required.

Radio

The following are the principal radio script elements with specifications for margin settings, content, capitalization, punctuation, and spacing:

Scene/Production Descriptions. Beginning at tab setting 20 and ending at tab setting 70, the writer could provide general guidelines and information about the mood, tone, pace, and overall interpretation of the script. The notation "SCENE (or PRODUCTION) NOTE:" should be in FULL CAPS followed by a colon (:). After two spaces, the description is written using regular upper and lowercase letters with double-spacing between lines. This kind of scripting notation is used primarily for commercials and announcements and only occasionally for other types of programs.

GARY
How would you like to save up to
three hundred and sixty dollars in
the next month just by going on a
diet? No -- it has nothing to do
with calorie counting. It's known
as "The Money Diet"...and that's the
title of a new book by our guest,
Janice Rotchstein, who's come up
with hundreds of practical tips for
cutting your cost of living.

QUESTIONS ROTCHSTEIN
Segment 4
(Gary, Janice)
Contact: Bob Carman

1. What inspired your "Money Diet" and who can use it?
2. Does the Money Diet change our way of living and make us
    give up a lot of our favorite necessities of life?
3. Well, let's get started on the Money Diet.

(JANICE WILL SHOW & DEMO THE TRICKS
AND SHORTCUTS AND SUBSTITUTES, TYPICAL
OF HER "MONEY DIET")

WEARING 2 PANTYHOSE, WITH 1 LEG REMOVED TO EXTEND
SNAGGED PAIR

BUYING BOX OF BIRTHDAY GREETING CARDS INSTEAD OF SINGLY

PLASTIC PRODUCE BAGS INSTEAD OF GLOVES

CHERRY TOMATO PLASTIC BOXES AS FLOWER FROGS

BAKING SODA & WATER INSTEAD OF COMMERCIAL MOUTHWASH

BOX OF MOTHBALLS FOR GARBAGE DEODORANT & INSECT KILLER

Figure 3-4 Semi-script for a program segment of *Hour Magazine* featuring host Gary Collins. *(Courtesy of Group W Productions, Inc.)*

CANDY IN BULK

CORNSTARCH FOR BABY POWDER

(SHE WILL BRING ALL PROPS PLUS
PRINTED CARDS INDICATING SAVINGS)

<u>CLOSE MONEY DIET</u>
Segment 4
(Gary)
Contact: Bob Carman

GARY
Thank you, Janice, for showing us
how to make our net income exceed
our gross habits...with the
money diet.

<u>TEASE DR. LEE SALK</u>
(Gary)
Contact: Bob Carman

GARY
When we come back, Dr. Lee Salk
talks about the relationship
between father and son.

Fig. 3-4   *(Continued)*

Talent Designations. Talent or character identifications begin at tab setting 13 and end at tab setting 19. Either generic or specific designations can be used. For example, TALENT #1, TALENT #2, or VOICE #1, VOICE #2 would be acceptable generic designations. The purpose of this script notation is to identify who is speaking. Each talent designation is written in FULL CAPS, underlined and followed by a colon (:).

Talent Interpretation Instructions. Between tab settings 25 and 70, the writer can include a brief suggestion about how the talent should interpret certain words, phrases, or sentences in the script. This information is to be included within parentheses immediately after the talent designation, using FULL CAPS. Such notations as (FURIOUS), (CALMLY), (SAD), and the like, placed just ahead of the words to be read by the talent, express the writer's perspective about the interpretation of key phrases and ideas. This type of notation may be helpful for commercials, announcements, and most dramatic and comedic radio productions.

Talent Directions. The same guidelines used for talent interpretation instructions are used to note physical movements by the talent or other talent-related production information. Notations such as (FADING OFF), (FADING ON), or (AS THOUGH HEARD ON A TELEPHONE) provide additional insight from the writer for production and talent personnel.

Words. Words to be spoken are written across a forty-five space typewritten line (using pica type) beginning at tab setting 25 and ending at tab setting 70. Regular upper and lowercase letters are used with double-spacing between each line of the script.

Music. Music notations are written in FULL CAPS and are underlined to distinguish music from sound effects notations. Music information begins at tab setting 20 and extends to tab setting 70. If music is to be inserted between the words spoken by the radio talent, the same scripting format guidelines would be followed except that the entire music notation would be enclosed within parentheses.

Sound Effects. The same scripting format guidelines provided for music are used for sound effects notations in radio. The obvious change would be the use of the term SOUND EFFECT or SOUND or SFX to alert those involved that a sound effect is to be heard at a particular point in the script. Also, sound effects notations would not be underlined.

Other Radio Script Elements. Depending upon the circumstances and scripting requirements, for longer radio scripts, the rewritten script could include consecutive numbers along the left margin to identify each audio element more clearly. This scripting notation is sometimes used for radio dramas and for documentaries.

In addition, some notion about the length or timing of each script segment or page can be included. If this kind of information is required, a consistent, standardized notation system should be used if the information is to assist production personnel.

Sample Full-Script for Radio. To better illustrate the standard style and format used for radio full-scripts, a sample commercial has been prepared. A radio commercial is used here as an example since this type of writing often makes use of many of the style and format guidelines just described. Although the script in figure 3-5 may not display all of the characteristics of an award-winning radio commercial, it does illustrate standard style for radio full-scripts.

Television

As in radio, the full-script for television must display standardization in the use, placement, and format for essential video and audio elements. The television script forms used must identify and clearly differentiate between video and audio elements and between talent and production assignments.

FIRST NATIONAL BANK
P-T-B System
FNB H-184-A
30 seconds
Jones   10/8

MUSIC: FIRST NATIONAL BANK JINGLE (INSTRUMENTAL -
           CONTEMPORARY BEAT) UP FOR TWO SECONDS AND
           THEN UNDER

ANNCR: (ENTHUSIASTIC) At the First National Bank, we've got
           a new sound for you!

(SFX: COMPUTER-TYPE SOUNDS - FEATURE BRIEFLY AND
           THEN OUT)

ANNCR: It's our new P-T-B System. Anytime, day or night, you
           can call the P-T-B number and have your bills paid from
           your First National Bank account...quickly, easily,
           conveniently -- and on time! No more hassles with
           checks, envelopes, stamps and record keeping. It's all
           done for you -- automatically...whenever you want to
           pay your bills, with P-T-B...

(SFX: TELEPHONE RECEIVER PICKED UP)

ANNCR: So, call now...5-5-5-21-21...

(SFX: SEVEN-DIGIT TELEPHONE NUMBER BEING DIALED
           ON PUSH-BUTTON TELEPHONE)

ANNCR: That's 5-5-5-21-21...Enjoy the savings and convenience
           of First National's P-T-B System of bill paying.

(SFX: ONE TELEPHONE RING)

VOICE: (AS THOUGH ON A TELEPHONE) P-T-B. May I
           help you?

MUSIC: FIRST NATIONAL BANK JINGLE (VOCAL -
           CONTEMPORARY BEAT) UP FULL TO THE END.

Figure 3-5 A sample full-script for a radio commercial.

Full-scripts for television are written in either two-column or one-column formats. The two-column format is used for virtually all principal types of television programs and announcements. The one-column format is used for feature-length television and motion picture dramas and comedies, action/adventure television programs, most regularly scheduled network television primetime program series, variety and game show series, and other types of television programming requiring large budgets, expansive facilities, and specialized production and talent personnel.

Two-Column Format. In this format, all video information is written in the left column (between tab settings 13 and 27) and all audio information is written in the right column (between tab settings 30 and 70). When deciding in which column to place script information, the writer simply determines whether the information relates to what is seen or to what is heard and places that information in the appropriate column.

All *video information* is written in FULL CAPS with single-spacing between lines. The precision and completeness of the video information or directions depends upon the nature of the program script, the production circumstances, and the requirements of your employer.

The writer places all the information for each video entry in the following order: the transition to the camera shot and then the camera shot (i.e., what is to be seen). For example, you could write

FADE TO LS OF OPEN FIELD

or

DISSOLVE TO WS OF HARRY

If the script is for an in-studio production, the information for each video entry would be placed in the following order: the transition to the camera shot, the specific studio camera to be used, and then the camera shot (i.e., what is to be seen). For example, you could write

FADE TO C-2 LS OF SET

or

DISSOLVE TO C-1 WS OF PAUL AND TOM.

Each video entry or change in the script must be placed adjacent to the corresponding audio entry. Do not cram all of the video information into one long, endless column and then spread the audio column information down the page using double-spacing. To ensure that video changes are made as scripted, some writers use various markings in the audio column to indicate when the video or picture is to change. Markings such as_____□ ,_____⌋, and ⊗ at the exact point in the audio where

Beltway Furniture
Clear the Store Sale
BF f-111-B
:30   Jones   10/10

VIDEO	AUDIO
QUICK FADE TO C-2 (WS OF ANNCR)	MUSIC: BRIGHT & CONTEMPORARY INSTRUMENTAL - UP FOR TWO SECONDS AND THEN UNDER
	ANNCR: (ENTHUSIASTIC)
	They're in a selling mood at Beltway
	Furniture! So they've slashed their prices
FOLLOW ANNCR	to clear the store! (ANNCR WALKS THROUGH
	STORE) You'll find great bargains on every item in
	stock --
SL #1 (SOFAS)	Luxurious occasional chairs and sofas...
SL #2 (LAMPS)	Beautiful lamps and paintings to add
SL #3 (TVs)	sparkle to any room... plus quality R-C-A
	appliances and T-V sets.
	It's all waiting for you during the
C-1 (H&S OF ANNCR)	special "clear-the-store-sale" at --
SL #4	Beltway...River City's finest furniture
	store.
	MUSIC: UP FULL FOR A FEW SECONDS AND THEN OUT

Figure 3-6 A sample two-column full-script for a television commercial.

the picture is to be changed can be used by the writer, although most often by the director, to avoid confusion and to ensure appropriate interpretation of the script.

All *audio information* is written with double-spacing between lines, following the same guidelines for capitalization, content and use of punctuation suggested for radio full-scripts. Because all audio notations must be squeezed into a forty-space typewritten line (using pica type), all audio entries for the two-column television full-script format begin at tab setting 30 and end at tab setting 70. The audio information for this scripting form must be just as complete as for radio. It is important to remember that *anything* relating to what is heard in the television announcement or program must be placed in the audio column of the script and not mixed in with video directions described in the left column.

To illustrate the key style and format characteristics of the two-column full-script for television, a television commercial has been devised (fig. 3-6). The same rationale has been used for the preparation of this script as was used for the radio commercial in figure 3-5.

One-Column Format. This script form is often called the "Hollywood format" because it is the most common script design used in major west coast production centers and because it evolved out of the earlier silent period of filmmaking when separate writers wrote the story line while others concentrated on the title cards containing the dialogue. In contrast to a theatrical play, a motion picture tends to stress the *actions* of major characters, and not necessarily the words they say, to move the plot or story line along. In this case, form follows content. The one-column script format provides more space and attention to such visual elements as scene headings and stage directions and less to dialogue and interpretation of dialogue. While the emphasis on these visual and auditory elements might shift in some specific situations, the basic one-column format will continue to emphasize visual over aural script information.

One page of a script written in the one-column format provides a little less than one minute of screen time. The action described may be extended or compressed to encompass more than one minute of real time, but actual viewing time would be about one minute. It is important to remember this concept when this format is used to prepare script material since the reader of the script anticipates pacing, timing, and length of screen time based on what is written on one page.

There are two types of one-column script formats used for television and motion picture production. The one-column one-camera format is used for some television comedy series and for practically all television and motion picture feature-length productions (teleplays and screenplays). The one-column three-camera format is used for most television situation comedy series and for practically all other television programs produced "live on tape" before a studio audience. There are noticeable differences between the two types of formats. While each contains the essential script elements necessary to produce a particular program, the placement, use and emphasis given to each element varies to better match the type of program.

It should be noted that subsequent rewrites of an original three-camera script are written in a "scene-by-scene" format while the one-camera script is usually rewritten in a "shot-by-shot" format. Consecutive numbers are placed in the left or right margins, or both, of each revised script page by the producer or director when the production or shooting script is prepared. The writer of the original script is not encouraged to use this consecutive numbering system when submitting first-draft script material. It tends to distract the person reading the script for the first time.

Here are the *specifications for the one-column one-camera script format:*

Scene Headings (Descriptions). This script information indicates what the audience should see and how they should see it. Scene headings are written in FULL CAPS between margin settings 14 and 73 (pica type) and placed in the following order with a hyphen (-) separating each element: (INT. or EXT. location - time of day or night - camera angle - what is to be seen. The scene description information provided is more extensive than in the one-column three-camera format. Single-space between lines of the same scene heading. But triple-space between separate scene headings. If a scene continues to the next page, double-space down and write "(CONTINUED)" at the bottom of the page at tab setting 61. Then at the begining of the next page write "CONTINUED:" at tab setting 14.

Stage Directions. The writer should provide only the essential information necessary to describe characters, scenes, camera shots, sound cues, and other elements needed to facilitate production of the script. Use regular upper- and lowercase letters to provide these directions between margin settings 14 and 73 (pica type). Single-space between lines of the same stage directions entry. But double-space between the scene heading entry and the start of the stage directions entry. Also double-space between the end of a character's lines and the start of a new stage directions entry.

Camera and Sound Directions. Only brief camera and sound cues should be included within stage directions entries placed between margin settings 14 and 73 (pica type). Camera and sound cues are highlighted by typing the words relating to such directions in FULL CAPS. Single spacing is used, just as for stage directions information. Double-space when separating one camera shot from the next camera shot and when separating the end of a character's lines from the start of a new camera direction notation.

Character Designations. It is important to name each character in the script to whom lines of dialogue have been assigned. This designation may be in the form of a first and/or last name or it may simply be a role description (e.g., policeman, fireman #1, receptionist, clerk, etc.). Such designations are typed in FULL CAPS when a particular character is first mentioned in a scene heading or stage directions entry. Character designations are typed in FULL CAPS between margin settings 41 and 54 to indicate the dialogue or lines assigned to that character.

Character Interpretation Notes. Suggestions for a particular talent (e.g., stands up, laughs, turns toward door, depressed, etc.) which would enhance the interpretation of specific lines of dialogue can be written between margin settings 35 and 51 (pica type). All words for these personal directions are written in lowercase letters, enclosed within parentheses, and single-spaced between the character designation and the first line of dialogue.

Dialogue. The words spoken by each character or talent are displayed in the exact center of the script page between margin settings 28 and 56 (pica type). Use regular upper- and lowercase letters to write dialogue with occasional FULL CAPS to indicate stress for specific key words. Use single-spacing between lines of dialogue assigned to one character or talent. Double-space between the end of lines assigned to one character and the next character designation or a camera or stage direction.

If one character's lines are interrupted by a stage direction, use "(continuing)," single-spaced down at tab setting 35 just under a repetition of the character's name, to indicate that this particular character continues to deliver his or her lines. If a character's lines continue to the next page, write "(MORE)" at tab setting 41 single-spaced down from the last sentence of dialogue on that page. Then, at the beginning of the next page, write "(cont'd)" beside a repeat of the character designation (on the same line).

Scene Transition Notes. The writer can choose from many visual transition possibilities to bridge between the end of one scene and the beginning of the next. Standard visual transition terms were discussed in chapter 2. If the writer wishes to indicate a specific technical direction to make such transitions (e.g., "CUT TO:" or "DISSOLVE TO:" etc.) and, thus, to achieve a specific visual effect, such directions are written in FULL CAPS followed by a colon (:), placed between margin settings 61 and 76 and double-spaced down from the preceding lines of dialogue. Before starting the next scene heading or description, triple-space down from the scene ending or transition notation.

Beginnings and Endings. To begin the script or a major division of a program, write "FADE IN:" at margin setting 14. After triple-spacing down, the first scene heading for the script is written as described earlier. In a teleplay divided into several acts, "FADE IN:" (FULL CAPS followed by a colon) would be written at the beginning of each act as well as at the beginning of a prologue or teaser segment if this is needed.

To indicate the end of the script, write "FADE OUT." (FULL CAPS followed by a period) at margin setting 61 after double-spacing down from the last line of stage directions or dialogue. Then write "THE END" (FULL CAPS and underlined) four spaces down and centered on the page. In a teleplay divided into acts, indicate the end of each act (except the last act) by following the same format guidelines just given, except write "END OF ACT TWO" (THREE, etc.) (FULL CAPS and underlined) instead of "THE END."

One-Column Sample Script Pages. Figure 3-7 illustrates many of the script format guidelines just outlined. Notice the placement, use and function of each item or entry in the script pages. Take special note of margin settings, capitalization, and spacing used both within and between each item. Remember that in this script format, as in most others, form follows content. Recognizing and using the scripting tools available in this and in other formats require careful observation and sustained practice.

Here are the *specifications for the one-column three-camera script format:*

Scene Headings (Descriptions). Scene headings serve the same function for the one-column three-camera format as for the one-camera format. Because of the types of programs produced from the three-camera, "live-on-tape" script format, scene heading information is abbreviated to indicate only "INT." or "EXT." and some notion of place or location written in FULL CAPS, underlined, and placed between margin settings 15 and 35 (pica type). The hyphen (-) is not used to separate each element in a scene heading. Although it is rare that more than one line is needed for a scene heading entry in the three-camera format, if necessary, single-space between lines within each entry. Double-space down between transitions at the end of a scene and the beginning of the next scene heading. Also double-space between a scene heading and the first line of a stage directions entry.

Stage Directions. Stage direction notations are also much more abbreviated in the three-camera script format. Write stage directions in FULL CAPS within parentheses between margin settings 15 and 46 (pica type). Single-space between lines in a specific stage directions entry. Use double-spacing to separate a stage directions entry and the next character designation or subsequent dialogue.

Camera and Sound Directions. In the three-camera script format, these directions are written as briefly as possible as separate entries and not included in stage directions notations (as in the other one-column script format). Camera and sound directions are written in FULL CAPS and are underlined. Both types of directions are placed between margin settings 15 and 35 (pica type). Only one line should be needed for each camera or sound cue. Such directions appear infrequently in this script format.

Character Designations. Regular upper and lowercase letters are used when referring to a specific character in dialogue. Character designations are written in FULL CAPS beginning at tab setting 30, directly above the lines assigned to a particular character. Character designations are written in FULL CAPS within stage directions to maintain style consistency. Double-space between scene headings or stage directions and a talent designation. Also double-space between the ends of lines assigned to one character and the next character designation.

Character Interpretation Notes. These brief interpretative notations are written in FULL CAPS and enclosed within parentheses between margin settings 15 and 36.

Dialogue. Words spoken by the talent are placed between margin settings 20 and 55 (pica type). Use regular upper and lowercase letters to write dialogue. Double-space between the character designation and the lines assigned to that character. Double-space between lines of dialogue within one character's speech.

If a character's lines continue to the next page, write "(MORE)" at tab setting 30, double-spaced down from the last line of dialogue for that character. Then, at the begin-

"MOLLIE"

ACT ONE

FADE IN:

EXT. CEMETERY - DAY - ESTABLISHING

It is a gray, cloudy day. Wind gusts blow dead leaves around a lone figure, MOLLIE SIMPSON, standing near a modest gravesite.

CLOSER - MOLLIE

Her features are pale and stiff as she stands next to the freshly turned earth. Her puffy, gnarled hands clutch her small, black purse.

INSERT - GRAVESTONE

The newly chiseled monument displays the usual obituary information and the name FRANK SIMPSON.

BACK TO SCENE

Mollie pauses for a moment.

SERIES OF SHOTS

A) Frank in earlier, younger days...smiling, laughing, talking in animated gestures.

B) the moment of a heart attack.

C) a hospital room with machines and monitoring devices.

D) CLOSE UP of Frank -- pale, expressionless, bedridden -- as we HEAR a minister whisper prayers in the darkened hospital room.

E) a small group assembled near an open coffin in a funeral parlor.

F) the same small group at a graveside religious ceremony.

DISSOLVE TO:

CLOSE SHOT - MOLLIE

She closes her eyes as if holding back the pain she feels at the sudden loss of her husband. She opens her eyes, shakes herself back to reality, and slowly walks away into the distance.

Figure 3-7 Sample pages from a one-column one-camera full-script for a television drama.

INT. MOLLIE'S DINING ROOM - DAY - CLOSE ANGLE - MOLLIE

Bank statements and financial records are spread out on the table as Mollie tries to muddle through the maze of bills, payments, etc. She is exasperated.

> BEE (o.s.)
> Yoo-hoo?

MED. TWO SHOT - MOLLIE AND BEE

Mollie's best friend BEATRICE LANG enters through the back screen door with a coffee cup in her hand. Bee is a full-figured woman, about 65, blurry-eyed and somewhat disheveled. Bee's cup contains a brew stronger than that usually derived from a coffee bean.

> MOLLIE
> (turns toward screen
> door; depressed)
> Hi Bee. Come in and give me a hand.

> BEE
> What's the problem?

> MOLLIE
> Oh these darned bills! I'm not sure
> what to do about them.

> BEE
> (in a sleepy, matter-
> of-fact manner)
> I used to worry about bills right
> after Sam died five years ago...But
> now my son Bill takes care of that
> whole terrible mess. He just gives
> me the money I need.

> (CONTINUED)

Fig. 3-7 *(Continued)*

ning of the next page, write "(CONT'D)" beside a repeat of the character designation (on the same line) to indicate that the character's speech continues from the preceding page.

   Scene Transition Notes. Scene transition notes are written in FULL CAPS followed by a colon (:), underlined, and placed within margin settings 15 and 25 (pica type). Triple-space between the end of dialogue, stage directions or a scene heading, and a scene transition notation.

```
#76185
(Bud)                           JUNIOR/MINNIE/SCHOOLHOUSE #01
(ADD LOTS OF LAUGHS AT TOP)
(MUSIC: INTRO)
(DISSOLVE THRU ART CARD)
(KIDS LAUGH AND THROW PAPER)


                          MINNIE

              Children! Children! All right now,
              Junior, last week I asked you to
              start making a list of every single
              thing you eat. Has this changed
              your diet at all?


                          JUNIOR

              It sure has, teacher! Now I don't eat
              anything that's hard to spell.


(KIDS LAUGH)


(Bud)                     ARCHIE/WILD LINE #11
(CIGAR PUFF)


                          ARCHIE

              Well, that means Junior won't eat
              anything with more than five or
              two syllables in it...and maybe not
              even alphabet soup!
```

Figure 3-8 Sample page from a one-column three-camera full-script for the television series *Hee Haw. (Courtesy of Gaylord Program Services, Inc.)*

Beginnings and Endings. To begin the script, write "<u>FADE IN</u>:" (FULL CAPS, under-lined and followed by a colon) at margin setting 15. After double-spacing down, the first scene heading for the script is written as described earlier. The same scripting format is used at the beginning of each major program division if the script is divided into prologue, act, and tag or epilogue segments.

To indicate the end of the script, write "<u>FADE OUT</u>:" (FULL CAPS, underlined and followed by a colon) at margin setting 15, triple-spacing down from the last line of stage directions or dialogue. Then write "<u>THE END</u>" (FULL CAPS and underlined) two spaces down at tab setting 15. In most cases, when this script format is used, "<u>END OF ACT ONE</u>" (<u>TWO</u>, etc.) is written instead of "<u>THE END</u>."

One-Column Three-Camera Sample Script Page. Figure 3-8 illustrates many of the script format guidelines just outlined. Notice that there is a slight modification of stan-dard margins and style in the *Hee Haw* script page shown.

CONCLUSION

This chapter has presented basic broadcast writing styles and techniques. The discus-sion of essential aural writing styles and techniques centered on how to select words, construct sentences, and integrate music and sound effects creatively into a broadcast script. The description of visual writing styles and techniques included suggestions for envisioning specific images (visualization) and combining images (sequencing) to visually convey a specific idea or perspective. There was an explanation of the mechanics of preparing broadcast script pages and the use of standard broadcast script-ing styles. A wide range of broadcast scripting formats, approaches, and techniques was described and illustrated. Both radio and television full-script formats were ex-amined in detail.

Preparing material in proper form is important for all writers, especially for broad-cast writers. Careful attention to details is a hallmark of all craftsmen and professionals; however, writing a script in proper form is a mechanical process readily grasped by most writers. Even more important than proper script form, the writer's scripts must display creativity, imagination, and innovation if they are to stand apart from many others.

SUGGESTED EXERCISES AND PROJECTS

1. Prepare a cover page for one of the following, using the guidelines provided in this chapter—a television drama (teleplay), a screenplay, or an instructional televi-sion series.
2. Prepare script identification information (which would be found at the top left cor-ner of a script page) for one of the following, using the guidelines provided in this chapter—a 30-second radio commercial for a local bank or automobile dealer-

ship, a 30-minute radio discussion program, or a 5-minute radio or television interview segment with the governor of your state.

3. Compile a list of five difficult-to-pronounce names or items from your area. These could be names of government officials, business leaders, athletes, coaches, street names, names of towns, and the like. For each name or item, provide both the regular spelling and your suggested pronunciation. Enclose each pronunciation notation in parentheses, using uppercase letters to emphasize stressed syllables.

4. Write each number in correct broadcast writing style:

   a. 1,218
   b. 215,750
   c. 618
   d. 1,800,000
   e. 2/3
   t. $20.50
   g. 16 ft.
   h. 33 St.
   i. 800-555-1212
   j. 1814 Briar Ave.

5. Use standard broadcast punctuation and editing marks to improve the effectiveness of each of the following sentences:

   a. Nate   you says id comein over tonite
   b. Boy   thats some tasty piz   za
   c. Its goiing to be a good day break for the races
   d. Tigers   elephants   and beers are featured in each performance
   e. He stopped   turned to face her   and suddenly began crying
   f. Is their a better reason to shop at Lakeside
   g. (Dialogue in a radio drama)
   Boy　　Struggling　　I know what you mean
   Girl　　Pensively　　Please come in now

6. Write five simple declarative sentences describing your hometown.

7. For 20 or 30 minutes, sit on a park bench, near a bus stop, or in any area where people gather to wait and converse. Report your observations about which topics or issues people discussed, the manner in which they selected and used words, how they constructed sentences, and how their conversations progressed. What are your conclusions about the current use of language based upon this experience?

8. Watch one of the following: a television drama or comedy program, or a current theatrical motion picture. Observe the use of language (words and sentences), music, sound effects, visualization, and sequencing. Report your observations and conclusions.

9. Monitor and, if possible, record several radio commercials. Report your observations about the use of words, voices, music, and sound effects in these commercials. If you recorded one of these radio commercials, try to write a full-script for the commercial to reflect what you heard on tape using the scripting guidelines, forms, and techniques discussed and illustrated in this chapter.

10. Watch one of the following types of television programs: a documentary, a music/variety, or a news magazine program. Prepare a television rundown sheet for 30 minutes of the program you watched. Prepare a semi-script for the same 30 minutes of the program viewed. Now, try to write a 2- to 4-minute sequence

from the program you watched. Your full-script should mirror approximately what was seen and heard during this short sequence and should follow the scripting guidelines, forms, and techniques discussed and illustrated in this chapter. The capability to record the program on videotape will make it easier to prepare the full-script for the 2- to 4-minute sequence.

11. For the same 30-minute program segment viewed in exercise 10, comment on the use and effectiveness of visualization and sequencing. In your judgment, which portions of the program were visually effective? Which portions were not effective? How would you have improved the scripting of these less effective portions of the program?

ADDITIONAL READING

Bates, Myrtle, and Stern, Renée. *The Grammar Game.* Indianapolis: Bobbs-Merrill Educational Publishing, 1983.

Berner, R. Thomas. *Language Skills for Journalists.* 2d ed. Boston: Houghton Mifflin, 1984.

Blum, Richard A. *Television Writing: From Concept to Contract.* Rev. ed. Stoneham, Mass.: Focal Press, 1984.

Brady, John. *The Craft of the Screenwriter.* New York: Simon & Schuster, 1982.

Bronfeld, Stewart. *Writing for Film and Television.* Englewood Cliffs, N.J.: Prentice-Hall, 1981.

Clifford, John, and Waterhouse, Robert. *Sentence Combining and Flexibility.* Indianapolis: Bobbs-Merrill Educational Publishing, 1983.

Coe, Michelle. *How to Write for Television.* New York: Crown Publishers, 1980.

Coopersmith, Jerome. *Professional Writer's Teleplay/Screenplay Format.* New York: Writers Guild of America, East, 1977.

Driscoll, John P. *Communicating on Film.* Champaign, Ill.: Stipes Publishing Co., 1984.

Edmonds, Robert. *The Sights and Sounds of Cinema and Television: How the Aesthetic Experience Influences Our Feelings.* New York: Teachers College Press, 1982.

Garvey, Daniel E., and Rivers, William L. *Broadcast Writing.* New York: Longman, Inc., 1982.

Haag, Judith H., and Cole, Hillis R., Jr. *The Complete Guide to Standard Script Formats.* Hollywood, Calif.: CMC Publishing, 1980.

Hilliard, Robert L. *Writing for Television and Radio.* 4th ed. Belmont, Calif.: Wadsworth, 1984.

Kessler, Lauren, and McDonald, Duncan. *When Words Collide: A Journalist's Guide to Grammar & Style.* Belmont, Calif.: Wadsworth, 1983.

Lee, Robert, and Misiorowski, Robert. *Script Models: A Handbook for the Media Writer.* New York: Hastings House, 1978.

Maloney, Martin, and Rubenstein, Paul Max. *Writing for the Media.* Englewood Cliffs, N.J.: Prentice-Hall, 1980.

Newman, Edwin. *Strictly Speaking.* New York: Warner Books, 1974.

Rothwell, J. Dan. *Telling It Like It Isn't: Language Misuse & Malpractice—What We Can Do About It.* Englewood Cliffs, N.J.: Prentice-Hall, 1982.

Strunk, William, and White, E. B. *The Elements of Style.* 3d ed. New York: Macmillan Co., 1979.

Willis, Edgar E., and D'Arienzo, Camille. *Writing Scripts for Television, Radio, and Film.* New York: Holt, Rinehart and Winston, 1981.

Wylie, Max. *Writing for Television.* New York: Cowles Book Co., 1970.

Zettl, Herbert. *Sight–Sound–Motion: Applied Media Aesthetics*. Belmont, Calif.: Wadsworth
      Publishing Co., 1973.
Zinsser, William. *On Writing Well*. New York: Harper & Row, 1976.

Chapter Four

COMMERCIALS AND ANNOUNCEMENTS

The basic principles and techniques of persuasion apply equally to commercials, public service, and station promotional announcements. The content in each type of message may vary, but the writer tends to approach each in a similar manner. Solid, effective, persuasive writing and production techniques are needed in PSA's, or public service announcements, and station promotional announcements as well as in broadcast commercials.

All commercials and announcements are intended to sell something. It could be a product, service, idea, concept, or even an emotion or feeling. An automobile manufacturer wants to sell more cars. A bank wants to sell potential customers on the benefits of a new type of checking or savings account. A social service agency tries to attract prospective volunteers by selling the concept of enhanced human values and lifestyles. A television station wants viewers to trust the station's news department to deliver the news objectively and in as comprehensive a manner as possible, so a promotional announcement is designed, written, and produced to sell this concept.

This chapter will describe how the planning document, called a copy rationale, helps writers generate more effective spot announcements by identifying the key elements to be used in the copy. Next will be suggestions about organizing an announcement— what to include and how to organize the material into an effective presentation. Several items relating to copy style and design will be discussed—utilizing to the fullest extent the standard broadcast copy lengths, how talent and production personnel styles of delivery influence the writer's work, and the importance of determining the most effective method of packaging or presenting the script material. Specific copywriting suggestions will be offered along with examples of various kinds of spot announcements from different types of broadcast advertising campaigns. Finally, techniques for writing effective on-air broadcast promotional announcements will be presented in an effort to show how the concepts, principles and techniques described for broadcast commercials and public service announcements transfer to writing promotional spots. Examples from various broadcast promotion campaigns will be presented to illustrate these techniques.

DEVELOPING A COPY RATIONALE

A discussion of the development of multi-media campaigns is beyond the scope of this book. It is important to realize, however, that broadcast commercials and announcements usually are only part of a comprehensive multi-media effort. Commercials, public service, and promotional announcements used on radio and television stations often use the same logos, music themes, and slogans to provide unity and to relate directly to efforts in other media by the same advertiser or client. To formulate and create multi-media messages for the same client, a campaign strategy and then a creative strategy are devised. Usually this is accomplished by advertising agency personnel in conjunction with the client or advertiser. The length of discussions and the volume of information collected generally are quite extensive.

A similar, although less extensive, process should be followed when writing one or a limited number of broadcast advertising messages for a particular client or advertiser. This planning document is called a "copy rationale." Other labels attached to this process and the resultant document are copy platform, copy strategy, and copy policy.

The copy rationale allows the writer and the client or advertiser to determine the key elements to be used in the broadcast announcement(s) to accomplish certain stated objectives. It is a kind of map or blueprint which points the way toward successful completion of a specific broadcast advertising goal. It is best to devise a copy rationale *before* writing broadcast advertising messages. Otherwise, commercials and announcements are written in a haphazard manner with no obvious unity within each message and between separate messages of a consolidated campaign for the same client. For the young writer, it is best to present a *written* copy rationale. Experienced writers for these types of messages usually can quickly devise a mental copy rationale without the need to commit such information to paper. Eventually, the copy rationale should be presented in written form, albeit abbreviated, for approval by the client or advertiser and to serve as a guideline for future messages for the same client, product, or service.

Several elements should be included in a short one- to three-page copy rationale:

• *Client/product/service analysis*
• *Audience analysis*
• *Statement of objectives*
• *Logical and emotional appeals*
• *Copy style and design*

•*Competition and competitive claims*
•*Positioning statement*
•*Central selling point*

The extent to which each element in a copy rationale is developed depends upon time restrictions as well as the amount of detail needed by the client or by the individual writing the announcements.

Client/Product/Service Analysis

It is important for the writer to know as much as possible about the client or advertiser as well as the product or service to be advertised. The more the writer knows, the easier it is to design effective spot announcements to meet realistic, identifiable goals.

Much of the information needed can be obtained directly from the client. Other information can be obtained about specific types of businesses and services from such organizations as the Radio Advertising Bureau, Inc., 485 Lexington Avenue, New York, NY 10017 and from the Television Bureau of Advertising, 485 Lexington Avenue, New York, NY 10017. Both the RAB and TvB provide information packets and booklets that contain useful national statistics and information on specific businesses. Industry periodicals and reference works directly related to a particular kind of business, client, product, or service also should be checked for additional background to assist in the writing process. Although such information usually provides a national perspective for the writer, the data will supply essential information and viable topic areas which can be applied later to the specific local advertiser or client.

Client Analysis. The list of questions to ask a client can be endless. Some of the crucial questions to ask, before writing the copy, are:

1. *What has been done in the past?* What types of media have been used? What were the results? What kinds of campaigns and promotions have been used with what results? What was the nature of the copy used? What has been the advertising or promotional budget in the past? What was the most successful campaign used? What was the least successful?
2. *What is now being done?* Type of media used? Kinds of campaigns and promotions? Nature of copy used? Current budget?
3. *What are the particulars about this business?* Hours of operation? When do most customers come in to the store or shop? When are most telephone calls received? What types of products or services are offered? Who are the owners and operators and what is their background? How long have they been in business? How much experience do they have in this particular field? What are the biggest sales events throughout the year? What are the special features of this particular business operation? What are the strengths and weaknesses of this business? What are the peak

sales months and peak sales days? How does the client or advertiser view business conditions, generally and specifically, in the areas of direct interest? What community projects receive participation from this advertiser? What are the major community problems, in his or her view? What are the client's short-term and long-term advertising goals and objectives? What are the *client's* opinions about the effectiveness of various media?

Product/Service Analysis. Important questions to ask to analyze a product or service are:

1. What exactly is the product or service to be advertised? What are its strongest and weakest selling points?
2. How is it used or made?
3. What are the special features or benefits of the product or service? Color and size of the package?
4. How has this basic product or service changed or evolved over the years? Or is this a new product or service?
5. When is it bought or used? Where?
6. By whom? How often? What days of the week? Months of the year?
7. How is the product or service distributed? Where?
8. How available is it?
9. Are there any restrictions on use?
10. What has been the pattern of development for this product or service (declining, growing, stabilizing)?

Audience Analysis

The writer must identify specific audience characteristics in relation to the marketplace to create effective broadcast advertising messages. Basic audience composition, as well as the characteristics of the target audience for the client's specific product or service, are significant facets of a thorough audience analysis. Not only will the writer discover the makeup of the current market, but he or she will also learn something about the untapped potential market. To create specific types of messages, it is important to identify a specific target audience or group. The results of the commercials or announcements can thus be effectively measured.

Here are some of the questions which should be asked to formulate a thorough audience analysis:

1. Who are the current customers? What are their demographic characteristics (age, sex, income level, education, family size, job status, etc.)? Who are the prime customers? Where are they from? When do they shop or come into the place of business? What comments have they made to the client about the business? About the quality and frequency of past and present advertising? What keeps these prime

customers coming back? What can be done to make them come back or to shop at this business more often? Does the client want to retain and strengthen his or her appeal to current customers?

2. Who are viable potential customers for the product or service? What are their characteristics? What are their shopping habits? What are their interests and priorities? What would attract them to the client's business or service? Should this be the target group for the commercials or announcements being written? What are the crossover characteristics of the current and potential customers?

3. How much do current and potential customers know about the client's product or service?

4. What are the attitudes of current and potential customers toward the client's product or service?

5. Which attitudes should be reinforced? Which attitudes changed? Why? How?

6. What are the common, identifiable, consistent traits (psychographics) of current and potential customers?

Much of the information needed to formulate both the client/product/service analysis and the audience analysis can be supplied through collection of marketing data. Clients can supply the results of internal research projects. Independent research companies can provide general or specific information from store audits, consumer panels, and surveys.

The results of marketing research can provide insight into the attitudes and behavior of consumers (product consumption, brand and image preferences, levels of product or service loyalty, etc.), determine product appeals and shortcomings (color, packaging, special features, convenience, etc.) and help determine the client's position in the marketplace by examining such items as sales volume, distribution patterns, and industry trends. Marketing research techniques can be used to test advertising concepts and entire campaigns both before and after the campaign is available in the market. Marketing research can be helpful when identifying problem areas, formulating objectives for future advertising, tracking current and future trends in the marketplace, and anticipating changes in the competition's strategies. It is an important tool in the decision-making process for the client and ultimately for the writer.

Statement of Objectives

The general purpose of any advertising message is persuasion. This broad objective must be more narrowly defined, however, to provide some means of measuring the results of the broadcast advertising and to save time and energy. The objectives of an advertising effort can be to create awareness or to inform consumers about a new product or service. For an established product or service, the objective might be to plant a name firmly in the consumer's mind and to motivate the consumer to buy the product or use the service advertised. If the client is facing stiff competition in maintaining customers, the advertising objective can be to provide information about the client, to shape a positive attitude in the consumer's mind, or to provide additional motivation for selecting the client's product or service over the competition.

To be an effective tool for the writer, the copy rationale statement of objectives must be:

•expressed as a clear, positive statement of the communications job to be accomplished, aimed at a specific target audience or group, with a specific result over a specified period of time
•realistic and capable of being measured
•capable of being translated into a specific plan of action and effective broadcast advertising messages
•based upon a thorough analysis of the marketplace, the client, the product or service, and the consumer
•agreed upon by the client or advertiser before any broadcast advertising is written or produced

The need to formulate a statement of objectives applies equally to commercials as well as to public service announcements for a non-commercial client and to promotional announcements written and produced by a broadcast station or network. Here are examples of statements of objectives for several different kinds of clients and writing situations:

•to create awareness about a new detergent product among women aged eighteen to forty-five who will buy 100,000 units of this new product in the next thirty days
•to enhance the image of Bill's Clothing Store among men between the ages of twenty-five and forty-five who will spend a total of $75,000 on items offered by the client in the next ten days
•to motivate adults between eighteen and fifty-four in the community to contribute $50,000 to the local United Way campaign in the next thirty days
•to convince women between eighteen and thirty-four in the local television market to watch Channel 2's Late Afternoon Movie series with the result that the size of this target audience for this program series will increase five rating points in the next ratings report for this market

Logical and Emotional Appeals

The writer must be able to identify and make effective use of basic motivators of human behavior. These motivators often are referred to as the logical and emotional appeals used in broadcast advertising to persuade current and potential consumers to follow a particular course of action. *Logical,* or *rational,* appeals are those which tap the intellectual, analytical, and thinking processes of the consumer. *Emotional* appeals relate to the non-logical, non-intellectual, humanistic, psychic, and personal aspects of the consumer. Logical appeals are effective when the product or service is being sold directly, without frills. Emotional appeals can be used to grab the audience's attention by presenting impelling motives and situations.

It is difficult to place a restrictive label on the wide variety of appeals which could be used in a commercial or announcement. For the sake of identification and classification, however, here are some of the major logical and emotional appeals available to the writer of broadcast advertising:

Self-Preservation. This is one of the strongest motivators of human behavior. Every individual is concerned about guaranteeing the continuation of life, personally and within a group or family. The listener or viewer wants to enhance the capability for self-preservation and to be alerted to situations which might threaten such enhancement. Public service announcements which appeal for funds to feed and clothe hungry and homeless refugees in a war-torn country use self-preservation as a primary appeal.

Security. Individuals want to be personally safe and comfortable, free from economic difficulties as well as psychological and social pressures. Security would be a primary appeal in spot announcements for smoke detectors, over-the-counter medicines, insurance company policies, and the use of automobile safety seat belts.

Reputation. Most people are concerned about the way others see them, how others feel and react toward what they own, as well as what they believe, say, and do. Most people seek some measure of recognition and approval from others. Reputation could be used as a primary appeal in announcements for a new automobile, furniture and interiors, appliances, and such personal items as bath soap, deodorant and foot spray.

Self-Respect. Most consumers set fairly high standards for themselves and their behavior and may be motivated to consider the purchase or use of a product or service because it would enhance this self-image. Hallmark's slogan "when you care enough to send the very best" tends to appeal to the self-image of the listener or viewer. A promotional announcement for a special television opera series could use this appeal to entice viewers to watch the upcoming programs since many viewers would want to consider themselves educated and refined, and naturally attracted to this type of high-quality television programming.

Status/Power/Prestige. The need to feel reassured, confident, able to persuade others, and to have direct control over their beliefs and actions may be overpowering in many consumers. Property, money, and power may be the overriding motivation in a person's life. Commercials for quality, exclusive stores and shops, special clothing items, expensive cars, and exotic vacation spots may center on this need for status, power and prestige.

Affection. Love, affection, loyalty, and sentimentality toward friends, family, church, school, country, or organizations are strong motivating forces for many people. When used expertly and creatively by the writer, this appeal can stir up strong, enduring feelings and emotions which are almost sure to inspire the listener or viewer. Commercials for Kodak and General Electric provide excellent examples of how this very strong, human, and emotional appeal can be effectively used in broadcast advertising.

Durability. This is one of the primary logical appeals the writer may decide to incorporate into a spot announcement. Every consumer wants to get the best value from each purchase—high performance and low maintenance costs. The consumer may be willing to pay more at the time of purchase if he or she can be convinced that the item will last for a long time. Durability is a primary appeal used in commercials for Jeep, Duracell Batteries, Maytag appliances, and Curtis Mathis television sets.

Economy. The initial or long-term low cost of a product item or service may be especially attractive to a consumer. Saving money is a continuing, growing concern among consumers. Economy could be the basic appeal used in commercials for gas-saving economy cars, energy-saving insulation, and low prices at specific supermarkets and food stores.

Sense of Adventure/Personal Freedom. Excitement, change, new experiences, adventure, and personal freedom to act, speak, write, and think at will with no restraints may be the appropriate appeal to make. Most people are curious about the unknown. They want to feel or experience something which normally is not available to them. Relief from the monotony of the daily routine may be a constant motivating factor for a specific group of listeners or viewers. Commercials for some personal products (e.g., toothpastes, mouthwashes, after-shave lotions, perfumes) could stress the unpredictable aftereffects of using a particular product. The exhilarating experience of owning and driving a sophisticated foreign sports car could appeal in a special way to an individual's sense of personal freedom.

Although placed into an arbitrary classification system, these logical and emotional appeals usually are not isolated for use alone in any one spot announcement. Rather, they are creatively combined or fused to produce a specific, predictable effect on the listener or viewer and to identify a unique benefit to be derived from the purchase of a product or the use of a service. It is the conscious, calculated use of these logical and emotional appeals which often determines the overall success of a commercial, public service, or promotional announcement.

Copy Style and Design

Implementation of the copy rationale or planning document is accomplished through the writing and eventual production of individual spot announcements. There are various presentational frameworks or design schemes available to implement the copy rationale effectively. These are described later in this chapter.

It is important that the copy style and design for each announcement match the product or service specifications identified earlier, implement the stated objectives, and incorporate specific logical and emotional appeals to make the message attractive and persuasive for the target audience. A decision may have been made to design announcements for use in several kinds of radio programming formats or for specific types of television programs. The copy style and design statement should specify the adjustments needed to provide this customization.

The copy style and design statement should determine the selection and use of music, sound effects, and voices. If television announcements are to be written, there should be specific references to the kinds of shots, scene transitions, and special effects to be used. All of the important aural or visual elements should be determined and identified and the use of each described and justified to create a particular mood, tone, color, or flavor in each announcement. Clarity and precision in the copy style and design statement are necessary for implementing the copy rationale document.

Competition and Competitive Claims

To place an advertiser or client in perspective in the marketplace, it is necessary to compile information and to form judgments about major competitors and competitive claims. It would be helpful to establish specific criteria for determining an advertiser's principal competitors. The criteria might include the amount of sales volume within the last year, visibility in the marketplace, and the amount of advertising purchased within a certain period.

Once major competitors have been identified, it is necessary to evaluate what each competitor is doing. It would be important to know the kind of advertising offered by each competitor—major brands sold, special sales, customer incentives, slogans used, claims made. Try to determine the identity of each competitor in the mind of consumers. Determine the specific niche in the marketplace for each competitor. It would be helpful to know what each competitor has done in the past as well as what each competitor is now doing. Track the development of each major competitor to better evaluate your advertiser or client. Information about competitors can be gathered by using market research techniques, through discussions with the advertiser or client or your station's sales account executive, and by your own careful analysis and observations of the marketplace.

The notion of identifying and analyzing competitors applies most obviously to commercial clients and advertisers. The same kinds of considerations, however, can be applied to promotional announcements where the competition is represented by the other stations and media outlets in the marketplace. Public service or non-profit clients do not usually identify competing agencies, but rather concentrate on other aspects of the copy rationale statement.

Positioning Statement

After analyzing the client, identifying the target audience, determining objectives and copy appeals, formulating an effective copy style and design, and evaluating major competitors, it is possible to devise a positioning statement for the client. A positioning statement explains or anticipates the client's niche in the marketplace and how the consumer will regard the client, product, or service after exposure to the soon-to-be-created spot announcement(s). Formulating a positioning statement forces the writer to identify a market vacuum and to determine how that vacuum can best be filled so that the client's products or services will be clearly set apart from the competition. Without a positioning statement, the client will blend into the competition and lose an effective means of marketplace identification.

Usually, there is a noticeable overlap between competitors in the mind of consumers. The positioning statement could incorporate attributes shared by competitors, but in addition should provide something unique or distinctive to set the client apart from the competition. The unique feature might be a jeweler who offers custom ring designs or a pharmacy which provides free home delivery of prescriptions and an end-of-the-year statement of medical expenditures for tax purposes. It is important to eliminate from a positioning statement the ineffective remnants from the client's past advertising efforts as well as the insurmountable strengths of major competitors. From this process should emerge a clear, distinctive, consistent, and memorable personality or identity for the client. With enough probing and analysis, practically every client, product or service can be positioned as offering something unique to its customers not normally provided by any of the competitors.

With a strong positioning statement, the client reaps the benefits: The client can match the competition now and anticipate future market developments from a position of strength and flexibility. A sound positioning statement should generate a main theme or stance from which sub-themes with multiple possibilities can be developed. Later in this chapter, a United Airlines campaign is described and illustrated which makes use of this positioning statement technique.

Central Selling Point

Once the positioning statement has been formulated, the writer can determine the central selling point or sales key. What is the central message, or sales pitch, to be delivered? How will the client's message be linked to the logical and emotional needs of the target audience? How can the statement of objectives and the client's position in the marketplace best be implemented? What will grab attention and sustain interest? How can the central sales message be expressed in a creative and interesting way? How can the listener or viewer best be persuaded to buy the product or use the service or shop at this particular store? What should be stressed in each spot announcement? Would it be best to stress a particular event (e.g., Christmas, Mother's Day, back-to-school), a specific product feature (e.g., uses, size, convenience), special client services (free delivery, no service charges, convenient parking, friendly sales personnel), or should these be combined for use in this set of announcements? Should emphasis be placed on the local client/advertiser or on the quality of nationally advertised and manufactured products available locally through the client?

These and many other questions must be answered before a strong, effective, and versatile central selling point or sales key can be formulated. All of the other copy rationale considerations culminate in the central selling point or sales key statement. In many instances, others will have determined the central selling point for the writer, who then takes what is given, what is known, and writes the spot announcements. In other situations (e.g., small broadcast stations and some advertising agencies), the writer is expected to help generate the central selling point or sales key as well as the actual copy.

ORGANIZING THE ANNOUNCEMENT

Despite the thorough analysis and careful documentation required to generate the copy rationale, the writer must still come to grips with the problem of what to include and how to organize each commercial, public service, or promotional announcement. The copy rationale should provide the answers for the writer. The primary function of such a planning document is to isolate and identify the information which *must* be included in each announcement and to suggest the most effective ways the information can be organized and presented.

What to Include

Three suggestions should help the writer determine what to include in each announcement:

1. Use key attributes.
2. Stress benefits.
3. Display both effectively.

Even a short, 10-second announcement should incorporate key characteristics identified in the copy rationale. While it will not be possible to use all of the key attributes identified, the one or two that must be used in every announcement should be obvious even in a 10-second message. The key attributes of a client, product, or service should generate specific individual benefits, which must be stressed in each announcement if the consumer is to be reassured that something positive and beneficial will come from the purchase of this product or the use of this service. Both attributes and benefits must be linked together in the consumer's mind by offering something tangible. What is included in each announcement must be organized and presented in an attractive, effective manner.

How to Organize

It soon becomes obvious that there are many ways to organize an announcement. The writer's challenge is to devise the *best* organizational pattern, the one which will create a message which is attractive, interesting, persuasive, memorable, and which fulfills the essential objectives and conclusions of the copy rationale. Many writers recommend the use of a five-step persuasive process based on observations and conclusions about consumer behavior. This five-step process can be readily identified in what knowledgeable observers have determined are effective and successful commercials and announcements, no matter what presentational framework eventually is used. While the five steps may not be presented in the same order as listed, all five steps should be incorporated into each announcement. The five-step persuasive process includes the following:

1. Get attention.
2. Hold attention.
3. Build interest.
4. Create desire.
5. Get action.

The first few seconds of a commercial or announcement are crucial. You must have the attention of the listener or viewer before any other information can be presented. The writer must use various devices both at the beginning and throughout the message to get and to hold attention. These attention devices include the following:

•an unexplained or unidentifiable sound or visual (later clarified in the announcement)
•a startling or provocative statement or picture
•an elaborate sound or visual effect
•a rhetorical question which involves the audience
•a well-known spokesperson respected by the audience
•a sound effect or piece of music which evokes emotions, images, textures, colors, and shapes
•a situation which immediately involves the audience because it relates to daily concerns

It is possible to build interest throughout the announcement by creatively using the elements of surprise, conflict, and suspense. Try to make the announcement somewhat unpredictable for the audience. Give them the unexpected. Create the impression that an important problem exists that must be resolved and hint that this problem could relate to the product, service, or client.

Using appropriate emotional and logical appeals the writer must create a desire for the product or service in the mind of the audience. The listener or viewer must want to purchase the product, use the service, or shop at the client's store. But this desire will be created in the audience's mind only if a tangible benefit is offered which impresses the individual consumer. The writer must plant in the audience's mind the idea that the problem presented earlier can indeed be resolved by the advertised product, service, or client. The individual listener or viewer must believe this connection can be made and that some personal benefit will result from the purchase of a particular product or the use of a specific service.

The last crucial step in the persuasive process involves getting a response or action from the audience. This response could be direct or implied. A commercial for a furniture store may conclude by urging the audience to buy specific items during a special sale. An institutional commercial for a major oil company may be written so that the audience understands and appreciates that company's efforts in finding new energy sources. The techniques used in a public service announcement may compel the listener or viewer to respond by being more sympathetic towards a certain cause or the announcement may ask for a more direct response, such as contributions to a central fund. The announcement must be clearly and precisely organized so that the audience has no doubt about the action needed. The message must build to this final step and be based on the key elements identified in the copy rationale.

METHODS OF PRESENTATION

An important part of the copy rationale document, copy style and design, requires more careful examination. The writer must consider many creative alternatives in order to select the best possible method of communicating the client's ideas and objectives. Some of the most important creative variables include: standard lengths for broadcast announcements; styles of delivery, which will be determined by talent and production personnel; and the packaging of the finished announcement, in which the number of talent featured, the presentational frameworks used, and the copy makeup selected become important considerations.

The classifications and terminology used here are meant to place this information into some order for the purposes of understanding the creative writing process. It is important to remember that many of these classifications overlap and that it is a common practice to combine several terms or classifications into one fused, cohesive announcement which displays a sense of unity and direction for the audience. It is the writer's responsibility to understand the various classifications and terms, to become aware of the potential use for each item, and to select the combination that best fulfills the goals and objectives of the copy rationale.

Standard Lengths

Several standard lengths for broadcast announcements and commercials have evolved over the years to accommodate scheduling demands, convenience, and the purchase of broadcast advertising time by the client. The length of each announcement may be the result of placement (i.e., where the announcement will be used in the broadcast schedule), the conclusions drawn from the copy rationale, the type of client or product or service featured, the nature of the program or the program format in which the announcement will be used, as well as a number of other considerations.

The use of standard lengths for commercials and announcements also provides the writer with some notion about the number of words needed. Nevertheless, only approximate word counts can be indicated for each standard copy length because individual words vary in length and in the amount of time needed to say them; some ideas are more complex and require a slower rate of speaking for the audience to understand and to digest the ideas; some words or phrases require more emphasis through pauses and variations in rate of speaking; the talent may read faster or slower than you would like or had planned; and the kind, length, and number of music and sound effects inserted in the script usually decrease the number of words needed.

To provide some assistance for the writer, each standard length is identified and an approximate word count and use for each length are suggested.

10-Second Announcement. Twenty-five words. The brevity of a 10-second announcement necessitates capturing immediate attention from the audience since the announcement must focus on only one sales item or point from the copy rationale. The name of the client or product or service and one consumer benefit are all that can be used. It is a length used infrequently in broadcast advertising.

20-Second Announcement. Forty-five words. A 20-second announcement can incorporate the name of the client/product/service, one or two consumer benefits, and perhaps squeeze in a slogan or additional client reminder.

30-Second Announcement. Sixty-five words. The length of a 30-second announcement can accommodate specific details about a company, product, service, or idea and expands the opportunity to present supporting claims and benefits. By a wide margin, this is the most common length used for both radio and television commercials and announcements on networks and on local stations.

60-Second Announcement. One hundred twenty-five words. The most elongated of the standard copy lengths, the 60-second announcement can be used to involve the audience longer and to disperse more information about the client/product/service. This length provides a broader canvas for the writer, allowing full development of the copy rationale as well as more complete development of characters, situations, mood, and atmosphere. It is a copy length used in the broadcast schedule about as often as 10-second announcements.

Other Lengths. There are other commercial and announcement lengths used for special reasons and under specific circumstances. For example, 15- and 45-second lengths have been created to accommodate special writing and broadcast sales needs (e.g., announcements used during program billboards or closing credits). Industry-wide, however, these cannot be considered standard broadcast copy lengths. Purchase of broadcast advertising time is made using the standard lengths already described.

There is movement within the industry toward commercials and announcements longer than 60 seconds. Programs that have been underwritten by a single sponsor often feature announcements lasting as long as two or three minutes. The growth of cable systems' capacity to provide still more broadcast advertising opportunities and the use of commercial underwriting for production of home video system videotape and videodisc programs should intensify the trend toward longer commercials and announcements.

Styles of Delivery

The manner in which talent and production personnel deliver the commercial or announcement is another important consideration. The writer should develop a versatility in writing that will allow him or her to prepare effective material for a specific kind of delivery style. This requires the writer to be flexible and to adapt such language usage components as word choice, sentence length, and syntax to different styles. While the writer may indicate in the script the characterization, mood, pace, tempo, and atmosphere that are most appropriate for a particular message, talent and production personnel often exercise a certain degree of discretion when producing the finished commercial or announcement. Just as a composer's music is subject to varying interpretations when performed, the writer's script may be delivered in any number of styles in an effort to further enhance the message.

Soft Sell. In the soft sell presentation style, the message is delivered in a relaxed, informal manner. The talent's voice projects a soft, intimate relationship with the audience. A television announcement using this style would emphasize close-ups, dissolves, slow motion action, soft focus, more music, and less narration or dialogue. The soft-sell approach stresses personal, human, intimate, and emotional appeals.

Hard Sell. The hard-sell style contrasts directly with the soft sell approach in the strong, direct, no-nonsense, almost overpowering manner of delivering the message. Visually, this style is characterized by quick cuts between shots as well as fast zooms, pans, trucking shots, and attention-grabbing special effects. The pace and tempo are fast. A large amount of information is crammed into a short amount of time. The hard-sell approach invokes immediate action in the audience.

Straight Sell. The moderate pace and tempo of the straight sell approach place it in the middle ground between the soft-sell and hard-sell delivery styles. The talent delivers the message in a conversational, yet persuasive, style. In a television commercial, the full range of visual possibilities is used. This is the routine, day-in-day-out style used in a large number of commercials and announcements.

New Wave. The newest delivery style to gain prominence within the advertising community has been labeled, perhaps for lack of a better term, "new wave." Although some use of this style is anticipated in radio, it has been television which has provided the vehicle for the full display of new wave techniques.

The new wave writing and production style stresses nuance and understatement, sophisticated visual effects, bold colors, often loud rock music, and characters who are emotionally cool, humorless, and on the edge of decadence and sadomasochism. The aim is to create a memorable mood or feeling. Unfortunately, this style often places the client's message behind the elegant, sophisticated, urbanized display of product user lifestyle. Technique tends to overshadow content.

This delivery style has been used to enliven a client's stagnant consumer image or to add extra zest to a product or service category which needs a different look and approach. Some advertiser categories may not find the use of new wave techniques beneficial or appropriate (e.g., corporate image announcements or life insurance commercials). Commercial clients who have used the new wave delivery style on television include: Diet Pepsi, Breyers yogurt, RC Cola, Avon, Chanel, Finesse hair conditioner, Lincoln-Mercury, Ford Mustang, Magnavox, Camaro, Honda, London Fog, Timex, Bon Jour Action Jeans, Thom McAn, and Candies shoes.

The full impact of the use of new wave advertising styles has yet to be determined. Like most emerging techniques, full acceptance by both consumers and clients will depend upon the quality and number of such commercials produced in the future. New wave techniques do provide an alternative for more traditional advertising styles.

Packaging

The writer must consider carefully the many variables that influence how an announcement is formulated and finally written. These variables include the number of talent featured, the presentational framework used, and the flexibility of the copy makeup selected. Each possibility must be explored completely and ultimately combined with other presentation factors to provide an effective, persuasive, memorable package.

Number of Talent. The three primary alternatives are: single voice, dialogue or interview, and multi-voice. Each can be an effective presentation tool. A *single-voice* announcement would be effective when using primarily logical appeals to convince the audience to buy a product or use a service; it allows an opportunity for strong one-to-one communication. *Dialogue or interview* announcements would be useful to create a realistic human situation or an imaginary, fantasy situation that brings out the attractiveness of the client's product or service; it permits development of two distinctive characters who interact in a conversation. *Multi-voice* presentations can be beneficial if a wide variety of characters and situations are to be used; a clear differentiation between voices and characters is essential to the effectiveness of this presentational format.

Any of these three alternatives can be combined with music or sound effects. For the purposes of classification, however, the writer might think in terms of emphasizing the talent and not necessarily the music or sound effects heard. The same designations can be used to classify television presentational forms. Whether the talent performs live or is recorded on film or videotape, each of these alternatives can be used both on-camera or off-camera in a voice-over.

Presentational Frameworks. A *dramatization* can be devised to provide further refinement of a dialogue or multi-voice presentation. In effect, the writer seeks to create a short playlet, a happening that creates suspense, develops characters, and reaches a climax. Despite the limitations and restraints of broadcast advertising copy lengths, this presentational form can be effective if the standard dramatic structure conventions are used: exposition, conflict, rising action, climax, resolution, or denouement. Often the structure is provided through a narrative approach using an announcer. Characters and plot must be developed quickly and well. It is one of the most difficult writing challenges because of the complexity of the dramatic structure needed. It has been used extensively, however, by such commercial clients as: Brim coffee, Miller's Lite beer, Biz presoak detergent, Colgate and Crest toothpastes, Shell Oil Company, Phillips Petroleum, Ivory soap, Birds Eye vegetables, AAMCO transmissions, and Jartran trucks.

Testimonials represent another kind of presentational framework. Well-known celebrities or personalities, ordinary consumers, or even the client could be featured. It is important that testimonials offer the audience someone whom they can trust, who can testify to the quality and effectiveness of the advertised product or service. Celebrities often are selected for such presentations in hopes of attracting those in the target group identified in the copy rationale document. Ordinary consumers can provide testimonials through in-the-store interviews or similar devices. Clients often insist on presenting their own messages, usually with mixed results. The goal is to humanize what is often a cold, impersonal approach. Commercial advertisers who have used testimonials in broadcast advertising include: Xerox (with its lovable Brother Dominic character), Rolaids (featuring Roger Staubach), Smith Barney and Chrysler-Plymouth (actor John Houseman), Remington shavers (featuring the president of the company), Midas shock absorbers (featuring several satisfied customers), Anacin (featuring actress Patricia Neal), Glad Trash Bags (Tom Bosley), Georgia-Pacific Company's Coronet towels (featuring Rosemary Clooney giving both a spoken and a singing testimonial), Eastern Airlines (with former astronaut Frank Bormann, president of the company, providing his personal endorsement), and Oldsmobile (actor Dick Van Patten and family).

Humor can be the basis for an effective broadcast advertising message. It can make a message stand out from many others. If the humor does not override the sales message, it can be a useful tool to get and hold attention and provide a memorable message for the audience. Humor tends to lower the audience's defenses, often makes the listener or viewer more tolerant of watching an advertising message, and can create a more positive attitude toward the product, service, or client. To be successful, humor in broadcast advertising must: reflect current lifestyles and events, involve the audience in the characters and situations presented, and explore the full range of subtle satire, parody, and offbeat, but believable, humor.

When selecting humor as the primary presentational framework, the writer should determine: whether humor is appropriate for this particular client, product or service; whether humor helps "sell" effectively; whether the humor used relates to human experiences and appeals to the target audience group; and whether the humor is indeed funny and attractive and enhances the message.

Writing humor is very difficult. It requires special writing talent that is developed only after many years of hard work and experimentation. Writing sharp, incisive, memorable humor for broadcast advertising messages requires the professional talents of such humorists as Stan Freberg, Bob and Ray, and Dick Orkin and Bert Berdis.

Jingles or musical announcements can add dimension and produce startling memorability and consistency in the minds of the audience. Although the writer is not responsible for composing the music, he or she must be aware of the various uses of music and how the writer's work can be placed in a musical setting through the creative talents of professional musicians. The writer can suggest that music be used alone to present the message or with other presentational forms to heighten the central sales message. Musicians can customize their compositions through adjustments in instrumentation, vocal stylings, tempo, length, and lyrics to better match various radio programming formats and to target the message for specific kinds of audiences. A great deal of time and money is spent developing jingles or musical commercial announcements that sell an image. In most cases, the effort and expense have produced worthwhile results. The commercial advertisers who have used this presentational framework include: McDonald's ("You Deserve a Break Today"), Vidal Sassoon, Burger King ("Aren't You Hungry?"), Alka-Seltzer, 7-Up, Pepsi-Cola ("Catch That Pepsi Spirit"), American Airlines ("Doing What We Do Best"), Coca-Cola ("Have a Coke and a Smile" and "Coke Is It"), Dr. Pepper ("I'm a Pepper"), Wrigley's gum, Meow Mix cat food, Band-Aid ("Stuck on Me"), and Oscar Meyer ("The Wiener Song").

A *demonstration* presentational framework allows the client to show or illustrate the uses or benefits of a particular product or service. Obviously, a demonstration would be effective on television, where the audience can see what takes place. Nevertheless, a creative writer should not discard the use of a demonstration on radio since the mind of the listener can be tapped by innovative use of voices, music, or sound effects. The sound of a steak sizzling, a motorcycle roaring off into the distance, and the street noise of an exotic location such as Hong Kong all produce vivid, memorable images for the radio listener. If combined creatively with other elements, such sounds can produce an interesting demonstration for the advertiser. Among the commercial advertisers who have used a demonstration as the primary presentational framework are: Stouffer's "Lean Cuisine," Texize's Spray 'n Wash, Michelob beer, Volvo, Bounty towels, Del Monte, Sears, Wilson hams, Zenith, and Dentu-Creme.

Animation is a presentational form used in broadcast advertising and is used, as well, in other media applications. Whether used alone or combined with live action, animation can simplify complex structures and processes, offer characters and situations which are more readily accepted by the audience, and provide an effective message which lasts over an extended period of time. Despite the high production costs involved, clients who have used animation generally agree that it is worth the cost, time, and precision necessary to produce an effective animated message. Commercial advertisers who have used animation in broadcast campaigns include: Planters peanuts, Green Giant niblets corn, Keebler cookies, Star-Kist tuna, Pillsbury, Michelin tires, and Raid Ant and Roach Poison.

The creative copywriter recognizes the value of the *combination* presentational framework in which no one method or form dominates; rather, a combination of methods is blended to produce the finished commercial or announcement. As indicated earlier, the combination format is more common. For the purposes of classification, however, we have isolated separate and identifiable presentational frameworks. Examples of this combination form include: Formby furniture products (demonstration and testimonial), American Dairy Association (musical and demonstration), Fram oil filters (dialogue and testimonial), Tombstone pizza (musical, demonstration, and testimonial), Kodak (demonstration and testimonials from celebrities), NAPA auto parts (demonstration, dramatization, and testimonial from Joseph Campenella), and Dristan (demonstration and dramatization).

Copy Makeup. Clients and advertisers continue to seek ways to use the writer's efforts in an efficient, flexible manner. The client usually is pleased when the writer finds ways to devise an announcement or commercial which offers the opportunity to present an attractive and persuasive message while at the same time providing flexibility, eliminating duplicate efforts, and saving money.

A "modulized" copy form has been found useful by many clients and advertisers. When a set of commercials or announcements is to be written, the writer generates the longest copy length (e.g., 60 or 30 seconds). From that long-form copy, the writer removes segments or pieces to produce the shorter lengths needed. This technique can be used in both radio and television applications.

In the "donut" copy form, there is a standard opening which remains the same each time the announcement is used. The middle portion, or hole, in the donut is where the client inserts the special item for sale or a special service feature or bonus. There is a standard closing which, like the opening, stays the same to remind the audience of the client or advertiser. There are several possible variations with the donut copy form: the length of each of the three segments can vary (:05, :15, :10 or :10, :10, :10 or any other time combination for a 30-second announcement, for example; a jingle could be used for the opening or closing segment or both; one talent could be featured in the opening and closing segments while another voice or voices could be heard in the hole segment. There are many other possibilities for the writer to explore. This is a very popular copy form for co-op messages in which the national manufacturer could provide the first and last segments and the local retail merchant inserts the middle segment to localize the client's message.

The "core" copy form also features three segments. The first and last segments may vary each time the announcement or commercial is constructed. The client can maintain various openings and closings in a library and select the particular segment necessary to give the message a flavor of difference while sustaining a strong identity with the audience. The middle segment forms the core and generally features an important sales point about the client (e.g., a unique service, established reputation in the business community, a special department, etc.). This middle segment remains the same when the core copy form is used. Using the core technique, the writer selects from the available opening and closing segments or generates new ones and blends these with the central sales point in the middle segment to produce a smooth, even presentation.

Another possibility is the "open-faced" copy form, which features a standard opening (usually longer than the opening segment in the donut and core copy forms) and a variable ending. It is in this short closing segment that the client tops off the message by emphasizing a different copy point each time (e.g., a special sale, a key service, or a product feature).

A copy form used often in co-op advertising is the "tag," in which the manufacturer's message is presented and then a short time is allowed for the listing of local dealers or distributors of the advertised products or services. In most cases, the national client or his or her representative insists on approving the local copy generated to ensure proper emphasis of national and local advertisers, and to provide access to valuable co-op dollars for local use.

Another popular copy form is the "lift," or "simulcast," in which the audio portion of a television message is lifted out and used in toto on radio. Many clients insist on this copy makeup to provide a readily available radio message and to enhance the uniformity of their multi-media campaign. When using this copy form, the writer must be aware that a lift is anticipated and devise the television copy to permit effective use of this technique. The sound portion of the television message must be strong enough to sustain interest and to deliver a strong, persuasive message when used alone.

An obvious writing hazard when using any of these copy makeup forms is the possibility that the various parts of the finished announcement or commercial will not blend together to produce an effective, smooth, persuasive message. Careful planning, skillful writing, attention to detail, high production quality, and intense coordination among those directly involved in the creation and production of such hybrid copy forms will prevent many of the potential problems from developing into insurmountable obstacles. These copy makeup alternatives offer additional options for the client or advertiser as well as the creative spirit of the writer.

COMMERCIALS AND ANNOUNCEMENTS—EXAMPLES

A number of commercial script and copy strategy examples will help to illustrate many of the concepts and techniques already discussed. A diverse selection of products, services, and clients is presented to show the wide range of copy design and format possibilities as well as the creative strategies incorporated into various kinds of copywriting situations.

United Airlines

Leo Burnett Company, Inc., developed for United Airlines a strong and versatile broadcast advertising campaign entitled "100,000 Mile Flier." The strength and flexibility of the copy rationale for this campaign generated many sub-themes highlighting specific services offered by United Airlines (fig. 4-1).

Each commercial in the campaign features a well-known personality or celebrity in a testimonial situation. The tone of the copy is friendly, but businesslike. It is written for a straight-sell style of delivery. Specific benefits and services offered by United Airlines are presented in each commercial. Each television commercial begins and ends with a voice-over announcer and a display of the campaign theme and client

---

BUSINESS CAMPAIGN - "100,000 MILE FLIER"

1. TARGET

   A. Business Traveler is

      - Extremely experienced
        (15 round trips a year)

      - Sophisticated ($40,000 + College Graduate)

      - Resentful of service declines due to cheapening of air travel.

2. STRATEGY

   Establish United as a preferred business travel airline on the basis of specific benefits provided to the business traveler. Business-like tone appropriate.

3. EXECUTIONAL FORMAT

   Individual executions will demonstrate specific services United offers.

Mileage Plus	(Rewards frequent fliers)
Advance Seat Assignments	(Convenience of reserving a specific seat/section)
Fares	(Inexpensive, competitive)

Figure 4-3 Script for a radio commercial based on the condensed copy rationale shown in figure 4-1. *(Courtesy of United Airlines and Leo Burnett Company, Inc.© United Airlines 1982)*

UNITED AIRLINES As Filmed & Recorded: 02/02/82 ms
30-Second Film
"JOSEPH PAPP NETWORK"
PASSENGER SERVICE
UAPC4170

VIDEO	AUDIO
1 MORNING, NEW YORK SKYLINE SUPER: "WHY DO 100,000 MILE FLIERS CHOOSE UNITED?"	ANNCR: Why do hundred thousand mile fliers choose United?
2 PAPP IN FRONT OF THEATER. SUPER: "JOSEPH PAPP, THEATRICAL PRODUCER."	PAPP: Y'know in this town, I never have a problem getting the best seat in the house. Particularly when it's my show.
3 WIDER SHOT. WE CAN READ "PIRATES OF PENZANCE" ON THEATER MARQUIS. PAPP ENTERS CAB	When I travel, I'm like anyone else but I can still get the seat I want. Anyone can. By reserving it in advance on United.
4 PAPP SHOWS FLIGHT ATTENDANT TICKET AS HE ENTERS PLANE.	STEW: Seat six B, Mr. Papp.
	ANNCR: Reserve your seat when you reserve your flight, United will hold it up to fifteen minutes before take off.
5 AS PAPP TAKES SEAT HE APPLAUDS UNITED.	PAPP: Row six on the aisle. Bravo, United.
6 AIR TO AIR. SUPER: "FLY THE FRIENDLY SKIES."	ANNCR: People who fly for a living fly United's friendly skies.

Figure 4-2 Script for a television commercial based on the condensed copy rationale shown in figure 4-1. *(Courtesy of United Airlines and Leo Burnett Company, Inc. © United Airlines 1982)*

UNITED AIRLINES   As Recorded: 09/21/82 ns
52/08 - Second Recorded   Revision #1: 10/04/82 ns
Radio Announcement
"PAPP/ADVANCE CHECK-IN"
PASSENGER SERVICE

05006-PASS-52/08

1	SING:	PEOPLE WHO FLY FOR A LIVING...
2	ANNCR:	Why do hundred thousand mile fliers choose United?
3		Theatrical producer, Joseph Papp.
4	SFX:	(SUBDUED LOBBY CROWD, ORCHESTRA PLAYING OVERTURE, INCLUDING "ONE".)
5	PAPP:	At the theatre, I can get the best seat in the house. Especially if it's "A CHORUS LINE."
7	USHER:	Row six, center. Enjoy your show, Mr. Papp.
8	SFX:	(THEATRE SOUNDS SEGUE INTO STREET NOISES: TRAFFIC, HORNS, ETC.)
9	PAPP:	When I travel -- taxi! -- I can still get the seat I want.
10	SFX:	(TAXI DOOR OPENS)
11	PAPP:	By reserving it with United's Advance Check-in.
12		Airport, please.
13	SFX:	(TAXI DOOR SLAMS SHUT)
14	PAPP:	And I avoid check-in lines, too. My boarding passes come with my ticket.
15	ANNCR:	Use Advance Check-In on any United flight, including
16		our fourteen daily nonstops to all three New York airports -- La Guardia, Newark and JFK.
17	SFX:	(AIRPORT TERMINAL BOARDING GATE, CROWD, BOARDING ANNOUNCEMENTS, ETC.)
18	UAL GATE EMPLOYEE:	Go right on board, Mr. Papp.
19	PAPP:	United's Advance Check-in is a hit with me. Because I
20		love "A Chorus Line," but not an airport line.
21	SING:	PEOPLE WHO FLY FOR A LIVING, FLY UNITED'S FRIENDLY SKIES.
22	TAG:	(LIVE ANNCR)

Figure 4-3 Script for a radio commercial based on the condensed copy rationale shown in figure 4-1. (*Courtesy of United Airlines and Leo Burnett Company, Inc.© United Airlines 1982*)

logo to provide continuity and emphasis. Figure 4-2 is the copy for one television commercial in the campaign.

The same specific service, advance seat assignment, and check-in is stressed in the radio commercial featuring theatrical producer Joseph Papp (fig. 4-3). Notice that the celebrity's copy has been expanded and that other audio elements (e.g., sound effects, music at the beginning and the end, other supporting characters such as the usher and the UAL gate employee) have been added to enhance the persuasive message in this 60-second commercial. An 8-second live tag across the United Airlines jingle ends the commercial with customized local information on United Airlines service.

Mutual of Omaha

The subject of cancer is a sensitive one to handle in a television commercial. It can be an automatic turnoff because people do not want to think about cancer. When developing the rationale for the Mutual of Omaha commercial entitled "Reassured," which discusses cancer insurance, Bozell & Jacobs, Inc., decided to portray someone else who has cancer, not the viewer. The objective was to let the viewer come to his or her own conclusion that having a Mutual of Omaha cancer insurance policy is wise (fig. 4-4).

The commercial starts at a dramatic low point and builds to a happy ending. The creators of this commercial want the viewer to be relieved at the end, left with positive thoughts about Mutual of Omaha, its products and services. The approach used illustrates the soft-sell style of delivery.

Neiman-Marcus

The annual Neiman-Marcus Fortnight occurs in late October and early November. Each year, the many images of a different country transform the store through special presentations, performances and exhibits. Foods, goods, crafts, and fashions related to the country featured delight store visitors.

All aspects of German culture were presented during the 1983 Neiman-Marcus Fortnight. Figure 4-5 is the storyboard for a 30-second spot announcement designed to remind customers that Fortnight was again running for three weeks (some years such observances have been two weeks), and that the end of Fortnight was drawing near. According to store management, the commercial was successful in increasing sales and store traffic during the third quarter.

Notice how very few words are used in the commercial. The images shown express the charm and wonder of the event. The clock featured in the opening and closing shots effectively reinforces the German Fortnight theme and the idea that time is running out for those who want to share the fun and excitement of the event. German food, decor, and transportation as well as Neiman-Marcus's participation in this annual event are combined into a stylish commercial that entices the viewer to come to the Fortnight.

BROADCAST PROMOTION

The concepts, principles, and techniques already described for broadcast commercials and public service announcements apply equally to broadcast promotion efforts.

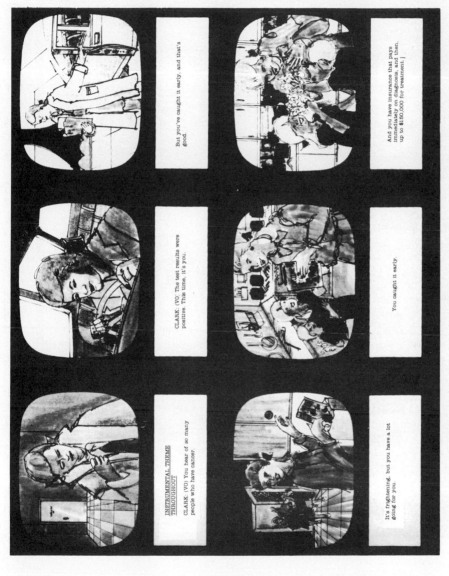

Figure 4-4 Storyboard for a Mutual of Omaha television commercial entitled "Reassured." *(Courtesy of Mutual of Omaha Insurance Company—Omaha, Nebraska)*

Fig. 4-4 *(Continued)*

The same basic creative process must be followed to produce effective and memorable promotional messages. Although this brief discussion of broadcast promotion will focus only upon on-air audience promotion since it most directly involves creative writing efforts, there are many other activities in which a broadcast promotion department is involved (e.g., sales promotion, community and press relations, and coordination of creative efforts between departments in a broadcast facility). At larger stations and networks, these responsibilities may be delegated to many employees working in the promotion area. In smaller operations, only one or two individuals may be available to handle all of the promotion responsibilities. As the concepts, types, and techniques of on-air promotion are described, notice the similarity to the creative process already outlined for commercials and public service announcements. Several copy examples will be presented to illustrate how these principles apply to on-air broadcast promotion efforts.

On-Air Promotion—Concepts

On-air promotion is the broadcast station or network use of its own air time to: create or enhance a specific image or profile for the broadcast facility among the audience; inform and attract audiences for programming; and develop awareness of the station or network's public service and community involvement.

The primary goal of on-air promotion efforts is building audiences. This is best accomplished by formulating a strong individual image for the station or network (similar to the positioning statement recommended in the copy rationale development for commercial clients), and then projecting this image prominently and consistently in all on-air as well as related multi-media promotional efforts (e.g., corporate identification items, stationery, order forms, billing forms, equipment, vehicles, etc.) Often this image is capsulized in a graphic look or logo. Once the station or network image or personality has become established in the minds of the audience, it is possible to accomplish other goals of on-air promotion—building audiences for programs and developing awareness and participation in a broadcast station's public service and community involvement projects.

Several companies provide customized versions of nationally distributed musical jingle and image packages. The station could choose to create its own image package and have appropriate IDs, music beds, and logo designed to provide the promotional consistency necessary. It is important that a station or network image be distinctive and indicative of a specific position in the market. This helps the copywriter focus each promotional announcement that is written. Often, a network-affiliated station will incorporate the network's image package into its own promotional efforts. This technique reinforces the strong network image usually projected and customizes the promotional message for local station use.

On-Air Promotion—Types and Techniques

Station Identification, or ID. These are required of every radio and television station. Legally, the ID must consist of the station's call letters and city of license or loca-

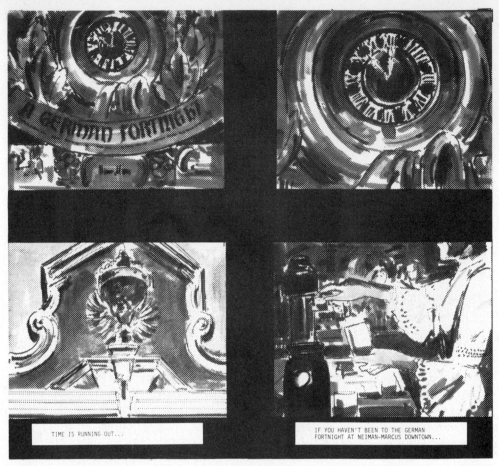

Figure 4-5 Storyboard for a Neiman-Marcus fortnight television commercial. *(Courtesy of Gary C. Grahnquist and Neiman-Marcus Advertising)*

tion; however, these mandatory IDs provide an excellent on-air promotion opportunity.

Station image or position can be reinforced by adding a short promotional statement from a station personality or celebrity, a slogan, a short musical jingle, or a logo to the required station ID information. For example:

> <u>ANNCR</u>: This is Radio 90, W-A-A-H, Central City...
> <u>your</u> country music station since 1965!

Or:

> VTR EXCERPT
> W/ LOGO/   <u>NET. NEWSCASTER</u>: Watch Channel 8 news
>   tonight at 11.
>
> ID SLIDE
> KEY-IN

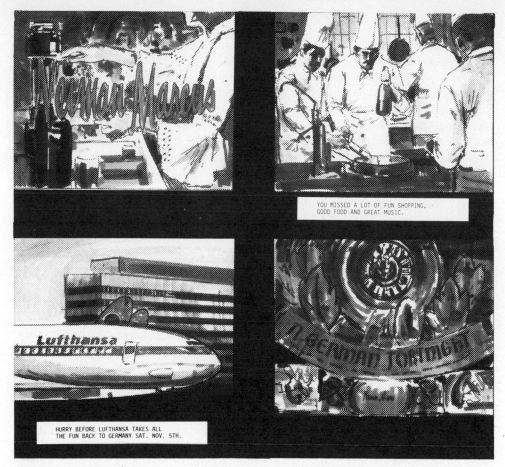

YOU MISSED A LOT OF FUN SHOPPING, GOOD FOOD AND GREAT MUSIC.

HURRY BEFORE LUFTHANSA TAKES ALL THE FUN BACK TO GERMANY SAT. NOV. 5TH.

Fig. 4-5 *(Continued)*

It is important to include the radio frequency (dial position) or television channel number in the station ID. Broadcast audiences will remember more easily "F-M 102" or "Radio 14" or "Channel 2" than specific station call letters.

Program and Personality Promos. Using the consistent image identified earlier, promotion personnel can create promos for specific programs or program series as well as personalities and celebrities featured in those programs. Using the umbrella station image adopted or developing sub-themes based on this image profile, on-air promos can be created to generate interest and to promote the acceptance of specific programs and personalities.

These promos could be developed for local programs produced by the station or for programs supplied by networks or program syndicators. Any type of program seen or heard on a station or network can be featured in such promos: newscasts, news specials, talk shows, live sports broadcasts, special events, music programs, children's shows, movies, network program series.

Program promos may be either generic or episodic. Generic promos are constructed for long-term use and to establish a program's image. Episodic promos tell the viewer or listener specific information about an upcoming episode or program in a series. Both types of program promos can be used effectively, although the episodic promo is preferred by many since a clear and specific benefit derived from the program can be emphasized for the listener or viewer. Just as in writing commercials, it is important to analyze the program and the target audience and then to construct the message to effectively provide an obvious benefit for the potential audience.

Personality promos can help establish station image and enhance the audience's attitude toward a specific on-air talent. This type of promo is used extensively to feature one or more members of a station's news staff and to highlight their strengths, summarize their achievements and, generally, to humanize their on-air presentation. Actors, performers, and well-known celebrities also could be featured in personality or testimonial promos which encourage the audience to watch for this individual in an upcoming program or to recognize that a certain program or station effort has been endorsed by someone who is trusted and respected.

The writer can choose from several *writing and production options* to construct effective promotional announcements. Practically all of the commercial copy presentational formats described and illustrated earlier in this chapter can be used. In addition, audience and celebrity testimonials could be featured in promos. Voice-overs—in which promotional copy is read over program credits, slides, film or videotape—are used extensively in television on-air promotion. Program excerpts or segments can be edited together to help convey the excitement, action and value of the program. Many of the writing and production techniques described earlier for commercials can be used to create a polished broadcast promotional announcement.

No matter what type of program or individual personality is featured in a broadcast promotional announcement, no matter which writing or production techniques are used, it is important that the information be presented clearly and directly, that the listener or viewer be given a good reason to tune in (benefit), and that where and when (day and hour) to tune in is stressed, especially at the end of the promo. As indicated earlier, the goal of the promotional copy writer is basically the same as that of the commercial copy writer. In broadcast promotional copy, the writer can focus consistently on one client—the station or network. The conceptualization, development, writing and production techniques, and strategies follow similar paths for commercials, public service announcements, and broadcast promos.

On-Air Promotion—Examples

WRC-TV. This NBC-owned and -operated (O and O) station based in Washington, D.C., designed a promotional campaign entitled "We Can't Wait to Show You" to correct a problem of station image. Research showed that audience opinion of NewsCenter 4 was negative. This opinion stemmed from an old series of problems that had been recently corrected. For example: the show was slow, lacking energy; sports coverage was dull; not enough videotape; not enough live coverage, and so on. WRC-TV knew the problems had been corrected, but the audience did not. Thus, the creation of the "We Can't Wait to Show You" campaign.

The campaign was designed to communicate enthusiasm for NewsCenter 4's people and product. Specific words like "new," "local," "love," and "tomorrow's news tonight" were used to sell formats and a positive image. According to Bob Casazza, WRC-TV's Director, Advertising and Promotion, "you might call our campaign 'corrective promotion.' Once we started changing audience attitudes, then we could continue to add messages."[1] Working with an advertising agency, Jacobs & Gerber, WRC-TV designed promotional announcements to convey a fresh new image necessary to build audience sampling. The campaign was presented in two phases. Phase I introduced the campaign with high-energy, although less informative, announcements. Phase II consisted of three spots, which won international awards from the Broadcasters Promotion Association, each promoting different newscasts: a 5:30 show that is all local and live; a 6:00 report that is in-depth; and an 11:00 show that gives the viewer tomorrow's news. Figure 4-6 is the production script used to create the promotional announcement entitled "Tomorrow's News." Several copy changes and location adjustments were made to produce a more effective on-air announcement.

Bob Casazza adds that

> As a marketing strategy, I feel that news should be sold as any consumer product. But, you must also balance this sell with day-to-day specifics on hard news coverage. Selling news with just songs and smiling faces is a mistake. Songs and smiling faces are fine for creating an umbrella image but you must support the reasons why people turn to news. I always sell an image and then support it with program benefits.[2]

After the introduction of the campaign in May of 1981, WRC-TV's news went from a third-place market position to first at 5:30 and 11:00 and was a strong second at 6:00.[3]

KNX. By associating with the winning image projected by the Raiders football team and by using an attention-grabbing gimmick (eating the microphone, which actually was charcoal-colored pound cake), KNX created an effective television message to attract radio listeners (fig. 4-7). This announcement has won thirteen major awards, including a Clio statue and first place awards in the Broadcasters Promotion Association, U.S. Television Commercial, and American Advertising Federation "ADDY" Awards competitions. Notice the creative use of a well-known sports figure and the closing moments of the announcement in which the call letters, station image, and radio frequency (dial position) are prominently displayed.

Y-100. WHYI FM's "Feel Like a Hundred" promotional campaign creates a humorous framework in which to emphasize dial position (Y-100) and music format and to create an identifiable, memorable campaign theme with multiple applications for the target audience. In the photoboard from one of the television spots in the campaign (fig.

FALL PROMOTION: "TOMORROW'S NEWS"

Scene 301:

Angle on Jim and Marty, exterior city. Camera dollies with them as they move through scene of news event. (Police come with flashing light -- cop is being interviewed by Barbara and Larry.)	Singers:	"NewsCenter Four can't wait to show you tonight." :03 sec.
Jim turns to camera, gesturing back to action. Camera keeps moving, discovers Barbara Allen, Larry Shainman and NewsCenter Four mobile unit.	Jim:	"Late breaking stories that get to you fast..." :02 sec.
Marty interrupts, gesturing back toward Barbara and Larry. :07 sec.	Marty:	"Because our NIGHTCREW gets to them fast..." :02 sec.

Scene 302:

Cut to George. Dolly shot in E. J. Tape Library. :03 sec.	Singers:	"NewsCenter Four can't wait to show you tonight." :03 sec.

Figure 4-6 Production script used to create the promotional announcement entitled "Tomorrow's News." *(Courtesy of WRC-TV and Jacobs & Gerber Advertising)*

4-8), notice the continual emphasis on dial position in the words heard, in frame three (with the car radio set on 100), and in the final frame in which Y-100's bold, distinctive, locally identifiable logo is displayed. Notice, too, the use of humorous situations punctuated by song lyrics heard on the station to highlight Y-100's program format. The repetitive copy line

...feel like a hundred -- Y-100

pounds home the theme and benefit for viewers and potential Y-100 listeners.

CKIQ. A unique copy style was used by CKIQ, Kelowna, British Columbia, Canada, for a year-long safe-driving community involvement campaign (fig. 4-9). If one accepts the premise that the public often develops an immunity to scare tactics used in announcements for such campaigns, then CKIQ's rather unique approach of macabre

Scene 303

George continues into control room "F." All screens are filled with action highlights, to which he gestures. :04 sec.	George:	"A late sports report that gives you the complete picture." :03 sec.
	George:	"Including the picture." :01 sec.

Scene 304

Cut to Arch, exterior theater at night.	Singers:	"NewsCenter Four can't wait to show you tonight." :03 sec.
Camera dollies with him.		
Arch continues to walk to camera, blithely unworried even though we hear crack of lightning, downpour, and he is dressed in his tuxedo.	Arch:	"Entertainment reports that are just as dependable..." :02.5 sec.
Arch steps out from under theater marquee into heavy downpour just as Bob steps into frame holding an umbrella, under which Arch continues to walk without interruption. :07 sec.	Bob:	"As my weather reports." :01.5 sec.
Cut to animation.	Singers:	"We can't wait to show you tonight."
Animation continues. Title holds.	Anncr:	"Get tomorrow's news tonight, weeknights at eleven on the new NewsCenter Four."

Fig. 4-6   *(Continued)*

parody of a game show becomes more understandable. Strong, fast-paced delivery coupled with the grim realities reflected in the copy help break through the apathy and produce a startling, memorable effect on listeners. The script is an excellent example of humor used effectively to communicate a serious message. "The Drinking Game" announcement has received awards from the Broadcasters Promotion Association, the Canada Safety Council, the Hollywood Television and Radio Society, and the Radio Bureau of Canada. The spot announcement also received a CLIO award for public service.[4]

KNX NEWSRADIO 10.70

World Champion Raiders (:10) Television Spot

BACKGROUND SOUNDS:
Football practice

ANNOUNCER:
"John Matuszak..."

...for the World Champion
Raiders."

MATUSZAK:
"Join me..."

...for a nice friendly
game of football."

(he bites mic)
SOUND EFFECT:
"Crunch"

ANNOUNCER:
"On KNX Newsradio,
ten seventy."

MATUSZAK:
"Good station, too."

KNX NEWSRADIO 10.70
6121 Sunset Boulevard
Los Angeles, CA 90028

Fred Bergendorff
Director of Advertising & Promotion

Agency: Bell Advertising

© MCMLXXXI
CBS INC All Rights Reserved

Figure 4-7 Photoboard for a KNX television promotional announcement. *(Courtesy of CBS Inc., KNX NEWSRADIO 10.70, and Bell Advertising)*

COPYWRITING SUGGESTIONS

The goal of a broadcast advertising copywriter is to create for a client, product, or service a positive, persuasive, and memorable commercial or announcement which effectively reaches a specific consumer target group with a central sales message. This is a challenging goal for the writer. But it is an attainable goal.

The following copywriting suggestions help capsulize some of the concepts and techniques discussed in this chapter. The list of suggestions which could be provided is extensive.

General Suggestions

1. *Keep the commercial or announcement in good taste.* Display your standards of creative professionalism and respect your audience. Let the goodwill of your client, product, or service come through in the copy you write. Avoid obvious exaggerations—unnecessary superlatives, false claims, and phony testimonials.
2. *Know the facts.* Know your client. Get the background information necessary to write in a believable, accurate manner. Know as much as you can about the client, product or service. Remember all of the key elements from the copy rationale.
3. *Be as specific as possible when relaying information on prices, products, and services.* Your specificity should be tempered by the overriding need to be clear, but also interesting, effective, and persuasive.
4. If known in advance, *adjust the style and content of the copy to the time of day and to the circumstances under which the announcement or commercial will be broadcast.* If appropriate, customize the copy to various program formats and uses.
5. *Stress benefits.* Tell the listener or viewer what is in it for him or her. Indicate why it is important to respond quickly to the commercial or announcement.
6. *Get and hold attention.* Know and use various writing techniques to get the message in front of the listener or viewer and into his or her consciousness. Build curiosity and suspense.
7. *Prepare the battle plan.* Know your objectives. Scrutinize the alternatives. Select the route carefully.
8. *Use slogans and catchwords effectively.* Often, these capsulize the central sales message.
9. *Use the right appeal.* Understand the emotions and lifestyle of the target group. Understand buyer motivation and audience self-perception. Select and use effectively the right blend of logical and emotional appeals in your copy.
10. *Use humor cautiously.* Make it work for the client, product or service. Discard the use of humor if it is inappropriate or less effective than other techniques and methods of presentation.
11. *Know the rules.* Know what is expected of you by the client, the audience, the law. Be aware of the parameters. Know the limits. Recognize the circumstances

Miami · Ft. Lauderdale

"It's not easy being a driving instructor."

"That's why I feel like a hundred -- Y-100."

(Car tires screeching)

"Things are tough all over."

"That's why more people all over..."

(Music: "Driving My Life Away")

Figure 4-8 Photoboard from one of the television spots in Y-100's "Feel Like a Hundred" promotional campaign. *(Courtesy of WHYI FM, Y-100)*

"...Than any other station in Florida."

"...feel like a hundred - Y-100..."

"It's not easy being a world famous brain surgeon."

"That's why I feel like a hundred - Y-100."

"Oooooooops"

"You feel like a million when you feel like a hundred - Y-100." (Music: "Another One Bites The Dust")

Fig. 4-8 *(Continued)*

JOHNNY: It's time once again for..."The Drinking Game." Now, here's
            your toastmaster, Al Call!

AL: Welcome to the Drinking Game. As you might remember, our
            contestant, Mr. Weaver, now has two impaired driving charges
            for a total of 20 big points! All he needs is another impairment,
            and he'll have another 10 points, a minimum three-month
            suspension and Johnny, tell him what else Mr. Weaver might
            get:

JOHNNY: It's a jail sentence!

SFX: CROWD CHEERS

AL: Alright, get ready to spin your wheels Mr. Weaver, and good
            luck! Remember, you can stop drinking at any time. If you
            drink too much, you could hear one of these sounds:

SFX: SIREN, CAR CRASH

AL: And if you do, here's what you'll get:

JOHNNY: It's a smashed up car!

SFX: AUDIENCE CHEERS

JOHNNY: But that's not all! You'll be driven in air conditioned comfort
            via ambulance for an extended stay in the Kelowna General
            Hospital!

SFX: AUDIENCE CHEERS

JOHNNY: Excellent accommodation and relaxation. Remember, KGH is
            hospitality at its best!

SFX: AUDIENCE CHEERS ENDING WITH ECHO

STRAIGHT: Every day, people play "The Drinking Game." They drink, and
            they drive...risking points, loss of driving privileges, fines, a
            jail sentence, or even injury or death. Don't play the Drinking
            Game, because when you do: You Bet Your Life.

Figure 4-9 Radio script of the announcement entitled "The Drinking Game." *(Courtesy of 1150/KIQ and Four Seasons Radio Ltd, Kelowna, B.C.)*

---

in which creative experimentation will be stifled and others in which rules can
be broken and creative energies can be released unimpeded.

12. *Work toward realistic creativity.* Expand your creative horizons. Become sensitive
    to as many of the creative options as possible. But know your limits. Know what
    is possible to accomplish and what will be acceptable to your employer, to the
    client, and to the audience. Temper your creative urges and talents with the realism
    of the competitive broadcast advertising environment.

13. *Make each message distinguishable.* Establish an identity with each commercial
    or announcement. Maintain a similar style, tone, theme, mood, and personality
    between commercials or announcements for the same client. Use the same logo
    or identification symbol. Use easily recognizable production techniques (music,
    voices, sounds, camera shots, etc.).

14. *Polish until it shines.* Read your copy aloud. Check every meaning and nuance. Make every word, every image work for you. Rewind and play back your copy in your mind's eye until there is no room for improvement. Put yourself in the place of the listener or viewer. Calculate the effect of each part of each message that you write. Make each commercial or announcement reflect your best personal and professional effort.

Copy Design Suggestions

1. *Use only one principal selling idea in each commercial or announcement.* Although the copy rationale statement may generate many viable selling points, it is necessary to focus the audience's attention on only one central idea in each message; otherwise, the audience's focus will be scattered and this will produce mixed results.
2. *Sell early and often.* Use every second to promote and enhance your client's central message. The first few seconds are especially crucial in gaining and holding the audience's attention. Make every part of the copy move the message statement forward.
3. *Emphasize the client, product or service.* Make it the star of the message. Keep the spotlight where it belongs. Repeat the product, service, or client name often.
4. *Create an affordable, attractive need in the audience's mind.* Make the audience want to buy the product or use the service. Make the need urgent.
5. *Put the audience in the picture.* Make the product or service relate to the audience's lifestyle and current needs by choosing carefully settings, moods, atmospheres, words, phrases, sentences, music, and sound effects. Show tangible consumer benefits. Involve the listener or viewer.
6. *Use production elements creatively and effectively.* Be aware of the immense power and flexibility offered by music, sound effects, voices, pictures, movement, and color. Know the reason each production element is used and the effect each will have when combined with other script and production elements.
7. *Keep in touch with the copy rationale.* It is the writer's blueprint. Your copy should be designed and constructed on the basis of the copy rationale statement.
8. *End the message with energy.* Build to a climax. Summarize the central sales point. Call for action or a change in attitude. Make the message end with strength.

Language Use Suggestions

1. *Talk the audience's language.* Write for the ear, even when preparing television messages. Always write in a conversational manner. Use contractions and sentence fragments when appropriate. Choose words which express ideas in a clear, simple, direct manner.
2. *Use positive action words.* Stress urgency and immediacy. Select words with care. Make every word count. Use active voice verbs and descriptive adjectives and adverbs.

3. *Do not overuse such verbal devices as alliteration, sibilants, fricatives, and plosives.* Consult your dictionary for definitions and examples of each of these.
4. *Make certain your grammar and spelling are correct.*
5. *Simplify your copy.* Make every idea as clear as you can. Nothing should be too wordy or too complicated to be easily understood. Make the copy simple, direct, and descriptive.
6. *Remember the consumer's perspective.* Talk to the audience in terms that they understand and in terms in which they think about the use of the product or service.
7. *Avoid clichés, indefinite pronouns, and unnecessary numbers* unless these help the audience remember the central sales message.
8. *Construct sentences carefully and with purpose.* Make each sentence track smoothly and move logically and clearly from point to point. Be conscious of how the words flow together in each sentence.

Visualization Suggestions

1. *Storyboard your message.* Even rough preliminary sketches will help the writer to visualize better and to formulate more effective use of each visual and aural element.
2. *Scrutinize visual sequencing.* Make certain each shot and each scene builds logically, clearly, and effectively to a strong visual conclusion. Eliminate visual elements which do not enhance a strong progression of ideas. Make certain each shot creates, sustains, and builds interest in the client, product or service.
3. *Eliminate shots and scenes which do not relate to the central message of the commercial or announcement.*
4. *Know the creative potential.* Be conscious of why each kind of shot is selected, how it is used, and what the effect of each will be. Anticipate the result when the various visual elements are blended into the final message. Fine tune each portion of the video in the script.
5. *Remember the audio.* Make the sound portion of the message complement, reinforce, or counterpoint the video. Transfer from radio to television copywriting your concerns and skills for using music, sound effects, and voices.

A considerable amount of research has been conducted to determine techniques which can be used in the execution of television commercials to increase their effectiveness. Some of the principal conclusions from this research were reported in a study by David Ogilvy and Joel Raphaelson of Ogilvy and Mather.[5]

Ogilvy and Raphaelson based their conclusions on results from tests on more than 800 television commercials by the research firm of Mapes and Ross. These tests measured the ability of commercials to change brand preference, a characteristic which Mapes and Ross have found to be highly correlated with the ability of commercials to produce sales.

Commercials were classified according to the techniques used in their execution. The change in brand preference produced by commercials which employed a particular technique was compared to the overall average for all commercials to determine whether the technique was above average or below average in effectiveness.

Television commercials which employed the following techniques were found to be above average:

•commercials that provide the solution to a problem
•commercials that start with the key idea or central sales point
•commercials that employ humor which is pertinent to the selling proposition
•commercials that include a candid camera testimonial or a slice-of-life enactment where a doubter is convinced
•commercials that provide news (about new products, new uses, new ideas, new information)
•commercials that include a demonstration
•commercials that use supers (but the words on the screen must reinforce the main sales or copy point)

Television commercials which employed the following techniques were found to be below average:

•commercials with extensive use of short scenes and several changes of situation or location
•commercials that do not show the package
•commercials that end without the brand name
•commercials that employ cartoons and animation were found to be below average with adults, but above average with children

Ogilvy and Raphaelson do not suggest that these conclusions provide a magic formula for success. But they do believe that judicious use of their findings will improve the writer's chances of creating an effective television commercial.[6]

SUGGESTED EXERCISES AND PROJECTS

1. Discussion topics:
    a. Evaluate the degree and quality of ethics and responsibility displayed in several local and area broadcast advertising campaigns.
    b. Discuss the use of deceptive and misleading advertising practices and techniques in several national and local broadcast advertising campaigns.
    c. Discuss the use of stereotypes in broadcast advertising. Cite specific commercials and announcements. How would you have changed the copy to eliminate the stereotyping, but still convey the same information and persuasive value?

d. Discuss the use of logical and emotional appeals in broadcast advertising copy. When is the use of each type of appeal appropriate? Inappropriate? Determine the products, services and clients which best use each type of logical and emotional appeal.

2. Monitoring projects:

a. Watch (and if possible record) several television commercials for national advertisers. Formulate an abbreviated version of a copy rationale for each commercial viewed. Comment on the effectiveness of each commercial—central selling point, positioning, organization of the copy, style of delivery, and other criteria which you feel determine the effectiveness of a commercial announcement.

b. Listen to (and if possible record) several radio commercials for national advertisers. Follow the process outlined in "a" and devise the copy rationale and provide comments on the effectiveness of each radio commercial heard.

c. Follow the process outlined in "a" but for a specified number of television public service announcements.

d. Follow the process outlined in "b" but for a specified number of radio public service announcements.

3. Examine carefully the style and content of a major metropolitan newspaper. Using standard reference material and your own observations of several issues of this newspaper, formulate a brief copy rationale for a set of commercials for this newspaper.

a. Write one 20-second generic radio commercial using a single voice/straight sell presentational format. This would be a commercial which could be used throughout the broadcast day with no seasonal restrictions.

b. Write one 30-second radio commercial for this same metropolitan newspaper using the donut copy design format. The middle segment of the commercial should be approximately 15 seconds long.

c. Write one 60-second radio commercial for this same metropolitan newspaper using one of the following presentational formats: dialogue, dramatization, humor, or testimonial.

4. Write two 30-second radio commercials for a specific local or area retail store which sells nationally advertised products and advertises regularly in your local or area newspaper. Clip sample newspaper advertisements and formulate an abbreviated copy rationale for the radio commercials. Construct the commercials so that they would be acceptable for co-op purposes; that is, your commercials should feature both a national manufacturer or advertiser as well as the local outlet or distributor for a particular brand of products. Use any of the following copy makeup formats: modulized, donut, core, open-faced, or tag. Types of clients which would best generate this type of broadcast copy include: hardware stores, automobile dealers, clothing stores, appliance stores, furniture stores, department stores, agricultural products distributors, and franchised operations. Attach the newspaper ads used to generate the copy rationale and to write the commercials.

5. Write one 30-second television commercial for a specific local or area retail store following the process and guidelines outlined in exercise 4.

6. Select a local advertiser whose business falls within one of the following client categories: furniture store, clothing store, shoe store, department store, pharmacy, carpet and floor covering, or jewelry store. Formulate a copy rationale for this client. Based on the copy rationale, write the following 30-second television commercials:

a. Voice-over copy for a single announcer. On-camera talent may be seen in the commercial, but may not speak. Any video production elements may be used. Music and sound effects may be used with the single announcer.

b. A commercial written for a radio lift, or simulcast. That is, the copy must be designed so that the audio portion can stand alone and be appropriate for effective use as a self-contained, radio-only commercial. The visual material in this television commercial, however, needs to be sufficiently interesting and creative so that the information for television provides an impact specifically designed to interest a television viewer/consumer.

c. Copy written in modulized form. The 30-second television commercial must be written so that one 10-second and one 20-second television commercial can be made from portions of the 30-second spot without substantial rewriting. Write the 10-second and 20-second versions as separate scripts.

d. Copy written in a non-verbal manner. The video portion of this commercial must convey the appropriate persuasive message with only music or sound effects heard in the audio. Animation techniques and graphics may be utilized; however, nothing more than music or sound effects may be heard in the audio portion of this commercial.

7. Select one of the following product or service categories: restaurants; appliance stores; real estate companies; banks or savings and loans; automobile dealers; sports, hobby, or toy stores; food stores and supermarkets. Compile as much information as possible about this product or service category and about a specific local commercial client whose business falls within the category selected. Prepare a one-page copy rationale for a set of commercials.

a. Write three 30-second radio commercials using three of the following presentational formats: demonstration, dialogue, dramatization, testimonial, or humor.

b. Write three 30-second television commercials using three of the following presentational formats: demonstration, dramatization, testimonial, or combination of formats.

c. Prepare a rough storyboard for one television commercial written in part "b."

8. Select one local social service agency active in your area. Compile as much information as possible on the goals and projects of this group or organization. Prepare a one-page copy rationale for a set of public service announcements. Prepare appropriate copy material as described in exercise 7 a–c, but for a non-profit, public service agency, group, or organization.

9. Follow the same procedures outlined in exercise 7 and/or 8, but work with others as a team to generate the specified copy rationale, spot announcements, and storyboard.

10. For a specified client, product, or service, prepare a 10-second, 20-second,

30-second, or 60-second radio commercial for use in one of the following radio programming formats: all-news or talk; beautiful music; country music; rock music. The commercial should be written to match the radio station program format selected and to attract and persuade a specific target audience.

11. For a specific radio or television station in your area, prepare the following promotional copy:

a. one 10-second legal station identification (ID) enhanced with a brief promotional message.

b. one 30-second news promo which would include specific information about the news resources, facilities, personnel, or programming available at this station. This should be a generic news promo for use throughout the broadcast day with no seasonal restrictions.

c. one 30-second program promo for a regular program series or for a one-time-only special program.

d. one 30-second personality promo featuring one prominent on-air talent who is heard or seen regularly on the station selected.

All of the information contained in each promotional announcement must be accurate. All of the promotional copy specified above would be for use *on* the particular station selected. Use standard broadcast industry reference material or contact appropriate station personnel as needed to compile information necessary to write these promotional announcements.

NOTES

1. Excerpts from a personal letter to the author, November 16, 1982, from Bob Casazza, Director, Advertising and Promoton, WRC-TV4, Washington, D.C.

2. Ibid.

3. Source: October 1982, NSI and ARB. (NSI is the initials for Nielsen Station Index; ARB, for Arbitron Ratings.)

4. A summary of comments contained in a personal letter to the author, July 15, 1982, from Dale Baglo, Production Manager, CKIQ, Kelowna, B.C., Canada.

5. See David Ogilvy and Joel Raphaelson, "Research on Advertising Techniques That Work—and Don't Work," *Harvard Business Review,* July–August, 1982.

6. Results of the Ogilvy and Raphaelson study reported by the National Association of Broadcasters, "Techniques That Increase the Effectiveness of Television Commercials" (Washington, D.C., 1982).

ADDITIONAL READING

Arlen, Michael J. *Thirty Seconds.* New York: Penguin Books, 1980.
Baker, Stephen. *Systematic Approach to Advertising Creativity.* New York: McGraw-Hill Co., 1979.

Barnouw, Erik. *The Sponsor: Notes on a Modern Potentate.* New York: Oxford University Press, 1978.

Bergendorff, Fred; Harrison, Charles; and Webster, Lance. *Broadcast Advertising and Promotion: A Handbook for TV, Radio and Cable.* New York: Hastings House, 1983.

Book, Albert C., and Cary, Norman D. *The Radio and Television Commercial.* Chicago: Crain Books, 1978.

Bunzel, Reed. *Guidelines for Radio: Copywriting.* Washington, D.C.: National Association of Broadcasters, 1982.

Busch, H. Ted, and Landeck, Terry. *The Making of a Television Commercial.* New York: Macmillan, 1981.

Conrad, Jon J. *The TV Commercial: How Is It Made?* New York: Van Nostrand Reinhold Co., 1983.

Heighton, Elizabeth J., and Cunningham, Don R. *Advertising in the Broadcast and Cable Media.* 2d ed. Belmont, Calif.: Wadsworth Publishing Company, 1984.

Jewler, A. Jerome. *Creative Strategy in Advertising.* Belmont, Calif.: Wadsworth Publishing Co., 1981.

Kleppner, Otto. *Advertising Procedure.* 7th ed. Engelwood Cliffs, N.J.: Prentice-Hall, 1980.

Malickson, David L., and Nason, John W. *Advertising —How to Write the Kind That Works.* Rev. ed. New York: Charles Scribner's Sons, 1982.

Murphy, Jonne. *Handbook of Radio Advertising.* Radnor, Pa.: Chilton, 1980.

Ogilvy, David. *Confessions of an Advertising Man.* New York: Atheneum Publishers, 1963.

Orlik, Peter B. *Broadcast Copywriting.* 2d ed. Boston: Allyn and Bacon, 1982.

Packard, Vance. *The Hidden Persuaders.* New York: Pocket Books, 1958.

Peck, William A. *Anatomy of Local Radio-TV Copy.* 4th ed. Blue Ridge Summit, Pa.: Tab Books, 1976.

Radio Copy Book. Vol. 2. New York: Radio Advertising Bureau, 1979.

Weaver, J. Clark. *Broadcast Copywriting as Process.* New York: Longman, 1984.

White, Hooper. *How to Produce an Effective TV Commercial.* Chicago: Crain Books, 1981.

Zeigler, Sherilyn K., and Howard, Herbert H. *Broadcast Advertising: A Comprehensive Working Textbook.* 2d ed. Columbus, Ohio: Grid, 1984.

Zeigler, Sherilyn K., and Johnson, J. Douglas. *Creative Strategy and Tactics in Advertising: A Managerial Approach to Copywriting and Production.* Columbus, Ohio: Grid, 1981.

Chapter Five

NEWS AND SPORTS

News and sportscasts represent a station or network's greatest daily commitment of time, effort, personnel and facilities. These broadcasts display the efforts of many individuals, working together to report the happenings of the day. For the writer, this work offers a stimulating challenge—to gather, digest, organize, and write reports quickly and accurately in standard form that can be used to effectively convey information and insight into events and personalities.

The principles and techniques of good writing described in this book (see especially in chapter 3, "Mechanics of Broadcast Writing Style" and "Aural and Visual Writing Styles and Techniques") apply to *all* broadcast writing, including the preparation of news and sports script material. The nature of news and sports reports requires some modification of these basic concepts, but the essential principles and techniques of effective broadcast writing remain intact.

The writing concepts and practices presented in this chapter are fundamental. They apply in all news and sports writing situations. It should be noted, however, that each broadcast news and sports facility will superimpose special writing and copy format guidelines to meet specific requirements. The news and sports writer must be prepared to adjust to these requirements.

This chapter focuses on the writing of individual "hard news" stories and placing them into news- and sportscasts. In addition, business and agriculture reports are examined since they require similar kinds of writing considerations and often are included in broadcast newscasts. The intent is to provide an overview of news and sports writing: where to obtain the necessary information; how to select, gather and compile information for news and sports coverage; how to write news and sports copy with particular attention to beginning the story effectively, structuring the information compactly, and presenting the copy in acceptable form; selecting and placing stories into an organized news or sportscast structure; and, finally, reviewing special considerations for writing sports, business, and agriculture reports.

The techniques for preparing broadcast news and sports material for other kinds of writing situations are examined elsewhere in this book. Specifically, these other writing situations include features, magazine programs, special events coverage, compilations, commentaries, documentaries, and investigative reports. Broadcast news and sports material can be written in any of these forms. The subject matter would relate to news or sports events or personalities.

SOURCES OF NEWS AND SPORTS INFORMATION

Wire Services

Domestic and foreign news services, distributed to broadcast newsrooms via satellite and leased land lines, supply reports on important stories as well as background pieces and features. Some wire services supply a wide range of material, while others specialize in only one type of coverage (e.g., sports, business and financial information, agricultural markets updates, comprehensive weather summaries and forecasts). Some broadcast newsrooms use the wire service stories as they receive them. Others rewrite the wire reports to provide a local angle to a story and to adjust story length and treatment.

Mailings and Handouts

Active broadcast newsrooms review regular mailings, handouts, and announcements about potential newsworthy events from governmental agencies, civic organizations, public service groups, private companies and organizations, and special interest groups. When this information is received it must be determined how newsworthy each item is and what kind of coverage is needed, if any.

Safety Service (Police) Monitors

Routinely, most newsrooms monitor the transmissions of police, fire, and ambulance units in their area. In a highly competitive market, this monitoring may extend to the transmissions of competing stations and news outlets. Federal law restricts the direct use of this information. Most newsrooms will use the information gathered by this monitoring as a "tip" and then dispatch one of their reporters to cover the story directly.

Newspapers and Magazines

While it is illegal to use stories on the air directly from newspaper or magazine accounts, such sources could be used as tips by reporters. The facts and comments contained in these print media stories provide additional details not otherwise available, but such reports must be verified and ultimately rewritten for broadcast use.

Reporters

The station or network's own reporters can be assigned to cover specific stories based on tips and information received from other sources. To generate stories with regularity, reporters may be assigned "beats," or subject areas (e.g., city government, education, finance, entertainment, sports, etc.), or may be assigned to cover various stories as the need arises. Newsrooms tend to use a combination of the two approaches.

Other Broadcast Outlets

Once alerted to a story which is of interest to its audience but which cannot be covered easily by available staff and facilities, a broadcast facility may request coverage from another broadcast outlet in the immediate vicinity of the event. Reciprocal coverage is provided as the need arises.

SELECTION OF STORIES AND INFORMATION

To determine which news and sports events to cover and which pieces of information to include in each report, it is necessary to identify the various elements of news. One or more of the following needs to be evident for an event or a specific piece of information to be considered newsworthy:

Timeliness. The information presented must be immediate. It must indicate what is happening now, what is about to happen, or what will happen in the near future.

Proximity. Items that affect the lives, welfare, or future of the immediate audience or which interest them directly command the greatest attention. Significant local information should be stressed as appropriate.

Prominence. Prominent or well-known people, places, and things interest the audience. The importance of the person involved or the place where the event occurred determines if an event or situation is newsworthy.

Significance. The item or event covered must be important to your audience. Knowing the characteristics and needs of your audience will help determine what is interesting and important.

Conflict. Broadcast journalism tends to report human conflict best. It uses the sounds, colors, emotions, and images of conflicting events and persons to present stories in a human and personal manner. While there are ethical concerns which should be raised about such coverage, this element is a strong criterion for deciding to cover a particular event and to include certain items in a news or sports report.

Human Interest. Practically anything which interests a majority of your audience can be considered newsworthy. Odd, unusual, or novelty stories often are used to conclude a newscast or sportscast.

GATHERING AND HANDLING NEWS AND SPORTS INFORMATION

There are several suggestions for gathering and handling news and sports information more efficiently and more effectively:

1. *Verify the date, time, place, and person to contact when assigned to cover a story.*
2. *Anticipate potential story coverage and angles.* Be aware of current developments, personalities, and issues.
3. *Know your deadlines.* You need to determine how much time you have to cover the story, write your report, and prepare the copy for the broadcast.
4. *Keep the newsroom informed.* Stay in touch by phone, two-way radio, or other means so that you are aware of late developments which might have an impact upon the story you are covering, and the newsroom is aware of where you are and what you are doing in case an emergency situation develops and you need to be reassigned to a more important event.
5. *Be professional in your manner of dress, attitude, and conduct.* The respect you need to engender in your news and sports sources comes primarily from your demeanor.
6. *Remain objective in your selection and treatment of story details and in your writing style.* Objectivity is a prime ingredient for noteworthy news and sports reporting.
7. *Get the facts.* Know the gist of the story. Probe and search until you have the essential information to prepare your report.
8. *Come prepared with the necessary reporting tools.* This would include pad and pencil, but probably also video and audio recorders, lights, and cameras.
9. *Observe carefully.* Absorb as much information about the news or sports event as possible. Take notes. If the event covered is a news conference or speech or group meeting, and if it is being recorded, make periodic notes about excerpts which might be used in your report. This could be accomplished by noting the approximate place on the recording where a newsworthy comment or statistics was presented.
10. *Organize your thoughts.* Check your notes as the story is covered, but certainly as you finish gathering the necessary information. Look for important ideas, new developments, unusual comments, statistics, etc. Determine what is important in the story, what is known, and what needs to be known to prepare a more ob-

jective and complete report. Try to determine the "why" as well as the "what" of the story.

WRITING BROADCAST NEWS AND SPORTS REPORTS

When preparing broadcast news and sports material it is important to understand the use of various types of "lead" sentences as well as how to structure a story and prepare the copy in proper script form. As indicated earlier, each broadcast newsroom will impose special writing and script format requirements to help standardize story selection, development, and presentation.

Leads

The lead begins each report. It sets the stage for the details to follow. It is important that the lead grab the audience's attention and motivate them to want to know more. There are various types of leads routinely used in broadcast news and sports reports.

Summary Lead. A summary lead conveys the essence of the story. It is used for hard-news items in which late-breaking developments are involved.

> Protesters continue to battle state police this morning at the Ord Nuclear Power Plant.
>
> The Bears beat the Wolves last night to capture the state basketball crown.

Interpretative Lead. An interpretative lead is used to gradually get into the specifics of a complex, unusual, or feature story. The label "interpretative" should not be equated with a lack of objectivity or the use of editorial comments. This type of lead is especially effective for longer, more involved reports and may be used to sustain audience interest throughout the story.

> Those battered cars you might have seen late yesterday afternoon at the corner of 44th and Maple could save your life tomorrow.

The story could then explain the city's new traffic safety campaign in which damaged cars are placed at intersections where fatality accidents have occurred.

> What began as a good day for quarterback Eric Smith ended in defeat.

The sports story could then detail the events which led to the unexpected defeat.

Question Lead. This should be used sparingly and only when the writer can be assured that it will not confuse the audience or stifle interest in the rest of the story.

How would you like to be the only person in town without a name? That's what happened to Mary Jones today when she discovered her name has been eliminated from the city records because of a quirk in the law.

What's it like to be the owner of a national championship team that has never defeated its crosstown rival?

Both of these leads could be used to begin feature stories which should interest the audience and perhaps momentarily provide a bit of levity.

Among the many types of leads which could be used, these are the most common. The special emphasis and treatment each story requires, as well as the nature of the event, the length of the story, how it is packaged or presented, where the story will appear in the news or sportscast, and the instructions given by newsroom supervisory personnel—all will interact to determine the type of lead used for each story.

Story Structure

After the lead sentence, the story should be written in a manner which best presents the basic facts. Perhaps a chronological arrangement would work best as in a story about a fatal car crash. A topical organization pattern would be useful for a meeting story in which several subjects are discussed. Opposing points of view could be presented in a report on a heated labor dispute. The writer needs to select a story structure which best matches the nature and importance of the story.

Broadcast news and sports stories must be written briefly and directly. One point should lead logically into the next point. Supporting information should be presented which explains, as briefly as possible, what happened, to whom, and with what result. Details should be held to a minimum and left for use in other, more extensive, broadcast reports or for reports in other media.

Broadcast reports are structured with an eye to how the story will be packaged or presented on the air. The newscaster might simply read the story written by the writer. Comments by newsmakers involved could be integrated into a story. In television, visual elements must be considered. Live reports from the scene compound the writer's problem in preparing such script material.

Formats

Radio. To illustrate both story structure and acceptable radio news and sports script formats, an imaginary fire story has been devised. The facts presented in each report remain the same, but the format or arrangement in which the information is presented and the use of various standard presentational forms vary.

Figure 5-1 shows how the fire story could be written if reported only by the radio newscaster or anchor. Figure 5-2 illustrates how the same fire story might be written if an "actuality," or comment, from the Fire Chief was to be inserted in the radio news

APEX FIRE
9/20.....9am
J. Jones

(10 lines)

Arsonists may have caused last night's big fire....Fire
Chief Bill Atkins today blamed arsonists for last night's fire which
destroyed the Apex Paint Company Warehouse on South Third Avenue.

Chief Atkins reports that ten empty gasoline cans were found
near the incinerator in the building. So far there are no clues
to the identities of the suspected arsonists.

City police are fingerprinting an abandoned car found near
the warehouse. There were no injuries. No damage estimate is
available at this time.

Fire and police officials continue their investigation.

Figure 5-1 Example of a single-voice radio news story report.

---

story. Another scripting possibility is to have the radio newscaster read an introduction to the report and then play a "voicer," or a summary of the story recorded by the reporter (fig. 5-3).

If the voicer scripted in figure 5-3 included an actuality from the Fire Chief, this would be called a "voicer wrap-around." The voice of the reporter would wrap around, or surround, the Fire Chief's comments.

A few copy format comments are needed for the scripts which appear as figures 5-1 through 5-3. Notice how each story is identified by a "copy slug" at the top left-hand side of each script page. The number of lines of copy or the line-count and the recorded length of the actuality or voicer appear at the top right-hand side of each piece of copy. This notation helps anticipate the length of each story in the broadcast news or sportscast. Material not meant to be read aloud is enclosed in boxes or circled. For each "cart," or recorded report, the first few words, the last words, the length, and a summary are written. The summary may be provided to ensure a smooth transition by the newscaster should there be technical difficulties or to provide a ready-made rewrite of the story for use in later newscasts or as headlines. Regular paragraphing and capitalization is used. Some newsrooms insist on no paragraph indentations and the use of FULL CAPS. To indicate that the story is finished, some kind of end mark is used (e.g., "-0-" or "end" or perhaps the initials of the writer).

The content and story structure of the scripts in figures 5-1 through 5-3 should not be neglected. Notice how a summary lead is used to provide a quick update on an important, ongoing story. The copy is relatively short, even when an actuality or voicer report is used. All of the essential information is attributed to a recognizable source. Notice how the details of this story update are unveiled—briefly, directly, one key

APEX FIRE
9/20.....9am
J. Jones

8 lines
PLUS :12 ACTUALITY

Arsonists may have caused last night's big fire....Fire Chief Bill
Atkins today blamed arsonists for last night's fire which destroyed
the Apex Paint Company Warehouse on South Third Avenue.

CART:	In Cue:	"From the evidence..."
	Out Cue:	"...was set on purpose."
	Length:	12 seconds
	SUMMARY:	Chief Atkins reports that ten empty gasoline cans were found in the building. Chief Atkins believes the fire was set on purpose.

So far there are no clues to the identities of the suspected arsonists.
City police are fingerprinting an abandoned car found near the
warehouse. There were no injuries. No damage estimate is available
at this time. Fire and police officials continue their investigation.

Figure 5-2 Example of the story in figure 5-1 written to include an "actuality" from the Fire Chief.

piece of information at a time, all relating to the lead sentence. The Fire Chief's comments provide the specifics about the new development in the story. The last few
sentences in each report take care of the related information about injuries and damage
estimates and note that the story continues to develop.

Television. Standard television script formats for news and sports reports perhaps
are best illustrated by copy style material from KIRO TV in Seattle (fig. 5-4). It is an
excellent description of the basic news script formats used by most television stations
across the country.

Figure 5-5 shows a "WRAP," or "wrap-around," report written for a fireworks story
and illustrates the application of the copy style guidelines contained in figure 5-4.
The number "502" indicates the position of this story in the newscast line-up.

Arsonists may have caused last night's big fire. Radio 90's Jeff Smith has details.....

CART:	In Cue:	"Fire Chief Bill Atkins..."
	Out Cue:	"...their investigation. Jeff Smith, Radio 90 News."
	Length:	32 seconds
	SUMMARY:	Radio 90's Jeff Smith reports that Fire Chief Bill Atkins blames arsonists for the Apex Paint Company fire last night. Gasoline cans were found in the building. An abandoned car is being fingerprinted. There were no injuries. The investigation is continuing.

Figure 5-3 Example of the story in figure 5-1 written to accommodate a "voicer," or reporter's summary, of the incident.

Suggestions

The following suggestions should help the writer provide more effective news and sports copy:

1. *Provide concise, accurate reports in an understandable form.*
2. *Work for clarity.* The audience is exposed to the story only once. The essentials of the story must be clear and memorable when heard or seen once and only once.
3. *Strive for simplicity.* Use short declarative sentences with an easy-to-follow subject/verb/object sentence arrangement.
4. *Use present tense and active voice.* Use present tense verbs to stress the sense of immediate or continuing action. Let the subject of the sentence perform the action; use the active voice.
5. *Remember attribution.* Be sure to indicate who is being quoted. Identify, by name or title or position, who is heard or seen during the report.
6. *Write for the ear and not the eye.* This is true even for television reports since the audio often carries the essential information for the story.

| LIVE TT _____ | COPY STORY | 5pm 2/22 jl |

LIVE TT _____
          Total Time

COPY STORY
(L) This is a compilation of the types of stories aired on Eyewitness News.

We've tried to anticipate the variety of pieces you'll write to correctly present the form they're to appear in.

This is an example of a story to be delivered "live" by one of the anchors.

Note that the upper right corner of all copy sheets should contain the show the copy is being written for (5pm in this example), the date, and the initials of the person writing it.

The story slug (title) should appear in all capitals and underlined at the head of the teleprompter column.

The word "live" should appear in the left hand column.

5pm 2/22 jl

- -

LIVE TT _____

VOICE OVER
(L) When you're writing a story which includes voiced-over video, use this form.

5pm 2/22 jl

CAS#_____ /NATSOC/VO
MATTE (at :01) locator

(VO) The instructions show a cassette (its number will be assigned by the show's producer and filled in by that person), and that the cassette contains natural sound which is being voiced-over by one of the anchors.

Mattes should be indicated on the sheet, with the times to be filled in by the editors.

The length of the cassette should be indicated at the end of the cassette read.

TCT- :30
TOTAL CASSETTE TIME

- -

LIVE TT _____

VO/SOC
(L) Stories during which the anchors read over tape until a sound cut are called "VO/SOC" stories here at KIRO.

5pm 2/22 jl

VOH - SOC

Figure 5-4 Television script format specifications for various types of news and sports stories. Broken underlining between these format specifications indicate the original pages received from KIRO TV. *(Courtesy of KIRO TV, Inc., Seattle)*

134

CAS# _____/NATSOC/VO MATTE (at :01) locator	(VO) Script them as you would straight voice-over stories. When it comes time for the sound cut, indicate accordingly.	
CAS/SOC at :06 MATTE (at :06) (INTERVIEWEE NAME) (Relation to Story)	<u>SOC AT :06</u>	
CAS/NATSOC/VO AT :35	<u>ENDS: "...END OF STATEMENT"</u> (VO @ :35) Note that you don't have to stay within teleprompter lines when showing outcues. Also note that tricky pronunciations should be shown on the right side of the page, as indicated earlier.	
TCT- :<u>45</u> LIVE	(L) Remember to show total time of the cassette. Should the sound cut end the video piece, indicate so by putting "TCT" on the same line as the underlined outcue.	
LIVE TT _____	ON-SET PIECES (L) Stories delivered "on-set" are to contain an anchor lead...	5pm 2/22 jl

LIVE/2-SHOT
(REPORTER @ _____IS.)
	(2-SHOT) and should also indicate a 2-shot of the anchor and reporter as the anchor explains "reporter _____ is here to fill us in" (or a similar variation of the handoff).
	    Leave the location (_____ is) blank. It will be filled in by the producer.
	            -more-	

LIVE/REPORTER MATTE - reporter name	(L) On a separate page, the reporter's on-set introduction to his story should be typed. Most on-set appearances consist of an anchor lead, a reporter lead, a packaged reporter piece, and an on-set reporter tag.	5pm 2/22 jl
CAS# _____/SOC	SOC AT :00	
MATTE (at :___) locator		

Fig. 5-4 *(Continued)*

MATTE (at :___) Interviewee
            relation to story

TCT-_____

LIVE/REPORTER

MATTE - reporter name

ENDS: "...END OF STATEMENT, OR TRACK."

(L) Note the reporter's name is matted both going into and coming out of his/her video piece.

Following the reporter's tag, a 2-shot is scripted for the mandatory "thanks" or question by the anchors. We call that "Horton."

LIVE/2-SHOT-------------------------------------- HORTON

LIVE TT _____

LIVE REMOTES

5pm 2/22 jl

(L) In the same way as on-set pieces are scripted, script live remotes with a lead and a tag 2-shot.

Only this time, the "2-shot" is with the TV monitor, and the reporter appearing in the live shot is on the monitor.

LIVE/WITH MONITOR

(MONITOR) Be sure to script that you're live and where you are.
            LIVE REMOTE

LIVE REMOTE

MATTE (at :01) LIVE/locator

MATTE (at :08) LIVE/reporter name

MATTE (at :16) LIVE

ROLL CUE: "...INDICATE THE SENTENCE YOU'LL BE READING TO GET TO YOUR SOUND CUT, VOICE-OVER VIDEO, OR WRAPPED INSERT."

CAS# _____/SOC

(or CAS#_____/NATSOC/VO)

MATTE (:___) whatever you need to

SOC AT :00

TCT-_____

LIVE REMOTE

ENDS: "...THE LAST THING ON THE CASSETTE."
            LIVE REMOTE

MATTE (at :01) LIVE/reporter name

MATTE (at :08) LIVE

LIVE/WITH MONITOR

REPORTER TOSSES BACK
            TO STUDIO

LIVE TT _____

WRAPS

5pm 2/22 jl

(L) Wraps should have the same information you'd show on voice-over or VO/SOC pieces.

Lead to all wraps with the name of the talent doing the wrap, with the wording a variation of "(name of reporter) reports."

CAS# _____/SOC

MATTE (at :___) location

SOC AT :00

Fig. 5-4 *(Continued)*

MATTE (at :____) reporter name ("reporting")	
MATTE (at :____) Interviewee relation to story	
MATTE (at :____) reporter name ("standup")	
TCT-____	ENDS: "...in/at (location), (reporter name), CHANNEL-7 EYEWITNESS NEWS."
LIVE	(L) All wraps should be signed off in the manner above. We don't normally give "Seattle" as a location, but we do use locations outside the city, faithfully.
	Use "reporting" mattes at times the reporter is not seen. Use "standup" mattes when the reporter is on camera.

- -

	MISCELLANEOUS	5pm 2/22 jl
LIVE	(L) Note that there is a fixed order of mattes. First, the locator. Second, the reporter's name. Third, other mattes.	
	Paragraphs should be indented two spaces.	
	Full screen mattes should be over video, or over a full-screen color rather than over the stomach of the anchor.	
CAMERA BLUE/VO	(VO) Camera blue/VO indicates a full-screen matte over blue.	
	You could just as easily matte it over a video cassette. But watch out for full screen mattes over rolling video. The two have a habit of clashing so that neither can be clearly seen.	
MATTE (at :01) $12 million	If you have to change	
CHANGE MATTE (at :10) $6 million	mattes...or add mattes	
-or-	fill-in additional	
MATTE (at :01) $12 million	information, indicate it	
ADD MATTE (at :10) $6 million	this way.	
	-more-	

- -

MISCELLANEOUS 2-2-2	When you reach the bottom of a page, make sure that your "slug" moves to the upper left and that you start on the top of the page with your copy.	5pm 2/22 jl
	No additional "live" or "VO" instruction is needed	

Fig. 5-4 *(Continued)*

as long as it doesn't change.

Make sure you slug <u>all</u> your stories.

The slug should appear only once on each page (above the scripted material on the first page, and in the upper left corner in subsequent pages of the same story).

The first line of copy should be the standard spacing from the slug line.

All information appearing in the margins not to be read by the anchor or reporter, must be typed in ALL CAPS.

This includes slugs, outcues, video information and instructions, and pronunciations.

All copy to be read by the talent must be kept within

-more-

<u>MISCELLANEOUS 3-3-3</u>

the teleprompter borders on the script form.

All video instructions should begin at the left margin.

Don't indent them.

Mattes should appear as indicated. Mattes should be typed exactly as they should appear on the air.

That's done so we can check the accuracy of the information as it's entered into the Chyron.

Feel free to turn in scripts without cassette and matte times.

It is the writer's responsibility, however, to tear off the last white script copy for the editors, as part of the story cutting instructions.

The editor will fill in the appropriate times, and pass them along to the show producer.

5pm 2/22 jl

Fig. 5-4 *(Continued)*

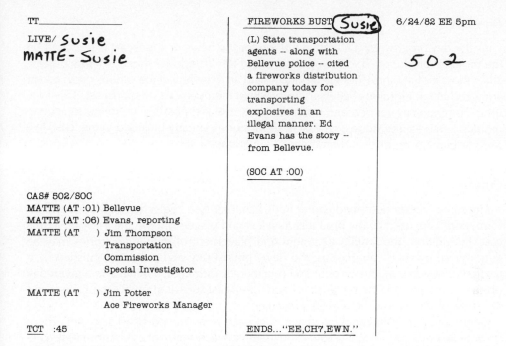

TT_____

LIVE/ Susie
MATTE- Susie

CAS# 502/SOC
MATTE (AT :01) Bellevue
MATTE (AT :06) Evans, reporting
MATTE (AT   ) Jim Thompson
            Transportation
            Commission
            Special Investigator

MATTE (AT   ) Jim Potter
            Ace Fireworks Manager

TCT :45

FIREWORKS BUST Susie   6/24/82 EE 5pm

(L) State transportation
agents -- along with
Bellevue police -- cited
a fireworks distribution
company today for
transporting
explosives in an
illegal manner. Ed
Evans has the story --
from Bellevue.

(SOC AT :00)

502

ENDS..."EE,CH7,EWN."

Figure 5-5 A "wrap-around" report illustrating the copy style guidelines in figure 5-4. *(Courtesy of KIRO TV, Inc., Seattle)*

7. *Read the copy aloud.* This is the best way to check the effectiveness, clarity, and length of the copy.
8. *Write within time limits.* Know the length of story needed. Suggest an appropriate story length if none is provided. But accept the fact that most radio stories are 20 to 40 seconds long, while television reports average one to two and one-half minutes. Learn to work within these story length constraints.
9. *Check legal points.* Read each story carefully with an eye toward avoiding problems involving libel and slander, objectivity, fairness, balance, and completeness (within the limits of time constraints).

NEWSCASTS

Long before the broadcast newscast or sportscast goes on the air, preparations are underway to produce the most complete and effective presentation possible. All of the various sources of information described earlier are monitored, information compiled, sorted, arranged, stories written and rewritten.

Line-Ups

As the day progresses, a tentative line-up for the news or sportscast is prepared by the program producer. The line-up (also called the "rundown sheet," "show order," and "show format") provides the producer with an overview of the various copy, talent, and production elements necessary to produce the newscast or sportscast. This line-up is continuously revised and updated, up to the last possible moment, to accommodate late-breaking stories, new facts about stories already included in the 'cast, live remote pick-up reports, and emergency situations.

Criteria

The same criteria described earlier in this chapter (see "Selection of Stories and Information") are used by the producer to select and place stories in the news or sportscast. In addition, the length, treatment and placement of individual stories may be determined by such variables as: the news philosophy and policy established by a particular newsroom, the amount and quality of information available in a given day or other time period, the on-air news and sportscast format already established, and the time of day when the 'cast is presented.

Generally, a specific length is assigned to each news or sportscast segment. There is some flexibility provided to adjust the length of each segment as circumstances dictate. Within each segment, the news or sportscast producer makes an effort to arrange stories so that there is an obvious bridge or connection between them. The content, pace and flow of the 'cast is controlled by adjusting the length and placement of each story, clustering related stories, and using obvious transitions between story or topic clusters.

SPECIAL CONSIDERATIONS—SPORTS, AGRICULTURE, AND BUSINESS

Sports

The comments made thus far in this chapter apply to sports as well as to news reporting and writing; however, there are additional considerations for generating sports copy.

Good sports writing evolves from good news writing. The principles of solid broadcast news reporting and writing should transfer easily to the sports area. Although sports often is treated in a lighter, more entertaining manner than news, the principles of objectivity, fairness, accuracy, completeness, and clarity of expression apply to both news and sports.

The contents of broadcast sports reports require special consideration. It is important to use sports items which are of direct interest to the audience. In a local station sportscast this means *local* and area sports coverage. People make news, whether it is sports news or general news on the local, state, regional, or national level. Other types of items which contribute to effective broadcast sportscasts are: those which offer simulated thrills and excitement for the audience, projecting them into the exciting and adventurous situation on the playing field or in the arena; those which stimulate opinion about controversial topics and issues; and those which help the audience analyze and appreciate sports developments (e.g., player trades, new game rules, strategies, etc.).

Sports reports may be in the form of news items (scores, game highlights, injuries, trades, changes in coaches and owners, awards, investigations, etc.); features and interviews with coaches, players and fans; commentaries; documentaries and special reports; magazine programs; compilations; talk programs; and play-by-play broadcasts. Except for play-by-play broadcasts, these types of programs and program segments are described elsewhere in this book.

Agriculture and Business

Regardless of the area of the country in which you live, agriculture and business information is important to you and your audience. Practically every area of the country is oriented to either agriculture or business, or both. The business side of agricultural activity continues to grow in importance. Consumer reports often are based upon agricultural and business interests. These two areas generate news which affects other news stories. Items concerning food supply, price supports, rising unemployment, falling stock market quotations, striking unions, mergers of companies, and agribusiness strategies and regulations have become a substantial part of broadcast newscasts because of the impact which these developments have on the general public. Events and conditions affecting agriculture and businesses are of interest to those both directly and indirectly involved in these related areas.

Business and agricultural information may be presented in various forms—news reports, features, spot announcements, interviews and talk programs, editorials and commentaries, magazine programs, documentaries, and investigative reports. The most common form used is the presentation of news reports. In most situations, full-scripts are prepared; however, other script forms can be used depending upon the type of program presentation.

Approaches for Agriculture Reports. When assigned to write agriculture news reports, consider incorporating the following items which have general appeal to the agricultural community: new discoveries or developments that make the agricultural environment safer, more efficient, and cost effective; agricultural events in your coverage area (i.e., fairs, expositions, and auctions); weather reports that are accurate, current, and comprehensive; national, regional, and local market price quotations for livestock, grain, and other agricultural products produced within the station's coverage area; and the issues and activities associated with agricultural groups and organizations (e.g., 4-H, Future Farmers of America, National Farmers Organizations, Farm Bureau Federation). A solid broadcast newscast, which includes items relating to politics and the economy and which incorporates world, national, and state activities, is of direct interest to this type of broadcast audience.

Some of the sources for agricultural information include: wire services (which provide daily summaries of items relating to agriculture); state and federal departments of agriculture (which mail to newsrooms the results of tests, surveys, and technological developments which are useful for many kinds of programs); extension services at nearby agriculture-oriented colleges and universities; specialized journals and publications; local and area agriculture organizations and representatives; and commodity market exchanges and reporting services. You will discover many additional sources of information as you begin working regularly with this kind of specialized information.

Approaches for Business Reports. Much of the material included in broadcast business reports involves business activities of the immediate past or emerging future. Another important ingredient are items that help the listener or viewer evaluate and respond to future activities based on past developments. This kind of approach is important for all material designed to provide information, but it is especially important when writing business news items.

The following kinds of items have general appeal for the business community: stock market quotations and trends; unemployment and inflation rate changes as well as prime and conventional loan interest rates; management trends; news of people in local and area businesses and industries; governmental regulations and judicial rulings that affect an entire industry or region; corporate mergers and acquisitions; and information about companies entering or leaving your immediate coverage area, or those expanding or restricting current business activities. As was true with agriculture reports, it is important to include world, national, state, and local news stories that could directly influence future business developments. A major policy shift in import/export quotas by the head of a key industrialized nation affects directly the decisions made by business and agricultural interests. Both agriculture and business audiences expect and require this broad base of information to make knowledgeable decisions about future investments and activities.

Excellent sources for business information and analysis include: business publications (e.g., *The Wall Street Journal, Business Week, Forbes, Fortune,* and Standard & Poor's *Index of Corporate News);* the wire services (which provide various kinds and levels of business and financial information); local and area Chambers of Commerce; stock brokerage houses and consultants; major employers in the area; and governmental publications.

Preparing Agriculture and Business Reports. The techniques and suggestions provided earlier for writing news and sports copy apply to the preparation of agriculture and business stories. In addition, the following guidelines should prove helpful when generating these special kinds of reports:

1. *Acquire the necessary background.* Through formal education or training and extensive personal experience the writer of such specialized information can prepare worthwhile and respected reports. However, the writer of such material must make a conscious and sustained effort to acquire the necessary background.
2. *Stay informed.* The trust and respect you need to instill in your audience comes only if you absorb the necessary information from pertinent trade and industry publications, professional organizations, and personal contacts (especially local experts whom you cultivate over an extended period).
3. *Cultivate reliable and flexible sources of information.* Continue to tap local, regional, and national resources and to develop new sources to enhance your reports. Stress local information sources since they tend to be more credible with your audience and reflect local and area perspectives and developments. Build trust and credibility with your sources.
4. *Fulfill your reporting responsibilities with an extraordinary amount of care, attention, integrity, completeness, and objectivity.*
5. *Remember the importance and impact of your writing.* Literally, the livelihood of many individuals and families may depend upon the accuracy and completeness of your reports.
6. *Write material for specialized as well as general audiences.* Prepare material which is interesting, understandable, and informative for those directly and indirectly involved in business and agricultural concerns. But tell the basic agriculture or economic story in terms that relate directly to a general audience. This might mean translating terms into understandable words and concepts. For example, showing how the inflation rate for the year translates into spending power for the middle-income family over the last several years. Or showing how a bumper grain crop will lower the price of bread for consumers. Always remember the general audience when preparing agriculture or business reports.

CONCLUSION

This chapter has presented an overview of the principles and practices necessary for writing effective news and sports copy. In addition, special considerations associated with generating agriculture and business reports have been reviewed. Specifically, this chapter has considered: appropriate sources of information; gathering, compiling, writing, and structuring story information to improve clarity and understanding; the selection, development, and placement of individual stories into an effective news and sportscast; and proper copy format for radio and television news and sports reports.

Several concerns should be remembered when writing this kind of material. The importance of such information cannot be overemphasized. Accuracy, completeness, clarity, objectivity, and balance should be watchwords for anyone preparing such information. The writer must work under constant and severe pressure to generate the volume of information needed. Format and copy style must become second nature to the writer. There is no time to second guess or mull over copy page formats and practices. The writing experience is intense because of the immediacy and volume of information that is processed. The exhilaration of writing at such a rapid rate must be tempered by the intrinsic desire to convey complex information in an interesting, informative, organized, and objective manner. The writer must remember to tell the basic facts of a story in a way that the ordinary listener or viewer can understand how this information relates to day-to-day living. For many writers, this is the only kind of writing worth doing regularly. Writing a solid news, sports, agriculture, or business report provides a unique kind of personal and professional satisfaction for the writer. Without the skill and care provided by the writer this kind of information would not be available to touch so many lives so directly with so much impact.

SUGGESTED EXERCISES AND PROJECTS

1. Rewrite the copy from a recent edition of a metropolitan daily newspaper to provide the following radio news script material: 3-minute world/national newscast; 4-minute state/local newscast; 4-minute sportscast.
2. Prepare a show format (rundown or routine sheet) for an hourly 5-minute local radio station newscast or sportscast.
3. Arrange to record two radio or television network newscasts which are broadcast simultaneously. Compare and contrast each newscast in terms of: selection, length, treatment, and placement of each story in the newscast; writing style; use of sound (and pictures for television newscasts); attribution; and news judgment.
4. Monitor a local station or network radio or television newscast. Provide the rundown sheet for the newscast.
5. Prepare the full-script for a 1- to 3-minute radio or television feature to be used in a local station's newscast. The feature may relate to news, sports, business, or agriculture items.
6. Attend a local sports event or a regularly scheduled local government meeting. Write a 20-second radio or a 60-second television news story summarizing the event or meeting. The copy would be read by the newscaster with no other production elements used.
7. Select a newspaper story at least six column inches long. Rewrite the story for use as a 20-second radio or a 60-second television report.

ADDITIONAL READING

Baker, John C. *Farm Broadcasting: The First Sixty Years.* Ames, Iowa: Iowa State University Press, 1981.

Chancellor, John, and Mears, Walter R. *The News Business: Getting and Writing the News as Two Top Journalists Do It.* New York: Harper & Row, 1983.

Fang, Irving E. *Television News, Radio News.* St. Paul, Minn.: Rada Press, 1980.

Gifford, F. *Tape: A Radio News Handbook.* 2d ed. New York: Hastings House, 1977.

Johnson, William O., Jr. *Super Spectator and the Electric Lilliputians.* Boston: Little, Brown, 1971.

Josephson, Larry, ed. *Telling the Story: The National Public Radio Guide to Radio Journalism.* Dubuque, Iowa: Kendall/Hunt Publishing Co., 1983.

Lovell, Ronald P. *Reporting Public Affairs: Problems and Solutions.* Belmont, Calif.: Wadsworth Publishing, 1983.

MacDougall, A. Kent. *Ninety Seconds to Tell It All: Big Business and the News Media.* Homewood, Ill.: Dow Jones-Irwin, 1981.

Matusow, Barbara. *The Evening Stars: The Making of the Network News Anchors.* Boston: Houghton Mifflin, 1983.

Newson, Doug, and Wollert, James A. *Media Writing: News for the Mass Media.* Belmont, Calif.: Wadsworth Publishing, 1984.

Powers, Ron. *Supertube: The Rise of Television Sports.* New York: Coward-McCann, 1984.

Shook, Frederick, and Lattimore, Dan. *The Broadcast News Process.* 2d ed. Englewood, Colo.: Morton Publishing Co., 1982.

Smeyak, G. Paul. *Broadcast News Writing.* 2d ed. Columbus, Ohio: Grid, 1983.

Stephens, Mitchell. *Broadcast News: Radio Journalism and an Introduction to Television.* New York: Holt, Rinehart and Winston, 1980.

Sugar, Bert Randolph. *The Thrill of Victory: The Inside Story of ABC Sports.* New York: Hawthorne Books, 1978.

Weaver, J. Clark. *Broadcast Newswriting as a Process.* New York: Longman, 1984.

Westin, A. *Newswatch: How TV Decides the News.* New York: Simon and Schuster, 1982.

White, Ted, Meppen, Adrian J., and Young, Steve. *Broadcast News Writing, Reporting, and Production.* New York: Macmillan, 1984.

Wimer, Arthur, and Brix, Dale. *Workbook for Radio and TV News Editing and Writing.* 5th ed. Dubuque, Iowa: Wm. C. Brown Co., 1981.

Chapter Six

EDITORIALS AND COMMENTARIES

At one time, broadcasting stations hesitated to express opinions on current controversial issues, problems, and personalities. Today, however, more and more stations recognize the value of expressing their opinions through editorials and commentaries. More than one-third of the broadcast stations in the United States now broadcast editorials, many of them daily. Although many of these are large facilities, located in urban areas, small- to medium-size broadcast facilities also recognize the value and responsibility of editorial comment prepared and delivered by the local station.

Many broadcasters are of the opinion that the broadcaster should and could take a stand on many important issues of direct concern to listeners and viewers. This sentiment is not universally shared since there are still some stations that do not editorialize under any circumstances.

The broadcasters who editorialize do so because they feel editorials and commentaries help fulfill their obligations as responsible community members, uphold the spirit of the FCC's Fairness Doctrine (discussed in chapter 1), provide additional viewpoints for people to think about, and increase station prestige and image in the community.

The stations that do not editorialize contend that they lack sufficient qualified personnel, facilities, and time for the necessary research to prepare editorial comment of consistently high quality on a regular basis. Also, some stations contend that tough editorial stands on crucial local issues often place the station management and sales staff in a delicate position with current and prospective advertising clients and some community leaders who may disagree with the station's editorial stance.

This chapter reviews briefly regulations that influence the writing process and techniques used to generate editorials and commentaries. Next, the difference between an editorial and a commentary will be explained so that the writer understands the kinds of messages to be written and the perspective from which each type of comment originates. News-related and special-purpose commentaries will be described and illustrated. The principal types of editorials will be examined to help the writer determine the specific purposes of such comment and to critically assess its impact.

The selection and development of editorial subjects will be traced to identify more closely the writer's participation in this process. Several editorial examples are presented to illustrate the writing suggestions offered.

It is important that broadcast editorialists and commentators not only understand the process involved in generating such material, but that they remember to consider certain ethical and moral obligations and responsibilities that should be an integral part of such writing. The power and impact of editorials and commentaries cannot always be measured by identifiable audience responses. The writer's often intangible influence on the audience must be remembered each time such material is prepared for broadcast.

REGULATIONS

Broadcast editorials and commentaries resemble newspaper editorial columns in nature except that the broadcaster must adhere to certain strict federal regulations while the newspaper does not. Although both media face the issues of libel and invasion of privacy, broadcasters must observe additional regulations enforced by the Federal Communications Commission. Because they bear directly on the preparation and broadcast of editorials and commentaries, it would be helpful to review the chapter 1 discussion on legal restraints and regulations which bear on such activity: rules and regulations governing defamation (libel and slander), invasion of privacy, the Fairness Doctrine (with particular attention to the Personal Attack Rule), and Section 315 of the Communications Act of 1934.

Editorializing by broadcasters is not only allowed by the FCC, it is encouraged. The regular broadcast of current, pertinent, and incisive editorials and commentaries can become an important part of a licensee's obligation and responsibility to offer ideas and opinions to its audience. This affirmative action of editorializing is but one way to fulfill the licensee's charge to serve the public interest, convenience, and necessity.

DEFINITIONS AND DIFFERENTIATIONS

"Editorial" has been defined variously as an expression of a licensee's opinion which usually consists of comments on current issues and events and as a statement which may criticize, praise, or simply discuss the actions and policies of some public official or group. An editorial is much like an essay in that it often reflects the personality of the author.

The FCC describes a station editorial as "a statement representing the view of the licensee of the station, such as its owner, a principal officer or the manager or another employee if he is permitted by the licensee to speak for the station."[1] As noted in chapter 1, the term *licensee* can be described essentially as the owner(s) of a broadcasting station.

A concise, workable definition of the term *editorial* is supplied by the National Association of Broadcasters. The NAB identifies an editorial as "an on-the-air expression of the opinion of the station licensee, clearly identified as such, on a subject of public importance."[2]

Commentaries are viewed as being distinct from editorial statements. Generally, commentaries reflect *individual* opinion rather than the official opinion of the station licensee. Many commentators are hired by individual stations, but more likely by group-owned stations, networks, and syndicated production companies, based on their background and reputation, their ability to write well, hold attention, and have something significant to say. While editorials may accomplish some of the same objectives, commentaries generally provide analysis of an issue or event and historical and contemporary perspectives on concerns of the day. Commentaries often focus on dominant national and international issues and events. The nuances, implications, and effects of people, places, and events in the news and on the minds of listeners and viewers are featured in commentaries. Commentaries provide a reflective perspective from an individual commentator who has examined the intricacies and implications of events.

COMMENTARIES

Although a large share of the commentaries broadcast today are news related and appear within or adjacent to the news broadcasts of a station or network, many special purpose commentaries are finding their way onto the airwaves. John Chancellor tends to emphasize politics in his commentaries for the *NBC Nightly News*. ABC's Howard Cosell specializes in sports commentary on related issues and personalities. Gene Shalit on NBC's *Today* and Pat Collins on *CBS Morning News* offer opinions and comments on current entertainment offerings and personalities. ABC's Dan Cordtz regularly provides economic analysis and perspective. Other special purpose commentary subject areas include health, religion, international affairs, and consumerism.

In figure 6-1, notice how John Chancellor eases into the controversial subject of social security and at the same time provides an insightful glimpse into the behind-the-scenes workings of federal officials during an election year. Short, grammatically incomplete sentences throughout the commentary create a staccato pace to emphasize key points and to sustain an effective conversational style. This commentary is especially noteworthy because of its logical organization, simple but effective word choices, smooth-flowing sentence structure and thoughtful observations by this experienced journalist who knows the political scene intimately.

A prominent type of special purpose commentary is the entertainment commentary. With sufficient background, training, preparation, and experience, an individual could be employed to provide regular reviews and observations on the entertainment industry. At the network level, Gene Shalit's "Critic's Corner" on NBC's *Today* has become a staple for early morning viewers. His crisp, biting, satirical writing style reflects his varied experience as a reviewer and observer of the entertainment scene.

HIT: 6:49:49

BROKAW: One thing the White House is not eager to talk about is the decision of Senate Republicans to put off plans for a forty billion dollars saving in Social Security over the next three years. That was the centerpiece in a compromise budget President Reagan was praising in a Rose Garden news conference just two weeks ago.

In his Commentary tonight, John Chancellor talks about why Social Security is getting so much attention these days. John.

HIT: 6:50:12

JOHN CHANCELLOR: Clout in politics is a word which means power, or influence. We've seen a lot of clout in the past few days exercised by a group of about twenty five million Americans, perhaps the most powerful group in the country when its own interests are involved.

The group: older people. The interest: Social Security. Their clout: they vote. Their Social Security system is in bad trouble. (Deficits of twenty billion dollars or more, predicted by 1985.) There are ways to fix Social Security, but they all seem to be politically suicidal. Pete Dominici tried; his Senate Budget Committee approved a plan early this month to save forty billion in Social Security costs over three years by reducing benefits or raising Social

Figure 6-1 John Chancellor's commentary for *NBC Nightly News,* May 19, 1982. *(Courtesy of NBC News)*

Notice in figure 6-2 how Shalit begins the entertainment commentary by clearly identifying the movie to be reviewed. It is important to be this specific early in such commentaries so that the audience is set up for the opinions that follow. Shalit then offers an overview of the movie and launches into his personal retelling of the story without revealing the ending so that viewers who want to see the movie will not have their experience spoiled. Shalit mentions noteworthy individual performances before concluding the review with his personal assessment of the movie and his recommendations for the audience. Notice the clever word choices, especially in the last sentence. The structural pattern for this type of commentary generally follows that shown in figure 6-2. Still photographs and film clips from the movie reviewed offer visual enhancement to the entertainment commentary. This kind of special purpose commentary is particularly suitable for reviews of radio and television programs, stage plays, musical performances, and even contemporary novels.

Security taxes. Dominici even got a reluctant White House to go along. Astounding!

Here's how it was done: all twelve Republicans on the budget committee approved the politically risky project. Why? Well, only one of the twelve is up for re-election, Hatch of Utah. These Republicans could run the risk of angering the aged. But everybody in the House of Representatives is up for re-election, so the idea was swiftly killed there, and when all the Republicans in the Senate thought it over, they rejected the idea of tinkering with Social Security. Just too risky.

There's a lot of talk about making a decision to solve the Social Security problem after the election, and brave pledges of keeping it solvent, but the fact is the Congress has copped out on this one, and the White House doesn't mind.

And so there it sits, Social Security, two hundred billion dollars a year, leaking at all of its seams, driving up the deficit, but beyond the reach of the government in an election year.

Tom.

HIT: 6:51:53

Fig. 6-1   *(Continued)*

TYPES OF EDITORIALS

It is sometimes easier to talk about types of editorials in the abstract without examining realistic problems and situations. By selecting a particular type of editorial writing approach, the opinions expressed can be formulated to match the nature of the topic discussed and to assure the editorial writer of an identifiable audience response. Knowing when to use a particular type of editorial approach often becomes a decision as crucial as selecting the topic and expressing the opinions.

While a given editorial may fulfill more than one purpose, most can be categorized on the basis of predominant purpose. There are basically five types of broadcast editorials.

The *informative editorial* restates the principal facts of a news story and tells of, or explains, a particular occurrence or series of related happenings. This type is used to lay the groundwork for future editorials on a subject or to give the station time

Gene Shalit
NBC TODAY Show
"Young Doctors In Love"
July 21, 1982

Remember all the fun you had watching "Airplane," that crazy spoof of
airport pictures? Now there's a new one that kids medical movies, and soap
operas like "General Hospital." It's called "Young Doctors In Love" and
it's not for your Aunt Matilda. It is rowdy, with gleefully terrible jokes:
sight gags, slight gags and gags that may make you gag, especially if you're
not into urology. The movie centers around a medical center, where
stethoscoped students are tyrannized by a greedy professor of surgery who
is more interested in riches than in stitches. And in stitches is what much
of this movie may keep you. There is also a weird pathologist (if "weird
pathologist" isn't redundant). As for the students, we have the fair-faced
Californian who wants to be a great surgeon but who's afraid to cut anything
(even though this movie is a slice of life). He's in love with the idealistic
woman student whose seemingly incurable affliction is up to him to cure.
Another student is a pill popper whose improper proposals are planned to
propel head nurse Sproket into surrendering her key to the narcotics
cabinet. Each intern has jokes in turn. Okay I'll admit that some of the jokes
are terrible, but some are awful. Be sure to sit through the closing credits
-- a kind of appendix -- in which the ultimate destiny of each character is
laughingly revealed. "Young Doctors In Love" is naughty nitwit silliness
in the manner of "Airplane" and "SCTV." In this movie-summer of fights
and frights, it's a release to be in this hospital staffed by disorderlies. These
merry medics give doctors the needle as they give us a shot of laughter in
the halls of I-V.

-END-

Figure 6-2   Gene Shalit's "Critic's Corner" for the NBC *Today* Show, July 21, 1982. (© *Gene
Shalit 1982)*

---

to research the topic in some depth and to determine the station's stand on an issue
or event.

The *interpretative editorial* presents the facts of a particular event briefly, and then
tells what the licensee feels is the real, vital, and hidden significance of the event.
This type may also present a conclusion for the audience to consider and may advocate a line of thinking for the audience to adopt.

The *argumentative editorial* takes a present condition or event and argues logically
what will happen from cause to effect. This type of editorial requires clear organiza-

tion, sufficient documentation, and convincing reasoning to be effective and to have impact on the audience. It is considered one of the most difficult types of editorials to write.

The *call-for-action editorial* states a problem or situation, details a solution, then finally calls for specific action by the audience or by a particular group, agency, organization, or individual. This is one of the easiest types of editorials to research and to write because the issue involved generally is well known. Its effectiveness, however, often is diminished by constant "calls to action" by the station on almost all issues considered.

The *entertaining editorial* employs satire, humor, and comedy in an effort to entertain, but also to gently persuade. This type of editorial strives to provide a light approach to the day's important and seemingly unimportant events and newsmakers.

SELECTING SUBJECTS

If a broadcasting station plans to editorialize regularly, it is best to select a person or to establish an editorial board to supervise editorial policy and to provide direction for selection and development of editorial opinions. At some stations, the licensee retains this editorial responsibility. Most stations, however, form an editorial board composed of a few or all of the following: the licensee or his or her representative, the station manager (if not also the licensee), the program director, public affairs director, editorial writer/researcher, and another member from the station's management team, or an individual from outside the station who is involved in community and philanthropic activities. A common practice is to keep editorial efforts separate from news department concerns to avoid potential conflicts. Topics for editorials, however, may be suggested by news department personnel as well as other station employees. The editorial writer often works through the ranks of the news department and, thus, continues to monitor local and state news events which provide the majority of editorial topics. The important thing is to have someone or some group in place to decide what subjects to discuss in editorials, who will write them, whether the final version of each editorial meets with station policy on each issue, when to broadcast the editorial, who voices the editorials, and who handles reaction and rebuttal to the editorial.

The process established by WCVB TV in Boston is typical of how most stations who editorialize regularly coordinate editorial efforts. Marjorie M. Arons-Barron, Editorial Director for WCBV TV, works with a researcher/writer. This editorial staff meets once each week with a ten-member editorial board. The staff makes presentations on about four issues they have selected. Recommendations are made regarding the position the station should take on each issue. Vigorous discussion among the board and staff usually follows and results in an editorial position. The editorial mandate is limited to a "sense of the board" (two or three principal points which are to be incorporated into each editorial). That is the end of the board's involvement. There is no board review of scripts.[3]

When you are called upon to help select and develop a subject for a broadcast editorial, the following suggestions should prove helpful:

1. *Select a topic or subject that has impact for your immediate audience.* Since your audience is more concerned about issues and problems which affect them directly, you should stress local, state, and area issues rather than national and international problems. If management is committed to a strong editorial policy, which is a necessary ingredient for successful editorializing, realistically, only local, state, and regional issues can be properly researched by the station's staff. Also, it is only these kinds of issues upon which the station can realistically have some impact within the community it serves. How the strike at a local steel factory affects the ten thousand employees and their families is more important than a Chicago transit strike which may affect more workers but has little or no impact on your local audience.
2. *Select a subject that is current, timely, and relates most directly to your audience's lifestyle.* Unless your audience can relate to the issue or problem discussed, your success as an editorial writer and the impact of the station on community concerns will be less than desirable.
3. *Select a subject which is important enough to discuss.* The audience must understand that the subject you are presenting is urgent and requires immediate attention. While occasional editorials on patriotic and safety topics may be regarded by some as part of the editorial service of the station, it is the hard-hitting, vibrant, sensitive, and tough subjects which command respect and attention from your audience and from the community at large.
4. *Select and develop an editorial subject which will gain and hold attention.* This may be accomplished by focusing on controversial subjects or perhaps by using striking graphics and visuals during a television editorial. Your audience deserves and expects only the best in topic selection, development, and presentation.
5. *Focus upon a problem or situation not yet resolved.* Although many excellent editorials have been written as reactions to events or situations, effective editorializing can also lead events rather than only follow them. Broadcast editorials can look to the future as well as assess events from the past.
6. *Limit the scope of the editorial subject.* The topic must be capable of being handled by the station's editorial staff. Station managers must recognize and accept the fact that sufficient staff and time must be provided if worthwhile editorial comments are to be offered regularly. If the subject is so broad that regular editorial staffers cannot handle it, more personnel should be assigned to help in the project or the subject should be limited in scope or dropped in favor of another topic which is more readily researched, written, and presented.
7. *Identify a subject in which the public interest conflicts with the interests of an individual or a special group.* Theoretically, when the station expresses an editorial opinion, it is seeking what is best for the public as a whole rather than for one particular individual or group. Editorials which express this attitude are usually the most effective.

When you are involved in the selection of editorial subjects, you can find excellent sources for ideas in the previous newscasts of your station, from other station staff members, from the station's last ascertainment survey of community needs, in files on previous meetings and decisions of local public bodies, in the library, from personal contacts and informed sources, unsolicited audience comments and opinions, and simply your solid editorial judgment acquired after many years of experience. Sometimes editorial subjects will be assigned by the station licensee or by the editorial board. As an editorial writer you may be in a position to suggest and help develop appropriate editorial subjects. Topics for station editorials may be suggested to you as you read an impressive magazine article or hear a startling local news story on the afternoon newscast. It is important to be aware of what is happening around you and to be sensitive to potential editorial subjects as you progress through your routine assignments.

DEVELOPING EDITORIALS AND COMMENTARIES

Once the editorial subject has been selected and the station's basic position on an issue confirmed, the editorial writer or staff then researches the subject in some depth and begins writing. When assembling information to be used in the editorial, you can tap basically the same sources used in selecting the subject. While the research for any given subject never will be complete, enough information must be compiled to formulate the first draft of the editorial and to allow the licensee or editorial board an opportunity to review the information and to confirm final approval of the station's opinion before any editorial stance is broadcast.

Once your essential research is completed, sift out the information to be used and organize the material in a clear and concise manner. Often, it is helpful to provide an outline of the information available and the tentative order in which the information in the editorial will be presented. At times this outlining process may indicate that a particular subject is not worthy of an editorial. The licensee or the editorial board should then be consulted and some kind of adjustment made in the selection or the development of the topic. Or at this juncture, the topic may be discarded and another editorial subject selected for development.

If the subject does seem to lend itself to a worthwhile editorial, write the first draft. Read it aloud and listen to how it sounds. Edit it for grammar, spelling, word choices, sentence structure and length, tone and treatment, persuasiveness, and, of course, content. Does the editorial gain and hold attention? Is it written in a conversational style? Is it written in a clear, concise, logical, and unified manner? Are the language mechanics of grammar and spelling used correctly and effectively? Do all of your word choices express precisely what you wish to communicate? Is the station's position on the issue or problem clear, especially after only the first reading? Does the editorial display a strong, persuasive, and constructive tone by offering thoughtful analysis and treatment of an issue along with practical ideas and solutions to the problems presented? Above all, does the editorial clearly express an opinion or stand on an issue of vital importance? If these and other concerns have been satisfied, then you can begin to prepare a subsequent or final draft of the editorial.

If the editorial is to be broadcast on television, consider the use of various types of visual material to accompany the written editorial comment. Nothing is so dull as a television editorial with only the presenter's face and a cold table top showing. Consider using charts, graphs, maps, and pictures to add visual reinforcement and information to the editorial statement. Stations often broadcast television editorials from a studio using chroma-key slides as the minimum visual support. B-roll from the station's news film/videotape library can be used. Shooting editorials on location periodically adds impact and a sense of immediacy to the presentation. Remember, the viewer has become accustomed to rather sophisticated television presentations. Any legitimate television production tool which will enhance the viewers' attention, produce a greater impact and supply essential supplementary information should be considered when designing, writing and producing television editorials.

Most often, radio editorials feature a single voice delivering the station licensee's opinion. On occasion, it may be appropriate to consider the use of other radio production tools to better communicate and reinforce the opinions expressed. Careful use of other voices, music, sound effects, or "location sound" could create in the listeners' minds a sharper, more graphic, and memorable impression than is possible only with a single voice delivering the editorial statement. Only occasional use of these additional production tools is recommended and only when appropriate for the circumstances.

Another factor to consider at this stage of the writing process is whether the station licensee wants a single editorial or a multi-part editorial series prepared. Besides presenting individual editorials on a variety of subjects, stations on occasion prepare a series of editorials on a major topic. These multi-part editorials may be presented on consecutive days or offered as events and issues develop over a period of weeks or even months. Some editorial writers question the advisability of consecutive day presentation since it presumes that the listener or viewer has been exposed to all portions of previous editorials in the multi-part series. On the other hand, consecutive day presentation allows the station to keep the issue before the audience, to follow through on developments, and to make it known that the station is committed to its stance and will continue to report and to editorialize on an issue of community importance. Careful planning and coordination are required to develop effective multi-part editorial series for broadcast.

EDITORIAL EXAMPLES

The technique of writing broadcast editorials is best illustrated by examining editorials from stations which have received awards from professional organizations and associations. The editorials in figures 6-3 through 6-5 are only a sample of each station's editorial efforts throughout the years.

Aired: 5/7/81

HER NIGHT ON THE STREETS

Tony Hirsh

Vice President & General Manager

The recent brutal death of 66-year-old Phyliss Ianotti demonstrates the tragic and desperate need for the City to provide the homeless proper lodging and supportive services.

Phyliss had been living at a shelter, the Dwelling Place...on West 40th Street...but the demand for their 12 beds is such that residents have been reluctantly forced to rotate between the shelter and the streets.

In spite of the fact that two months earlier she had been beaten and raped, Phyliss accepted her turn on the streets without complaint the night she was killed...amid a litter of broken wine bottles in the Port Authority parking lot.

Sister Naureen Marie Kelly of the Dwelling Place, asks the right question regarding this disgraceful situation:

VOICE CUT

"How, when the City owns hundreds of sound buildings taken over for nonpayment of taxes, can they say they have so little space to lodge our homeless?"

On behalf of all those who may some day meet the same fate as Phyliss Ianotti, WINS calls upon the Human Resources Administration to explain why they are able to provide only 200 beds for the City's 6,000 homeless women.

This is Tony Hirsh for WINS.

CLOSE

Call the WINS Editorial Hotline with your comments: 557-5183.

Figure 6-3   Example of an informative editorial. *(Courtesy of WINS Radio)*

The WINS editorial in figure 6-3 relates the tragic details of a particular human problem in New York City. Notice the use of an audio insert or actuality within the copy. This can be an effective technique if used judiciously by the editorial writer. Although the editorial closes with a direct challenge to rectify the situation, the primary purpose of the editorial is to inform listeners.

Religion, Morality and the Political Process   Reference No.

Philip Scribner Balboni, Director of Editorials and Public Affairs   127

September 22:   6:30 AM,   12:28 PM,   6:55 PM,   3:00 AM 1980
September 27:   6:58 PM,   3:55 AM

Morality and politics are frequently inextricable. That's why members of
the clergy are often obliged to speak out on moral issues in the political
arena. When and how they do it, however, can distort the political process
and sow discord among persons of different religions.

For the Catholic Church and some fundamentalist Protestant sects, banning
abortion is a moral imperative. Others, however, maintain that abortion is
a private matter, to be decided by a woman and her doctor. Disagreement
is inevitable when public policy affecting everyone is based on what is a
matter of religious faith for some but not for others.

But where a candidate stands on abortion should not be the sole basis for
deciding his or her fitness to represent voters on a wide range of issues.
A representative must also deal with such matters as defense, the economy,
criminal justice and civil liberties. Given the complexity of the job, we believe
the political process is ill served by voting on the basis of a single issue.

When any religious institution urges such a course on the eve of an
election, it risks creating antagonisms which divide otherwise reasonable
people. Abortion is already an emotional issue. So the ill-timed pre-primary
exhortation by Cardinal Medeiros served to polarize many.

Democracy permits any person or group to advocate almost any cause. But
the system works best when voters choose candidates not on the basis of
a single cause, such as banning abortion, but on the basis of how
the candidates will address the many difficult problems facing their
constituents.

Figure 6-4 Example of an argumentative editorial from WCVB TV, Boston. *(©WCVB TV/Metromedia, Inc.)*

WCVB TV in Boston has received numerous awards for its editorial work, including
National Broadcast Editorial Association awards. Figure 6-4 shows a WCVB TV editorial
on religion, morality, and the political process. It is an excellent example of an argumentative editorial. It logically analyzes the interrelationships between religion and political
activity and comments on one of the most controversial contemporary topics—abortion.
The editorial displays excellent organization, documentation, logic, and persuasiveness.
    WHIO-TV in Dayton, Ohio, has received a Society of Professional Journalists, Sigma

Delta Chi (SDX) Distinguished Service Award for Editorializing on Television. The city of Dayton transferred administration of the city jail from the police department to a civilian human services agency in an effort to trim expenses and pick up additional funding. What ensued shocked the Dayton community. WHIO-TV strongly editorialized against the changeover and reported what was happening in clear, unmistakable language. Although the station was pressured by advertisers and the Mayor to soft-pedal its campaign because it could damage the city's image, WHIO-TV reminded its critics that it could be one of their sons or daughters suffering under these conditions while in jail for relatively minor offenses. The city of Dayton later returned the administrative responsibility for the jail to the police department. Several former jail employees have been indicted. One of the striking editorials from this multi-part editorial series is shown in figure 6-5.

#100 2:45
April 13, 1981

The incidents and words coming up are not pleasant and they will almost certainly offend many people. But ignoring them won't stop them from coming up again.

Listen carefully:

> <u>Forced</u> to perform oral sex on other men
> <u>Forced</u> to drink urine
> <u>Forced</u> to eat cigarette butts
> <u>Burned</u> with cigarettes
> <u>Punched</u> and <u>Beaten</u>
> <u>Physically</u> and <u>Psychologically</u> degraded and humiliated

These aren't accusations or descriptions out of some cheap novel or out of Attica State Prison, New Mexico State Prison, Lucasville or some Prisoner of War Camp.

These are allegations and descriptions of what transpired over several days in the <u>Dayton City Jail</u>. Two men sexually abused and assaulted repeatedly while in custody in the <u>Dayton City Jail</u>. It's the second time since the jail was taken over by the Dayton Human Rehabilitation Center staff that there have been serious allegations of sexual abuse. The earlier incident allegedly involved some guards and city employees demanding sexual favors from male prisoners.

All of this under the label of "Human Rehabilitation." In this case the name of the unit is ludicrous. Many people housed in the Dayton City Jail

Figure 6-5 Example of a call-for-action editorial from WHIO-TV, Dayton, Ohio. *(Courtesy of Jack Hurley and WHIO-TV)*

have not yet been convicted of doing anything. Right after the incidents came to light, Human Rehabilitation officials talked about "doing everything they could, noticing nothing irregular and being short staffed."

In a matter of days, the Human Rehab staff investigated the incidents and concluded today that while there should be some minor changes...there were no major violations of policies or procedures. That conclusion is more than a little self-serving. While expressing some concerns, city officials are being, in our opinion, incredibly blasé about the abuse and degradation of two persons for whose safety and well-being they are ultimately and indisputably responsible. Perhaps the Human Rehabilitation Department has been given a job it's not capable of handling. Fine! Then let's correct that and give the job to someone who can.

Think about it. That could have been you or any member of your family who had a brush with the law.

And one more thing, if it had been you...Mr. Mayor, you...Mr. Commissioner, you...Mr. City Manager, or you...Mr. Superintendent of Rehabilitation...We think you'd be falling all over yourselves correcting the problem and making sure it doesn't happen to anyone else.

The Human Rehab staff has investigated itself and pronounced itself innocent. It's also proved itself incapable of handling the City Jail. And if the City Manager, the Mayor and the Commission accept these bureaucratic excuses and condone this bureaucratic whitewash...then they too must share in the responsibility for ineptitude and insensitivity.

If the sexual abuses involved one of them or theirs...you can be damn sure they'd be doing something about it...right now.

Fig. 6-5 *(Continued)*

CONCLUSION

With strong managerial support and encouragement plus sufficient time, personnel, and research facilities, broadcast editorials can be an effective tool to enhance station image and to provide a catalytic spark for community improvement. A strong editorial policy on the part of a broadcast station indicates its strength and commitment within the community.

Jack Hurley, then News Director of WHIO-TV at the time of the multi-part series on Dayton jail conditions, feels strongly about the role and function of broadcast editorials.

The willingness to take on tough, controversial and unpopular issues is all too often left to newspapers whose circulation and influence have long been diminishing. The research, writing and presentation of a strong TV editorial can have tremendous effect on a community and an issue . . . if the station follows through, and makes it known it will follow through and continue reporting and editorializing on issues of importance.[4]

SUGGESTED EXERCISES AND PROJECTS

1. Critique several commentaries broadcast on national radio or television networks. Comment on the selection and development of subjects, writing and presentation style, tone and treatment of the subject, documentation presented, persuasiveness, impact, and compliance with broadcast editorial regulations.
2. Write a short radio or television commentary on a current national or international topic of importance.
3. Write a short radio or television entertainment commentary on a current motion picture, stage play, or musical performance in your area.
4. Prepare an outline and then write a short radio or television editorial on a current local or state topic of importance.
5. Write a series of three radio or television editorials on the same topic. Prepare the editorials to be used in sequence, on consecutive days, on a local broadcast station.
6. List five viable topics or issues suitable for local station editorial comment. Indicate why you selected each topic or issue for potential development and use as a broadcast editorial.
7. Compile a list of ten key community leaders in your area who you feel should receive advance copies of editorials broadcast by local and area broadcast stations. Indicate why you would recommend each person on your list.

NOTES

1. From *The Law of Political Broadcasting and Cablecasting.* Federal Communications Commission, Federal Register, Vol. 43, No. 159, August 16, 1978, 36387.
2. National Association of Broadcasters, *Radio and Television Editorializing* (Washington, DC: National Association of Broadcasters, 1967), p. 2.
3. Summarized from a letter by Marjorie M. Arons-Barron, Editorial Director for WCVB TV in Boston, to the author. Letter dated June 30, 1982.
4. Quotation from a letter by Jack Hurley, News Director for WXIA-TV in Atlanta, to the author. Letter dated July 20, 1982.

ADDITIONAL READING

National Association of Broadcasters. Legal Department. *The Editorial Director's Desk Book.* Washington, D.C.: NAB, 1980.

Routt, Edd. *Dimensions of Broadcast Editorializing.* Blue Ridge Summit, Pa.: TAB Books, 1974

Stonecipher, Harry W. *Editorial and Persuasive Writing.* New York: Hastings House, 1976.

Chapter Seven

DOCUMENTARIES AND INVESTIGATIVE REPORTS

A substantial portion of the programming efforts by networks and local stations today consists of the production of public affairs broadcasts, which include documentaries and investigative reports. Unfortunately, such programs often do not attract as large an audience as broadcasts which appeal to general entertainment tastes. Nevertheless, large sums of money as well as a substantial amount of time, energy, and talent continue to be invested in the production of documentaries and investigative reports because of their inherent value for the public and the broadcasting industry.

This chapter examines documentaries and investigative reports. It will be a basic examination focusing on the writer's participation in the creative process involved. There will be a description of the basic types of documentaries as well as the criteria used to evaluate such creative efforts. The chapter outlines the progressive steps used by the writer to generate a documentary and investigative report: selecting and developing meaningful subjects, gathering information, preparing script material, developing a program structure and organizational pattern, and working with narration. Script examples are presented at the end of the chapter to illustrate the writing principles described.

DEFINITIONS AND DIFFERENTIATIONS

Documentaries

Documentaries present facts about a relevant subject from actual or real events, persons, or places to reflect, interrelate, creatively interpret, or comment upon current concerns and realities. Documentaries should be designed to create a cohesive, dramatic presentation with intellectual and emotional impact. Reality is the basic criterion for a documentary.

Documentaries may be classified according to the ultimate objective of such presentations—information, interpretation, persuasion. Certainly such classifications can be combined and altered to provide an even more effective documentary presentation. If the intent is information, a documentary may simply explore a subject in an organized manner; facts would be carefully selected and organized to provide as complete and objective a report as possible. Interpretation may evolve from this informational base; the documentary presentation could be designed to provide insight and perspective into a sensitive or controversial subject. A documentary could be designed which arouses concern and presents solutions to specific problems which have been factually and objectively identified and outlined and creatively interpreted. In effect, the persuasive documentary incorporates information and interpretation to convincingly present persuasive arguments.

Two developments have provided additional dimensions for these primary documentary classifications. In "cinéma vérité," the audience is allowed to witness an event for themselves and, thus, to form their own inferences, perspectives, and interpretations of what the camera simply records. The documentarian controls, to some extent, the view of the event by selecting camera angles, editing long sequences, and omitting some material, but it is the viewer who ultimately determines the impact of what is seen and heard. "Docudramas" are essentially fictional accounts based upon actual events, persons, and situations. They are a hybrid program form which usually emphasizes fictional dramatic entertainment and plot structure.

Investigative Reports

Investigative reporting is a form of documentary. It requires the acquisition and presentation of carefully documented facts to substantiate specific charges, to explain changes in society, and to serve as a guidepost for societal ethics and standards. It should lead to a direct knowledge of events, actions, and facts which usually have been concealed. Revelation is the essential characteristic of investigative reports.

Good investigative reporting requires an emphasis on accuracy, objectivity, and documentation. These are acquired only through hard work which is painstaking, careful, logical, thoughtful, and as complete as possible. The ability to gather pertinent facts from various kinds of sources and to present these facts in a logical, understandable, and interesting manner is the mark of a good investigative reporter.

The selection and development of a topic often determine the success of an investigative report. Engaging and effective investigative reports tend to focus upon corruption, fraud, hypocrisy, and illegality by public officials and agencies, private corporations, political organizations, charities, and foreign governments. Other viable topics may evolve from personal injustices, scandals, intimate details about notorious celebrities, and societal inequities. Later in this chapter, specific suggestions will be presented to help select and develop effective topics for investigative reports.

Ethical and legal concerns often impinge upon the use of certain investigative reporting techniques and practices. These concerns include: the methods of gathering information; how human sources of information are treated and rewarded; the personal integrity, objectivity, and perception of the individual investigative reporter; how information is prepared for presentation; balancing the individual's right to privacy against the public's right to know and react to certain kinds of information; and the formulation of composite persons who typify real characters. The investigative reporter faces the difficult challenge of deciding what actions and practices are illegal or unethical and then following a carefully documented path which leads to the objective presentation of previously concealed facts. The investigative reporter continually walks a tightrope, balancing delicate moral and ethical standards and the documentation and interpretation of complex issues, events, and actions.

DEVELOPING THE DOCUMENTARY AND INVESTIGATIVE REPORT

Selecting Subjects

The program topic must capture and sustain the attention and interest of the audience. The most effective topics usually relate directly to contemporary lifestyles and affect the heart, health, and pocketbook of the audience. Topic selection is the crucial first step in generating an effective, engaging documentary or investigative report.

The initial idea for such presentations may come from any number of sources. A conscious effort to become aware of current developments and concerns usually yields many viable subjects. Excellent sources include: regular reading of pertinent magazines, newspapers, and books; audience research information compiled for program ratings or community ascertainment purposes; unsolicited audience comments and reactions; routine review of available public records; regular newscast reports of the station or network which indicate the spark of an idea which could be more fully developed; and suggestions and comments by fellow staff members or from a formally established advisory board.

Developing Subjects

The idea for the documentary or investigative report must be developed or fleshed out. How the idea is developed usually depends upon such variables as established developmental procedures within the broadcast facility, the nature of the topic, available personnel and production resources, and the writing and production timetable. No matter what process is used to develop a subject, generally this scheme is followed:

information $\longrightarrow$ knowledge $\longrightarrow$ understanding $\longrightarrow$ exposition

Each essential step leads to the next. Information provides knowledge which leads to understanding and ultimately to an exposition of the material in a clear, logical, poignant manner. Although an experienced documentarian or investigative reporter may combine or even bypass some of the specific steps to be outlined, the recommended procedures are isolated for the purposes of discussion and evaluation by the novice writer. These procedures are only recommendations based upon general practices within the industry. Usually several steps are under development simultaneously.

Gather Preliminary Information. Many of the same sources used to select a topic can be tapped to gather preliminary information to formulate a tentative plan of action for further development. At this point, it is necessary to complete enough research to know something about the topic, but not so much that you form a prejudicial perspective and, thus, preclude alternate methods of presentation and development. In effect, this phase should be a *preliminary* examination of the topic. The writer/researcher should remain objective and alert to identify the parameters of the topic and the sources of information that will be pursued at a later time. Research continues as the documentary or investigative report is developed and finally produced.

Besides the sources already listed for selecting a subject, it might be helpful to seek out experts or technical advisers or people who have lived through a particular experience, to visit certain places or locales which might be used in the final presentation, to complete a preliminary examination of relevant written material and documents, and to determine the availability and usefulness of archival material—films, slides, pictures, newspaper accounts, historical objects, etc.

Prepare a Treatment. The treatment for a documentary or investigative report contains the same kind of descriptive information all treatment statements provide—purpose of the program, intended audience, content and length of each major sequence, and the style, mood, emphasis, and shape of the presentation. In addition, a treatment for a documentary or investigative report should reflect the preliminary information gathered and indicate a tentative point of view which will be explored, developed, and adjusted later by the writer and production staff.

Complete Research. At this point, the writer returns to those fertile research sources identified earlier. Now each source is explored fully to refine and focus the topic. Specific material is gathered, recorded, filed, and organized. There should be a continual review of the accumulated material and the treatment (if one was prepared) to determine what is known and what needs to be known to provide a more complete report. Every reasonable effort should be made to examine and probe all available resources which relate to the subject.

Formulate an Outline. At this point the writer/researcher begins to place each piece of information into perspective, to determine its place and function in the program. The program outline could be written as research progresses. Often, it is written after most of the research has been completed. It must be a dynamic outline, one that progresses dramatically and remains reasonably flexible. The outline serves as a guidepost for writing the documentary or investigative report. It must be a "living" document, adjusting to new information and new perspectives. The outline must be clear, concise, and cohesive and must logically display the relationship between main points and supporting ideas. As a developmental step, the outline may substitute for a treatment statement.

Determine Program Structure. A thoughtful, carefully written outline normally will suggest the most effective program structure for a particular documentary or investigative report. It is important that such programs be structured dramatically—with a beginning, a middle, and an ending progressing to a climax. The beginning must capture audience attention and clearly indicate the nature of the program. The middle must examine the topic, issue, or event in practical, human terms. It should explore the subject in a compelling manner. The ending must provide the essence of the program as well as focus and interpretation which adds meaning to what has been presented. It should make the audience think about the significance and impact of the subject. It may be appropriate to suggest a course of action to resolve a problem or issue.

Various organizational patterns can provide a clear and logical program structure and allow a progressive exposition of the topic. Some of the more common patterns are: problem-solution, cause-effect, chronological, geographical or spatial, topical, and various classifications (e.g., age groups, political subdivisions, etc.). Selection of the appropriate organizational pattern must reflect the nature and anticipated development of the topic.

Several kinds of program formats can be used to structure the program. Short-form formats include news magazine and mini-documentary reports. Long-form formats include news specials and full-length programs. The use of each kind of program format will influence the shape and style of the final presentation.

Short-form formats are used frequently. *News magazines*—which display diversity, flexibility, and fast pace—tend to attract large, loyal audiences. When structuring a news magazine presentation, the intent is to provide short but complete reports on a variety of topics of direct interest to the audience. The reports or segments are positioned during the presentation to attract and sustain audience interest. *Mini-documentaries* are a series of brief, interrelated presentations on a subject of prime importance to the audience. Mini-docs can provide coverage of immediate, emerging topics not requiring full-length program treatment. Mini-docs create interest and suspense as the various parts or episodes are presented, usually on successive newscast programs, building to the final, climactic episode. Each episode is usually 2 to 6 minutes long. Three to twelve episodes may be presented within regularly scheduled newscasts or public affairs program series over a period of one week or even several weeks. Each episode must be able to stand alone and yet still interrelate to all other episodes in the series to provide a complete and unified perspective of the topic. Since it is unrealistic to expect that the audience will see or hear all parts of the mini-doc series, each episode (except for the first) begins by briefly recapping previous episodes and placing the upcoming episode into perspective. Each episode (except the last) usually ends with a preview of the next installment to help arouse audience interest. The final episode could review the entire series and offer additional insights.

Long-form formats are useful for a full exposition of a topic within a single program. *News specials,* which usually are broadcast in primetime or just after the late-night newscast, are programs which explain or interpret the significance and impact of a particular contemporary news event or development. Such specials concern an event, person, or action which significantly dominated the news events of the day (e.g., the death of a nation's leader or a popular entertainer, military or political changes in a developing story, a natural disaster, or human tragedy). Archival material as well as various prerecorded reports often are used during such broadcasts. *Full-length programs* are the more traditional 30- and 60-minute documentary or investigative reports centering on one specific topic for the entire broadcast. The dramatic program structure outlined earlier would be used to develop such programs.

It is possible to combine short- and long-form program formats into an effective program structure. For example, it would be possible to develop a five- to ten-part mini-doc series on a particular topic. These episodes could be written and produced to be used as "interlocking modules." That is, the individual mini-doc episodes could be consolidated or combined into a unified, long-form, full-length 30-minute documentary program. The opening and closing sequences of each installment would have to be deleted, but there should be no obvious need to change the crucial middle portion of each episode. When combined, the episodes would present the full exposition of the subject, just as though they were originally designed for broadcast in this way. Thus, a station or network could present the mini-doc series in its entirety and also offer the opportunity to see or hear all of the parts in one, consolidated program. Careful writing and production planning are necessary to make this multiple-use possibility feasible.

Select the Production Process. It is necessary to determine how the documentary or investigative report will be produced before the appropriate kind of script can be written. The writer often serves not only as a researcher (as noted earlier) but also produces or directs such broadcasts. Thus, the production process must be selected carefully and early.

Many documentaries are *field-produced programs.* After the outline for the program has been completed, interviews are conducted in the field with the principals involved. These remarks are transcribed and reviewed. Useful recorded comments are underlined and numbered to permit retrieval from the production work tapes. Then, narration can be written and additional visual and aural material recorded to further illustrate what is said in the field recordings and to bridge gaps between program segments. These elements are then assembled in the editing room into the final program. Field-produced programs generally rely upon a carefully devised outline to begin the production process. Since the final assembly of the program is done in the editing room, a full-script may or may not be developed. After the program has been assembled, a transcript of the broadcast may be prepared for record-keeping purposes and a final check on program content.

Studio-produced programs can make use of a full-script since they normally include the use of prerecorded reports (which can be produced in the field), archival material, and a primary anchor. This is a more carefully controlled production environment which allows the pre-scripted use of already available, timed material.

Write the Script. A full documentary script cannot always be written in advance because usually it is not possible to anticipate every content and production possibility precisely. Enough preparation and scripting must be done in advance, however, to keep the documentary on track and still provide an opportunity to react, in a flexible manner, to evolving situations, and to adjust the content and structure of the broadcast accordingly. Whatever form of scripting used (outline, semi-script, or full-script) it must at least indicate the parameters of the subject and the particular program elements to be emphasized. But the script still must permit future creative involvement to mold and shape the final documentary presentation. Most documentaries use the standard scripting formats already described and illustrated; however, these standard scripting formats often are modified to accommodate specific writing and production situations.

Several suggestions may be helpful for preparing scripts for field-produced programs and segments:

1. Prepare as detailed an advance script as possible. It may be only an outline, but make the outline as comprehensive as possible.
2. Divide program elements into those which are under your control and those which are not. Prepare script material for what can be controlled or anticipated.
3. Make the controllable elements serve as pegs or building blocks for the rest of the program or segment structure. A usable, "dynamic" program outline is essential.
4. If possible, provide a full-script for the opening and closing sequences. Pre-scripting these two crucial parts will help determine the shape and tone of at least some of the broadcast.

Narration is used often in both field- and studio-produced programs and segments. It is important for the writer to understand the functions and techniques of narration since narration can be used effectively in many kinds of programs.

The basic functions of narration are to clarify, interpret, enhance, and reinforce what is presented. In general, narration should be expository, explaining what is seen or heard. It can help control the flow of information, forming bits and pieces of information and comments into unified segments, and ultimately into a recognizable whole. To be considered effective, narration must be an obvious, integral, justifiable part of the program structure. Narration has several specific applications: to establish a scene or situation; to make effective transitions between ideas and program segments; to keep the audience on track; to provide additional information; to call attention to something easily overlooked or misunderstood; and to preview or review what is presented. If used properly, narration can be an effective tool for the writer.

There are several techniques recommended for writing effective narration:

1. *Narration could be written for either on- or off-camera use.* A mix of the two can also be effective.
2. *Involve the audience.* Present the subject matter in meaningful, human terms. Use second person and active voice.
3. *Provide narration which sounds natural and conversational.* When using material taken from the printed media (e.g., excerpts from books, magazines, newspapers, or poems), it may be necessary to adapt or "translate" such material for use in a broadcast situation or to use only short excerpts from such material.
4. *Avoid unnecessary statistics, long lists, complex terms, specialized jargon, and trite and hackneyed expressions.* These distract the audience easily and usually add nothing significant to the narration or the overall exposition of the subject.
5. *Make the narration clear, precise, and easy to understand.*
6. *Stick to the subject.* Each piece of narration must relate directly to the structured development and exposition of the subject.
7. *Use controlled experimentation.* This might include the use of contrasting narrators, the voices of people directly involved in the subject or the use of human voices for inanimate or even animalistic situations and characters.
8. While narration usually matches what is seen or heard, *consider using narration as a contrasting element, counterpointing aural or visual material.* For example, stark pictures of a war-torn city could be juxtaposed with a soft, melodic, poetic narration about what the city used to resemble.
9. *Do not inundate the program with too much narration.* This usually causes the audience to become confused, bored, distracted, and irritated.
10. *Make the narration sparse.* Let the pictures (real or imagined), sounds, actions, and situations create the mood, convey the meanings, shape perspective and interpretation, and move the program along. Narration should supplement and complement the main body of information. It should not dominate the program.
11. *Leave some breathing room.* Allow time for the audience to think about or digest what is said, especially after a provocative or startling statement.
12. *Do not use narration when a picture or sound will communicate the information or mood more meaningfully.*

The procedures used for writing narration are as varied as those used to formulate an effective outline for a program. Each project involving narration will necessitate a slightly different process. Some of the factors which interact to determine the narration writing process used include: the nature of the subject, the production timetable, the timetable for research work, the division of production and writing team responsibilities, and the preferences of the individual writer.

Bits and pieces of narration may be written as material is collected. The narration can then be rewritten to fuse with the other program elements to produce a solid, unified program structure. The narration style and approach may change as new material is gathered and as the script moves through the various development stages. A certain degree of flexibility is necessary. The intended function of the narration must be determined early, as the treatment and outline are developed. It is not uncommon, however, for the material or content of the program (pictures or sounds) to mold and shape the specific length, style and mood of the narration.

The narration should not dominate and determine program content. On the other hand, neither should program content dictate, unilaterally, the nature of the narration. Both must work together to produce an effective program.

Timing is an important consideration when writing narration. In some situations, the narration is written first and then the visual or aural material is edited to fit that predetermined length. In other cases, the narration is written after this editing step has been completed. In most situations, the narration is written or rewritten as other program material is assembled, usually in the editing room. An important variable is the reading speed and other vocal characteristics of the narrator. A rapid, light, almost flippant, narration style will necessitate a different kind of writing style and approach than if the narrator bellows the words in a slow, deliberate, dramatic style.

The writer does not select the narrator unless the writer also serves as the producer for the program. Narration may be written and then the narrator is selected; if the narrator is already determined, an effort is made to write the narration to match the predetermined narrator's voice characteristics. Unfortunately, the writer often does not always know who will read the narration. Patience and flexibility are necessary in this all-too-common situation. The best test for the effectiveness of broadcast narration is to evaluate how well the edited program material and the narration come together in the final assembly of the program and then to adjust each program element as necessary.

PROFILES

Two local station programs are examined to illustrate the application of many of the principles and techniques already outlined. Each illustrates a different writing, research, production, and program format approach. Each involves the development of a different kind of subject.

Newsfile: A Bankrupt Court

WJR-AM, Detroit, produced a series of investigative reports on that city's Federal Bankruptcy Court. David L. White, then WJR News Director, explained how the investigation started, what it revealed and how the three series of reports were prepared for broadcast.

> Rod Hansen, now acting News Director of WJR and Gene Fogel, federal beat reporter, were tipped by interested parties of some "problems" in the conduct and relationships of certain officers of U.S. District Bankruptcy Court and certain attorneys practicing in the court. When cross-checking verified these "problems," which were only peripherally connected to the more serious scandal uncovered later, hard news stories were broadcast by Fogel.
>
> The airing of these stories generated a series of allegations from within and without the Bankruptcy Court—establishment of cronyism, irregularities in procedure and judgments, sexual favoritism and apparent judicial incompetence.
>
> Rod and Gene investigated these charges, checked scores of case-files, interviewed judges, lawyers and court clerical employees for more than two months before writing rough drafts of the first series of special reports. The drafts were submitted to me and I then wrote the programs as they appeared on the air, starting in March of 1981. Each subsequent series was handled largely the same way. And after each series was written it was submitted to a lawyer retained by WJR for comments and suggestions to protect the station from any potential libel, slander, defamation or invasion of privacy judgments. Due to the thoroughness of the reporting and the care taken in writing the programs, there were few suggestions for rechecking or revision of elements of the series.[1]

In a departure from standard scripting and production practices, the 3-minute reports were written in "newspaper form"—all narration, with no actualities. White explained that the decision to use straight narration in these series was made early and for a variety of reasons.

> 1. Most of the sources could not be quoted by name and would not be interviewed on tape.
> 2. The story was a difficult and complex one to tell. Actualities would only have made it longer and required unwarranted "set-up" verbiage.
> 3. In running the programs as three-minute segments outside of newscasts, straight narration using Rod's and Gene's voices, we felt, would keep the story concise and clear.
> 4. The process of securing and editing tape would add many employee-hours of work for two valuable news staff members who were being called upon to handle normal assignments on many days in addition to carrying on their investigation.
>   We felt, and still feel, that if the writing did its job and the reporters did theirs, on the air, the programs would be interesting and understandable without the inclusion of tape.[2]

The complete script for one report in the third series of reports by WJR on the Federal Bankruptcy Court is shown in figure 7-1.

The WJR investigation led to the removal or resignation of two federal judges, the removal and conviction of the chief federal court clerk, the removal of all Detroit

NEWSFILE: A BANKRUPT COURT. I'M GENE FOGEL WITH A SERIES OF REPORTS ON THE UNUSUAL WAYS THE SCALES OF JUSTICE ARE BALANCED IN DETROIT'S FEDERAL BANKRUPTCY COURT.

IN OUR INITIAL SERIES, CONSIDERABLE TIME WAS SPENT EXAMINING THE BLIND DRAW SYSTEM IN THE COURT. SOME DESCRIBE THE BLIND DRAW AS THE CORNERSTONE OF THE COURT'S INTEGRITY. BUT THERE ARE SERIOUS QUESTIONS IN FEDERAL BANKRUPTCY COURT IN DETROIT AS TO JUST HOW BLIND THE DRAW HAS BEEN.

YOU MAY RECALL THAT IN THE FIRST SERIES IT WAS DISCLOSED THAT THE PROMINENT BANKRUPTCY LAW FIRM HEADED BY IRVING AUGUST HAD UNCANNY SUCCESS IN KEEPING ITS SIGNIFICANT CASES OUT OF THE REPUTEDLY TIGHT FISTS OF JUDGE GEORGE BRODY. WJR NEWS DISCOVERED THAT IN THE MORE THAN ELEVEN MONTHS THAT HIS GIRLFRIEND WAS HANDLING THE BLIND DRAW AS INTAKE CLERK, ONLY ONE OF AUGUST'S 44 CHAPTER ELEVEN CASES FOUND ITS WAY TO BRODY. A UNIVERSITY OF MICHIGAN STATISTICS PROFESSOR CALCULATED THE ODDS OF THAT HAPPENING IN A TRULY BLIND DRAW AT ONE IN 100-THOUSAND.

SUBSEQUENT TO THAT FINDING, WJR NEWS ANALYZED THE ASSIGNMENTS OF ANOTHER LARGE BANKRUPTCY FIRM, GOLDSTEIN, GOLDSTEIN AND BERSHAD, AND FOUND THAT IT TOO WAS EMINENTLY SUCCESSFUL IN AVOIDING JUDGE BRODY. COURT FILES INDICATE THAT DURING THE SAME TIME SPAN, NOVEMBER FIRST, 1979 TO MID-OCTOBER, 1980, THE FIRM FILED 19 CHAPTER ELEVEN REORGANIZATION PETITIONS. TWO WERE CONSOLIDATED INTO ONE -- AND THAT LEFT EIGHTEEN. ONLY ONE WENT TO BRODY, WHILE FOUR WENT TO JUDGE DAVID PATTON AND THIRTEEN WENT TO SENIOR JUDGE HARRY HACKETT.

COURT RECEIPTS INDICATE THAT IRVING AUGUST'S GIRLFRIEND DREW THE VAST MAJORITY OF THE ASSIGNMENTS FOR THE GOLDSTEIN, GOLDSTEIN AND BERSHAD FIRM. IN FACT, AVAILABLE RECORDS SHOW THE FIRM NEVER FILED A CHAPTER ELEVEN CASE WHEN SHE WAS NOT ON THE JOB.

BASED ON THE BLIND DRAW ASSIGNMENT FORMULA GIVEN HIM

Figure 7-1 One of a series of investigative reports on the Federal Bankruptcy Court in Detroit. *(Courtesy of WJR, Capital Cities Communications. © 1981 by Capital Cities Communications)*

NEWSFILE SERIES III - program 3...page Two

PREVIOUSLY, U OF M STATISTICS PROFESSOR MICHAEL WOODRUFF PLACED THE ODDS AT ONE IN 300 THAT THE GOLDSTEIN FIRM'S CASES WOULD HAVE BEEN DISTRIBUTED AS THEY WERE IF THE DRAW HAD BEEN BLIND.

SEVERAL PERSONS WORKING CLOSE TO FEDERAL BANKRUPTCY COURT HAVE TOLD WJR NEWS THAT WITH CO-OPERATION IN THE RIGHT QUARTERS IT WOULD BE RELATIVELY EASY TO SUBVERT THE BLIND DRAW. AS DESCRIBED TO WJR, A PETITIONING FIRM WOULD ARRIVE AT THE INTAKE WINDOW WITH SEVERAL CASES, ONE OR MORE COULD BE CHAPTER 11 BUSINESS REORGANIZATIONS AND SOME OF THEM RELATIVELY SIMPLE CHAPTER SEVEN BANKRUPTCIES. IN CASUAL CONVERSATION, THE PERSON FILING MIGHT SAY SOMETHING LIKE..."I NEED A JUDGE." THE NEXT BLIND ASSIGNMENT CARD IS DRAWN. IF IT'S NOT THE JUDGE THE LAWYER WANTS, FOR THE IMPORTANT CHAPTER 11 RE-ORGANIZATION CASE, HE HANDS THE CLERK A MINOR CASE TO WHICH TO ATTACH THE CARD. THE PROCESS IS REPEATED UNTIL THE RIGHT JUDGE COMES UP...AT WHICH TIME THE CHAPTER 11 CASE IS HANDED THROUGH THE WINDOW TO THE CLERK, WHO ATTACHES THE ASSIGNMENT CARD.

CONTACTED BY WJR NEWS...STANLY BERSHAD OF THE GOLDSTEIN FIRM SAYS HE WAS NOT EVEN AWARE THAT THE ASSIGNMENTS MIGHT BE OUT OF BALANCE ADDING HE DOESN'T CARE WHAT JUDGE HE GETS. BERSHAD SAYS, "IF YOU DO A GOOD JOB YOU DON'T HAVE TO WORRY ABOUT WHAT JUDGE IS HEARING IT." ASKED IF HE THOUGHT IT WAS UNUSUAL THAT THE SAME CLERK ALWAYS SEEMED TO DRAW HIS FIRM'S CHAPTER 11 CASES, BERSHAD SAID HE WASN'T AWARE OF IT, THAT SEVERAL OF HIS FIRM'S EMPLOYES FILE CASES AND IT WOULD BE IMPOSSIBLE TO KNOW WHO DREW THEM ALL.

TOMORROW AN UNUSUAL CHAPTER 12 RE-ORGANIZATION CASE WHEN OUR NEWSFILE SERIES CONTINUES...I'M GENE FOGEL, FOR NEWSFILE.

Fig. 7-1   *(Continued)*

bankruptcy trustees and the disbanding of their panel, an FBI investigation of the way certain bankruptcy cases have been conducted, several significant changes in the "blind draw" assignment of judges, and a tightening of codes of conduct and lines of authority for those working in the bankruptcy court system. This WJR investigative report series received not only George F. Peabody and Sigma Delta Chi national awards, but also the National Headliners Public Service award, the grand award of the Investigative Reporters and Editors, the Radio-Television News Directors Association International Award for investigative journalism and the American Bar Association Silver Gavel award.

CloseUp: Police Shooting

Each weeknight, following its 11 P.M. local newscast, KIRO TV, Seattle, broadcasts a 30-minute public affairs program entitled *CloseUp*. The producers for the series try to prepare an in-depth report on the most important or most interesting news story of the day. On June 24, 1982, as final preparations were underway for a *CloseUp* program on a local park bond issue controversy, it was decided to change topics and prepare a special report on the killing of a local county policeman. This was obviously the day's most important local and area news story. The full resources of KIRO Television's staff and facilities were called into action as visual material was assembled and copy written for the broadcast of this news special less than six hours later. This sudden shift in program topics is not uncommon for series which try to present meaningful reports on current events.

Figure 7-2 shows the opening segment for this KIRO Television broadcast. It captures attention, indicates clearly the topic of the program, and hints at the continuing nature of the story. The writing is terse, but dramatic.

The main body of the broadcast brings the viewer up to date as the shooting incident is reconstructed, the suspects identified, and the emergency run to the hospital described. The anchor prerecorded a voice-over narration of the quickly-assembled visuals. There was a report on protective gear worn by the murdered officer and how it was not designed to withstand the force of the weapon used. This was followed by a report from the police command post on the continuing manhunt involving police and sheriffs' deputies from two counties. This led to a brief profile of a new and sophisticated piece of electronic hardware used in the search, and an update on the story from a KIRO TV reporter in the field who was asked questions by the anchor (fig. 7-3).

The closing segment of the broadcast, delivered on-camera by the anchor, summarizes the news event, provides additional insight, interprets the story in striking, human terms, and offers viewers something to think and talk about—the value of a human life (fig. 7-4).

This *CloseUp* broadcast provided meaningful information on a significant news story of direct interest to KIRO TV viewers. The program structure allowed the in-depth report to present relevant facts in a clear, precise manner through excellent writing and strong visualization.

CONCLUSION

An effort has been made in this chapter to describe and illustrate the basic writing and organizational process for documentaries and investigative reports. It is impor-

```
CLOSEUP/SET UP                          For the first time
11:30/6-24-82bc                         in 28 years, a King
                                        County police officer
                                        has been shot and killed
                                        in the line of duty.
                                          Tonight the search
                                        for his murderer goes on.
                                          More about the
                                        killing of Sam Hicks and
                                        the manhunt that
                                        followed in tonight's
                                        CloseUp report.

VTR/SOT - SHOW OPEN/EFFECTS               Welcome to CloseUp.
                                          The call on a police
                                        radio "Officer shot" brings
                                        an immediate response. All
                                        available units will go
                                        to the scene.
                                          Late this morning,
                                        such a call came in on the
                                        King County Police radio.
                                        And before the day ends,
                                        an officer is dead, a
                                        suspect is on the loose,
                                        and the largest manhunt
                                        in this area in recent
                                        history is continuing.
```

Figure 7-2 Opening segment for the KIRO TV *CloseUp* program on the killing of a local county policeman. *(Courtesy of KIRO TV, Inc., Seattle)*

```
CLOSEUP/BURFORD REMOTE -                  Earlier this evening,
NIGHTSCOPE                              King County authorities
11:30/6-24-82bc                         turned a new and
                                        sophisticated piece of
                                        electronic hardware on
                                        the search:
CAS    SIL/VO                           (VO)  This device amplifies
                                        light rays, making it
                                        possible to see in almost
                                        total darkness. It's
                                        called a nightscope.
                                        And what you are seeing
                                        is a picture taken after
CAS:  30 sec.                           dark in the search area.
LIVE:  MARLER & REMOTE                  (LIVE)  Brooks Burford
                                        has been standing by at
                                        the Command Post. Let's
                                        go back for one last
                                        report. Brooks...
                                        anything new to report?
                                          Will the search
                                        effort continue all night
                                        in some form?
```

Figure 7-3 A middle segment for the KIRO TV *CloseUp* program on the killing of a local county policeman. *(Courtesy of KIRO TV, Inc., Seattle)*

CLOSEUP/FINAL NOTES
11:30/6-24/82bc

A final note
The headlines...
television newscasts...
and programs like this
tell the story.
A police officer
shot and killed. A family
left alone. Fellow officers
mourning the loss of a
colleague. And still to
come, the arrest of a man
believed to have fired the
fatal shot. Then the trial.
But there's more to
this story: the incredible
risk that police officers take;
the fact that they put their
lives on the line regularly.
People like Sam Hicks
know the risk...hoping
they won't become a statistic
but knowing they might.
And tonight you can't
blame some of Sam Hicks'
fellow officers if they are
asking...if the risk is
still worth the job.
It is to their credit
that people like Sam Hicks
serve on the force.
It is the loss of all
of us that people like Sam
Hicks are killed in the line
of duty.
That's our report for
tonight.
I'll be back with another
edition of CloseUp again
tomorrow.

VTR/SOT - SHOW CLOSE

Good night.

Figure 7-4 Closing segment for the KIRO TV *CloseUp* program on the killing of a local county policeman. *(Courtesy of KIRO TV, Inc., Seattle)*

tant to remember that each step in the process leads logically, progressively, and dynamically to the next step until an engaging and cohesive presentation is achieved. Topics for such programs must be selected carefully and developed in a manner that clearly indicates the contemporary significance for the audience. Sufficient information must be gathered and then organized to provide convincing documentation and to devise a flexible treatment or outline of the subject and eventually a finished script for the presentation. A clear, logical, and flexible program structure and format must be developed to allow a progressive exposition of the topic. The production process to be followed must be determined before the appropriate kind of script can be written. The effective use of narration provides still another tool for the writer of documentaries and investigative reports.

SUGGESTED EXERCISES AND PROJECTS

1. List five subjects or topics which you believe could be developed into effective documentaries and investigative reports for use on a local radio or television station. Explain why you selected each topic.
2. Prepare a schedule of interviews and tentative research sources you would suggest to help develop further one of the topics listed in exercise 1.
3. Gather preliminary information, prepare a treatment, and complete research for one of the topics listed in exercise 1. Then, prepare an outline for a five-part (2 to 4 minutes per part) mini-documentary or a full, 30-minute documentary on the same topic.
4. Write the full-script for the documentary or investigative report outlined in exercise 3. The script must be written in one of the following ways:
   a. entirely in a voice-over, narration form.
   b. for effective use on both radio and television.
5. Write the full-script for a five-part radio or television mini-documentary using one of the topics generated in exercise 1. Then, indicate how this script could be modified for use as a full-length, 30-minute documentary or investigative presentation using the interlocking module scripting format technique described in this chapter.
6. Complete the research and write the script for a prospective radio or television documentary news special on a current prominent world leader.
7. Monitor a network documentary or investigative report. Prepare a report in which you critique: the selection and development of the subject or topic; the effectiveness of the program structure and the organizational pattern or scheme used; the accuracy and completeness of the information presented; and overall writing and production style.

NOTES

1. Quoted from a letter (dated July 9, 1982) from David L. White to the author.
2. Quoted from a letter (dated July 9, 1982) from David L. White to the author.

ADDITIONAL READING

Atkins, Thomas R. *Frederick Wiseman.* Monarch Film Studies. New York: Monarch, 1976.

Baddeley, W. Hugh. *The Technique of Documentary Film Production.* 4th revised ed. New York: Hastings House, 1975.

Barnouw, Erik. *Documentary: A History of the Non-Fiction Film.* New York: Oxford University Press, 1974.

Barsam, Richard Meran, ed. *Nonfiction Film Theory and Criticism.* New York: E. P. Dutton and Co., 1976.

Baum, Tom. *The Invention of the Television Documentary: NBC News 1950-1975.* NBC News Brochure, 1975.

Bluem, A. William. *Documentary in American Television: Form; Function; Method.* New York: Hastings House, 1965.

Bolch, Judith, and Miller, Kay. *Investigative and In-Depth Reporting.* New York: Hastings House, 1978.

Cook, David A. *A History of Narrative Film, 1889-1979.* New York: W. W. Norton and Co., 1981.

Field, Stanley. *The Mini-Documentary—Serializing TV News.* Blue Ridge Summit, Pa.: TAB Books, 1975.

Fielding, Raymond. *The American Newsreel: 1911-1967.* Norman, Okla.: University of Oklahoma Press, 1972.

Friendly, Alfred W. *Due to Circumstances Beyond Our Control.* New York: Random House, 1967.

Griffith, Richard. *The World of Robert Flaherty.* New York: Duell, Sloan and Pearce, 1953.

Hage, George S.; Dennis, Everette E.; Ismach, Arnold H.; and Hartgen, Steven. *New Strategies for Public Affairs Reporting, Investigation, Interpretation, and Research.* 2d ed. Englewood Cliffs, N.J.: Prentice-Hall, 1983.

Hammond, Charles Montgomery, Jr. *The Image Decade: Television Documentary: 1965-75.* New York: Hastings House, 1981.

Hardy, Forsyth, ed. *Grierson on Documentary.* Winchester, Mass.: Faber & Faber, 1979.

Jacobs, Lewis, ed. *The Documentary Tradition.* 2d ed. New York: W. W. Norton and Co., 1979.

Kendrick, Alexander. *Prime Time: The Life of Edward R. Murrow.* Boston: Little, Brown, 1969.

Rosenthal, Alan. *The Documentary Conscience: A Casebook in Film-Making.* Berkeley, Calif.: University of California Press, 1980.

Scott, William. *Documentary Expression and Thirties America.* New York: Oxford University Press, 1973.

Snyder, Robert L. *Pare Lorentz and the Documentary Film.* Norman, Okla.: Oklahoma University Press, 1968.

Williams, Paul N. *Investigative Reporting and Editing.* Englewood Cliffs, N.J.: Prentice-Hall, 1978.

Wolverton, Mike. *Reality on Reels: A Handbook on Radio–TV–Film Documentaries.* Houston: Gulf Publishing, 1982.

Chapter Eight

TALK PROGRAMS

Among the first types of programs to appear on local station and network program schedules, when regular radio broadcasting began in the 1920s, were those which featured interviews with prominent celebrities and discussions of contemporary ideas and issues. These talk programs (interviews, news panel programs, and discussions) have remained on the broadcast schedule. Usually, they are placed under the general program category "public affairs" or "community affairs."

Most talk programs are regularly scheduled broadcasts. Many network talk program series initially are produced as television shows with the audio portion "lifted" and used for radio purposes. Often, these programs generate comments from newsmakers which can be used on regularly scheduled newscasts. For example, you will notice that most of the news panel programs are broadcast on Sundays when very few of the regular news sources are active and readily available. Skillful editing of comments from these programs usually produces several newsworthy excerpts for use in Sunday evening newscasts.

An interesting hybrid talk program format, *This Week with David Brinkley*, was developed in 1981 by ABC. This hour-long Sunday morning broadcast features a brief newscast of events "since the Sunday morning newspaper" as well as two news panel interview segments (usually on related topics) and a discussion or round table segment led by David Brinkley in which news reporters and correspondents freely express their views on events and issues of importance. Although the program segments appear in a regular pattern in each broadcast, there is flexibility to expand or contract portions of the program to maintain viewer interest. Thus, in one program, several types of talk program segments are featured—interviews, news panel interview or discussion, and round table or panel discussion.

In many talk program situations, the writer's work is combined with other on-air production responsibilities. In very large production facilities and situations, the writer may simply be expected to provide only the necessary abbreviated pre-scripted material and leave the on-air duties to appropriate production personnel. But at smaller broadcast stations and facilities, and even in a few network and syndicated program production situations, the writer carries a hybrid title (e.g., writer-interviewer, writer-producer, or even writer-producer-program host or moderator). Thus, the writer should be prepared to participate fully as needed in the preparation of material for talk programs—helping to select guests, researching a guest or topic, devising an outline of topics to be discussed or a preliminary list of questions to be asked during a program. This combined set of responsibilities provides the full creative vehicle for the writer to accomplish the tasks necessary for successful production of various types of talk programs.

As noted in other chapters, the work of the writer still must precede the production of such programs since some degree of preparation, even if minimal, is needed to ensure the success of each broadcast. The nature of talk programs usually requires that the writer, who works with the script on the air, perform the largest share of his or her task orally and spontaneously as the program progresses, rather than in a formal, fully scripted manner.

This chapter considers the major types of talk programs related to the work of the broadcast writer—interviews, news panel programs, and discussions. For each type of talk program situation, there will be a description of the nature of such broadcasts and the kinds of preparations involving the writer plus suggestions for the writer to use when approaching such assignments. Although the writing techniques required are minimal, it is important to master such techniques because talk programs are a staple in the broadcasting industry.

INTERVIEWS

Each of us does several interviews every day. We ask questions to find out information, to determine feelings, to get reactions, to solicit comments. It is a basic part of our everyday human communication pattern and routine.

In a similar way, interviews constitute a basic element or part of many types of broadcast programs—feature programs, music and variety shows, live sports broadcasts, game shows (when contestants are interviewed on the air by the host), documentaries, and investigative reports. While interviews may constitute the entire program, often they are used as part of a larger program format or concept. The importance of this basic programming form cannot be overemphasized. For the writer, a firm grasp of the principles and techniques of preparing effective broadcast interviews will pay dividends when other types of broadcast programs are developed.

Types

There are three primary types of interviews commonly used in broadcasting. Precise delineation of each type is difficult since there are obvious similarities among the three. Nevertheless, knowing the primary types of interviews will help determine the principal purpose or function of each interview situation and, thus, the nature of the script needed.

The *information interview* focuses on factual material. No opinions are expressed overtly, and no attempt is made to delve into the personality of the person being interviewed. Broadcast news reporters as well as public service, civic, and institutional organizations use the information interview extensively.

The *opinion interview* centers upon the ideas and beliefs of an individual. While information or background on a topic or subject is provided during the interviews, the primary purpose of such interviews is to obtain specific viewpoints, beliefs, and opinions. Such interviews may consist of man-on-the-street comments on a particular contemporary issue or topic, audience phone-in or write-in responses to editorials or programs or simply interviews with individuals on controversial issues in which opinions are expressed.

The *personality interview* features a public figure or well-known celebrity in a human interest situation. The interview subject or guest often is selected because of past events or activities, recent developments involving this individual, or simply because of the position this guest currently holds in the public eye. Motion picture stars, television personalities, sports figures, artists, and comedians are some of the groups which fit this category best. The interviewer in this situation must be flexible and sensitive in approaching the guest and in discussing topics. Also, the interviewer must carefully adjust language and delivery style to complement the background and temperament of the guest.

Approaches

Whether you are preparing an information interview, an opinion interview, a personality interview, or some combination of the three, there are essentially five methods, systems, or ways of approaching the task. Each approach is isolated for the purpose of description; however, each can be combined with another approach to prepare a particular broadcast interview.

Several factors determine the approach or method the writer uses to prepare a broadcast interview:

•the individual style of the interviewer
•the comfort and wishes of the guest(s)
•the time available for preparation of the interview
•the nature of the topic or guest(s)
•(at times) the interview policies of the individual station or network. Some broadcasting outlets prefer spontaneous, unrehearsed interviews. Others prefer a more structured, predictable interview situation.

If at all possible, the writer should strive to prepare at least a show format (rundown sheet or routine sheet) if not a semi-script (introduction and closing to the interview, specific written questions and approximate timing for each interview segment) for each broadcast interview. The amount of preparation needed or desired and the result of such preparation efforts are influenced by the factors just listed.

Here are the five basic approaches used for broadcast interviews:

The *ad-lib method* involves virtually no preparation by either the interviewer or the interview guest. This can be a deadly approach, especially for an inexperienced interviewer. More than one interviewer has made a serious mistake in an interview because there was no time to meet with a guest and to discuss in advance the topics and issues featured in the interview.

A more desirable approach involves the preparation of an *outline of the topics or points* to be covered during the interview. The interviewer ad-libs or formulates questions from the outline as the interview progresses, while the guest ad-libs the responses.

A highly recommended approach entails *preparation of specific questions* as the interviewer expects them to be used in the interview. When combined with other elements of a show format or semi-script, the approach allows the interviewer to prepare material in a more precise manner, but still incorporate the elements of informality and spontaneity necessary for an effective broadcast interview.

Another approach is to *prepare specific questions and then brief the guest(s)* about the topics or areas to be discussed. Some interviewers show the questions to guests in advance, while others prefer only to indicate the general line of questioning prior to the actual interview. At such a briefing, the guest may prefer only to preview the topics; others prefer to make brief notes to use in answering some or all of the questions, especially questions which require a precise response. Once briefed, some guests may inform the interviewer of the general line or tone of responses. The danger of such a practice is that the guest will over-rehearse responses and not provide a spontaneous, informal response to the question when asked in the actual on-air interview. Such pre-interview comments by a guest may, however, help the interviewer to correlate prepared questions and to discover other pertinent topics which could be included in the interview.

The *full-script approach* usually results in what often is referred to as a "canned" interview. That is, the interview, when broadcast, usually sounds or looks artificial and preplanned and lacks spontaneity and liveliness. When using this approach, the writer prepares a complete script (introduction to the interview topic and guest(s), specific questions, word-for-word responses for each guest, transitions between topic areas or guests and the formal conclusion to the interview). The full-script approach is *not* recommended for effective broadcast interviews.

Preparations

First, *obtain as much information as possible* about the topics to be discussed and the guest(s) to be interviewed. This may require detailed and exhaustive research in the local library, examination of old newspapers or broadcast newscasts, or conversations with the guest's friends and acquaintances. See chapter 1 for a discussion of basic research techniques for the broadcast writer to apply to interview situations.

Next, *sift the accumulated information* so that only the most important topics or issues remain. Keep in mind the approximate length of the interview so that a sufficient amount of interesting information is available. As you sift through the information compiled, keep two important questions constantly in mind:

1. *What questions would the audience want to ask or be most apt to ask if given the opportunity to talk to this guest?*
2. *How can I create a desire for information on the part of the audience?* How can I motivate them to want to know more? Select only the most important, potentially interesting and significant information which will have a direct impact upon the audience—emotions, beliefs, lifestyle, and pocketbook.

Finally, *prepare for the interview* using one or a combination of the approaches already described. Organize the interview using one of several schemes: by geographical location (north, south, east, and west or uptown, downtown or national, regional, statewide, and local or any other similar pattern); by chronology of events (before, during, and after or past, present, and future, etc.); by divisions of the subject matter (problem, solutions, results or background of the issue, personalities involved, issues, prospects for the future, etc.); or by divisions of the audience (men, women, and children or elementary, junior high, and high school students, etc.).

The important thing to remember is to make your planning for an interview orderly and systematic to produce an effective broadcast interview presented in an easy-to-follow, recognizable pattern. Strive to have the interview planned and organized for the benefit of the interviewer and the interview guest as well as the audience. Systematically explore issues, problems, and topics of interest. A systematic approach to broadcast interviews will make your work as a writer more efficient and will enable the interview to look and sound more professional when finally broadcast.

Guidelines and Suggestions

Virtually an unlimited list of recommendations can be made to better prepare for and to interact in a broadcast interview. Essential recommendations have been included to reflect the primary concerns of the writer and interviewer:

1. *Select the topic carefully.* If you are responsible for selecting the interview topic, be certain the subject is important enough to interest the audience. You should feel comfortable about the selection and potential development of the topic. You should not feel embarrassed to discuss a sensitive or potentially controversial topic.
2. *Know as much as possible about the topic.* Become an informed surrogate member of the audience. The more background and information you have available, the better the interview questions that can be formulated.

3. *Limit the topic.* It is better to cover a few items well than many items poorly. Expand or contract the subject to match the time available for the interview. Focus only on key areas to better guide the audience in connecting ideas and absorbing information or opinions.
4. *Establish and reinforce the importance of the topic.* This must be done early in the interview and at appropriate junctures throughout the dialogue. Give the audience reasons for listening or viewing.
5. *Formulate developmental questions.* Devise questions which bring out the crux of the situation or issue and which point up the guest's information or opinions about the history of the problem, the people involved, current procedures, and proposed solutions.
6. *Pace the exposition of the topic.* Prepare background questions to familiarize the audience with the scope, nature, importance, and direction of the topic. Formulate a "break" question which will be the high point of the interview, the culmination of responses up to that point. This should be planned in advance, even if a better break question turns up in the course of the interview. Then the interviewer has the choice of using either break question. It is best to build up to the explosive and controversial question (if this is to be used) than to ask this important question at the beginning of the interview and then have nothing worthwhile or interesting for the audience for the rest of the dialogue. On occasion, the break question may be asked at the beginning of the interview for dramatic effect or for shock value.

NEWS PANEL PROGRAMS

A special type of interview situation is the news panel program. The producers of such programs invite a current prominent newsmaker to be questioned by a panel of newspeople drawn from the station's or network's news staff and from newspapers and the news wire services. The panelists question the guest on current topics, issues, problems, and concerns of direct interest to and under the jurisdiction of the guest. The newsmaker questioned by the panelists may be from government, labor, business, the arts, the sciences, or any number of fields.

Prominent examples of network news panel programs include CBS's *Face the Nation*, portions of ABC's *This Week with David Brinkley* and NBC's *Meet the Press*. Figure 8-1 is the semi-script prepared for the production of one program in the *Meet the Press* series. Notice the precision with which this 30-minute Sunday program series is scripted. The script is prepared for the broadcast to begin at 30 minutes after the hour and to conclude at the beginning of the next hour. Specific camera shots are noted. The opening, closing, and transitions into and out of each major segment are fully scripted. Backtiming cues are noted for the last 3 minutes of the main portion of the program to provide a smooth transition to the final segment of the broadcast. The last segment of the program (from 56:30 to 58:24) is fully scripted. Notice the use of a voice-over promotional announcement at 57:50 to entice viewers to watch the next day's *Today* program. The *Meet the Press* script is an excellent example of the written preparation needed to produce a successful news panel program series.

Approaches and Preparations

The format for news panel programs usually is simple and direct. Generally, the format consists of an opening question, introduction of the guest and panelists by the moderator (who may or may not participate in the questioning), a continuation of questioning, intermittent commercials or public service announcements, and a brief summary by the moderator or a final comment by the guest.

The general approach used to prepare most news panel programs is rather conservative. A subdued setting and straightforward format allow the audience to concentrate on the guest's comments and the issues raised by the panelists' questions.

For a news panel program, the writer may serve as the producer or moderator. Producing such a program involves selecting panelists and arranging for interesting guests who are in the news. The writer/producer must also gather and organize research material related to the guest(s)—interests, activities, previous comments and positions, current issues, and so on.

DISCUSSION PROGRAMS

Broadcast discussion programs allow for the purposeful, systematic, and oral exchange of ideas, facts, and opinions by a group of individuals. Such programs follow a variety of patterns in their structure and presentation to fulfill the overall objective of a discussion or interchange between individuals.

Types/Formats

Each type of broadcast discussion program sustains the overall objective just described, but permits the ideas, information, and opinions to be presented or expressed in a slightly different way. Each type is a legitimate broadcast talk program format.

Panel Discussion. In a panel, or round-table, discussion, a small group of participants provides expert analysis of a problem or issue for the benefit of the audience. The participants, who should represent various backgrounds and perspectives appropriate to the topic(s) under discussion, should engage in open, informal interplay. A specific solution to the problem or issue does not necessarily have to be presented. The moderator may summarize the position(s) taken by each participant at the end of the discussion.

Group Discussion. In a group discussion, participants attempt to solve a problem or reach a conclusion about an issue by objectively and cooperatively examining all

VIDEO	AUDIO
C__1__: CU Monroe Zoom out to two shot	Monroe: This is Bill Monroe inviting you to Meet The Press with -- Jeane Kirkpatrick, U.S. Ambassador to the United Nations.
C__2__: Wide shot of set Chiron: Meet The Press (KEY)	ANNCR: MEET THE PRESS, THE WORLD'S OLDEST NETWORK TELEVISION PROGRAM IS A PUBLIC AFFAIRS PRESENTA-TION OF NBC NEWS.
VT: Open Billboard ADM	SILENT VT.......ANNCR V/O....... :10 sec. ANNCR: MEET THE PRESS IS SPONSORED BY ADM. USING AMERICA'S ABUNDANCE TO FILL THE WORLD'S NEEDS. TO BLACK
VT: ADM QADM-0698	Sound on tape.................:60 sec. TO BLACK
C__2__: CU Monroe	Monroe: Our guest today on Meet The Press is the
C__1__: MCU Guest Zoom into CU	United States Ambassador to the United Nations, Jeane Kirkpatrick. A former political science professor at Georgetown University, she is a specialist in

Figure 8-1 Director's script prepared for a *Meet the Press* broadcast. *(Courtesy of NBC Television)*

		Latin American politics and author of numerous books on foreign policy, including a book on Argentina.
C 2 :	CU Monroe	Monroe: Meet The Press returns today to its original format, with moderator distinct from the panel, which will enable us, among other things, to include more newspaper panelists. Marvin Kalb is on assignment. Our reporters today are:
C 3 :	CU Delaney/PAN CU Nelson/PAN CU Geyer/PAN CU McLaughlin	Steve Delaney of NBC News, Lars-Erik Nelson of the New York Daily News, Georgie Anne Geyer of the Universal Syndicate and, to open the questioning, Bill McLaughlin of NBC News.
	CU McLaughlin	(McLaughlin opens questioning)
C 2 :	Two Shot Zoom out to Wide over/shoulder	Thank you, Ambassador. We'll be back with more . . . . questions for Ambassador Kirkpatrick.
		TO BLACK
VT:	United Technology UGTC-6126	Sound on tape......................1:00
		TO BLACK
C 2 :	Two shot	Monroe: Meet The Press continues with Georgie Anne

Fig. 8-1 *(Continued)*

		Geyer questioning Ambassador Kirkpatrick.
C <u>3</u> :	CU Geyer	(Geyer continues questioning)

MAIN PORTION OF PROGRAM

3:00.....52:20	:30.....54:50
2:00.....53:20	:15.....55:05
1:00.....54:20	

CUT AT 55:20

AT 55:20

C <u>1</u> :	Two Shot	Monroe: (I'm sorry to inter- rupt but our time is up). Thank you, Ambassador, for being with us today on Meet The Press.
	Zoom out to wide over/shoulder	I'll be back in a minute.............. with a look at letters.

AT 55:30 TO BLACK

VT:	ADM QADM-0668	Sound on tape......................1:00

AT 56:30 TO BLACK

C <u>1</u> :	CU Monroe	Monroe: Commenting on last week's program,
C <u>3</u> :	MTP Sign (out of focus)	Bettie Campbell writes from New
Chiron:	Name #1 (KEY)	Mexico, "Secretary (of the Treasury)
Chiron	Name & Quote #1A (KEY)	Regan should forgo a saucer of cream occasionally and learn how those of us among the ten-plus million unemployed.....are subsisting on skim milk.....Not so

Fig. 8-1 *(Continued)*

Chiron:	Name & Quote #1B (KEY)	many of us are pro-Reaganomics as he is counting on.''
Chiron: Chiron:	Name #2 (KEY) Name & Quote #2A (KEY)	Justine Walker writes from Illinois, ''How long does it take for Congress and Tip O'Neill to get the American people's message -- that we back President Reagan's budget and want to get on with it.''

AT 57:00

C__3__:	MTP Sign (out of focus)	Monroe: The special address to write to, if you would like to comment on today's program is: Meet The Press, NBC, Washington, D.C. 20016. (We cannot answer all the postcards and letters, but we do read them all).
Chiron:	MTP address (KEY)	

AT 57:10

Chiron:	Transcripts (KEY) 50 cents Stamped envelope	ANNCR: FOR A PRINTED TRANSCRIPT OF MEET THE PRESS, SEND 50 CENTS...AND A STAMPED SELF-ADDRESSED ENVELOPE TO .....KELLY PRESS, BOX 8648, WASHINGTON, D.C. 20011.
Chiron:	Kelly Press Address (KEY)	

AT 57:25

C__1__:	CU Monroe	Monroe: Next Sunday on Meet The Press another headline figure in the news will be our guest. Now, this is Bill Monroe, saying goodbye
C__2__:	Wide shot of set	for Ambassador Jeane Kirkpatrick and Meet The Press.

Fig. 8-1   *(Continued)*

LIGHTS

AT 57:40

VT: Close Billboard   SILENT VT.......ANNCR V/O.......
             ADM   :10 sec.

ANNCR: MEET THE PRESS HAS
BEEN SPONSORED BY ADM.
USING AMERICA'S ABUNDANCE
TO FILL THE WORLD'S NEEDS.

AT 57:50

C 2 :   Wide shot of set   ANNCR: TOMORROW MORNING
                                      ON "TODAY", CHRIS WALLACE
Chiron: Credit Crawl (KEY)   REPORTS FROM ROME AS
                                      PRESIDENT REAGAN MEETS
                                      WITH THE POPE.....ALSO ACTOR
                                      JOHN SHEA FROM THE MOVIE
                                      "MISSING".....AND CONTINUED
                                      COVERAGE OF THE FALKLAND
                                      ISLAND CRISIS. THIS IS MAURY
                                      HIGDON.

AT 58:10

VT: NBC News Logo   Sound on tape..........in BG..........

ANNCR: MEET THE PRESS
HAS BEEN A PUBLIC AFFAIRS
PRESENTATION OF NBC NEWS
AND HAS COME TO YOU LIVE
FROM OUR STUDIOS IN
WASHINGTON, D.C.

AT 58:24 TO BLACK

CLOSING IN FROM NEW YORK

Fig. 8-1 *(Continued)*

facets of the situation, and then forming a consensus. This type of discussion program shares some of the characteristics of the panel discussion format. It is important that each participant share available information and opinion and that the discussion be approached without preconceived notions. The group must reach a collective decision by defining and limiting the problem or issue to be discussed, determining the causes of the situation, reviewing available solutions, and then selecting a solution or course of action to follow.

Symposium. Just as in the panel discussion, a small group of participants in a symposium presents expert analysis of a policy, process, problem, or issue. The presentational framework differs from a panel discussion, however. In a symposium, each participant delivers a reasonably short prepared speech without interruption. Each speech explains a particular viewpoint, explores one aspect of the problem or issue, or offers an individual approach or solution to a complex problem. Speakers follow each other in turn until all participants have been heard. Usually, the same amount of time is provided to each speaker. The moderator simply introduces the topic of discussion, introduces each participant, and then closes the symposium at the conclusion of the last speech.

Forum. A forum consists of general audience participation usually after some type of presentation has been made (e.g., panel or group discussion, symposium or debate) except that the audience may participate in the discussion from the very beginning. Thus, forum can be attached to other discussion program designations to indicate that the audience participates in some way. The choice of when and how the forum portion of the program will be integrated into the discussion rests with the program producer and the moderator.

Debate. Two distinctly opposite points of view should be obvious in a debate. The debate could be between candidates for public office or proponents and opponents of a particular policy, process, problem, or issue. Usually, the moderator briefly introduces the topic(s) for debate and the participants and may summarize the principal points made by each side at the conclusion of the debate. Each side presents an initial prepared argument or point of view. Then, each side gets an opportunity to rebut or argue against the opponent. Finally, each side usually is provided an opportunity to make a final statement in which the main arguments are highlighted for the audience.

Combinations. It is often appropriate to combine the different types of discussion programs to produce a more lively and flexible program format. A forum, perhaps the easiest format to integrate with others, usually enlivens the discussion by including input from the audience. The audience may contribute to the discussion directly in the studio, or through the moderator, or perhaps via telephone lines from a remote location. Another combination format would be a symposium–group discussion in which the standard symposium portion of the program is followed by interaction between the symposium participants in an effort to arrive at a solution collectively. Other combinations are possible. The topic(s), the type of participants, the setting for the discussion, the length of the program, and the kind of interaction desired should govern the design of a combination discussion format.

KETV Television of Omaha, Nebraska, developed an interesting combination discussion program format in 1982. 7TV sought to create a weekly 30-minute program in which community people would actually take part in the direction of the show. The result was *Sunday Friends*. After an intensive search, 7TV selected three people from the community (with no prior television experience) to host the program series. Their disparate backgrounds, careers, and family situations gave each a different perspective on a variety of personal and social issues. Topics discussed on *Sunday Friends* have included: sexual harassment, teen contraceptive regulations, nuclear freeze, the

SUNDAY FRIENDS

Taping Date ___June 16, 1982___

Air Date ___July 18, 1982___

Topic ___Incest___

Angles: (1) ___Establish problem and numbers affected___

(2) ___Focus on appropriate treatment. Do we deal with incest___

(3) ___as a crime? an illness? a family problem? what works?___

Guest: ___Helen Swan - Clinical Director of Johnson County (Kansas)___

Affiliation & Angles ___Child Sexual Abuse Treatment Program___

___Her program is a positive, diversionary one.___

Audience: Person   Affiliation & Angles

(1) ___Husband and Wife___   ___Incest Family___

(2) ___Janet Gilfoyle___ } ___Group Therapist with___

(3) ___Jim Poppert___   } ___Parents United___

Figure 8-2 An information sheet prepared for one program in the *Sunday Friends* series. *(Courtesy of KETV Television, Inc., and the Pulitzer Broadcast Group)*

insanity defense plea, non-payment of child support, treatment of Israel by the media, and restriction of farm land ownership.

The format of *Sunday Friends* permits the hosts to express their opinions on the weekly issue (a privilege not afforded most television discussion program moderators). The program begins with a brief (five-minute) outline of the topic or issue by the hosts. After a commercial break, a guest expert answers the hosts' questions and challenges their viewpoints for approximately five minutes. Another commercial break precedes the final and longest program segment, comments and questions from a preselected studio audience. The result is a stimulating free-for-all exchange of views.

To provide some focus and direction for the discussion and yet not encumber on the hosts the task of formal script preparation, an information sheet is prepared for

(4) Melissa Rau — Douglas Cty. Juvenile Probation officer

(5) Mary Mitchel — Cat & Mouse! A program for the Prevention of Sexual Abuse at North Omaha Girls Club

(6) Pam Curry — Child Protective Services worker, Sarpy Cty.

(7) Phyllis Wachler — " , Douglas Cty.

(8) Julie Mallory — Therapist at Nebr. Psychiatric Institute

(9) Sue Oakes — Therapist, Parents United

Tentative   (10) Police Investigator and/or County Attorney

Notes & Special Instructions:

In the past, treatment has been punitive, ie. father (offender) is prosecuted, family is separated. Many Therapists now are working for a system in which courts refer offenders and families to counselling and support groups like Parents United. They strive to keep families together. In 95% of Incest cases, Therapists say offenders are not sexual deviants, but part of a "family dysfunction." They are different from child molesters. A "positive" program brings more people forward.

Parents United groups now exist in Douglas and Sarpy Counties; Lincoln trying to form one. They get referrals from the courts WHAT DO YOU THINK?

Fig. 8-2   *(Continued)*

each program in the *Sunday Friends* series. Each sheet itemizes the topic and angles or approaches to be used, the scheduled guest expert, suggestions for selecting the studio audience together with affiliations and backgrounds related to the topic, and brief notes about the parameters of the topic and potential areas for discussion. Figure 8-2 shows the information sheet prepared in advance for the program on incest.

Approaches

In most cases, for the types of discussion programs described, it is best to prepare at least an outline of the topic areas if not a structured show format (rundown or routine sheet) or semi-script. Such programs could be produced live or recorded for later broadcast on radio or television. The writing and production approach should reflect the kind of interaction, informality, and spontaneity desired in the program. Generally, the more informality and spontaneity desired, the less structured the script and program format should be.

Preparations

The same kinds of preparations outlined for the broadcast interview and news panel program should be followed by the discussion program participants. Background on the topic must be compiled and organized. An outline should be prepared. Then, depending upon the specific discussion program format used, each must prepare to participate based on the parameters established by that format. For example, participation in a debate will require a different kind and level of preparation than that used in a group discussion or symposium-forum.

CONCLUSION

Although the amount of formal scripting required for the production of talk programs is limited, it is important for the writer to understand the types of talk programs constantly used by broadcast outlets and to use specific kinds of techniques to generate the necessary script material. If appropriate script material is prepared for such programs, it will assist production and on-air personnel who continually strive for a smooth, organized, and interesting talk program presentation. The writer must know the needs of the program before effective script material can be written.

SUGGESTED EXERCISES AND PROJECTS

1. Prepare a list of five significant contemporary subjects which would stimulate local audience interest when featured in an interview or discussion program broadcast on a local or area radio or television station. Explain briefly why each subject or topic would be interesting to the broadcast audience.

2. Prepare a radio or television semi-script for an eight-minute information interview with a guest of local, area, or national importance. The introduction and closing to the interview must be fully scripted and should serve to highlight the guest's background as well as the importance of the topics to be discussed. All questions must be written in full and should anticipate the development and progression of the broadcast interview. If possible, record and then critique the interview.

3. Follow the directions given in exercise 2, but for an opinion interview.

4. Follow the directions given in exercise 2, but for a personality interview.

5. Select one person to interview. Prepare a show format (rundown or routine sheet) for a 5-minute information interview with this individual. The interview could be for either radio or television. Then, using the same guest, prepare separate show formats for an opinion interview and a personality interview. If possible, record and then critique one of the interviews.

6. Monitor (and if possible record) a network radio or television interview. Comment upon the effectiveness of the interview: selection and development of the topics discussed; completeness and accuracy of the information presented; the interviewer's opening, closing, transitions, and comments; the effectiveness of the questions asked; the organization of the interview; other favorable and unfavorable comments about the interview; and suggestions for improvement.

7. Monitor and, if possible, record a network radio or television news panel program. Comment upon the effectiveness of the program: selection of the guest and the panelists; format of the program; selection and development of the topics discussed; effectiveness of the questions asked; other favorable and unfavorable comments about the program; and suggestions for improvement.

8. Prepare a semi-script for a local 30-minute television news panel program. The guest is the mayor of your city. Identify four local and area news reporters who, realistically, could be the panelists. Create a name for the program. Provide a full-script for the: introduction to the program (introducing the guest, panelists, and topics to be discussed if appropriate), closing to the program, and transitions to and from two 1-minute commercial breaks inside the program. Provide approximate timing cues for each significant program segment. Use the *Meet the Press* script included in this chapter as a model.

9. Select one of the following types of discussion programs: panel discussion, group discussion, symposium or debate (between candidates for a national political office). Select a topic suggested in exercise 1. Prepare a show format (rundown or routine sheet) for a local 30-minute radio or television discussion program of the type selected.

ADDITIONAL READING

Brady, John. *The Craft of Interviewing*. Cincinnati: Writer's Digest, 1976.

Broughton, Irv. *The Art of Interviewing for Television, Radio and Film*. Blue Ridge Summit, Pa.: TAB Books, 1981.

Cavett, Dick, and Porterfield, Christopher. *Cavett.* New York: Harcourt Brace Jovanovich, 1974.

Downs, Cal W. *Professional Interviewing.* New York: Harper & Row, 1980.

Hilton, Jack, and Knoblauch, Mary. *Oh Television! A Survival Guide for Media Interviewers.* New York: Amacum, 1981.

Keirstead, Phillip O. *Modern Public Affairs Programming.* Blue Ridge Summit, Pa.: TAB Books, 1979.

King, Larry, with Yoffe, Emily. *Larry King by Larry King.* New York: Simon and Schuster, 1982.

Walters, Barbara. *How to Talk with Practically Anybody About Practically Anything.* Garden City, N.Y.: Doubleday and Co., 1970.

With the Nation Watching: Report of the Twentieth Century Fund Task Force on Televised Presidential Debates. Lexington, Mass.: Lexington Books, 1979.

Chapter Nine

MUSIC AND VARIETY PROGRAMS

One chapter covers both music and variety programs because each requires similar considerations and uses approximately the same type of script. Also, various elements of both these types of programs often are integrated into a composite program or series. For example, variety programs often include musical segments. Music programs need to display the same qualities of pacing, unity, and variety necessary for a successful variety program.

For each type of program, this chapter will present the following information: an overview and current perspectives; the role and function of the writer; the process and techniques recommended for preparing such material; and examples of scripting techniques. From this discussion it is hoped the writer will obtain sufficient insight into the skills necessary to accomplish such writing tasks.

MUSIC PROGRAMS

Overview

Music is the basis for much of the programming seen and heard on television and radio. It can be combined with other program elements in variety shows. It can be used to convey certain kinds of moods and meanings in commercials and announcements as well as in documentaries, dramas, and game shows. It is the primary component in a program showcasing musical talent. For the writer, the ability to work effectively with music becomes almost as important as the ability to communicate meanings, ideas, information, and feelings through words.

Music has become a primary ingredient which often determines the success of a commercial radio station. In television, the number and quality of music program series and specials produced for syndication to local stations and for distribution on cable systems continue to increase. Music producers continue to show versatility and ingenuity by offering a music program product which meets and often anticipates the needs of the audience.

Music on Radio

Formats. Format is an important concept to understand when considering any radio station music programming. Essentially, it is the kind of programming offered by a station. A more complete definition of the term is the preplanned control of all elements in a station's presentation which develops the consistency necessary for that station to exist effectively in a competitive climate.

A special label is attached to a music format by the radio station's management team to focus the projected image of the station and to pull together specific ingredients to help mold and shape that image and to instill it in the mind of the listener. Listeners also have attached a label to each radio station's programming efforts. Ideally, both the format designation of the station and the format label assigned by the listening audience are the same. Often, they are not. It is important for everyone involved with the station, including writers, to know the intended as well as the perceived format of the station.

Role of the Writer. On a radio music program, an announcer or D.J. ad-libs most of the comments made between music selections. The announcer becomes an "oral writer," creating material spontaneously. Scripting becomes more formalized and extensive when special effects, gimmicks, prerecorded dialogue, or humor is used or when an engineer operates the equipment for the announcer and it becomes necessary to provide some kind of script material to avoid confusion.

Some degree of preparation is necessary to ensure the success of any program; however, most radio music formats require minimal preparation. The announcer selects or is given the music to be played based on the format and offers comments, as appropriate, on the recording artist, the music, upcoming station programs and activities, and very frequently simply provides the time and temperature. Even nationally syndicated program music services usually do not prepare fully scripted material for the many formats distributed. They employ knowledgeable announcers who provide appropriate extemporaneous comments about the music as the program is recorded for distribution. Stations receive only a rundown or cue sheet for the music contained on each tape.

Preparing Radio Music Programs. It should not be inferred that formal script preparation is not necessary for music programs. Each broadcast requires, if not a written, then certainly a firm mental rundown sheet. A semi-script or even a full-script may be appropriate for such programs as a musical year-in-review or a special broadcast which highlights the musical progression of a particular musical era, recording artist, or composer. In these circumstances, precise information and timing are important. This precision can best be achieved through formal script preparation.

For *any* radio music program it is necessary to

•plan the musical selections
•check the music clearances (ASCAP and BMI uses)
•note the timing of each selection
•prepare for emergencies
•follow the format consistently

When *preparing contemporary music programs,* consider these recommendations:

1. Select music which is appropriate for the format and which consistently reinforces a specific, predetermined image.
2. Know the music by keeping abreast of current developments through the music trade press.
3. Know the available music library, its contents, and cataloguing system.
4. Be aware of scheduled breaks for announcements, station ID's, and other programs (e.g., newscasts).
5. Pace the program by controlling the general intensity of the music—tempo, lyrics, groups featured, etc.—and by providing a smooth continuity of sound.
6. Remember the audience. Analyze the potential target audience. Take them seriously. They take you and the music seriously. It is an important part of their musical lifestyle.
7. Match the language used to the type of program prepared.
8. Keep it simple. Provide only the essential facts. Make "information with a purpose" your watchword.

All of the suggestions for preparing contemporary music formats apply to some degree to several of the other standard radio music formats.

Additional suggestions should be considered when preparing jazz and classical music programs since often these types of music shows require more extensive scripting preparations:

1. Know the music thoroughly. Regular listeners for these kinds of programs expect intelligent and informed comments and musical interpretations since often they are very familiar with the music already. This audience is unforgiving when, for example, in an introduction to a musical selection, an important fact is omitted or a prominent composer's name is mispronounced.
2. Use standard music reference works. Assemble your own personal music literature library.
3. Read the back of album jackets. Often, valuable and interesting information is provided.

4. Provide comments and biographical information about the composer. Also, be sure to include a pronunciation guide for difficult-to-pronounce names.
5. Provide information about the musical composition (anecdotes, the historical circumstances surrounding the music, other musical developments during the same period, analysis of the construction of the composition, etc.).
6. Provide comments about the performer(s) (background, previous recordings, repertoire, etc.)
7. Prepare brief "filler" material to accommodate time requirements and equipment difficulties (if the program is broadcast "live").

To better illustrate the process and many of the principles and techniques used to prepare a radio music program, let us examine a year-in-review country music special produced by Kenny Bosak for William B. Tanner, Inc. During the year, as particular country music selections gain popularity and show increases in sales, Bosak writes rough draft or "unpositioned" script fragments for each music selection. Although he knows these fragments will have to be rewritten for content and length and then fused with other program elements when the eight-hour show is produced later in the year, Bosak has found that by writing these fragments early instead of waiting until the crunch of final production he can weave into his introduction of each selection interesting and pertinent background material gathered from music trade publications as well as his own rich country music background. Figure 9-1 is an example of such an "unpositioned" script fragment. Notice how he provides the name of the recording artists and the music selection only after the background information is given. This technique encourages the listener to participate in the program by trying to determine who is being introduced before the name is supplied.

When it comes time to assemble the final year-in-review program, all of the "unpositioned" script fragments are reviewed and adjustments made as necessary in content and length. But to make these adjustments it is necessary to determine: the placement and length of all the music to be used, the amount of commercial matter to be inserted, the length of the opening and closing to the program, and the length and placement of musical jingles as well as introductions, interviews and program segment transitions. Figure 9-2 is the rewritten version of the unpositioned script fragment shown in figure 9-1. Notice how the previous program selection is identified before the next selection is introduced. This provides a smooth flow and continuity between musical selections. The hand-written notation "→1 :38" indicates the first recording of this copy by the narrator lasted 38 seconds and is the recording to be used in the final program. Years of experience at producing such year-in-review programs show through when one notices that very few changes were needed in the final version of this script fragment. It is obvious the writer knows the music well. Sentence length and vocabulary help establish the pace and create the intensity needed for the selection introduced. The copy is crisp, succinct, and in tune with the musical lifestyle of the potential target audience.

HAGGARD, MERLE & G. JONES "YESTERDAY'S WINE"

COUNTRY '82 SCRIPT   CUT #_____

NOW, HERE'S A DUET BY TWO PERFORMERS WHO AS SOLOISTS HAVE CAPTURED JUST ABOUT EVERY MAJOR AWARD THAT THE COUNTRY MUSIC INDUSTRY HAS TO OFFER. ONE HALF OF THIS SINGING TEAM WAS THE COUNTRY MUSIC ASSOCIATION'S MALE VOCALIST OF THE YEAR, AS WELL AS ENTERTAINER OF THE YEAR IN 19-70, WHILE THE OTHER HALF HAS NAILED DOWN THE MALE VOCALIST AWARD TWICE...IN 19-80 and 19-81. THE DUO IS, OF COURSE, MERLE HAGGARD AND GEORGE JONES. THIS YEAR, THEY COMBINED THEIR TALENTS FOR SONG NUMBER _____ IN OUR SHOW...HERE'S "YESTERDAY'S WINE."

Figure 9-1 Example of an "unpositioned" script fragment for a year-in-review country music special. *(Courtesy of Kenny Bosak, Producer,* Country '82)

COUNTRY '82 SCRIPT   CUT # 1/6

"WHEN YOU FALL IN LOVE" BY JOHNNY LEE, NUMBER 80 ON COUNTRY 82. NEXT IS A DUET BY TWO PERFORMERS WHO AS SOLOISTS HAVE CAPTURED JUST ABOUT EVERY MAJOR AWARD THAT THE COUNTRY MUSIC INDUSTRY HAS TO OFFER. ONE HALF OF THIS SINGING TEAM WAS THE COUNTRY MUSIC ASSOCIATION'S MALE VOCALIST OF THE YEAR, AS WELL AS ENTERTAINER OF THE YEAR IN 19-70, WHILE THE OTHER HALF HAS NAILED DOWN THE MALE VOCALIST AWARD TWICE...IN 19-80 and 19-81. THE DUO IS, OF COURSE, MERLE HAGGARD AND GEORGE JONES. THIS YEAR, THEY PUT THEIR TALENTS TOGETHER FOR THE NUMBER 79 SONG OF THE YEAR...HERE'S "YESTERDAY'S WINE."

⟶ 1:38

Figure 9-2 Rewritten version of the "unpositioned" script fragment shown in figure 9-1. *(Courtesy of Kenny Bosak, Producer,* Country '82)

Figure 9-3 is the final rundown sheet for the first three segments in the program. Segment, or "element," times are noted in the far right column. The running time for the program tape appears in the far left column. The script fragment examined earlier is used in segment 1/B, 8 minutes and 22 seconds after the first hour of the program begins. Notice how a musical jingle is used either side of each commercial insert to reestablish the name and theme of the program.

Music on Television

Music programming has been an integral part of public television programming since its inception. Local stations and the PBS network system have provided a wide range of dazzling music programs over the years for its diverse viewing audience.

Two of the longest running and most successful music programs seen on commercial television are Dick Clark's *American Bandstand* and *The Lawrence Welk Show.* Despite modest adjustments and concessions to contemporary music styles and more sophisticated television production techniques, both series have remained essentially the same in their viewer appeal. Each uses a proven formula which works consistently and with longevity.

There have been other television music series and occasional music specials offered by networks and syndicators, most featuring contemporary music. Some feature the talents of a single entertainer, while others showcase a number of stars. These programs, often combination music-and-variety programs, are traditionally seen during special holiday periods.

The amount and diversity of music available on cable systems and in the home video market continue to grow. Pay-television systems produce several music specials and limited series, most featuring rock and country music performers. So-called "music video" is now part of the music industry lexicon. Recording artists now incorporate video as well as audio conceptualizations into their plans for new recordings.

Generally, the writer's contribution to the preparation of music material for television is limited. The writer might be involved in the preparation of short musical introductions or transitions, a rundown sheet for the music featured in a broadcast, or a semi-script for an interview with a music performer. In many situations, the actual full musical score becomes the script used by production personnel with only minimal scripting added to provide some measure of continuity.

The principles and techniques presented earlier for radio music programs transfer with little modification to similar programs for television. The writer still must emphasize pacing, continuity, unity, and diversification in the selection, placement, and use of the music. The tastes and expectations of the audience remain a primary concern. The obvious difference between radio and television music programs is the visual presentation of the music.

If the writer becomes directly involved in the production of music presentations for television, then a different kind of contribution can be made. The intensity and fullness of the music can be visualized. The music can be enhanced by effective visualization and the visuals can display new dimensions because of the music. The

SCHEDULED START TIME	ACTUAL START TIME	ELEMENT	ELEMENT TIME

00:00		1/A
		COUNTRY '82 THEME AND OPENING OF
		    HOUR 1
		#82 WHATEVER/Statler Brothers
		INTERVIEW/Larry Gatlin
		#81 IN LIKE WITH EACH OTHER/
		    Larry Gatlin & The Gatlin Brothers Band
		COUNTRY '82 JINGLE
			6:52

6:52		COMMERCIAL INSERT	1:30

8:22		1/B
		COUNTRY '82 JINGLE
		#80 WHEN YOU FALL IN LOVE/Johnny
		    Lee
		#79 YESTERDAY'S WINE/Merle Haggard
		    & George Jones
		EXTRA: ALMOST PERSUADED/David Houston
		    (#1 of 1966)
		COUNTRY '82 JINGLE
			9:43

18:05		COMMERCIAL INSERT & COUNTRY '82 CUSTOM LOCAL ID	2:10
20:15		1/C COUNTRY '82 JINGLE INTERVIEW/Ed Bruce #78 LOVE'S FOUND YOU AND ME/Ed Bruce #77 HEY! BABY!/Anne Murray COUNTRY '82 JINGLE	7:03
27:18		COMMERCIAL INSERT	1:30

Figure 9-3 Final rundown sheet for the first three segments in the *Country '82* year-in-review country music special. *(Courtesy of Kenny Bosak, Producer,* Country '82*)*

music can be visually interpreted based upon the lyrics, a suggested locale or theme, or even the personality of the performer. The variety of interpretations is limited only by the imagintion. The full range of visual alternatives can be tapped and new dimensions offered by the use of such art forms as dance, pantomime, slides, films, videotapes, drawings, sketches, paintings, buildings, abstract representations, colors, and shapes.

VARIETY PROGRAMS

Overview

At one point in the development of radio and television programming, regular variety series were an industry staple. These shows featured music, dancing, and drama/comedy sketches often with well-known vaudeville and stage stars who brought their entertainment magic to the airwaves to delight millions across the country. Programs such as *The Ed Sullivan Show, Show of Shows, The Carol Burnett Show, The Jack Benny Show* and *The Hollywood Palace* (to mention only a few) for many years consistently filled the audience's need for entertainment. These kinds of shows were just plain fun to watch and often were used by young entertainers to sharpen their performing skills.

Today, variety program series are rare. Because of high production costs and a lack of general audience appeal, only networks, syndicators, and packagers (an individual or company which assembles the creative talent necessary for a production) now produce such programs. Variety shows tend to be produced as specials rather than as a series. These specials feature a theme or a celebrity. Hybrid variety program forms have evolved in which diversified elements are presented to attract and hold audience interest. The talk/variety program and magazine programs now fulfill many of the same audience needs once served by the more traditional variety program forms.

Categories

Besides the fact that a variety program can be produced either as a special or as part of a regular series, such shows can be categorized as:

• *Performer oriented.* Here the emphasis is on the performance of one or more entertainers. This emphasis could be displayed as a vaudeville or music hall show (e.g., *The Ed Sullivan Show* or *Hollywood Palace*); a solo performance by such talents as Barbra Streisand or Diana Ross or Loretta Lynn; or a program which features one main performer or regular cast of performers along with other special guests (e.g., Bob Hope's periodic NBC-TV specials, Christmas specials by the Osmond Family or Perry Como, *Saturday Night Live, The Carol Burnett Show,* and *Hee Haw).*
• *Theme oriented.* Here the subject or topic dominates rather than individual performers. These variety program specials have used such themes as patriotism (ABC-TV's *I Love*

Liberty which featured music, dances, speeches, and even dramatic readings to heighten a patriotic American spirit); holidays (numerous Christmas season programs as well as occasional programs for various other special events); nostalgia (ABC-TV's *Whatever Became of...* and limited specials which bring information about favorite stars up to date); and television (Dick Clark's popular limited program specials entitled *TV's Censored Bloopers* and *TV's Greatest Commercials*). A locale or setting could be used as a variety program theme. For example, the exotic environment of Hawaii could be featured or the plain, homespun people of the Tennessee mountains could be the backdrop and connecting link between program segments for a country music variety program.

Networks and syndicators have found the *talk/variety program* an attractive alternative to the traditional variety show format. Syndicated programs such as *The Merv Griffin Show* and *The Regis Philbin Show* (both winners of Emmy awards) as well as network entries such as *The Tonight Show Starring Johnny Carson* and *Late Night with David Letterman* offer viewers entertaining, often informative, conversation as well as guest appearances by singers, dancers, musicians, actors, athletes, authors, and specialty performers. Often, comedy sketches are featured. On some series, co-hosts share the spotlight with the featured talent and provide a sense of continuity for a limited set of programs. Talk/variety is a hybrid program form offering elements of comedy, music, and entertainment as well as conversations with interesting guests.

One of the dangers of placing all variety programs into a limited number of classifications is the implication that each type of program must be developed in isolation, with no attempt to blend creative elements into the finished program. Obviously, a variety show frequently emphasizes both performers and theme. For example, the Perry Como Christmas specials feature both performers and a Christmas theme in music, guests, and locales. In this situation, both performers and a theme blend into the fabric of the program. It should be noted too that music often serves as the basis for many variety programs.

Role of the Writer. Practically all variety programs are staff written. That is, established writers who have worked on similar programs in the past are contracted to write material with other writers sharing similar backgrounds. For a variety program series, a staff of six to ten writers generates the majority of the material for the entire series. The writers of a variety program special usually have worked with the program producer or packager on previous programs or series.

Generally, the writers inherit the program idea presented by the packager or producer as well as the general content and approximate length of each major program segment. Rarely does a staff writer help formulate the original program idea or even the general nature of most of the program segments.

The writers can function as program enhancers, however. Research may be needed for a particular segment. The specifics of each segment must be determined (e.g., the specific song to be sung, the length of the dance routine, the words and movements needed for an effective comedy sketch or monologue, how a guest will be introduced, etc.). Precise script material must be prepared for interviews as well as music and drama/comedy segments. Writers may suggest alternate segment ideas which may or may not be accepted. It is a unique writing environment since in most cases the individual writer must interact with and respond to the suggestions of other writers and offer individual insights but still conform to the consensus agreed upon for a successful program. This situation requires a strong, seasoned writer who has faced the turmoil and inevitable compromises inherent in this kind of program development.

Preparing Variety Program Material

Despite what may appear to be limitations placed on the writer in developing the idea or concept for the program, it is the writer who places the flesh on the bones of the variety program outline. Working with others, the writer contributes significantly to the success of the program by providing specific script material and ideas to make each program segment work. Several techniques and suggestions may help the writer accomplish this task:

1. *Know the audience.* It is important to know the target audience for the program. This is true not only for variety programs but also for any other form of communications, especially in the mass media. Once the audience is identified, the purpose or intent of the program also becomes clear. For a variety program, a wide and diverse audience is the goal with entertainment the ultimate objective. On the other hand, a variety program format could be used effectively to reach elementary school students, for example, with specific kinds of information from any number of subject areas.
2. *Know the available resources.* Aside from your own personal writing resources, you must know about the creative and production talent. As you write specific script material for the program, you should be aware of the range of talents and skills as well as preferences which have been expressed or implied by each major performer. On the production side, you ought to discover what is possible to produce and what is not. You might find that the personal preferences of key production personnel or the availability of the production facility or equipment will impose certain limitations.
3. *Work with the schedule.* Variety programs are produced under severely compressed time constraints. While some of the writer's work can be completed before production begins, it is during the grueling six to ten days of production that the writer's metal is tested. It is important to know the complete development and production schedule, but especially the writer's participation in that schedule to avoid unnecessary conflicts and a reduction in expectations by the writer or by the producer or packager. The more you work on this kind of program, the better you can evaluate the progress that is being made and the level and quality of your contributions.

4. *Stress teamwork.* Writing a variety program normally is not a solo effort. It is done within the pressure cooker environment of human interaction. There are disagreements, conflicts and, sometimes, constant bickering. But also there is the sense of accomplishment as several individuals pull together to create something which, by themselves, they could not have achieved. Variety program development, as well as most of television production, requires a concerted group effort to produce consistent, high-quality work.

5. *Build program unity.* Even if the variety program is destined to be performer oriented, a clear central theme must exist to connect and unify the various program segments. The unity expected in a variety program is not unlike that of a drama or comedy show. Each program segment must exhibit unity and excellence within itself. Each segment hinges on the effectiveness of the segment which precedes and follows it. Together, all of the segments provide a sense of unity for the audience and build to a final climactic segment, which features the principal performers in a dazzling display of technical quality and high entertainment value.

6. *Maintain program diversity.* Allow each segment to shine with its own special qualities and contribute to the general effect of the program. If the show is to be considered variety, it must exhibit some degree of contrast and diversification, but all with the ultimate goal of effectively joining together all of the program segments. The diversity or variety provided by each segment should fall into place under the unifying umbrella of the program idea or concept.

7. *Monitor continuity and pacing.* A key to the success of any program is conscious control over the continuity and pace of the show. The various program elements must flow and blend together in some way. Initially, continuity and pacing are established by the order, length, and content of each segment. For example, two comedy segments normally do not run back to back. The same would be true of musical or dance segments. Instead, these segments are mixed together, blended as it were, to provide a smooth, easy movement throughout the program. The writer can enhance the "flow" of the program by providing carefully written transitions between segments and appropriate introductions to guests and by working with others on the creative staff to drain as much as possible out of each performer and program segment. Without continuity and pacing, the program will appear disjointed. But when these two characteristics are displayed in the program, the creative staff, and more important, the audience, will attain a firm sense of organization and unity among program elements.

To better illustrate many of the principles and techniques used to prepare an effective variety program, let us examine the NBC-TV music/variety special entitled *Texaco Star Theatre...Opening Night.* This one and one-half hour salute to the American musical featured top celebrities from the stage, movies, and television. The columns on the two pages of the rundown sheet (fig. 9-4) indicate the consecutive numbering of each segment, the content of each segment along with the names of the performers, the original script page (in parentheses) where each segment begins, the length of each

"TEXACO STAR THEATRE...OPENING NIGHT"   REV   8/23/82
SHORT RUNDOWN

1. NBC SPECIAL PEACOCK PREEMPT	(1)	:10	:10
2. TEXACO STAR THEATRE LOGO ANIMATION	(2)	:30	:40
3. PARTY INVITATION (Anncr V/O) (Music Underscore)	(2A)	:08	:48
4. OPENING MEDLEY (Full Cast) (SC-1-37)	(3)	4:37	5:25
5. OPENING TITLES & GUEST BILLBOARDS (Anncr V/O) (SC-43)	(18)	:55	6:20
6. COMMERCIAL POSITION #1	(20)	1:02	7:22
7. PARTY INTRO (Into Broadway Baby) (Zsa Zsa Gabor, Donald O'Connor, Carol Burnett, Sammy Davis Jr., Loretta Swit, Bernadette Peters, ANNIE cast, Ann Jillian, John Schneider, Pam Dawber) (SC-38B-42)	(21)	1:10	8:32
8. BERNADETTE PETERS PERF. "Broadway Baby" (SC-43)	(26)	3:19	11:51
9. PARTY INTRO (Into Annie) (Zsa Zsa Gabor, Donald O'Connor) (SC-64)	(56)	:20	12:11
10. ANNIE SEGMENT (SC-65) a. "Tomorrow" (Annie) (:56) -------------------- b. "You're Never Fully Dressed" (Cast) (Lead-In :16) Song (2:17)	(57) (59)	3:41	15:53
11. COMMERCIAL POSITION #2	(38)	1:32	17:25
ANIMATED BUMPER	(39)	:03	17:28

Figure 9-4 Rundown sheet from the NBC-TV special *Texaco Star Theatre...Opening Night.* *(Courtesy of Pasetta Productions, Inc.)*

12. PARTY INTRO   (40)   :44   18:12
    (Into Oklahoma) (Robert Guillaume,
    Loretta Swit, Steve Allen, Debbie Allen,
    Charles Nelson Reilly) (SC-59)

13. JOHN SCHNEIDER/PAM DAUBER PERF.   (42)   5:38   23:50
    "Oklahoma Medley" (SC-60)
    ─────────────────────────
    a. "Oh, What a Beautiful Morning"
    (John Schneider) (1:50)
    ─────────────────────────
    b. "Many a New Day"   (44)
    (Pam Dawber) (1:06)
    ─────────────────────────
    c. "People Will Say We're in Love"   (46)
    (Pam, John) (1:34)
    ─────────────────────────
    d. "Oklahoma" (Ensemble) (1:01)   (48)

14. PARTY INTRO (Into Bewitched) (Steve   (51)   :32   24:22
    Allen, Charles Nelson Reilly) (SC-62)

15. LORETTA SWIT PERF.   (53)   2:40   26:59
    "Bewitched, Bothered & Bewildered"
    (SC-63)

16. PARTY INTRO   (30)   :30   27:32
    (Into Adelaide's Lament) (John Schneider,
    Ken Berry, Pam Dawber) (SC 46-47)

17. CAROL BURNETT PERF.   (32)   3:18   30:49
    "Adelaide's Lament" (SC-48)

18. ANIMATED BUMPER   (65)   :03   30:52

19. COMMERCIAL POSITION #3   (66)   1:02   31:54
    7 SEC. S.I.   (67)   :07   32:01

20. STATION BREAK   (68)   1:46   33:47
    7 SEC REJOIN   (69)   :07   33:54

21. PARTY INTRO (Into Diamonds) (Zsa Zsa   (70)   :18   34:12
    Gabor, Sammy Davis Jr.) (SC-44)

Fig. 9-4 *(Continued)*

segment, and the cumulative or program running time. This revised rundown sheet reflects the "as broadcast" program. Since program segments were recorded out of sequence, the page numbers are not consecutive.

This theme oriented variety special appeals to a wide cross section of the audience because of the way the music and performers are featured. The rich, diverse range of talent available is used well in the program. Notice how the musical party theme is reinforced throughout the show and used as the transition into single and group performances of music and comedy. The quality of each segment shines through and contributes to the overall effectiveness of the entire program. The structure of the program displays good contrast, diversification, continuity, and pacing. Notice how the emphasis continually shifts from group performances (segments 4, 10b, and 13) to individual spotlight segments (segments 8, 15, and 17), all connected by the party settings (segments 7, 9, 12, 14, 16, and 21) as well as animated "bumpers," or transitions. The various program segments flow and blend together well to present a strong, diversified but still unified presentation.

To show specific writing formats and techniques for two of the most common segments featured in this as well as most variety programs, let us examine the script pages for segments 12 and 13 from this same program (fig. 9-5). Segment 12 (PARTY INTRO) begins 18 minutes and 12 seconds into the program. Notice the use of a slightly modified three-camera scripting format described in chapter 3 to create a feeling of rehearsed spontaneity. The dialogue or patter is light and paced quickly in an effort to bridge easily and naturally into the upcoming Oklahoma medley. Segment 13 (original script pages 42 and 43) illustrates how a musical number in the show was written. Triple spacing and FULL CAPS are used for song lyrics. Talent directions are in FULL CAPS enclosed in parentheses. Sufficient space is provided for the director to note camera shots, singer/dancer movements, and technical changes.

CONCLUSION

This chapter has examined music and variety programs and the writer's work associated with each type of presentation. While the preparation of each kind of program calls for distinctive writing techniques, the writer can approach each of these writing opportunities with a similar set of concerns and interests: creatively selecting elements that enhance to the fullest each program segment but that still provide a unified presentation which blends creatively and coincides with the expectations of the audience; providing the variety, contrast, and diversification necessary to sustain audience interest and involvement and to control the pace and intensity of the presentation; making full use of available resources (talent, music, settings, etc.); and using simple, direct language and syntax to guide and hold audience attention throughout the program.

Music and variety programs offer still another opportunity for the writer to work

PARTY INTRO #7 "OKLAHOMA"
(Debbie Allen, Steve Allen,
Charles Nelson Reilly, Robert
Guillaume, Loretta Swit, Bartender)

PARTY INTRO #7 "OKLAHOMA"
(Debbie Allen, Steve Allen,
Charles Nelson Reilly,
Robert Guillaume, Loretta Swit)

(UP ON PIANO AREA, WE SEE DEBBIE ALLEN,
STEVE ALLEN, LORETTA SWIT, ROBERT GUILLAUME,
CHARLES NELSON REILLY)   SC-59

STEVE

Okay, guys. Check what I'll do.
Guess what song this is. I'll
give you five notes.

(HE PLAYS THE SAME NOTE 5 TIMES)

DEBBIE

I know what it is. I know.

STEVE

Ah huh.

DEBBIE

1937. Rodgers and Hart. "Babes
in Arms".

JOHNNY COULD ONLY SING ONE NOTE
AND THE NOTE HE SANG WAS THIS

(BEFORE DEBBIE CAN SING NEXT NOTE
STEVE INTERRUPTS HER)

STEVE

(SINGING)

WRONG!

Figure 9-5 Script pages from the NBC-TV special *Texaco Star Theatre…Opening Night. (Courtesy of Pasetta Productions, Inc.)*

DEBBIE

Your momma was wrong.

STEVE

Well, I guess so. Anyway, I'll tell
you what. Here's a little easier shot.
Six notes.

(HE PLAYS THE SAME NOTE 6 TIMES)

STEVE

(PLAYING AS HE SINGS)

CHICKS AND DUCKS AND GEESE
BETTER SCURRY

LORETTA

"Oklahoma".

ALL

(AD LIBS)

Oh, "Can I take you out in the
surrey with the fringe on top".

(INTO: JOHN SCHNEIDER/PAM DAWBER PERFORMANCE - "OKLAHOMA")

"OKLAHOMA" SEGMENT
"OH WHAT A BEAUTIFUL
MORNING"
(Pam Dawber, John Schneider)

"OKLAHOMA" SEGMENT
"OH WHAT A BEAUTIFUL
MORNING"
(Pam Dawber, John Schneider)

(UP UPON SHOW POSTER,
THEN DISSOLVE TO...)

SC. 60

Fig. 9-5 *(Continued)*

214

(JOHN SCHNEIDER ENTERS OPEN
PRAIRIE FIELD)

<u>ORCHESTRA INTRO 4 BARS</u>   (4)

JOHN

THERE'S A BRIGHT GOLDEN HAZE

ON THE MEADOW

THERE'S A BRIGHT GOLDEN HAZE

ON THE MEADOW

THE CORN IS AS HIGH

AS AN ELEPHANT'S EYE

AN' IT LOOKS LIKE

IT'S CLIMBIN' CLEAR UP

TO THE SKY...

OH, WHAT A BEAUTIFUL MORNIN'

OH WHAT A BEAUTIFUL DAY

I GOT A BEAUTIFUL FEELIN'

EV'RYTHIN'S GOIN' MY WAY

ALL THE CATTLE ARE STANDIN'

LIKE STATUES

ALL THE CATTLE ARE STANDIN'

LIKE STATUES

THEY DON'T TURN THEIR HEADS

AS THEY SEE ME RIDE BY

BUT A LITTLE BROWN MAV'RICK

IS WINKIN HER EYE

OH WHAT A BEAUTIFUL MORNIN'

OH WHAT A BEAUTIFUL DAY

Fig. 9-5 *(Continued)*

I GOT A BEAUTIFUL FEELIN'

EV'RYTHIN'S GOING MY WAY

OH

WHAT A

BEAUTIFUL

DAY

(INTO: "MANY A NEW DAY")

Fig. 9-5   *(Continued)*

---

cooperatively to prepare entertaining and, surprisingly, often informative material. Because of the different elements involved, the writer for such programs has to stretch, creatively and professionally. It is a challenging writing opportunity.

SUGGESTED EXERCISES AND PROJECTS

1. Select a popular music recording group. Write a full-script for a 30-minute radio or television program which features several of the group's recordings and which traces the musical style and development of this group.
2. Follow the steps outlined in exercise 1 but for a prominent composer or composer/performer.
3. Select a theme, motif, or special event for a 30-minute radio music program. Select music and write a full-script that will develop the theme, motif, or special event.
4. Write a full-script for a two-hour radio music program to be distributed nationally to local stations. The script must include specific information about the recorded music used (title and length of each selection, composer, performer, and record label). The program must feature one of the following types of music: rock, country, jazz, or classical.
5. Read one of the major articles or special feature stories in a current issue of one of the following publications: *Billboard, Cash Box, Radio & Records, Variety.* Provide a brief summary of the article.
6. For a special holiday or event (e.g., Christmas, New Year's, Valentine's Day, Easter, Fourth of July, Labor Day, seasons of the year, festivals, etc.) prepare a show format (rundown or routine sheet) for a 1-hour music or variety program for radio or television. Then, write a full-script for one segment of the program.

7. Assume that you have access to your choice of leading show business performers. Design a 1-hour television variety program. Write a show format (rundown or routine sheet) for the show. Provide a brief justification for your program design.
8. Follow the directions given in exercise 7, but work with other members of the group. Each member of the team concentrates on developing and writing the material for one segment of the program, but all participate in the overall planning. Each member could be assigned a specific job associated with the show (e.g., producer, director, talent coordinator, writing supervisor, music coordinator, comedy coordinator, technical adviser, etc.) but each must participate in some way in the writing of the program. An oral or written group presentation should be made and evaluated.
9. Monitor (and if possible record) a one-hour television network or syndicated variety program. Prepare a rundown sheet for the show. Then, critique the program using the writing techniques and suggestions contained in this chapter.

ADDITIONAL READING

Eastman, Susan Tyler, Head, Sidney W., and Klein, Lewis. *Broadcast/Cable Programming: Strategies and Practices*. 2d ed. Belmont, Calif.: Wadsworth, 1984.

Eberly, Philip K. *Music in the Air: America's Changing Taste in Popular Music 1920-1980*. New York: Hastings House, 1982.

Galanoy, Terry. *Tonight*. New York: Warner Paperback Library, 1974.

Hall, Claude, and Hall, Barbara. *This Business of Radio Programming*. New York: Billboard, 1977.

MacFarland, David R. *The Development of the Top 40 Radio Format*. New York: Arno Press, 1979.

Routt, Edd, and others. *The Radio Format Conundrum*. New York: Hastings House, 1978.

Shemel, Sidney, and Krasilovsky, M. William. *The Business of Music*. 4th ed. Lakewood, N.J.: Billboard Books, 1979.

Current broadcast industry information relating to radio and television music and variety programs is available in many of the periodicals and trade publications listed in Appendix B. Of particular interest are the following: *Billboard, Broadcasting, Cash Box, Radio & Records, Television/Radio Age,* and *Variety*.

Chapter Ten

SPECIALIZED FORMS OF
BROADCAST WRITING

Although each type of broadcast writing included in this chapter could be expanded into a separate chapter, it is felt that such depth is outside the scope of this book, which is only an introduction to the principal forms of writing for the broadcast media. The special skills necessary to write material for many types of programs will be acquired at a later stage in the writer's professional development. The information in this chapter, however, provides some insight into potential writing career specializations (discussed in chapter 12). The suggested readings at the end of this chapter provide detailed explanations and illustrations for many of these writing assignments.

The types of programs included in this chapter often interrelate and utilize similar preparation and scripting techniques and procedures. For illustrative purposes, however, each type of writing form has been isolated. A diverse group of script examples illustrates writing principles.

The specialized forms of broadcast writing examined in this chapter include: compilations, magazine programs, special events broadcasts, programs for special audiences, religious programs, children's programs, animation projects, and game shows. For each writing situation, the content and purpose of such programs will be examined, and specific writing techniques and suggestions will be offered.

COMPILATIONS

Compilation is the creative process of combining appropriate program elements to construct an effective, synergistic composite presentation. The broadcast writer functions as a creative compiler, pulling together various bits and pieces of material from numerous sources to write the finished script. Each part of the scripting puzzle is examined critically to determine what is known and what is still to be determined. Sometimes, the pieces fall easily into place. Often, composite pieces must be forged and meshed into the fabric of the script. This synergistic process should yield an enhanced combination of program elements resulting in a cohesive, balanced presentation offering a new perspective for the broadcast audience.

Compilation, a necessary organizational broadcast writing technique, is used in research, to gather material to write a script (see chapter 1) and in various kinds of writing projects. Most of the types of programs discussed in this chapter make use of compilation. In addition, compilation techniques are useful for commercials, interviews, music programs, documentaries and investigative reports, features, instructional programs, year-in-review, and "instant" news specials (i.e., same-day coverage of significant news events).

Approaches

The writer's approach to the compilation process is determined by the interaction of several variables:

* *The nature of the writing project.* Each writing assignment requires a different kind and level of compilation activity. Documentaries, for example, necessitate extensive research. Variety programs, on the other hand, entail minimal information compilation efforts.
* *The writer's depth and diversity of experience.* Steps which both save time and energy and produce more effective results become part of the work habits of a person who writes more and more scripts for different kinds of programs.
* *The number of writers/compilers involved.* A different level and type of compilation activity is required when a writer works alone on a script than when a team of writers works together.
* *The writing and production timetable.* The time available for compilation may be unlimited or restrictive. The time factor often determines the depth and extensiveness of compilation activity. Usually, writers complain that they never have enough time to gather material or to think through a complex or emotionally charged sequence. A professional writer's continuous quest for excellence produces the unsettling concern that detailed knowledge about the subject of a script is incomplete.
* *Budget constraints.* Meaningful compilation activity requires adequate time, money, and personnel. Sufficient funding should be provided to complete the compilation process. Despite budgetary limitations, the writer should use ingenuity and innovation to complete the necessary compilation work.
* *The nature and extent of available resources.* The writer must determine the quantity and quality of the available material, and ferret out less obvious, but valuable, sources of information and comment.
* *Quality requirements.* While most writers contend that they strive for quality at all times, the exigencies of deadlines and budgets often force compromise. Ideally, both

deadline and script quality demands always will be satisfied. Realistically, quality often is a secondary concern, a worthwhile bonus, but not the primary concern.

There are several methods for approaching the compilation process:

1. If the fundamental idea or premise for a program script is established, this will determine the contents and depth needed in preliminary research, the tentative outline, initial treatment statement, and subsequent drafts of the script. This is a very common sequence for the writer who develops the finished script from an idea already accepted. Industrial, educational, and instructional scripts follow this pattern of development. The editorial writer often works from ideas initially generated by the station manager. Generalized ideas, concepts, and issues often form the basis for dramas.

2. If only a large volume of material on a topic or subject area is available, and if no specific program concept or premise has been established, then it is the writer's responsibility to determine the nature, quality, organization, and depth of the material compiled. From this determination, the specific program script idea can be formulated. This leads to a distillation of resource material so that only appropriate items are included. At the same time, a tentative, flexible script outline should be devised. A treatment statement may be prepared before initial and subsequent drafts of the script are written. This compilation approach is useful for year-in-review programs in which significant events and personalities are featured. The year-in-review could highlight music, entertainment, news, sports, medicine, finance, laws, or any number of other subjects and topic areas. "Instant" news specials also use this approach when it is necessary to quickly produce a program which places a complex issue or series of events into proper perspective. While the general idea or objective for the program may have been determined in both types of program applications before compilation began, it is the results of the compilation process which provide the means to identify and crystallize the unique aspects or features of the topic or subject.

3. The material to be written may be compiled all at once, in the aggregate, or cumulatively over time. For example, a year-in-review music program, featuring the top artists and recordings in a particular music format, can be prepared at the end of the year when final record sales and recording awards have been determined. Within a short period, the writer can assemble the necessary material, determine the appropriate music selections and write the necessary script fragments. Another approach is for the writer to formulate preliminary comments for each top-selling recording and artist throughout the year. At the end of the year, these preliminary script fragments can be reviewed, the language and length of each fragment adjusted to fit timing constraints and to accommodate late industry developments and new material written for additional top artists and recordings. All of the fragments are then pulled together into a smooth, cohesive, finished script. See figures 9-1 and 9-2. A similar process could be followed for year-in-review programs

featuring news, sports, or entertainment items. At the end of each week, a short summary can be written of the top events and personalities featured in daily reports. At the end of the year, these preliminary weekly summaries are reviewed, rewritten, and forged with other events, personalities, and topics from other weeks. An alternative method is to wait until the end of the year and then review the top stories in each report. This delay sometimes provides a better perspective of the year, but is more time consuming and allows for a less critical analysis of the material.

4. The writer may complete the compilation process alone or in a group. Working alone provides the freedom to explore new concepts and techniques without constraints and to avoid some of the confusion and duplication of effort which often occur when others are involved. Nevertheless, the volume of work may be overwhelming for the single compiler who runs the risk of losing perspective and who does not derive the usual benefits resulting from interaction with others. The success of joint writing ventures often hinges on the individual's willingness to cooperate, share, and coordinate information and to contribute a strong personal sense of organization and dedication to quality.

These approaches to the compilation process are most effective when combined creatively to meet the requirements of each writing situation. For example, the writer may come up with an idea for a short feature on a community project. The specific premise, tack, or angle for the feature may be determined after conversations with people involved in the community or the specific project, a short visit with the news director, or informal talks over coffee. Several individuals may conduct the research. The writer, whether working alone or with another writer or the program producer, distills this information and prepares a tentative outline or treatment for the feature. Short segments could be written as the information falls into logical sequence. The initial scripted segments are edited and rewritten to meet time, budget, production, and quality requirements. Other writing situations often necessitate a similar combination of compilation approaches to produce the best possible script.

Writing Techniques and Suggestions

1. Remember the purpose of the script to be written. Understand the writing objective. Then, compile only essential and pertinent information and material to reinforce key ideas associated with this identified objective.
2. Explore viable leads. Gather as much pertinent material from as many sources as possible.
3. Work from a flexible, evolving outline which allows meaningful accumulated material to form and shape the final effective treatment of the topic or subject.
4. Continually analyze and evaluate material, allowing each piece of information to find its niche and to help shape the flexible outline that continues to evolve.

5. Remember the value of script, audio, and video archival material. Know what is available and how to obtain such material for use in current broadcast script projects.
6. Rewrite continuously. A new fact, a startling archival voice or picture remnant, a fleeting image or impression, a significant new development—all should cause the compiler/writer to re-examine the collected material, the manner in which it is organized, the style of presentation, and the length of specific segments. The compilation process is a continual, progressive effort to provide the most complete, effective presentation possible.

The American Sportsman

An excellent example of the compilation process is ABC's *The American Sportsman*. This Emmy Award–winning limited sports series has presented a unique profile of outdoor adventure and has showcased the courage and leadership needed to maintain the spirit of the outdoors.

The narration is written by a series production assistant/writer or by a freelance writer who reviews the film or videotape segments, completes additional research as needed, and shares notes and impressions compiled by the segment's field producer. The narration is adjusted to complement the edited video sequences and to maintain the proper pace and flow of the segment. Often, the narrator will adjust specific words or phrases to better communicate the sequence of events and to enhance the spirit of outdoor adventure. The length of each narration insert is specified in the script. The narrator may record several "takes" for each insert. These are numbered sequentially and enclosed in circles on the script. The notation "*" is used by the producer to indicate the most effective take for each narration insert. Music and sound effects are added as needed. Similar scripting notations and compilation techniques could be used for other kinds of compilation situations.

Figure 10-1 is a script excerpt from a program segment featuring an American/British team trying to become the first in seventeen years to scale the top of Ama Dablam in the Himalayan Mountains. After a profile of team members and the preparations needed for the climb, the segment traces the dangerous trek up the steep mountain peak. During post production, the climber's comments (recorded on location) were inserted between the narrator's remarks. Curt Gowdy, the series host, is the narrator. This climactic sequence provided the viewer with an intense and vivid image of the danger involved and the spirit and courage of the climbers. Notice how the jubilant spirit of the moment is captured by the writer and how the sequence builds dramatically to a strong and memorable conclusion. The writing is terse. This intense human struggle is allowed to develop and be revealed by the courageous actions of the participants. The writer, working with others, has combined crucial pieces of material from various sources to forge an impressive, dramatic, and cohesive presentation offering a new perspective for the television viewer.

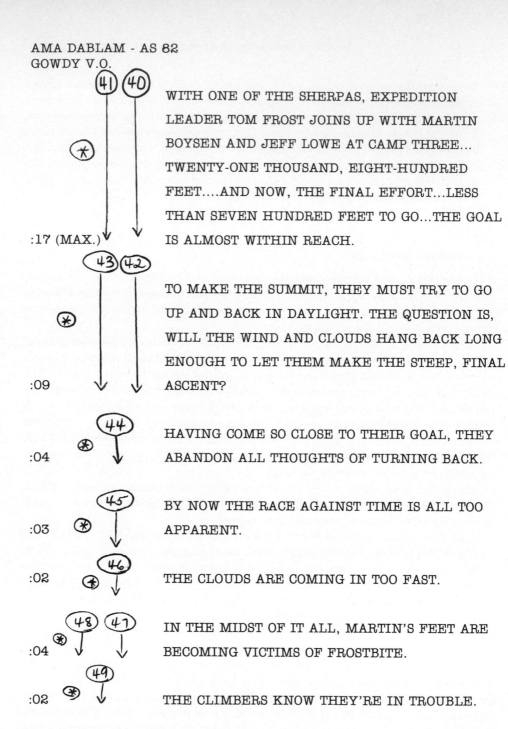

AMA DABLAM - AS 82
GOWDY V.O.

WITH ONE OF THE SHERPAS, EXPEDITION LEADER TOM FROST JOINS UP WITH MARTIN BOYSEN AND JEFF LOWE AT CAMP THREE... TWENTY-ONE THOUSAND, EIGHT-HUNDRED FEET....AND NOW, THE FINAL EFFORT...LESS THAN SEVEN HUNDRED FEET TO GO...THE GOAL IS ALMOST WITHIN REACH.

:17 (MAX.)

TO MAKE THE SUMMIT, THEY MUST TRY TO GO UP AND BACK IN DAYLIGHT. THE QUESTION IS, WILL THE WIND AND CLOUDS HANG BACK LONG ENOUGH TO LET THEM MAKE THE STEEP, FINAL ASCENT?

:09

HAVING COME SO CLOSE TO THEIR GOAL, THEY ABANDON ALL THOUGHTS OF TURNING BACK.

:04

BY NOW THE RACE AGAINST TIME IS ALL TOO APPARENT.

:03

THE CLOUDS ARE COMING IN TOO FAST.

:02

IN THE MIDST OF IT ALL, MARTIN'S FEET ARE BECOMING VICTIMS OF FROSTBITE.

:04

THE CLIMBERS KNOW THEY'RE IN TROUBLE.

:02

Figure 10-1 Excerpt from the Ama Dablam segment of the telecast of *The American Sportsman*, April 4, 1982. *(Courtesy of ABC Sports, Inc.)*

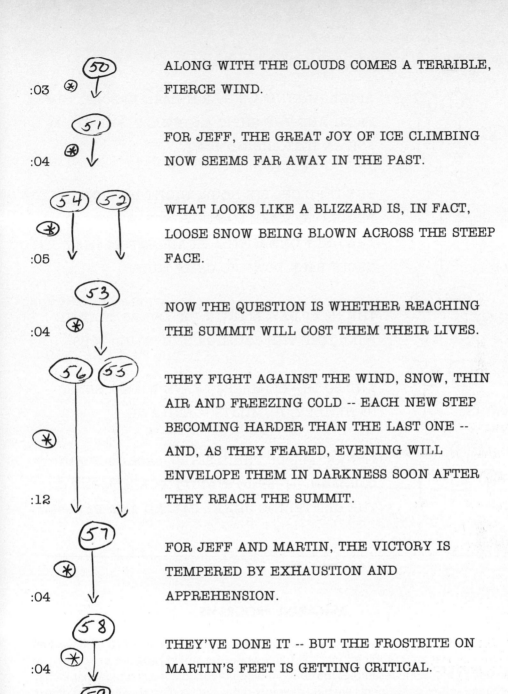

:03 ⊛ 50 ↓   ALONG WITH THE CLOUDS COMES A TERRIBLE, FIERCE WIND.

:04 ⊛ 51 ↓   FOR JEFF, THE GREAT JOY OF ICE CLIMBING NOW SEEMS FAR AWAY IN THE PAST.

54 52
:05 ⊛ ↓ ↓   WHAT LOOKS LIKE A BLIZZARD IS, IN FACT, LOOSE SNOW BEING BLOWN ACROSS THE STEEP FACE.

:04 ⊛ 53 ↓   NOW THE QUESTION IS WHETHER REACHING THE SUMMIT WILL COST THEM THEIR LIVES.

56 55
⊛
:12 ↓ ↓   THEY FIGHT AGAINST THE WIND, SNOW, THIN AIR AND FREEZING COLD -- EACH NEW STEP BECOMING HARDER THAN THE LAST ONE -- AND, AS THEY FEARED, EVENING WILL ENVELOPE THEM IN DARKNESS SOON AFTER THEY REACH THE SUMMIT.

57
⊛
:04 ↓   FOR JEFF AND MARTIN, THE VICTORY IS TEMPERED BY EXHAUSTION AND APPREHENSION.

58
:04 ⊛ ↓   THEY'VE DONE IT -- BUT THE FROSTBITE ON MARTIN'S FEET IS GETTING CRITICAL.

:03 ⊛ 59 ↓   AS IF APPARITIONS SUDDENLY APPEARING...

Fig. 10-1 *(Continued)*

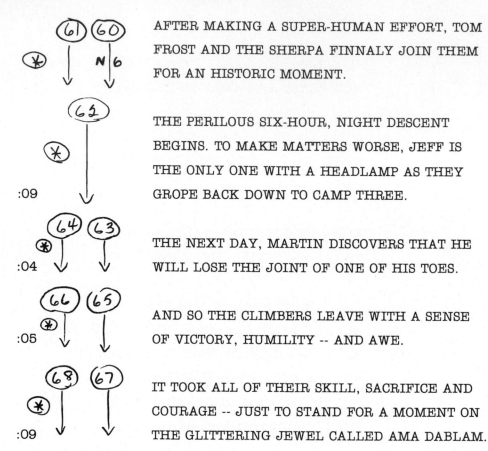

AFTER MAKING A SUPER-HUMAN EFFORT, TOM FROST AND THE SHERPA FINNALY JOIN THEM FOR AN HISTORIC MOMENT.

THE PERILOUS SIX-HOUR, NIGHT DESCENT BEGINS. TO MAKE MATTERS WORSE, JEFF IS THE ONLY ONE WITH A HEADLAMP AS THEY GROPE BACK DOWN TO CAMP THREE.

THE NEXT DAY, MARTIN DISCOVERS THAT HE WILL LOSE THE JOINT OF ONE OF HIS TOES.

AND SO THE CLIMBERS LEAVE WITH A SENSE OF VICTORY, HUMILITY -- AND AWE.

IT TOOK ALL OF THEIR SKILL, SACRIFICE AND COURAGE -- JUST TO STAND FOR A MOMENT ON THE GLITTERING JEWEL CALLED AMA DABLAM.

Fig. 10-1   *(Continued)*

MAGAZINE PROGRAMS

In a broadcast magazine program, several separate topics are featured in individual segments that are combined into the framework of a single program or series. The broadcast magazine resembles the conventional print media magazine format in that separate stories or segments are fully developed but always placed within the context or framework of the entire magazine's objectives or goals. While the objective of a broadcast magazine program may be to entertain, particular program series and specific segments within a magazine show may also inform, persuade, or provoke action on an issue or topic. "Reality programming" has become the label attached to these programs which have captured the attention and interest of broadcast audiences. The nature of magazine programs provides a unique opportunity for writers and program producers to identify specific target audience groups and to fashion program content to meet specific tastes and interests.

Various kinds of magazine programs, both regular series and specials, produced at all levels of broadcast production and distribution, offer audiences a wide selection of program content. Such programs are produced by print magazine companies as well as by cable systems, local stations, networks, and syndicators. Segments may focus on such diverse topics and subject areas as news, sports, entertainment, exercise, food and nutrition, gardening, fashion, personal enhancement, lifestyles, travel, medicine, health, science, finances, consumerism, and celebrity and human interest profiles. The length and objectives of the entire magazine program as well as the number and placement of each program segment will determine the kind of development of each topic or subject within individual program segments.

Approaches

A wide range of scripting and production formats and techniques is used. Individual segments may be designed as interviews, discussions, call-ins, regular newscast-type reports, etc. Segments, and even entire programs, may be produced live, recorded on tape or by a combination of production methods. Most magazine programs are produced as a regular series for use five days each week, generally in late afternoon or early evening time slots. Regular series hosts provide visible continuity for the programs, while special contributors may be featured in individual program segments.

Effective magazine programs are carefully planned, designed, and structured. They display cohesiveness as well as flexibility. Segment themes can be designed in advance and may be utilized in the programs either "vertically" (that is, in each program) or "horizontally" (that is, inserted periodically and regularly but not in each program). For example, regular vertical segments might be those featuring news headlines, an interview, local entertainment notes, or a health tip. Horizontal segments, included regularly on specific days of the week, might include personal finances on Mondays, exercise on Tuesdays, travel on Wednesdays, and so on. Thus, the magazine program could be designed to use the skeletal structure provided by the vertical theme segments to establish stability and continuity for the series, and then each program could be "fleshed in" with horizontal theme segments. This approach provides an excellent method to maintain the pace and flow of the program series, but still permit the inclusion of immediate and contemporary issues, topics, concerns, and personalities.

Regular magazine program series generally are prepared from a standard rundown sheet, which is used to map out the various segments for each program. The length of each segment is determined in advance and ranges from one to five or six minutes. Other script forms (described in chapter 3) are used to write and produce each segment. The choice of script form depends upon the nature, topic, or subject of the segment as well as the availability and requirements of production and talent personnel, budget, timetable, and facilities. For example, an interview segment could use a routine sheet. A cooking segment might be produced from a semi-script. See figure 3-4. Full-scripts would be useful for entertainment or lifestyle commentaries, news or sports features recorded in advance. The standard opening and closing to the program could be fully scripted and often is preproduced on tape to begin and end the program in an effective manner.

Writing Techniques and Suggestions

1. Keep program objectives in mind at all times. Information program series and segments should stress information. Entertainment programs and segments should spotlight entertainment news and features.
2. Remember the audience. Give them what is interesting, important, innovative, and expected from the type of magazine program produced.
3. Offer the innovative, with reference to the familiar. Unusual, startling, or controversial material can be presented, but always should be clearly linked to more familiar, easily accepted information and concepts. A thorough, practical knowledge and acceptance of your audience's characteristics will help present the unfamiliar in terms of the familiar.
4. Make abstract information concrete by presenting specific, real life material which can be easily identified and understood by the audience.
5. Prepare program segments which provide a flexible, contemporary approach to modern living.
6. Organize each program segment. Get and hold audience attention and interest. Present supporting material that logically and effectively moves the listener or viewer from point to point, idea to idea. End each segment smoothly and climactically, with an eye to how the ending of each program segment will make an effective transition to the next portion of the magazine program.

SportsWorld

An interesting example of a sports magazine program is NBC's *SportsWorld*. This Saturday afternoon sports anthology series is structured in a "collapsible" position behind live broadcasts of sporting events. As necessary, adjustments are made in *SportsWorld* segments to end the program on time. A "short routine" or rundown sheet is prepared for each scheduled one-and-a-half-hour telecast to provide a quick overview of each broadcast so that prerecorded segments can be lengthened or shortened to meet time requirements.

Figure 10-2 is one page of the "short routine" for a *SportsWorld* telecast. Notice how several prerecorded features and reports are used around the main event of the broadcast—the Ayala/Herrera fight. Transitions and short promos of upcoming program segments provide continuity and reinforce the structure of the broadcast.

SHORT ROUTINE
SPORTSWORLD #204   December 4, 1982

1.	TEASE	(1:00)	4:00:00-4:01:00
2.	SPORTSWORLD OPENING	(1:00)	4:01:00-4:02:00
3.	MR. OLYMPIA-ACT I	(7:07)	4:02:00-4:09:07
4.	BUMPER: AYALA	(:09)	4:09:07-4:09:16
5.	Co-op Bumper/COM'L POS #1	(1:39)	4:09:16-4:10:55
6.	MR. OLYMPIA - ACT II (w/bumper at end to tease Ayala feature)	(6:33)	4:10:55-4:17:28
7.	COM'L POS #2 + :15 Promo	(2:15)	4:17:28-4:19:43
8.	AYALA FEATURE (w/boxing bumper at end)	(5:46)	4:19:43-4:25:29
9.	COM'L POS #3	(2:00)	4:25:29-4:27:29
10.	RING INTROS/ROUND 1 OF AYALA/HERRERA FIGHT	(4:31)	4:27:29-4:32:00
11.	COM'L POS #4	(1:00)	4:32:00-4:33:00
12.	ROUND 2	(3:03)	4:33:00-4:36:03
13.	COM'L POS #5 + :30 Promo	(1:30)	4:36:03-4:37:33
14.	ROUND 3/END OF FIGHT	(4:42)	4:37:33-4:42:15
15.	COM'L POS #6	(2:00)	4:42:15-4:44:15
16.	AYALA INTERVIEW/REPLAY (w/promo of Olympia & lead to Volleyball)	(2:25)	4:44:15-4:46:40
17.	VOLLEYBALL - NEW ACT I (w/:12 Olympia bumper tied to end)	(8:04)	4:46:40-4:54:44
18.	COM'L POS #7	(2:00)	4:54:44-4:56:44

Figure 10-2 One page of the "short routine" for a *SportsWorld* telecast. *(Courtesy of NBC SportsWorld)*

19. MR. OLYMPIA - ACT III   (6:27)   4:56:44-5:03:11
    (w/lead to SJ)

20. SPORTSJOURNAL   (3:57)   5:03:11-5:07:08

21. COM'L POS #8 (SJ) + :15 Promo   (2:15)   5:07:08-5:09:23

22. VOLLEYBALL - NEW ACT II   (7:45)   5:09:23-5:17:08
    (w/Mr. Olympia bumper
    tied to end)

Fig. 10-2   *(Continued)*

Details about each program segment are provided on individual "master seg. reel" sheets. Figure 10-3 is the master seg. reel sheet for item #3 on the rundown sheet shown in figure 10-2. The time indicated under the heading "time code" indicates the place on videotape #81542D where this particular prerecorded segment begins. The center column on the sheet displays information about the segment in abbreviated form. Under the repeat of the segment listing from the rundown sheet, a quick visual and aural production summary of the segment is written in parentheses. Next is a notation about how the segment begins and ends—"IN Q" and "OUT Q." This is followed by the time on the videotape when this segment ends. Because of the collapsible nature of the program, however, and the need to adjust the length and placement of individual program segments at the last minute, alternate in and out points are provided. For example, to save 1 minute 29 seconds, the Mr. Olympia segment could begin further into the prerecorded videotape (at 11:07:29). To eliminate 37 seconds from the program, this segment could begin at the original designated point on the videotape but end early, at the point where the master seg. reel displays the time 11:12:30. Thus, the writer/producer is provided more flexibility for timing and structuring the final program. *SportsWorld* is a unique broadcast magazine series because of the need to quickly respond to the time restraints caused by a live sports event going overtime.

SPECIAL EVENTS

The special event is the broadcast of a particular actual happening whose outcome often is undetermined. Many special events are witnessed by all media rather than just the broadcast media. The event must be distinctive, out of the ordinary and of direct interest to a substantial number of listeners or viewers. It is heard or seen in "real time," as the event unfolds. The broadcast may be a recording, but the sequence of events follows the pattern of the actual or real occurrence. The final result or outcome often is unknown to the audience until the final, climactic moments (e.g., the winners declared in a sporting event; an election; a beauty pageant; or the safe return of astronauts, which is not assured until the final camera shot at the landing site). There are many events which might be labeled as special. Some of the types of occurrences which could be classified as special events, worthy of broadcast coverage consideration, are: special news coverage (late breaking news stories reported from the scene of the event, election-night reports, funerals of public figures and political conventions), news conferences, speeches, political candidates' debates, sporting events, parades, dedications (of such things as buildings, shopping centers, transit system facilities improvements, a special wing in a library, etc.), banquets, awards presentations, beauty pageants, fairs, expositions, telethons, and auctions or fund-raisers.

SPORTSWORLD #204 _____   Master Seg. Reel NYBH 81542D

Dec. 4, 1982 _____   Rec. Date: 12/2/82 _____

NBC SPORTSWORLD
MASTER SEG. REEL

TIME CODE	ITEM	SEG. TIME

11:06:00   MR. OLYMPIA - ACT I   (7:07)
                (music montage/OC open/Makkawy/
                 talking heads)

        IN Q: "(MUSIC)"

        OUT Q: "...(MORE)...Mr. Olympia competition from
                           Wembley, England."

            @ 11:13:07 (+ :18 A/V PAD)

        ALTERNATES

        ALTERNATE IN @ 11:07:29 (WITHOUT OPENING MONTAGE)
          IN Q: (MUSIC) LYRICS: "Muscles, muscles..."
        (SAVES 1:29)   (SEG TIME = 5:38)

        ALTERNATE OUT @ 11:12:30 (WITHOUT BODY COMMENTS)
          OUT Q: "...in Wembley, England."
        (SAVES :37)   (SEG TIME = 6:30)

                    COMING UPS:

                    UL 11:11:07 - 11:11:12

Figure 10-3 "Master seg. reel" sheet for item 3 on the rundown sheet shown in figure 10-2. *(Courtesy of NBC SportsWorld)*

Under the proper circumstances, these and many other occurrences could be considered special. This designation hinges on a determination of the nature of the event, the degree and quality of interest in the unfolding or development of the event, the importance of the final result and its impact on the audience. The decision to cover a particular event as a special is made by programming or sales personnel who have considered the situation carefully and determined that such coverage would be beneficial. The writer then helps prepare material which makes the special event broadcast interesting and worthwhile.

Approaches

The immediate, spontaneous, and developing nature of most special events generally prevents thorough planning and complete scripting. Nevertheless, some minimal level of program preparation is necessary to adequately anticipate the exigencies of the event and the special circumstances involved. Ad-libbed rather than full-scripted comments are used to communicate information in these situations. Thus, most special events broadcast are produced using a show format (rundown or routine sheet) or a semi-script.

Like many other types of programs already discussed, the approach used to prepare script material for a specific special events broadcast often is contingent upon several interrelated factors.
Among these factors are the following:

- *The nature of the event.* For example, experienced sports play-by-play announcers require a minimum of prepared script material to provide an interesting sporting event broadcast. On the other hand, the live broadcast of a parade or an awards presentation requires more precise anticipation of events and, thus, more complete scripting.
- *The availability of information.* While some information can be accumulated for each special event, there may not be enough information available in advance of the broadcast for the writer to prepare detailed script material. As always, the writer should use whatever pertinent information is available and prepare the type of script needed for an interesting and effective broadcast.
- *The timetable.* Working under a deadline, there may not be sufficient time to prepare extensive script material, even if this would be desirable. For example, a late breaking local news story which occurs during the early evening newscast permits the preparation of only a very brief introduction to the reporter at the scene who then ad-libs the information about the incident.
- *The preferences of talent and production personnel.* Extensive script material may be unnecessary and perhaps confusing to those responsible for producing the program. They may be accustomed to and expect to encounter less formal, more spontaneous script and production formats.

Writing Techniques and Suggestions

1. Adhere to the predetermined concept for the broadcast. If the special event is a local community awards presentation, prepare script material to provide essential

background information on recipients. If special election night coverage is prepared, gather and prepare background information for pre-produced segments on major candidates, campaign issues, and political party policies.

2. Allow the special event to be the focal point for the broadcast. Write material that enhances the immediacy, reinforces the structure or organization, and anticipates the conclusion of the special event.

3. Collect as much information as possible about the event—what is planned, who is involved, when and where specific parts of the event are scheduled to occur.

4. Abstract pertinent and interesting items of information for use in preparing script material.

5. Prepare "digests," or summaries, of the abstracted information in the form and length to be used by the on-air talent. This could be done on either standard-size paper or on index cards. Using index cards provides the talent with immediate access to essential script material and makes it easier for the producer to accomplish last-minute program line-up adjustments by simply shuffling the index cards into the revised order.

6. Anticipate as much as possible. Prepare script material for openings, closings, and transitions as well as for possible emergency situations. Thoughtful, well-written, brief "filler" material, prepared in advance and not during the heat of the emergency situation, has rescued many special events broadcasts.

7. Prepare script material for short, prerecorded program segments that can be used to overcome inevitable delays and production problems and to control the pace and tempo of the broadcast.

8. Keep the script material and coverage interesting, timely, and informative so that the audience does not become bored or distracted.

9. Work with the special events program producer and director to adjust the coverage if necessary if the event develops or turns in a direction not already anticipated. Be prepared with alternative methods of adjusting to the changing events. If necessary, prepare script material to accommodate these alternatives.

Academy Awards

The annual Academy Awards telecast is a premium special events broadcast and one of a growing number of annual awards presentations shown on national television. The writer's preparations for this kind of program parallel those needed for other types of special events (e.g., parades, banquets, beauty pageants, and telethons). The broadcast of such special events has become more commonplace on national networks as well as local stations.

Figure 10-4 is one page from the thirteen-page rundown sheet used to produce "The 54th Annual Academy Awards" telecast on ABC-TV. The standard program information is included in each rundown sheet page (i.e., program segment number and description, script page number in parentheses, segment length and cumulative or program running time). In the column labeled "DESCR.," the abbreviation "VTPB WINNER" indicates a videotape playback of the winner of that particular category.

"THE 54TH ANNUAL ACADEMY AWARDS"
SHORT RUNDOWN (CONT'D)   (2:50:35)

ITEM	PAGE	DESCR.	TIME	CUM TIME
87. AWARD #20 DIRECTOR (Jack Lemmon, Walter Matthau)				
a. TALK	(190)		2:45	2:53:25
b. NOMINATIONS & PRESEN- TATION OF AWARD				
c. WINNER ACCEPTANCE	(192)		2:25	2:55:45
88. INTRO JERZY KOSINSKI (Johnny Carson)	(194)		0:57	2:56:42
89. AWARD #21 ORIGINAL SCREENPLAY (Jerzy Kosinski)				
a. TALK	(195)		2:28	2:59:10
b. NOMINATION & PRESENTA- TION OF AWARD		VTPB WINNER		
c. WINNER ACCEPTANCE	(197)		0:46	2:59:56

Figure 10-4   One page from the rundown sheet used to produce the telecast of "The 54th Annual Academy Awards." *(Courtesy of Academy of Motion Picture Arts and Sciences)*

For an illustration of how the awards presentation process unfolds for the writer working on the project, see figure 10-5, which shows the "as broadcast" script pages for program segment number 89 (script pages 195–197). The script pages for each awards presentation display the same page format or layout: the program segment number is provided at the top center of the page, enclosed in parentheses; the script page number is at the top right; the program segment is identified just as on the rundown sheet and written in FULL CAPS and underlined; the presenter or introducer is indicated in parentheses just under the identification of the segment and again in FULL CAPS in the center of the script page; staging and production notes are written in FULL CAPS and enclosed in parentheses or underlined. The comments by the presenter are brief and pertinent to the award being presented. The excitement and

90.	AWARD #22 SCREENPLAY ADAPTATION (Jerzy Kosinski)				
	b. NOMINATIONS & PRESEN- TATION OF AWARD	(198)	VTPB WINNER	1:30	3:01:26
	c. WINNER ACCEPTANCE	(199)		1:49	3:03:15
*** 91.	COMMERCIALS #16 & #17 (Orchestra Plays to house)	(201)		2:02	3:05:17
*** 91a.	LEAD-IN STATION BREAK (Announcer (V.O.))	(202)		0:11	3:05:28
*** 91b.	NETWORK TIME (Black)	(203)		1:23	3:06:51
91c.	REJOIN	(204)	VTPB	0:07	3:06:58
	ACT XI 91d. FILM BUMPER #9	(205)	VTPB	0:19	3:07:17
92.	INTRO JON VOIGHT (Johnny Carson)	(206)		0:26	3:07:43

Fig. 10-4 *(Continued)*

anticipation of the moment are heightened by showing excerpts from each nominee's work as each is named. The recipient's comments are also brief and help maintain the quick pace and even flow of the program. Obviously, the writer cannot control all of the comments made during such broadcasts, but as much pre-scripted material as possible should be generated.

SPECIAL AUDIENCES

Most broadcast programs are aimed at general audiences who share common tastes and preferences and who have money to spend on a variety of advertised products and services. There are special groups within this general audience, however, with unique needs, problems and concerns which are not always fulfilled in general audience programs. Some might believe that it is still unrealistic to expect to find programs that address these special audiences regularly. The proliferation of cable systems,

AWARD #21 - ORIGINAL   AWARD #21 - ORIGINAL
SCREENPLAY   SCREENPLAY
(Jerzy Kosinski)

JERZY KOSINSKI

My experience as an actor has taught
me the importance of a writer. We
who act owe so much to those of us who
write. The Bible tells us that in
the beginning was the word. When
the universe was in complete disorder,
Moses was called to the mountain. A
warning bolt of lightning, an
overture of thunder, the skies
parted and a mighty hand reached
down to give Moses the stone
tablets. That was the first
script. Some critics thought it was
over-produced for just ten lines.
But, but, by following it, mankind
restored order out of disorder. If
succeeding generations had stuck to
that original script, instead of ad-
libbing around it so much, this
would be a better world to live
in. The original scripts nominated   APPLAUSE
this year as Best Screenplay Written
Directly for the Screen are...

(MORE)

- -

AWARD #21 - ORIGINAL
SCREENPLAY
(89)   (CONT'D)

JERZY KOSINSKI (CONT'D)

(4-7-9-4)   "Absence of Malice," by <u>Kurt</u>   C#146
              <u>Luedtke</u>.
(4-7-3-4)   "Arthur," by <u>Steve Gordon</u>.
(4-7-5-4)   "Atlantic City," by <u>John Guare</u>.
(4-7-7-4)   "Chariots of Fire," by <u>Colin</u>
              <u>Welland</u>.

Figure 10-5 "As broadcast" script pages for one segment from the telecast of "The 54th Annual Academy Awards." Broken lines across the pages in figure 10-5 indicate original script pages. *(Courtesy of Academy of Motion Picture Arts and Sciences)*

(2-6-1-1)   ...and "Reds," by Warren Beatty
(4-7-1-4)   and Trevor Griffiths.
             I admire all of you. And the
             winner is...

(OPENS ENVELOPE, READS WINNER)

             Colin Welland for "Chariots of Fire."

MUSIC: WINNER PLAYON

                                       APPLAUSE

(WELLAND TO STAGE)

(INTO: PRESENTATION OF AWARD)

                                      197.
                            AWARD #21 - ORIGINAL
                                  SCREENPLAY
          (89)   (CONT'D)
             COLIN WELLAND

        What you've done for the British
        Film Industry!
        I'd just like to thank David
        Puttnam for having the wisdom to
        ask me to write it in the first
        place, Hugh Hudson for respecting
        me and my script, which is a very
        hard thing to find in our business,
        as you know. All the actors for
        getting fit enough to appear like
        olympic athletes, and to British
        Television where I learned my craft.

        I'd like to finish with a word of
        warning -- you may have started
        something...
        ...The British Are Coming!!!...

                                            APPLAUSE

MUSIC: PLAYOFF

(INTO: AWARD #22 - SCREENPLAY ADAPTATION)

Fig. 10-5 *(Continued)*

however, and the development of technologies such as videodisc and home computer learning and information centers provide an opportunity to "narrowcast" to such special audiences as shut-ins, the elderly, the retired or unemployed or infirm, the hearing impaired, and various ethnic groups. Women, too, often find that their special needs and concerns are neglected and that their interests have been stereotyped as shallow so that only a limited range of program types is believed to appeal to them (provocative programs, soap operas, cooking, and exercise shows). For these and many other special audiences, much of broadcast programming is unrealistic, stereotypical, and often denigrating.

The broadcast media command attention and have the capability of realizing the goals and objectives of most special as well as general audiences. The process begins when there is a commitment to do something about the situation. Commitment is the result of attitude acquired through knowledge and understanding. It is beneficial not only to know but to experience the needs and concerns of special audience groups. The writer must cultivate this kind of sensitivity as an individual, in a personal way.

As a writer, there are several steps which can be taken to improve the treatment of special audiences in broadcast scripts:

1. Avoid stereotypes as much as possible. Usually, they are unrealistic and an unnecessary writing shortcut.
2. Avoid insensitivities and affronts to the needs, problems, and concerns of special audiences.
3. Present the interests of special audiences in programs intended for general audiences. Without sermonizing, bring the message of special audiences into the consciousness of general audiences. Offer new alternatives and perspectives.
4. Use your writing to relate the positive and unique contributions and activities of special audience groups. Stress the community awareness and involvement of such groups.
5. Project a positive attitude. Show the diversified success achieved by such groups through concentrated effort and determination. Present a strong, consistent, positive, uplifting spirit worthy of imitation.
6. Stress the individual as well as the group. Show how self-awareness, a sense of personal dignity and self-respect, and individual problem solving can have a lasting, positive impact on improving the visibility and treatment of special audiences in broadcast programs.
7. Provide subject matter which addresses special audience concerns and problems. Make the content, language, style, and manner of presentation appropriate for the intended audience.
8. Relate contemporary developments to the interests, concerns, attitudes, feelings, and motivations of special audiences.

All types of programs and scripting forms can be used to reach special audiences. Basic scripting formats do not vary. But the skill, style, and sensitivity of the individual writer is important if special audience programming is to be considered worthwhile and effective.

The needs of special audiences can be fulfilled through the broadcast media. But it is necessary to change the way these special needs and concerns are now addressed. That change begins once an individual recognizes that a problem exists, and specific steps can be taken to rectify the situation. It requires a high level of personal and professional dedication and determination to offer pertinent, quality programming despite ratings or financial consequences. Once the process begins, it is the writer who is in a primary position to make positive, enduring contributions to present uplifting programming for special audiences.

RELIGIOUS PROGRAMS

Religion is a dominant influence in society next to family and peer groups. Nationwide surveys continue to document strong church affiliation despite declines in church attendance.

A large portion of current religious programming is of the fundamentalist variety. Mainline churches acknowledge the success of these fundamentalist groups in raising funds and staying on the air with their messages. There have been efforts at combining forces in production and distribution facilities so that programs of all faiths can be offered to local stations and nationwide through syndication, network, cable, and satellite distribution systems.

Religious programming is designed for specific audiences and purposes. Among these are: children, youth, adults (married and single), divorcees, peer groups, specific social and moral issues, interpersonal relationships and concerns within the family or workplace, human values and freedoms, and essential religious beliefs and principles. The goal of a religious program may be one or more of the following: entertainment, information, persuasion, inspiration. Such programming may be produced by a particular denomination and then offered to stations, networks, and cable systems, or these same distribution outlets may also produce the programs with the assistance, endorsement, and underwriting of a particular religious group.

In an effort to make religious programming as attractive and acceptable as possible, virtually all forms of broadcast programming and scripting are used. These would include: spot announcements, talk programs and interviews, religious news reports, magazine and feature programs and segments, the broadcast of religious services and sermons, music and variety programs, editorials and commentaries, documentaries and investigative reports, instructional material, cartoons, dramas, and comedies. All of these forms of programming are used to present a religious message in a relevant, contemporary setting with the hope that the audience will accept the message and act upon its implications. Religious dramas, for example, portray contemporary, real-life situations and problems in which religious solutions are offered. The same scripting formats described elsewhere in this book can be used to develop a variety of religious program material. The scripting format used would depend upon the type of script and program developed.

Several techniques and suggestions can be offered to help develop more effective religious broadcast scripts:

1. Use the strongest possible writing techniques to make the content and style of religious programming attractive, interesting, thought provoking and acceptable. Except for special dedicated program services, such as the Christian Broadcasting Network and PTL (People That Love) distributed via cable systems, the majority of religious programming is offered outside of prime broadcast airtime. This makes the job of the writer even more difficult and challenging.
2. Identify and remember your audience and objective. What are you trying to say? To whom? Keep these objectives firmly in mind as you write.
3. Prepare script material in which relevant contemporary concerns are fused with a strong, but subtle, display of religious spirit and insight. Make an effort to break through the distractions, frustrations and day-to-day concerns of most listeners and viewers and offer a clear, effective, and practical religious solution.
4. Become conscious of the religious significance of everyday events. Be sensitive to the application of religious principles to contemporary concerns.
5. Be aware of current religious issues and interests through professional and religious contacts, reading, and so forth.
6. If script material is written for a particular denomination, be aware of specific beliefs, principles, and preferences.
7. A deep, abiding religious spirit should permeate the work of the writer of religious program material.

Except for financial contributions to help sustain such broadcasts, the impact of religious programming is difficult to determine in terms of the lives affected and of changes in human and social interaction. The style and form of religious programming continue to evolve to respond to contemporary demands.

CHILDREN'S PROGRAMS

The mass media, particularly television, have been scrutinized over the years in an effort to determine the impact on consumers of the media, especially children. More studies and surveys have focused on this one audience group than perhaps all others combined. Although the results of such research are important and should influence, to some degree, the work of the broadcast writer, the reporting and analysis of such research results are not within the scope of this book. See the readings at the end of this chapter for pertinent research studies.

Characteristics of Children

The writer must identify basic characteristics of children (under twelve years old) and use this information when designing and writing specific kinds of children's programs:

•*Vulnerability.* Most children willingly trust and depend upon those in positions of authority. This pristine state of vulnerability provides an opportunity to mold and shape youngsters in a positive or negative manner.

•*Impressionability.* Children imitate what they see and hear from parents and peers. A child begins as an empty reservoir of human experiences, which is soon filled with specific attitudes, concepts, priorities, and lifestyle preferences.

•*Need for a protective environment.* Most children learn and react within a sheltered environment. A child's needs are fulfilled as concepts, ideas, and morals are developed within a close-knit group.

•*Simplistic notions.* For most children, life's complex problems and concerns are resolved in a simple and direct manner. Initially, children display a certain degree of naiveté about what they see and hear in the world around them. This simplistic approach erodes as the child matures and begins understanding and accepting the complexities of life. One of the principal complaints about children's television programming is its unrealistic, misleading, and simplistic approach to human situations. It is usually difficult for a child, and even a young adult, to accept the fact that all of life's problems cannot be resolved in sixty minutes divided into four acts and interrupted periodically by commercials. Separating reality from fiction, and even program content from commercials, is a giant mental leap for most children.

•*Short attention/interest span.* For children, the world is so vast, with so many interesting things to see and do, that they have only a short attention span. It is important for the broadcast writer to capture the child's attention and then present information and concepts quickly and effectively to enhance retention by the child.

•*Fondness for repetition and uniformity.* The child, like most adults, appreciates a certain degree of repetition. It helps us to learn and to reinforce basic concepts and ideas. Knowing what will happen next is often reassuring. Consistent structuring of particular program segments allows the child to anticipate program content and to develop a sense of uniformity.

•*Imaginative spirit.* The desire for uniformity and predictability is tempered with a free, uncluttered, imaginative spirit. Entire make-believe worlds—complete with sinister characters, unbeatable heroes, and villainous plots and schemes—are created by the child. It can be a wondrous time of life, probably never fully recaptured because of the world's complexities except perhaps later in life when an adult views the world vicariously through another child.

•*Curiosity.* Although younger children soon develop an egocentric attitude, this attitude eventually matures in later years into an almost insatiable curiosity about the world, its people, objects, and processes. This curiosity is shaped and developed by home, school, and peer group environments.

• *Love of humor and involvement.* Most children enjoy various levels of humor. They like to experience happy, exhilarating events and people. They laugh at clichéd comedic pratfalls. They quickly become involved in chase scenes and imaginative mystery and adventure situations to which they can relate. They often verbalize rhetorical questions asked in school or on television. They sing the lyrics of commercial jingles after seeing a particular announcement many times. They may clap their hands, dance around the room, sing and perform other activities which allow them to fully participate in what is presented.

Children have many other characteristics, and the writer of children's programs should reinforce his or her background and information about children through formal instruction as well as extensive observation and reflection. The writer faces a difficult challenge in attempting to capture the mind and spirit of a child, but it is a challenge that must be accepted if worthwhile children's programs are to be written.

Content and Format/Approaches and Methods

Children's television programs feature a wide range of content and scripting formats. There are very few live-action series produced for children. Superhero and science fiction animated programs dominate Saturday morning commercial television. Children's programming employs many other formats—including newscasts, variety and game shows, dramas, comedies, and spot announcements. The scripting format for each is the same as described and illustrated elsewhere in this book, but to adjust for content and style of presentation requires some adaptation of these basic scripting forms.

The writer of children's programs should strive to provide engaging and uplifting script material. The child's environment includes the mass media, particularly television, and children learn from their environment. Recognition by television legitimizes the status of particular groups, individuals, issues, and concerns in society. The writer must resolve the dilemma of providing commercially acceptable script material while sustaining a personal and professional sense of ethics and responsibility when writing for this unique, impressionable audience. Meaningful, realistic, and engaging script material should be the broadcast writer's goal.

Writing Techniques and Suggestions

To write quality scripts for children's programs, the writer must learn to apply the characteristics of children creatively to each writing project to reach this special impressionable young audience in a meaningful and memorable way. Several suggestions are offered to achieve these objectives.

1. *Be imaginative.* Expand your creative horizons by generating innovative and stimulating scripting and production techniques. To a certain extent, become childlike in your approach and perspective.

2. *Enhance realism.* Children tend to relate to what they see and hear in their own environment, circumstances, and personalities. Characters and situations are more convincing and effective if the audience (children included) can identify with these elements.

3. *Relate the known to the unknown.* Introduce new concepts, information, and attitudes by connecting them to real or easily imagined situations and characters. Extensive research may be necessary to achieve this objective consistently.

4. *Use a simple, direct, cohesive program structure.* This should provide the opportunity to vary the content and pace of the program, and still make it a consistent, interesting, and meaningful experience.

5. *Respect your audience.* Children are more perceptive and intelligent than most adults believe. Children quickly reject programs and personalities which tend to patronize them.

6. *Stress self-worth.* It is important for the child to know and to appreciate the value and importance of each individual. Respect for others leads to self-respect and strong personal moral development.

7. *Engender confidence.* It is important for every child to know that certain skills and pieces of information can be learned and that it is possible to succeed.

8. *Provide action.* Make something significant and interesting happen. Children tend to be visually oriented and stimulated. In your scripts, capitalize on this characteristic. Make the action clear, simple, meaningful, and progressive (building to a climax).

9. *Watch the violence.* Use it cautiously and only when necessary to reflect important, real-life situations and values.

10. *Avoid undue emphasis on romance.* Such situations generally hold no interest for younger children and often embarrass young viewers. When such situations occur, most children become anxious to return to the main story line or to move on to the next program segment.

11. *Promote a positive, creative, and developmental spirit.* Try to enlighten and entertain rather than confuse or bore your young audience. Provide constructive entertainment. Sustain positive standards and values of conduct, morals, ethics, behavior, and language.

Sesame Street

One of the outstanding children's program series provided by Children's Television Workshop is *Sesame Street.* This award-winning series has helped children adjust to different situations and experiences, develop positive human values and attitudes, and establish healthy curiosity about the world around them.

The scripting process for *Sesame Street* is unique. For each program segment, the writer is first given an assignment sheet with specific educational goals. After the first draft of each segment is written, the head writer for the series reviews the material and discusses the necessary revisions with the writer. The head writer then discusses the script with the research department to ensure educational goals are properly im-

Any day of the week.

TELLY: That's amazing! I can fly! *He's some teacher isn't he, maria?*

~~WOMAN ON PHONE: Would you like to fly first class?~~
MARIA: He certainly is.
~~TELLY: Wow!~~

~~MARIA REACTS~~

MUSIC BUTTON

FADE

3...PROF. GROVER LISTENS (LISTENING)

SCENIC: MEADOW, WITH LARGE TREE
TALENT: PROF. GROVER, A.M. LUMBER
JACKS *& Jill*
PROPS: MUPPET ~~CHAIN~~ *2 man* SAW.
WARDROBE: CAP AND GOWN FOR GROVER.
EFX:
SFX: CHAIN SAW, TREE CRASH.

OPEN TO PROF. GROVER IN A MEADOW.
BEHIND HIM IS A LARGE OAK TREE.

PROF. GROVER: Good day. Professor
Grover here, and today, we're going to
talk about listening....

ENTER 2 A.M. LUMBER JACKS

PROF. GROVER: Listening is very
important. Because if you do not
listen, you will not hear ~~anything.~~ *many important and fun things.*
FIRST LUMBER JACK: This it, ~~Pete?~~ *Jill*
SECOND LUMBER ~~JACK~~ *Jill*: Yeah. ~~Too bad.~~ *This is one we gotta cut down.*

Nice lookin' tree.

Figure 10-6 Suggested rewrite comments on a segment from Sesame Street. Broken lines across
the pages in figure 10-6 indicate original script pages. *(Courtesy of Children's Television
Workshop. ©Children's Television Workshop)*

FIRST LUMBER JACK: Well, ~~when they get~~ let's get started. ~~diseased, they gotta go.~~

THEY START ~~TO READY THE~~ to SAW with 2 man saw.

PROF. GROVER: For example, if you did not listen, you would not have heard how to get to Sesame Street. ~~So, as you can see, listening is a very good way to pick up information, and learn things.~~

continue to saw
THE LUMBER JACKS ~~GET THE SAW STARTED.~~
GROVER IS OBLIVIOUS.

If you did not listen you would also not know that I am Professor Grover and today I am talking about listening Ha Ha.

PROF. GROVER: ~~Listening is also a lot of fun, too. Like when you listen to a joke...~~

THE LUMBER JACKS START TO CUT THE TREE.
GROVER IS OBLIVIOUS.

PROF. GROVER: ~~Or, when you listen to music.~~ Now, there's one more thing about listening that is very, very important. Listening is a very SAFE thing to do. Because if you're listening, you can hear ~~things~~ warnings about around you ~~like automobiles, and bicycles, and~~ that might be ~~your mommy calling.~~ dangerous like ⟶

bicycle horns honking for you to get out of the way.
sefx: Bicycle horn
Grover: Like that.
(Grover steps out of the way as a riderless bicycle passes through)
Grover: (Does a take) ~~Did you see that? There was nobody riding on that bicycle.~~ or automobile horns
sefx: Auto horn
Grover: Like that one.
(Grover steps out of the way as a driverless car passes through)

LUMBER JACKS: Timber!

(has not heard lumber jacks)
PROF. GROVER: ...or someone yelling "Timber!", which means a tree is about to fall. get out of the way because

LUMBER JACKS: Timber!! (They run out and the tree begins to sway.)
PROF. GROVER: So remember, for information, fun, and safety, open your ears and listen. Timber? Timber!? Did someone say timber?

Fig. 10-6 (Continued)

(off)

LUMBER JACKS: Timber!!!

TREE FALLS PROF. GROVER JUMPS CLEAR
JUST IN TIME.

AFTER A MOMENT, PROF. GROVER RISES
THROUGH THE BRANCHES.

PROF. GROVER: Class dismissed.

GROVER FAINTS OVER BACKWARDS.

FADE

Fig. 10-6   *(Continued)*

---

plemented in the script. Final revisions are made based on this conversation. This script is then written in its final form.[1]

Figure 10-6 shows the suggestions made for rewriting a program segment featuring muppet character Grover dressed as a professor and two muppet lumberjacks ("A.M. Lumber Jacks"). The specific educational goal of this segment is to teach the child the value of listening. Notice how the change to a Lumber *Jill* helps the young girls in the audience identify with the muppet character and, thus, be more likely to feel that the information on listening applies to girls as well as to boys. The word change (early in the segment) from "...anything" to "...many important and fun things" reinforces the educational goal and sets up the situation that develops later. By eliminating the brief reference to why the diseased tree is being removed, the tree cutting action can start that much sooner. Prof. Grover's lines are changed to emphasize the importance of listening carefully. The action and audience involvement in this segment intensify as Grover finally remembers to apply the principles of effective listening to his immediate situation and narrowly escapes injury.

ANIMATION

Animation techniques are used in many different kinds of productions and programs. Advertising clients often use animated television commercials to present their messages effectively. Animation may be incorporated into informational, educational, training, and public relations presentations by businesses, institutions, and government agencies. Television music and variety specials, newscasts, children's shows, and many other dissimilar types of programs have used prerecorded animated program segments or elements. Many art films, theatrical short subjects, and feature-length motion pictures are produced using animation techniques. The majority of children's program-

ming on Saturday morning commercial television uses animation production techniques.
There are several reasons animation is considered an effective presentation tool.[2]

•it offers a human or real-life element which appeals to the emotions of the audience
•characters tend to become more acceptable, lovable, and entertaining when shown
in animated form
•animation does not share the physical limitations of other media; it thus allows
animated figures to defy the laws of time, space, and, often, reason and still be accepted by the audience—which suspends reality and temporarily accepts the fantasy
of an animated world
•animation helps simplify and explain complex structures and processes (e.g., how
a human heart works, the inside of an automobile engine, the various stages in the
formation of human life); concepts and ideas can be isolated, dissected, reassembled,
and reviewed through the innovative techniques of animation
•although production costs remain relatively high for quality animation work, this
presentation form is financially competitive with other available formats (e.g., live-
action, narration, etc.)
•it has longevity: animated programs and segments tend to avoid the perishability faced
by most broadcast programs; engaging animated characters and situations can be used
to communicate an idea or an emotion in a universal and timeless manner

Approaches

It is important that the writer for an animation script anticipate every visual and aural
detail. Once production begins, it is too late to add new script ideas or production
concepts. The cost and complexity of animation preclude this luxury.

An animation project normally begins with an idea for a story line, a character, or a
situation. The idea might be original or adapted from some other medium (e.g., books,
comic books, comic strips, silent films, theatrical plays, magazine articles, etc.). A story
treatment is developed, especially for longer, more complex, animated projects. It is
helpful for the writer to outline the story idea including key action and plot points,
characters, situations, action, dialogue, music and sound effects. A rough storyboard
can then be prepared to visualize the various sequences and to arrange them into
a logical progression. Dialogue is then written, recorded, and plotted on "barsheets,"
which provide a visual display of the sound track, later matched with the animated
pictures. Background music and narration can be added later. From the storyboard
sketches and the script, camera shots, special visual effects, transitions, and movements
are plotted on "exposure sheets," which are a visual display of the action to be filmed once the animated material has been prepared for shooting.

For a Saturday morning animated series, a one-page idea or premise statement for
each episode is prepared to obtain approval from the network that broadcasts the series.
Once the initial idea has been approved, a ten- to twelve-page outline or treatment
is written. The story editor for the series works with the program's director, the

storyboard artist, and the writer to create and refine the storyboard and script that eventually are used to produce the animated program.

The script page format used for animation projects is similar to live-action formats. In animated projects, however, *two* pages of script are required to provide approximately 1 minute of screen time. Animation particularly calls for this two for one ratio because, as a predominantly visual medium, it requires the writer to develop a director's eye and to indicate when to move the camera, what to show, and how to present the characters and situations effectively. The animation script, more than other script forms, requires the writer to provide many more production details.

Writing Techniques and Suggestions

In addition to the suggestions already provided, several others should assist the writer of animated projects.

1. Let animated humor grow naturally out of inherently logical situations and characters.
2. Clearly delineate each animated character to provide recognizable contrast, consistency, predictability, and believability in all situations.
3. Develop concepts which extend beyond human limits and abilities.
4. *Suggest* rather than show blatant violence in animated projects. This approach avoids potential censorship and content clearance problems.
5. Avoid including harmful actions in the script which could be duplicated by audience members.
6. Avoid including material which might unduly date the script. Make your script fresh and universal in anticipation of multiple reruns over an extended period of time.

Thundarr the Barbarian

This series, produced by Ruby-Spears Productions, Inc., won critical acclaim and captured a large audience of both children and adults when it first aired. The opening narration sequence (fig. 10-7) provides a quick, vivid, and enticing introduction to the characters and setting for the series.

In the pilot episode for the series, entitled "Secret of the Black Pearl" (storyboard by Dick Sebast and script by Steve Gerber), Thundarr, Ariel, and Ookla rescue Tyronn, courier of the Black Pearl, from a swarming tribe of Groundlings (hairy mutant man-rats with burning red eyes). Because of his weakened condition, Tyronn asks them to take the magical Black Pearl to the humans who dwell in the Ruins of Manhatt (the ruins of the borough of Manhattan). They accept the challenge. Meanwhile, the Chieftain of the Groundlings is given a command by Wizard Gemini—destroy Thundarr and recover the Black Pearl or the Groundlings will pay a terrible price.

The Groundlings attack on motorcycles, swinging laser-firing metal clubs. Thundarr

THUNDARR OPENING NARRATION

The year is 1994 -- from out of space comes a runaway planet, hurtling between the earth and moon -- unleashing cosmic destruction!

> (<u>VISUAL</u>: EARTH AND MOON SEEN FROM SPACE. RUNAWAY PLANET PASSES BETWEEN THEM. MOON CRACKS IN TWO. RUNAWAY PLANET SHATTERS. PUSH IN ON EARTH.)

Man's civilization is cast into ruin!

> (<u>VISUAL</u>: ON EARTH. TIDAL WAVES, EARTHQUAKES, VOLCANIC ACTIVITY DESTROYS CITIES, RESHAPES THE FACE OF THE GLOBE.)

2,000 years later, earth is reborn! A strange new world rises from the old -- a world of savagery and super-science, a world of sorcery and slavery!

> (<u>VISUAL</u>: ACTION SHOTS OF NEW EARTH. IN RAPID-FIRE SUCCESSION - THE MUTANT JUNGLES, MARSHLANDS, FORESTS AND THEIR STRANGE NEW CREATURES, THEN ONE OF THE SORCERERS' CITADELS WITH ITS ENSLAVED HUMANITY.)

But one man bursts his bonds and dares to fight for justice!

> (<u>VISUAL</u>: THUNDARR, LITERALLY PULLING APART THE SHACKLES AND CHAINS THAT BIND HIM WITH HIS BARE HANDS.)

With his companions, OOKLA THE MOK and the PRINCESS ARIEL, he pits his strength, courage, and his fabulous SUNSWORD against the wizards' tyranny and the forces of evil! He is -- THUNDARR THE BARBARIAN!

> (<u>VISUAL</u>: ACTION SHOTS OF THUNDARR, OOKLA, AND ARIEL. THUNDARR FIGHTING WITH SUNSWORD. ARIEL CASTING SPELLS, OOKLA RIPPING THROUGH A WALL. THUNDARR ON HORSEBACK, IN ACROBATIC ACTION, ETC.)

Figure 10-7   Opening narration sequence for the *Thundarr The Barbarian* series. *(Courtesy of Ruby-Spears Productions, Inc.)*

---

soundly defeats the Groundlings and their Chieftain. The Wizard Gemini vows to recapture the pearl and crush Thundarr.

Gemini's Knights capture Ariel while she, Thundarr, and Ookla explore the Ruins of Manhatt. The Knights threaten to kill her unless Thundarr gives them the Black Pearl.

As Act II begins, Thundarr discovers that the Black Pearl protects its holder from magical attacks. Thundarr and Ookla defeat Gemini's Knights and steal their twentieth-century helicopter. The human dwellers of Manhatt show themselves and agree to welcome Thundarr and his allies as friends. Meanwhile, Ariel remains a captive in Gemini's stronghold as the Wizard waits for Thundarr's attempted rescue.

Just as Thundarr is about to present the Black Pearl to the Manhatt humans and to tell them of its magical powers, Gemini appears against a background of rolling black clouds and jagged lightning bolts, thunder crashing, and lightning slicing across the sky. The humans refuse to release the magical pearl despite the fatal consequences. Gemini's sorcerous blasts strike the Statue of Liberty. The aged metal giant shudders and then moves its limbs, fully animate. The Statue's torch blazes with a sorcerous flame which spurts like a Roman candle at Thundarr and the Manhattanites. The final battle begins (figs. 10-8 and 10-9).

The intense battle ends as Thundarr remembers the magical powers of the Black Pearl and hurls the gem at the Statue. As the pearl strikes the Statue, the blue flame at the center of the pearl spreads over and then engulfs the metal giant. Gemini, standing at the base of the statue, suddenly writhes in the mystical energy of the blue flame. Gradually, Gemini disappears and with him the imminent danger to the Manhatt humans.

A celebration follows. Thundarr is melancholy because he had to destroy the pearl to save their lives. In the closing sequence, Thundarr draws his Sunsword, lifts it forward in a "charge" position and shouts "Onward! A world of wonders lies before us!"

This episode of *Thundarr the Barbarian* as well as many other animated program series and projects illustrate the magic and wonder of animation. For the writer, animation provides still another creative outlet. But, quality animation work requires skilled,

---

THE STATUE

aims its torch downward. SHOT WIDENS as its sorcerous flame SPURTS like a Roman candle at Thundarr and the Manhattanites!

ARIEL

gestures magically. A SILVERY BURST flashes from her palms, hurtling UP AND OUT OF FRAME.

WIDE SHOT - THE RUINS

As Ariel's magical burst and the statue's spurting flame COLLIDE IN A MAGICAL EXPLOSION over the heads of the humans, each neutralizing the other!

Figure 10-8 Full-script excerpt from the *Thundarr The Barbarian* episode entitled "Secret of the Black Pearl." *(Courtesy of Ruby-Spears Productions, Inc.)*

TIGHT ON THE STATUE

About to launch another burst, it REACTS to the FWASSSH of Thundarr's Sunsword, and looks down. CAMERA PANS DOWN the Statue's body to its feet, where Thundarr, the pearl in one hand, the sword in the other, is HACKING AWAY at its metal gown.

> THUNDARR
> (shouting)
> It's still a thing of metal!
> It's not alive! How can it
> move?!

OOKLA

snatches a length of twisted metal out of the muck and comes running toward the Statue. CAMERA TRACKING.

> OOKLA
>
> (MOK GROWL: "Smash first, ask
> questions later!")

SHOT WIDENS as he dashes past Thundarr, leaps, and gloms onto the Statue's copper form! CAMERA TRACKS as he begins a strange climb up the Statue's body and OUT OF FRAME.

ANGLE THE STATUE'S HEAD

As Ookla climbs UP INTO FRAME, over the Statue's chin...and lips...over its nose...and brow...onto its noggin. PUSH IN as Ookla wields the length of metal like a club and WHAPS the Statue repeatedly on the noodle! SFX: WHACKAWHACKA-WHACKAWHACKA!!!

> OOKLA
> (MIGHTY MOK ROAR)

Fig. 10-8   *(Continued)*

---

professional specialists working with patient exactitude over an extended period of time.

GAME SHOWS

Game shows are an important part of commercial television networks' daytime schedule and often form the basis for local station programming during access time (i.e., the time just after the early evening newscast and before primetime network pro-

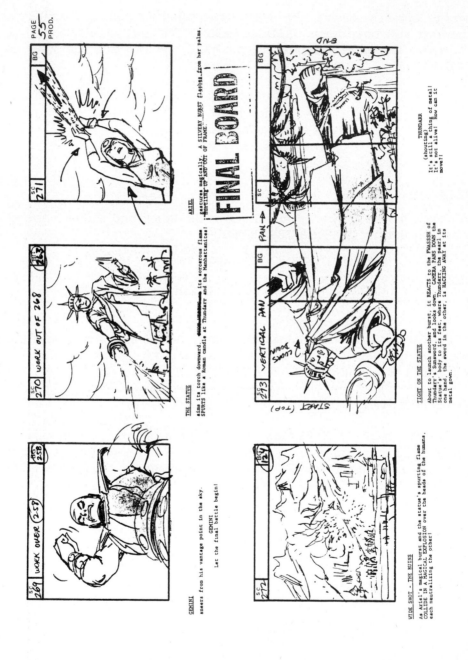

Figure 10-9 Storyboard for the full-script excerpt shown in figure 10-8. (*Courtesy of Ruby-Spears Productions, Inc.*)

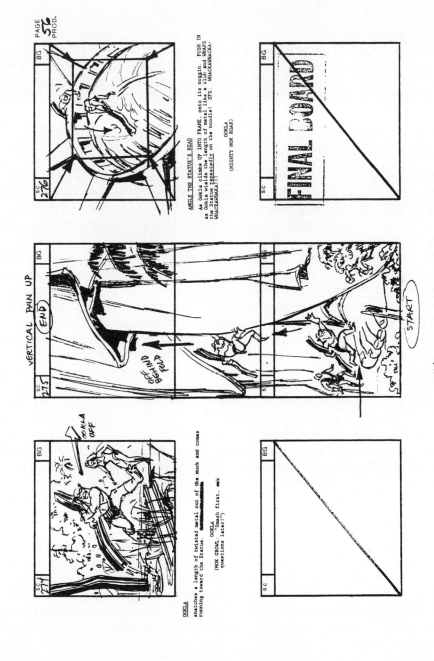

Fig. 10-9 *(Continued)*

gramming begins). Game show series are produced for network television use only, syndication only or, sometimes, for both network and syndication use.

To begin to explain the creative process involved and to place this programming form in perspective, a definition may be helpful. A game show involves a participant competing with others or alone against another contestant or group of contestants, working against time, under an established set of rules, to perform a specific skill in hopes of winning (money, prizes, merchandise, prestige). It is a contest of some kind where the rules of the game are laid out beforehand and then the participants simply join in the action.

Approaches

While it may appear to be easy, developing a strong game show series entry is difficult and extremely competitive. Most of the game show series now on television are produced by a handful of production companies. The precision and efficiency observed in long-running game show series comes only after careful and thoughtful planning and development.

The concept or idea for the game show series comes first. Then, the structure and rules for the game are developed in a master script for the series. In most cases, the fundamental concept remains constant throughout the life of the series, but variations or adaptations may be added during successive years to enliven and freshen the original program concept or idea. Most game show details are finally decided upon after the program has been pitched in a proposal and the program idea initially accepted. This process may require months and sometimes years before the game show sees "the light of day."

The concept or idea for the game show must be developed, tried, improved, adjusted, refined, and polished to produce a combination of elements which work consistently and effectively. Every detail must be considered: precise rules of the game (with all possible variations and alternatives); the logistics of handling tie games and interrupted games carried over from the previous show; the format and timing of each program segment; the pace and tempo to be established and maintained in each program; production quality and technical requirements; the selection and use of contestants as well as the host or M.C.; the amount and type of participation desired by the in-studio and at-home audiences; the amount and type of prizes to be awarded; and, most important, the marketability of the game show series.

Game show proposals may be written but generally are presented in a verbal pitch to a production company representative, a packager (who pulls together the various components necessary to produce the show), or occasionally to a network representative. Whether presented in written or verbal form, the proposal becomes a hard sell, practical description of the basic program series idea or concept. The proposal must generate excitement for the concept and anticipate basic questions and details about the game show series.

Most often, the writer is involved in writing only the rundown or routine sheet for the game show. The concept or idea for the program series is developed by the packager or production company. Writers who regularly work on game show development function as both writer and producer and, thus, do not have to separate writing and producing activities. Also, staff writers, employed by the game show production company, may be involved in the evolution of the master script as well as the material needed for individual programs.

It should be emphasized that there is a minimal amount of writing required for a continuing game show series. These programs are games and to all intents and purposes do not require what traditionally might be regarded as "writing." The key writing activity is the development of the master script for the series.

Writing Techniques and Suggestions

As the game show concept evolves, the writer helps develop a master script for the series. This basic document provides a blueprint to ensure consistency among programs in the series, but still allows for the spontaneity necessary for each program. The master script is revised and refined throughout the development process and even after the series is on the air. Material for individual programs is prepared by other writers or production assistants using the parameters and requirements established in the master script.

The master script details, in either a semi-script or show format, such program elements as: opening, closing, introduction and interviewing of contestants, statement of the game rules and categories, transitions between segments, introductions to commercial breaks, announcement of winners and losers, and essential stage directions for getting the host or M.C. as well as contestants on and off the set.

Although the standard semi-script or show format script form is used, the master script for a game show is written so that specific kinds of information are included: each program segment must be clearly identified on each script page; succinctly written material must be provided for each segment; a modified two-column television format is used in which the left column is kept blank for directorial and production notations while the right column contains audio, video, and talent directions written in FULL CAPS and enclosed in parentheses plus the words read by the program talent written in regular upper and lowercase letters; key words (relating to crucial game rules), requiring emphasis, are underlined; and throughout the script, blanks should be provided, as appropriate, to help customize each program in the series.

The New $25,000 Pyramid

Dick Clark hosts this popular Bob Stewart production which has won an Emmy Award and which has been seen on network television since the early 1970's. It is a variation of the successful *Password* series. On *The New $25,000 Pyramid,* however, celebrities work as co-contestants to provide clues to guess a subject area or phrase rather than a specific word. The prize money at stake increases as the game progresses and builds to the climactic "big board" segment in which up to $25,000 can be won. A special set area is used to heighten the intensity and excitement for the try at the big money.

Figure 10-10 is the rundown sheet for the show. Notice how each major segment is identified and both segment and continuous program running time are indicated to ensure proper pacing and flow for the program. The rundown sheet is prepared as a parallel to the series master script.

Figure 10-11 is the master script page for the opening to segment number 3 of *The New $25,000 Pyramid* game show series. It illustrates the special scripting techniques described earlier for writing an effective master script.

"THE $25,000 PYRAMID"

RUNDOWN

		SEGMENT TIME	RUNNING TIME
1.	OPENING - INTERVIEWS - GAME #1		8:10
2.	COMMERCIAL BREAK	(1:03)	9:10
3.	BIG BOARD #1 ($10,000 TRY)	(2:00)	11:20
4.	COMMERCIAL BREAK	(2:05)	13:25
5.	GAME #2	(7:00)	20:25
6.	COMMERCIAL BREAK	(2:26)	22:50
7.	BIG BOARD #2 ($10,000/$25,000 TRY)	(2:00)	25:35
8.	COMMERCIAL BREAK	(1:03)	26:20
9.	CLOSING - A. GOODBYE	(:35)	
	B. PLUGS	(:50)	
	C. DISCLAIMERS	(:10)	
	D. CREDITS	(:20)	28:22

Figure 10-10 Rundown sheet for *The New $25,000 Pyramid*. *(Courtesy of Bob Stewart Productions)*

```
DICK:     (OUT OF COMMERCIAL)

          CONTESTANT. You're going for
          $_____. To win it all,
          you must name the six subjects on
          the Pyramid in less than 60 seconds.

          CELEBRITY. You're only allowed
          to give a LIST of the things that
          fit the subject. If you use your
          hands to describe _____or give
          a clue -- or mention part of the
          subject, you'll hear this sound:

          (BUZZER)

          Which means you give up the chance
          to win the $_____.

          You have one minute to win $_____.
          -- Here's the first subject....GO!
```

Figure 10-11 Master script page for the opening to segment 3 indicated in the rundown sheet in figure 10-10. *(Courtesy of Bob Stewart Productions)*

CONCLUSION

The brief examination of specialized forms of broadcast writing in this chapter had the purpose of outlining the content and objectives of such programs and of explaining methods used to prepare specific kinds of scripts. This chapter also offered suggestions and techniques for preparing the written material. Although each writing situation is different, there is a noticeable overlap in the writer's approach to the preparation of such diverse scripts as well as to the final writing and presentation of the script material.

Each situation offers unique creative opportunities to develop specialized writing skills. The experienced, seasoned writer should find such opportunities interesting enough to pursue under certain circumstances. The novice writer should find these opportunities challenging and look forward to working on these kinds of scripts after mastering basic broadcast writing skills. Some writers work in these specialized areas exclusively. They continue to refine their special writing talent and strive to become master craftsmen in a restricted writing area. Other writers diversify their efforts and use the special writing techniques and approaches outlined for various kinds of writing.

The information in this chapter points up the need to identify the specific writing requirements of a situation, acquire the necessary writing skills, integrate the successes and failures of past writing experiences with each new undertaking, and approach each new writing opportunity with confidence, enthusiasm, and a strong creative spirit willing to explore a new writing outlet.

SUGGESTED EXERCISES AND PROJECTS

1. Write a full-script (length to be determined) for one of the following compilation programs: (a) a musical year-in-review for one of the standard radio format designations; (b) a world and national news year-in-review; (c) a sports year-in-review for one team or for one sport at the college or professional level; (d) an entertainment industry year-in-review.
2. Design a thirteen-week radio magazine feature program series. The subjects or topics featured in the series may include any of the following: consumerism, home repairs, personal finances and investments, crime prevention, health and medicine, nostalgia, religion, news or sports personalities or events, agriculture, children, entertainment news items and personalities, and issues related to specific and identifiable minority or ethnic groups. Submit the following material: (a) a brief prospectus for the thirteen-program series (title; suggested program length, adjacencies and day/time of the broadcasts; purpose, justification or need, and marketability of the series); (b) a routine sheet for the series; (c) a brief description of the content of each segment of each program in the series; (d) the full-script for the first program in the series.
3. Follow the steps outlined in exercise 2, but for a *television* magazine feature program series.
4. Submit the rundown sheet for a radio or television magazine program you have monitored.
5. Prepare a routine sheet and appropriate filler material for the live radio or television broadcast of one of the following special events: the next major athletic event in your community; a news conference by the governor of your state; election-night coverage for the next scheduled statewide election; a one-night telethon for a local non-profit, charitable organization; a special local or statewide awards presentation.
6. Watch several programs in one of the following series: *Sesame Street, 3-2-1 Contact, The Electric Company, Powerhouse.* Report your observations on: writing and production style and techniques; story lines; characters or talent presented; program diversity and pacing; and entertainment value. Provide the rundown sheet for one of the programs.
7. Watch at least 2 hours of Saturday morning commercial network children's programming. Follow the reporting steps outlined in exercise 6.
8. Compare and contrast the children's programs viewed in exercises 6 and 7.

9. Individually or as a member of a writing team, prepare a rundown or routine sheet for a new half-hour children's television program. Then, write the full-script for this program.

10. Write a full-script for a current Saturday morning commercial television network animated children's program series.

11. Write the full-script and, if possible, provide a preliminary storyboard for a 1- to 3-minute animated segment to be used in a television program series aimed at children seven to ten years old. Then, show how the script can be adjusted for use in series aimed at children three to six or eight/ten to twelve years old.

12. Write the full-script and, if possible, provide a preliminary storyboard for a 5- to 15-minute animated art film or short subject.

13. Use a popular Sunday newspaper comic strip as a storyboard to write the full-script for a short animated or live-action sequence. Then, create other short sequences, in full-script form, for the same comic strip.

14. Watch two different television network or syndicated game show series. Critique each program using the suggestions and techniques contained in this chapter.

15. Develop a game show idea or concept based upon or patterned after one of the popular arcade or home video computer games or a popular card or board game. The two- to five-page proposal for your half-hour television game show series should include information about: the title of the series; the rules of the game (with all possible variations and categories); the format or order of events to be followed in each program in the series; the approximate timing of each principal segment; the recommended characteristics of the program host or M.C. to be selected; the selection and use of contestants; the types of prizes to be awarded; the technical requirements and tentative production schedule for the series; and a brief description of why your game show is entertaining, marketable, and distinctive from other current television game show series.

16. Individually or as a member of a writing team, prepare the rundown sheet and then the master script in semi-script form for the pilot program in the game show series developed in exercise 15.

NOTES

1. Summary of a portion of a letter (dated September 20, 1982) from Arlene Sherman (Associate Producer, *Sesame Street*) to the author.

2. Summary of information from Paul da Silva, *The World of Animation* (Rochester, N.Y.: Eastman Kodak Co., 1979), pp. 35, 99–110.

ADDITIONAL READING

Anderson, Kent, ed. *Television Fraud: The History and Implications of the Quiz Show Scandals.* Westport, Conn.: Greenwood Press, 1978.

Bryant, Jennings, and Anderson, Daniel R., eds. *Children's Understanding of Television: Research on Attention and Comprehension*. New York: Academic Press, 1983.

Butler, Matilda, and Paisley, William. *Women and the Mass Media*. New York: Human Sciences Press, 1980.

Doerken, Maurine. *Classroom Combat: Teaching and Television*. Englewood Cliffs, N.J.: Educational Technology Publications, 1983.

Fabe, Maxene. *TV Game Shows*. Garden City, N.Y.: Doubleday and Co., 1980.

Fates, Gil. *What's My Line: The Inside Story of TV's Most Famous Panel Show*. Englewood Cliffs, N.J.: Prentice-Hall, 1978.

Friedwall, Will, and Beck, Jerry. *The Warner Brothers Cartoons*. Metuchen, N.J.; Scarecrow Press, 1981.

Hadden, Jeffrey K., and Swann, Charles E. *Prime Time Preachers: The Rising Power of Televangelism*. Reading, Mass.: Addison-Wesley, 1981.

Hayward, Stan. *Scriptwriting for Animation*. New York: Hastings House, 1977.

Horsfield, Peter. *Religious Television: The Experience in America*. New York: Longman, 1984.

Lesser, Gerald. *Children and Television: Lessons from "Sesame Street."* New York: Random House, 1974.

Liebert, Robert M.; Sprafkin, Joyce N.; and Davidson, Emily S. *The Early Window: Effects of Television on Children and Youth*. 2d ed. Elmsford, N.Y.: Pergamon Press, 1982.

National Association of Broadcasters. Television Office. *Kids' Stuff: A Resource Book for Children's Television Programming*. Washington, D.C.: NAB, 1980.

Turow, Joseph. *Entertainment, Education, and the Hard Sell: Three Decades of Network Children's Television*. New York: Praeger, 1981.

U.S. Federal Communications Commission. *Television Programming for Children: A Report of the Children's Television Task Force*. 5 vols. Washington, D.C.: FCC, October, 1979.

Winick, Mariann Pezzella, and Winick, Charles. *The Television Experience: What Children See*. Beverly Hills: Sage, 1979.

Winn, Marie. *The Plug-in Drug: Television, Children and the Family*. New York: Grossman, 1977.

Woolery, George W. *Children's Television: The First Thirty Five Years, 1946-1981; Part I: Animated Cartoon Series*. Metuchen, N.J.: Scarecrow Press, 1983. *Part II: Live, Film, and Tape Series*. Metuchen, N.J.: Scarecrow Press, 1984.

Chapter Eleven

INSTRUCTIONAL, EDUCATIONAL, INDUSTRIAL, AND CORPORATE PRESENTATIONS

A vital and growing area of the telecommunications industry is the design and production of instructional, educational, industrial, and corporate presentations. Many diverse groups and organizations use various media to inform, train, persuade, and even entertain specific targeted audiences.

Governmental agencies and educational institutions long have recognized the importance of quality audiovisual material for instruction and education. Business and industry have enhanced the technological capabilities to design, write, produce, and deliver worthwhile material to train employees, upgrade skills, and present complex material in an interesting, well-organized manner. "Corporate Video" and "Professional Video Specialist" have begun to replace the more restrictive "non-broadcast," "ITV," and "A-V Specialist" designations. Private companies, corporations, professional and special interest organizations, trade associations, medical and health service groups, religious organizations, and independent production companies are generating a larger quantity and generally a higher quality of material for instructional, educational, industrial, and corporate applications.

Programs and presentations are being designed and produced for various purposes including internal communications, public education, public service, community relations, sales and marketing, training, education, and employee morale. The content is varied—company news, employee profiles, updates on internal forms and procedures, current issues and policy statements, historical vignettes and profiles, reports on positive programs and projects, introduction of new product lines, effective sales techniques and procedures, the use of new technology, repair and maintenance of equipment, job safety.

Many of the presentational forms discussed in this book (e.g., dramas, talk shows, magazine programs, documentaries, and investigative reports) incorporate education or instruction in their program design. "Industrial or corporate video," "educational program," or "instructional presentation" refer to the context or setting in which certain kinds of presentations are used. Almost any type of program or presentation can be used in various contexts. For example, a television drama or documentary which examines the causes and consequences of child abuse could be useful for a sociology or criminal justice class studying this subject or a community service organization beginning to train new volunteers for self-help activities in this area. A talk program featuring leaders of major industrial nations may be the initial stimulus for further discussion of current issues and developments by political science or international relations students or perhaps executives in an import/export business.

Many forms of media are used in these kinds of presentations. The most common are slides, filmstrips, audiotapes, videotapes, motion picture films, multi-media presentations, and various kinds of print material. Each form requires specialized writing skills and presentational techniques.

This chapter will focus on the visual media, specifically motion picture films and videotapes. Except in only a few situations, audiotapes are not used extensively for formal instructional or educational purposes nor for most industrial or corporate applications. Slides, filmstrips, multi-media presentations and print material require unique skills and procedures that are beyond the scope of this book. Some of the suggested readings listed at the end of this chapter touch on writing for these media.

In this chapter, the emphasis will be on the role and function of the writer in the preparation of script material for instructional, educational, industrial, and corporate motion picture film and videotape presentations. The basic design process used for these types of presentations will be outlined with particular emphasis on establishing and accomplishing specific goals and objectives to reach an identifiable audience with an effective, organized message using available resources. The scripting process involved for such presentations will be traced with emphasis placed on how to apply standard scripting steps to the preparation of such material and how the writer needs to become involved early in the planning and development of such scripting. Case studies or profiles will be presented at the end of the chapter to illustrate the principles and techniques discussed.

THE DESIGN AND SCRIPTING PROCESSES

The design and scripting processes to be described applies most directly to independent production companies. In-house production units follow essentially the same process, but often modify, condense, or even bypass some of the steps outlined. A large share of the presentations prepared for industrial, corporate, educational, and instructional purposes are produced by in-house production units. Each kind of situation and application requires some adjustment. With some modification, the standard broadcast writing and production techniques already described and illustrated in this book are used for these special kinds of programs and presentations.

The writer should be actively involved in these early stages of project development since the decisions made will determine how the writer molds and shapes the presentation to exact specifications. The writer must be aware of how these important decisions are made and what concepts and strategies are accepted and rejected. The writer can then use the most effective scripting approaches and techniques.

Contact the Client

A client may approach a production company or independent producer to design a specific presentation. The client's selection usually is based on the quality of previous work or perhaps the reputation of the individuals or the company involved. In some situations, the production company or independent producer may bid on a project already formulated by the client or may generate the initial idea for a presentation and then approach the client to secure acceptance of the idea and funding for further development.

In-house production units have only one client—the company, organization, institution, or agency which employs them. In this situation, the initial idea for a presentation may come from the production unit or from a particular individual or division within the organization. Often, regular contact is maintained to ensure systematic development of worthwhile proposals and projects.

Consult the Client

This is a crucial stage in the development of a presentation. It will lay the foundation and set the course for the rest of the design and scripting process. It must be a cooperative effort between representatives from the production unit and the client. If at all possible, the writer should be involved in these discussions. The ideas and comments which come from these meetings will help guide the writer later on. Several important decisions must be made at this point: goals and objectives, intended audience, organization of content, resources available, presentation design, media to be used, budget, timetables and deadlines, and approval points.

Goals and Objectives. The intent or purpose of the presentation must be determined. Does an important problem exist which might be solved by designing a special presentation? What is the communications task to be accomplished? What should the viewer get from this presentation? What should be the result after this presentation is seen? What should the viewer know, feel, or be able to do after the presentation is shown?

A general goal could be identified first—information, instruction, training, enrichment, inspiration, motivation, persuasion, or entertainment. These general goals often overlap and fuse into a combined set of goals; however, it is best if only one primary goal is selected.

The general goal should be refined into a specific statement of behavioral objectives. These objectives should be placed in written form and approved by the client before scriptwriting begins. This will help the writer select, organize, and present the material effectively. This procedure will also ensure the accountability of the script and the resultant presentation.

Behavior objectives can be grouped into three primary categories or "domains":

• *Cognitive.* Here information is presented to convey knowledge and stimulate learning. Examples include the orientation of new students or employees, an overview of a company's or institution's goals and projects, and the history or geography of a particular country.
• *Affective.* In this case thoughts, feelings, emotions, attitudes, values, and certain actions are stimulated or motivated in a certain direction. Examples include convincing students to discontinue the use of harmful drugs, improving employee morale, and accepting the reality of cancer treatment.
• *Psychomotor.* Specific skills and procedures are presented. Examples include presentations on how to use a drill press, how to fill out an income tax form correctly, and the proper hand grips used in tennis.

Each behavioral objective category or domain comprises several levels. For example, the cognitive domain includes knowledge, comprehension, application, analysis, synthesis, and evaluation. Select the appropriate level within each domain and use specific language to formulate that particular kind of behavioral objective.

Three components are included in an effective statement of behavioral objectives—action, condition, and standard. It is necessary to determine what someone must do (action) under what circumstances (condition) with what degree of accuracy or skill (standard).

A few examples should help illustrate how a variety of specific behavioral objectives can be formulated for the same topic. See figure 11-1. The writer will need to select a specific behavioral objective to prepare script material at a later stage of development.

Not all projects can be based upon stringent behavioral objectives. Many topics are very abstract and elusive when it comes to identifying and measuring behavioral objectives. But the effort involved in formulating such objectives in clear, simple, specific, and straightforward language will help crystallize ideas and provide a sound basis for writing the script and producing the presentation.

Intended Audience. During this preliminary meeting with the client, it is necessary to identify the target or intended audience for the presentation. To whom will the presentation be directed? Preliminary research or information may have to be gathered to determine such items as the intended audience's educational level, background,

A presentation on a new employee group insurance plan

Cognitive Objective. After viewing this presentation, employees will be able to accurately compare and contrast the old and the new group insurance plans.

Affective Objective. After viewing this presentation, employees will be motivated to sign up for the new group insurance plan.

Psychomotor Objective. After viewing this presentation, employees will be able to fill out the necessary forms to activate the new group insurance plan coverage.

A presentation on new technology and equipment in a company

Cognitive Objective. After seeing this presentation, viewers will be able to list the new technology and equipment available to company employees.

Affective Objective. After seeing this presentation, viewers will be motivated to accept the new technology and equipment available to improve job productivity.

Psychomotor Objective. After seeing this presentation, viewers will be able to enter inventory information into the company's computer system.

A presentation on musical notations

Cognitive Objective. After seeing this presentation, the student will be able to identify correctly the symbols used for bass and treble clefs, sharps, flats, and natural signs.

Affective Objective. After viewing this presentation, the student will be motivated to appreciate the precision used in making basic musical notations.

Psychomotor Objective. After seeing this presentation, the student will be able to write, in proper form, the musical notation symbols for bass and treble clefs, sharps, flats, and natural signs.

Figure 11-1 Examples of the three principal types of behavioral objectives prepared for various topics.

---

interests, current knowledge and attitudes about the client or subject matter, learning requirements, language, and visualization usage.

In addition, it would be helpful to determine why the intended audience would watch the presentation. Will it be required? Will the presentation be viewed voluntarily? Will the viewing of the presentation be considered crucial to personal or professional development and fulfillment? The more that is known about the intended audience, the better the material can be written and presented to meet specific behavioral objectives.

Organization of Content. Determine what will be included in the presentation. List the primary and secondary points to be made. The goals and objectives statement should guide in the selection and treatment of each primary idea. Limit each presentation to only two or three major points. If more than two or three primary points emerge at this stage, consider redirecting or restructuring the presentation. It is better to present a few ideas well than to try to cram too much information into a single presentation. At a later development stage, the writer will expand the major points identified in this preliminary meeting with the client.

Resources Available. At this same client conference, available resources relating to the project should be identified. These resources might include: access to archival material; pertinent research data gathered by the client or by outside sources; the services of a technical adviser, content specialist, or program consultant; assistance from a research assistant or a typist; and other material, programs, and presentations available to the client and relating to the project under development. The resources may be extensive or limited. They could include people, facilities, equipment, information, or services.

Presentation Design. An important strategy consideration involves deciding how to present the material. Should the material be arranged into a single presentation or a series of presentations? What should be the length of the presentation(s)? Should the presentation(s) be designed for individualized instruction or for small or large group use? At home or work, in school, in a social or business environment? Although the writer generally does not decide how the material will be used, it is important that the writer understand the various considerations used in making that kind of decision. This type of information will help the writer mold and shape the material to exacting specifications.

Media to Be Used. Generally, how the presentation will be utilized will determine the media used to deliver the content effectively. Select the best medium or format for the specific communications task. (See, in chapter 2, "Selecting the Medium.")

Budget. Even at this preliminary stage it is necessary to have an estimated budget in mind so that the production unit and writer can operate at a realistic level of development. Some clients already have a budget in hand for each project. A budget or several versions of a budget may have to be devised before further development of the project can continue. Formal approval of the project's budget generally comes at a later stage of development.

The writer should be aware of the budgeting process and of the final budget for each project. Many writers function in a hyphenated role (e.g., writer-producer or writer-director). Knowing the budget for a project allows the writer to anticipate constraints and to control the eventual shape and quality of the final product more effectively to meet project specifications and expectations.

The availability and even the source of funds may cause certain writing and production limitations and constraints. Very effective and creative presentations, however, have been written and produced on relatively low budgets.

Timetables and Deadlines. Tentative deadlines should be established for each major step in the design and scripting process. These can be formalized later when a written bid or proposal is submitted for the client's approval. It is important to consider all of the factors relating to the project before trying to establish realistic deadlines which satisfy the needs of the client, the production company, and the writer.

Approval Points. There are several points or stages during the development process when the client may exercise approval rights. Identifying the specific approval points with the client and placing them into the formal contract, bid, or proposal will help ensure that everyone involved in the project is communicating properly on a regular basis and that satisfactory progress is being made. The approval points might include: the final budget, each major stage of scripting development (treatment, sequence outline, first and subsequent drafts of the full-script), selection and use of on-camera talent (voice and picture) and graphics, the use of locations and production sites, and the final edited version of the presentation. Other approval points may be needed in particular instances.

The use of numerous approval points slows the development process as more people get involved in clearing or approving such items as content, policy, format, security, and usage. Determine who ultimately will own the rights to duplicate and show the finished presentation. This may help to identify the key people who should be involved at each approval point.

Prepare the Proposal

The production and creative staff, including the writer, discuss and evaluate the determinations made during the client consultation. A proposal, sometimes called a "bid," is then prepared for presentation to the client.

The proposal is formulated based on the information supplied by the client and the capabilities and interests of those preparing the proposal. The proposal may be for any combination of further development steps—budget, goals and objectives, treatments, full-script, production of the finished program or presentation, postproduction evaluation, and the like. For example, the proposal may be made to develop only a goals and objectives statement for use in supplemental material, or it could be made to develop only the final script for the presentation. A full service unit will prepare a complete proposal which details goals and objectives, costs, timetables and deadlines, approval points, promotion, evaluation, the skeletal outline of the presentation, and special needs, objectives, and concepts related to the presentation.

The proposal, written in a concise and direct manner, should reflect the primary concerns of the client. Even for in-house clients, it is important that a proposal be written in the style and language the client expects to see. It must reflect a special interest and insight into the client's needs and expectations. When structuring the proposal, ask yourself what the people reading the proposal will want to know. More than likely their primary interest will be the results they can anticipate from their investment. Thus, you should list the results or benefits of the project in the first section of the proposal. Present the remaining information in a decreasing order of importance. An effective proposal clearly delineates the client's primary concerns and interests and shows the client the quantitative and qualitative benefits to be derived from the presentation.

Review the Proposal/Finalize the Contract

The client reviews the proposal and may reject it, request changes, or accept it as written. If the client rejects the proposal, the writer may either have to abandon the project or prepare a new proposal after further consultation with the client. If the client requests changes, the proposal may be adjusted and resubmitted to the client for approval.

If the client accepts the proposal, a formal contract is prepared. The contract becomes a legally binding document and details such items as costs, approval points, timetables and deadlines, policies and procedures to be followed, general responsibilities of all parties, and control of the rights to the finished program or presentation. In-house projects do not require a formal contract, but some type of statement may be drawn to clarify the responsibilities and expectations of the in-house units involved.

Prepare Script Material

If the writer has been involved in the early stages of development, he or she knows the requirements of the project. Otherwise, the writer should be briefed thoroughly about the client's requirements, interests, and concerns. The specific information contained in the proposal and the contract now requires review and evaluation from the scriptwriter's perspective.

The scripting steps listed may not apply in all cases; however, this description should familiarize you with how the majority of such programs and presentations come together. Chapter 3 provides more details about these scripting steps.

Complete Research. In as short a time as possible, the writer must become thoroughly familiar with the subject. This involves using traditional research methods as well as tapping the available resources identified earlier in the client consultation. This is the first phase of script development.

Technical advisers, content specialists, and program consultants are a valuable resource for such presentations. They can fill in information gaps, update your research and information, help interpret complex or confusing details and specialized terminology and, often, refer you to other experts with even more specialized interests, information, and backgrounds. These resource people usually are thoroughly familiar with the subject matter, but they are not writers and often are not able to think visually in terms of what the writer needs. The writer must work with such resource people to refine the main points and goals of the presentation, clarify ambiguities, identify material that needs special emphasis or treatment, and organize the subject matter into an attractive and effective arrangement. Alternative methods of presenting the material should be discussed. Attention should be focused not only on the technical information, but on the precise wording, sequence of ideas, and visualization techniques. All too often, resource people will concentrate only on the technical information and neglect to respond to other important components of the presentation.

Field research may be appropriate. Get into the subject by becoming part of the environment you will write about. Talk to those who eventually will see the presentation. Scout locations which might be used in the script and later in production. Placing yourself in such an environment might call to your attention a unique camera angle, a distinctive sound, or an interesting person or image to include in the script.

Continue to do research throughout the writing process and maintain contact with the client or the client's representative to obtain a specific fact or detail as you assemble the script. Do not allow lack of information to be the reason for a poor script. Determine what you need, and then go find it right away.

Prepare the Treatment. As indicated in chapter 3, a treatment is a concise statement of the content of a program or presentation and explains what is planned and how it will be presented. It is not a simplified shooting script. Much of the treatment should explain *why* the material is being handled a certain way. The treatment should be written by the person who eventually will write the final shooting script for the presentation.

For the kinds of presentations under consideration in this chapter, the treatment is an efficient way for the client to review the content and to recommend changes in concepts and approaches. It is more efficient and less costly to make changes during this early development stage than to disrupt production later on when objections to the organization or visualization of the material cause unnecessary turmoil and delays. It is best to take the time to rewrite the treatment to bring the idea into harmony with the client's wishes.

The treatment needs to indicate the presentational approach that will be used. Many of the successful presentational formats described elsewhere in this book are used for corporate, industrial, educational, and instructional presentations. The once standard "talking heads" approach has been supplanted by newscasts, magazine programs, documentaries using archival material and host-narrators, reenactments, product demonstrations, role-playing exercises, dramas, simulated game shows, humor, puppets, and animation. The writer is no longer confined by a limited range of presentational approaches. The approach selected must reflect the appropriate level of visual and aural language. It must not only be interesting but high-powered to capture the increasing intensity and sophistication of today's audiences.

The organizational approach used for such presentations must arrange the material or content into logical sequences which progressively increase interest and provide proper emphasis of important points. In a single-concept instructional presentation, for example, the beginning must peak audience interest and curiosity, establish the nature and importance of the subject, and hint at how it will be developed. The middle portion needs to develop the subject in an ascending order of importance, interest, intensity, and impact so that the audience moves through the subject matter logically, clearly, naturally, and memorably. The conclusion should reestablish the main points of the presentation, interpret information and form conclusions as necessary, and provide a final thought or image to ensure the impact and memorability of the presentation.

Evaluate the Treatment. Several checkpoints or criteria should guide the writer, client, and production staff as they evaluate the treatment. Does the treatment provide a clear and concise image of the finished presentation? Is the subject matter presented clearly, simply, directly, and in the manner desired by the client? Is the eventual presentation likely to spark and sustain interest? Will it stimulate and involve the audience, motivate its members to think and react creatively and to want to learn more about the subject? Will it be memorable and eventually produce measurable, tangible results? Is the treatment realistic in its content development and production implications? The development and evaluation of the treatment should bring all parties involved in the project to mutually acceptable terms.

Prepare and Evaluate the Sequence Outline. If the treatment is prepared properly, a sequence or step outline may not be necessary. This optional, intermediate scripting step may be needed, however, if the presentation is extraordinarily complex, if the content requires even more refinement, or if the client requires it.

Write the Shooting Script. All of the writer's work and preparation lead to the writing of the shooting script. By this time, the writer has considered thousands of possibilities for presenting the subject matter. The treatment and sequence outline steps should have helped the writer focus and crystallize the presentation. At this point, the writer gets even closer to the subject, tries various scripting techniques, adjusts and fine tunes each shot and sequence—all in an effort to find the best way to present the material to the audience.

The shooting script can be written in any of the standard scripting forms described and illustrated in chapter 3. In practically all situations, a full-script is prepared. In some circumstances, however, a semi-script or a show format may be appropriate. For example, a semi-script or a show format might be appropriate for segments which include interviews, panel discussions or role-playing exercises. Use the script form that is most appropriate for the kind of segment or presentation planned and that meets or exceeds the requirements of the project and the client.

Evaluate the Shooting Script. Evaluation of the shooting script is an important approval point for the client as well as the writer and production team. The client needs to determine whether the script meets or exceeds expectations, and if each of the primary objectives identified and finally approved during the initial consultation and in the preliminary scripting stages has been realized in the shooting script.

The production team needs to determine the technical requirements and feasibility of the presentation. Thus, the writer should remember to use standard production terminology in proper form to ensure clear understanding of what is to be seen and heard.

If changes in the shooting script are required, one responsible person (preferably the producer) should synthesize the comments made by the client or the production team, present these comments to the writer, and help rework the shooting script into acceptable form. The writer should be told why a specific change is needed. Adjustments in one part of the script usually necessitate changes in other parts. If all parties involved in the project have approved the treatment or sequence outline, the changes requested at this point should be minor and should not disturb the overall approach used in the script by the writer. Nevertheless, the writer should be prepared to rewrite the script as often as necessary to refine and polish it, to give it continuity, and to make it worthy of enthusiastic acceptance by the client and ready for production.

Production Begins

Strictly speaking, the writer's work is finished once the shooting script has been approved for production unless the writer also serves as producer or director of these kinds of presentations. Combining these functions is common practice, especially for in-house production units.

Production of the script involves specific steps and procedures which require detailed explanation and illustration. For this kind of information, consult the appropriate books listed at the end of both this chapter and chapter 2.

Presentation Is Approved and Evaluated

An essential approval point for the client is the screening of the finished presentation. Changes made at this juncture are costly—in time and money. If all other development stages have gone well and received client approval, the screening of the finished presentation should provide only pleasant surprises for all involved.

The evaluation process should extend beyond cursory approval by the client. The presentation should be analyzed critically to assess how well it fulfilled the communications task identified earlier in the design process. The client should determine the cost effectiveness of the presentation as well as the increased level of productivity and the certainty of attitude changes. The production team should scrutinize audience response to specific visual and aural techniques. The writer should assess how well essential concepts and information were understood and accepted by the audience. The *results* of the presentation need to be determined. Various techniques can be used— questionnaires, surveys, pretests, posttests, and field-tests of the presentation— before it is widely distributed. This kind of evaluation should provide additional insight into the most efficient and effective means to convey messages in various situations.

PROFILES

High Feather

This series of ten 30-minute programs is

> designed to assist children [aged eight to fourteen] in developing sound nutritional habits while making them aware of nutrition-related health problems. The programs, dramatic in nature, follow a group of children through their daily activities at summer camp. Each episode contains nutrition information to enlighten young viewers while they are entertained. The continuing cast of characters is representative of the population in many towns, cities and states....*High Feather* demonstrates that dieting practices affect the way one looks and feels, and the way one behaves and learns.[1]

Nutrition topics in the series include: sugar and its effects, comparative shopping, wilderness diets, balanced low-cost meals, teenage drinking, ethnic foods, and the importance of fruits and vegetables.

The series, and individual programs from the series, won a number of awards for production excellence from such organizations as the American Academy of Pediatrics, Action for Children's Television, the Information Film Producers of America, and the New York Chapter of the Academy of Television Arts and Sciences.

Kroyt-Brandt Productions, Inc. was hired by the New York State Education Department to produce the series. Yanna Kroyt Brandt explained how the series was developed:

> Initially, there were a series of meetings with a group of five nutrition consultants and myself as executive producer, the producer, and associate producer. We asked them to make a list of 100 nutrition issues they felt were important to get across. Out of those hundred in discussion we developed those issues which everyone felt were the most important.
>
> At this point the producer, associate producer and I sat down in a series of meetings and discussed various series ideas. After arriving at a series concept and leading characters we all felt were viable, we then developed story lines for each show in the series. Each story line was coupled with a series of nutrition education objectives. We then met again with our nutrition consultants and went over concepts.
>
> An educational researcher also worked with us on creating goals and objectives for each program that could be tested. At this point the story lines and character descriptions and educational goals were sent to the writers.
>
> The scripts were gone over for dramatic value and educational goals both by us and the consultants. Most of the scripts went through at least three drafts.[2]

An excellent teachers' guide was prepared for the series to help teachers plan nutrition activities which would help shape positive attitudes, develop abilities, and increase knowledge. The guide also provides learning objectives for each program in the series, background information on nutrition topics, a cookbook, and a resource index of pertinent booklets, filmstrips, guides, and posters.

In "Swifty," the third program in the series, everyone is preparing for the camp race. Tom ("Swifty") joins in reluctantly. After a few mishaps, he learns much about self-image, diet, exercise, and teamwork. The objectives of the "Swifty" episode are

> To help students:
>
> 1. analyze how they feel about themselves (their body, diet, and exercise habits).
> 2. realize that people of varied cultures, upbringing, and geographic location have varied eating patterns.
> 3. recognize the importance of eating a nutritious breakfast.
> 4. recognize the value of a regular exercise program in maintaining optimum health.[3]

The opening scenes from the "Swifty" episode, written by Alan Seeger, are shown in figure 11-2.

Merck Focus

Corporate video news magazine programs are becoming an essential part of many companies' employee communications efforts. Such programs can efficiently present several pertinent contemporary topics in a visually interesting manner tailored to the specific requirements of corporate and industrial audiences.

At a meeting in November 1980, executives at Merck & Co., Inc., a major pharmaceutical firm, decided to produce this kind of television program for its seventeen thousand employees based in the United States. The objectives of the program were to: foster a feeling of unity among employees in a diverse company; improve employees' conceptions of company benefits; inform employees about company activities (e.g., new plant additions, job openings and pertinent legislation affecting the company); enhance employee understanding of the various facets of the company's operations, departments and divisions; show company involvement in community affairs; and present information useful to the individual employee. It was decided to make this a regular program which focused on the employees and their interests, humanized top management, and concentrated on lower and middle management employees. At least one of the three to four segments in each 13-minute program was to include humorous or lighthearted material.[4]

Besides establishing goals, objectives, and content guidelines for the program, company executives also formulated a timetable and budget and determined a flexible delivery system for the program, the initial criteria for selecting on-camera talent, approval points, promotion activities, and evaluation steps. It was a thoughtful and efficient plan, well-conceived and well-executed.

Although the first few programs were produced entirely outside, a combination of outside professionals supervised by an in-house corporate video department producer

FADE IN:

1. EXT. PATH TO BOYS' BUNK.
   DOMINGO RAMOS is running along the path towards the bunks.

2. EXT. BOYS' BUNK
   STAN LIPTON, LEO BARTLETT, CARL KERN and BRUNO BONOMO
   are lounging on the porch.

   DOMINGO comes running down the path, shouting to Stan and Leo
   as he approaches.

                    DOMINGO
          Come on, Hawks. Let's put it on.
          Got to meet the girls in five.

Domingo springs up and enters the cabin.

                    CARL
          Who are the Hawks?

                    STAN
          Our Olympic Day Team.

                    CARL
          We're the Tigers.

3. INT. BOYS' CABIN.
   TOM PAGE, a rather pudgy camper, is sitting on his bunk reading a
   rock magazine. His cassette recorder is playing and he is munching
   on a bag of potato chips. DOMINGO enters.

                    DOMINGO
          Come on, Tom. All Hawks to the
          practice field.

                    TOM
          I'm no Hawk.

Figure 11-2 Full-script for the opening scenes from the "Swifty" episode. *(Courtesy of Alan Seeger, Yanna Kroyt Brandt, Dr. Bernarr Cooper, and the Center for Learning Technologies, The New York State Education Department)*

                    DOMINGO
You sit at our table, don't you?
We're all Hawks there...the girls
and us. Let's go. Have to start
practicing if the Hawks are going to
win.

                    TOM
I never won anything in my life.

                    DOMINGO
I'll teach you.

Domingo runs out the door with Tom following somewhat
unenthusiastically.

4. EXT. BOYS' CABIN.
DOMINGO runs from the cabin, jumps from the porch, and runs off
down the path. STAN and LEO follow on his heels. TOM hurries from
the cabin and looks for his friends. CARL and BRUNO laugh.

4. EXT. PATH TO FIELD.
DOMINGO, STAN and LEO come trotting down the path. SUZANNE
FREESTONE, ANN CAMPBELL, LESLIE REYNOLDS and CATHY
EHLERS are jogging along an intersecting path. The two groups meet
and run off together happily.

As the group disappears from view, TOM appears, running awkward-
ly after his friends.

5. EXT. MESS HALL.
Sitting on the steps are NAT SHAPIRO, BOBBY RAINWATER and
BONNIE CONSTANZA. To the left of the steps are several vending
machines.

DOMINGO and SUZANNE come running down the path...past the
Hall. ANN, LEO, CATHY, STAN and LESLIE follow.

NAT, BOBBY and BONNIE cheer the runners on sarcastically.

                    BONNIE
Hey, don't strain yourselves.

Fig. 11-2 *(Continued)*

NAT

We got a kitchen table that runs faster than that. Betcha the Hawks are gonna lay an egg.

As the runners vanish from view, TOM huffs and puffs into view. He's obviously pooped and his trot slows to a walk and then, when he reaches the vending machines, he comes to a complete stop.

BONNIE
(teasing Tom)
Hey, one of the Hawks got lost.

BOBBY
That's Swifty..."Swifty" Hawk.

Tom ignores the taunting and buys himself a coke and a candy bar from the vending machine.

NAT
What'cha doing, Swifty? Getting a little quick energy?

Tom jogs off down the path toward the practice field. He juggles the soda and candy, attempting to consume them as he hurries to catch up with the others.

NAT
Go ahead, go with your little Hawks, Swifty. C'mon, run Swifty, c'mon.

6. EXT. HAWKS ON THE PRACTICE FIELD.
DOMINGO holds up a mimeographed sheet and seems to have taken charge of the group.

Fig. 11-2   *(Continued)*

---

and assistant now package the programs. A permanent staff of company employees is used for narrating program segments. Merck employees were also involved in naming the program. More than eight hundred submissions were received before *Merck Focus* was selected for the program and *TeleVisionMerck* was chosen for a Merck video network. *Merck Focus* is now seen on cable television on the Cable Network of New Jersey (the interconnect of all New Jersey cable systems) and on a system in Pennsylvania near a major plant.

Figure 11-3 is the script for one of the *Merck Focus* programs which won top awards from the International Television Association (a non-profit organization for professional video communicators). The script demonstrates how effective a magazine program format can be for corporate and industrial presentation applications. The segments display good pacing, flow, and entertainment value and provide the type of material that fulfills the program objectives listed earlier.

CONCLUSION

This chapter has examined the writer's work in helping to design and prepare script material for industrial, corporate, educational, and instructional motion picture film and videotape presentations. It is important for the writer to participate actively in the design and scripting process so that specific objectives can be identified, agreed upon, and then activated in the final script. The standard script development process traced in chapter 3 can be used to generate material for such presentations. It is important for the writer and all others involved in such projects to evaluate rigorously each step in the design and scripting process. This kind of critical evaluation should provide insight into techniques that will produce even more effective presentations in the future.

A bright future is predicted for these kinds of presentations. The optimism is based on developing technology. New transmission technologies are eliminating the costly and wasteful restrictions of conventional broadcast, corporate, industrial and educational communications practices, thus permitting faster, more convenient, reliable and more effective communications capabilities. Electronic mail, computer-based graphics and instructional systems, interactive cable systems, videodiscs, videocassette recorders (VCRs), word processing, videotext, teletext, and satellite teleconferencing have expanded the potential delivery system capabilities available. As these and other delivery systems become even more feasible, the result is expected to be a savings in time and money, an increase in accessibility to material, a noticeable sense of unity and cohesiveness in presentation of such material, more accurate and more efficient measurement of learning capabilities, and increased human productivity and interaction. Refinement of these delivery systems should expand the capability to present such material to individuals as well as to small or large groups for various purposes in a variety of settings (in the home, at school, in the work environment).

SUGGESTED EXERCISES AND PROJECTS

1. Using the criteria described in this chapter, evaluate the effectiveness of three motion picture film or videotape presentations from your local library or media center which relate to industrial, corporate, educational, or instructional topics.
2. Obtain authorization from a nearby company, business, agency, or institution that

((FADE UP ON ANNOUNCER, TINA DOUGHERTY, STANDING OUT-DOORS. MUSIC HELD UNDER BACKGROUND.))	TD: Welcome to Merck Focus.
((CUT TO SEGMENT OF ARLENE FRANK. TITLE: PROFESSIONAL REPRESEN-TATIVE))	TD (VO): In this program, we'll look at a day in the life of one very unusual professional sales represen-tative.
((CUT TO SEGMENT OF MERCK PEOPLE. TITLE: MERCK PEOPLE))	TD (VO): We'll hear our fellow em-ployees and find out if one of them has said the secret word.
((CUT TO SEGMENT OF JAPAN STORY. TITLE: NEW LABORATORY))	TD (VO): And we'll travel half way around the world to Japan, for the dedication ceremony of a new re-search laboratory.
((CUT BACK TO TINA DOUGHERTY))	TD: I'm your moderator, Tina Dougherty. And those are the stories we'll cover in this edition of Merck Focus.
((FADE UP MUSIC. LOGO/TITLE. MUSIC UNDER AND OUT))	TD: Our first story starts in New York City.
((CUT TO LONG SHOT OF ARLENE FRANK WALKING UP BLOCK. IN-CLUDE TRAFFIC AND SOUND.))	TD (VO): This is bustling Manhattan, with its apartment buildings and brownstones. This is the place where Arlene Frank, an MSD Professional Sales Representative comes every day to conduct business.
	But the noise of New York doesn't distract her. At eighteen she lost most of her hearing and became legally deaf.
	There are many important jobs at Merck, and a Professional Represen-tative is one of them. They're the people who bring our products to

Figure 11-3 Script for one of the *Merck Focus* programs. *(Courtesy of Jeffrey M. Goldstein, Merck & Co., Inc.)*

physicians. Representatives explain how Merck products may benefit their patients as well as inform them of possible adverse reactions.

Arlene tries to see about seven doctors and three pharmacists each day.

((CUT TO INSIDE OF DOCTOR'S OFFICE))

TD (VO): One of the most difficult parts of the job is the waiting. Arlene is an active woman and sitting isn't one of her favorite activities. But when it happens, she can catch up on her business reading and get ready for her presentation.

Before you can become a Professional Representative, you have to go through an extensive training program. You learn about Merck products and associated diseases. Arlene concentrates on knowing her products very well. Her objective is to find out the physician's concerns. Then she can gear her talk directly to the points that interest him.

((NURSE WALKS IN AND MOTIONS THAT THE DOCTOR WILL SEE HER NOW))

She lipreads the doctors in order to understand them, and lip reading forces direct eye contact.

((CUT TO APARTMENT, AF SETTING UP VU-PHONE))

TD (VO): Arlene is in frequent contact with her District Manager, Paul Cottone. The phone system they use is a telephone typewriter for the deaf called the Vu-Phone. It's a valuable tool because it allows her to hear with her eyes.

((CUT TO PAUL COTTONE AT HIS VU-PHONE. ON IT READS: "HOW ARE YOU? I'M GOING TO PUT YOU IN THE MACHINE."))

Fig. 11-3 (Continued)

PC (VO): Arlene, like most of our Professional Representatives, does an outstanding job. It's a tough job, requiring both physical and mental stamina. But she gives it her all. We're really glad she's on our team.

((CUT TO AF AT VU-PHONE. ON IT READS: "I FINALLY GOT TO SEE SEVEN DOCTORS AND I ALSO GOT AN ORDER FOR FIFTY VIALS OF PNEUMOVAX."))

((CUT TO PC TYPING ON VU-PHONE. WE SEE HIM TYPE "LOOKS LIKE WE'RE GOING TO MAKE PLAN FOR THE QUARTER."))

((CUT TO TD ON CAMERA))

TD: A lot of you have told us that you like our new added feature of the "secret word," so we're going to do it again! We have one rule and it's quite easy: The first person who says the secret word, wins the prize.

((CUT TO DUCK WITH WORD IN MOUTH))

TD (VO): It's a common word, something you'd hear every day. Today, the secret word is SAILING.

((CUT TO MERCK PEOPLE))

TD (VO): We asked two questions. The first was "What do you think is a good investment for the future?"

Our second question was "Do you have a hobby?"

((CUT TO TD ON CAMERA))

TD: Our congratulations to Betty Posner for saying the secret word and winning two tickets to The Valley Forge Music Fair. Next time it might be your turn to say the secret word on Merck People.

For our last story, we go to Japan.

Fig. 11-3 (Continued)

280

((CUT TO FOOTAGE OF NEW LAB))	TD (VO): Recently, senior officers of Merck traveled to Menuma, Japan, 45 minutes northwest of Tokyo. There they took part in the dedication ceremony of our newest research lab.
((CUT TO EXTERIOR OF LAB))	Japan is the second largest phamaceutical market in the world. In Japan, we are part of a joint venture with the Banyu Pharmaceutical Company, known as Nippon Merck-Banyu Co., Ltd.
((CUT TO HUSKEL EKAIREB SPEAKING AT CEREMONY))	The new laboratory is vital to the introduction of new products into Japan. The Japanese government requires extensive testing and often requires the company to replicate the findings of animal and clinical tests elsewhere in the world. So under strict controls, our products are analyzed and tested.
((SHOTS OF LAB TECHNICIAN))	The guests at the dedication saw a laboratory with some of the most modern technical equipment in operation. At a cost of $15,000,000, it's a sign of Merck's determination to be a leader in all of its worldwide markets.
((CUT TO ELECTRON MICROSCOPE))	Of course, a serious occasion will have its lighter moments too. At a reception following the dedication ceremony, there was the traditional opening of the barrel of sake.
((CUT TO SHOTS OF RECEPTION, CLOSE-UPS OF WOMEN IN KIMONO, AND BREAKING OF BARREL))	Sometimes our company officers don't know the amount of power they have!

Fig. 11-3 *(Continued)*

281

((CUT TO TD ON CAMERA))

TD: This will be our last edition of Merck Focus until the Fall. We hope you've enjoyed them and we look forward to seeing you again in September.

((ALL SHOTS FROM CEREMONY, JAPANESE MUSIC THROUGHOUT: WASHING OF HANDS, HORAN OFFERS GIFTS, TRUCK SHOT OF MSD OFFICERS, OFFERING OF SAKE. EXTERIORS: GLOVES AND SCISSORS GIVEN TO HORAN AND JAPANESE OFFICERS, CUTTING OF RIBBON AND RELEASE OF DOVES.))

We'll close with the actual dedication ceremony of the laboratory in Menuma, Japan. It's an event full of custom and tradition -- a Shinto ceremony with symbols of nature and ancestry.

((FREEZE ON LAST FRAME. FADE TO BLACK.))

Fig. 11-3   *(Continued)*

---

regularly produces in-house industrial, corporate, educational or instructional presentations to monitor the complete process involved in planning, designing, writing, producing, distributing, and evaluating one program or presentation. Maintain a log book or diary of your observations and experiences. Accumulate written material used in the project. Finally, provide a report on your experiences.

3. Write a treatment for a presentation based on one of the following statements of objectives:
   a. After viewing this presentation, preschool children will be able to write on paper, in proper form, numbers one through twenty.
   b. After viewing this presentation, field sales representatives of this company will be able to list on paper ten positive steps to increase sales of the new product line.
   c. Upon completion of this orientation program, nurses in this hospital will be able to correctly fill out standard inventory forms for medications issued to patients.
   d. After seeing this presentation, new cooks hired by this restaurant will be able to prepare properly the eight standard sandwiches offered to customers.
   e. After viewing this presentation, assembly line factory workers of this company will be able to correctly demonstrate standard cardiopulmonary resuscitation techniques and procedures.
   f. After seeing this presentation, the employee will be able to list five specific steps taken by the company to improve employee morale.

4. Write a treatment and then a full-script for a presentation which explains the goals

and projects of an organization to which you belong. The target audience could be current or potential members or the general public.

5. Prepare a full-script for a presentation based upon the annual stockholders' report of a national company or organization.

6. Prepare a treatment and then the full-script for a series of short presentations in which the basic skills and procedures associated with one of the following jobs are presented:

    a. a cook at a local restaurant

    b. a waitress or waiter at a local restaurant

    c. a cab driver

    d. a specific assembly line position

    e. a poolside lifeguard

    f. a clerk in a hardware or a department store

    g. a summer camp counselor

    h. a service station attendant

7. Follow the steps, procedures, techniques, and recommendations contained in this chapter and design and write one presentation which would be appropriate for use by a local or area business or company, school, non-profit organization, hospital, or governmental agency. You determine the presentation's objectives, target or intended audience, expected results, length, medium to be used, uses of the finished presentation, and so on. Prepare a treatment and then the full-script for this one presentation.

NOTES

1. Rebecca Grimshaw Gardner, *High Feather,* Teacher Guide (Albany, N.Y.: New York State Education Department and The University of the State of New York, 1981), pp. iii, v.

2. Quoted from a personal letter from Yanna Kroyt Brandt to the author, dated November 17, 1982.

3. Gardner, p. 14.

4. Summarized from a Merck & Co., Inc., meeting agenda on internal video, November 1, 1980.

ADDITIONAL READING

Burder, John. *The Work of the Industrial Film Maker.* New York: Hastings House, 1974.

Edmonds, Robert. *Scriptwriting for the Audio-Visual Media.* 2d ed. New York: Teachers College Press, 1984.

Fleming, Malcolm L., and Levie, W. Howard. *Instructional Message Design.* Englewood Cliffs, N.J.: Educational Technology Publications, 1978.

Gayeski, Diane M. *Corporate and Instructional Video: Design and Production.* Englewood Cliffs, N.J.: Prentice-Hall, 1983.

Gordon, George N. *Classroom Television: New Frontiers in ITV.* New York: Hastings House, 1970.

Hilliard, Robert L., and Field, Hyman H. *Television and the Teacher: A Handbook for Classroom Use.* New York: Hastings House, 1975.

Iuppa, Nicholas V. *Practical Guide to Interactive Video Design.* White Plains, N.Y.: Knowledge Industry Publications, 1983.

Klein, Walter J. *The Sponsored Film.* New York: Hastings House, 1976.

Lesser, Harvey. *Television and the Preschool Child: A Psychological Theory of Instruction and Curriculum Development.* New York: Academic Press, 1977.

Mercer, John. *The Informational Film.* Champaign, Ill.: Stipes Publishing Co., 1981.

Roth, Dorothy H., and Price, Donel W. *Instructional Television: A Method for Teaching Nursing.* St. Louis, Mo.: C. V. Mosby, 1971.

Sambul, Nathan J. *The Handbook of Private Television.* New York: McGraw-Hill, 1982.

Strasser, Alex. *The Work of the Science Film Maker.* New York: Hastings House, 1972.

Van Nostran, William. *The Nonbroadcast Television Writer's Handbook.* White Plains, N.Y.: Knowledge Industry Publications, 1983.

Periodicals which occasionally contain articles of special interest to the writer of industrial, corporate, educational and instructional scripts include: *Audio-Visual Communications, Journal of Communications, Sightlines, Videography,* and *Video Systems.* See Appendix B for a brief description and mailing addresses of these publications.

Chapter Twelve

DRAMAS AND COMEDIES

Dramatic principles are universal. They apply equally to dramas and comedies written for the stage as well as those written for theatrical motion pictures, radio, and television. Special techniques must be used by the writer when constructing a serious drama and when devising a light comedy. The medium used will also influence the writer's approach. This chapter will focus on basic dramatic principles with the understanding that they encompass both drama and comedy and that special techniques are used to apply these principles to various writing situations.

Unfortunately, the genius and inspiration needed for effective dramatic writing cannot be taught in a single chapter in a book such as this. Many years of training and practice are necessary to acquire the background and to refine and perfect the skills needed by the successful dramatist. Many of the books listed at the end of this chapter focus, in depth, on these special writing skills. What can be presented in this chapter are the basic principles of dramatic writing, the various steps used in generating dramatic script material, and the application of dramatic principles to specific kinds of writing situations. The emphasis will be on the fundamentals of dramatic writing for the electronic media, especially television.

Because of the length and nature of dramatic and comedic scripts, only excerpts from various kinds of dramas and comedies will be presented to help the reader understand basic principles and concepts and to cultivate some measure of dramatic insight and intuitiveness. Since it is the scripting format used most often for broadcast dramas and comedies, the reader should review the standard one-column, full-script format described and illustrated in chapter 3.

SOURCES OF DRAMAS AND COMEDIES

Ideas for dramas and comedies may come from any number of sources. The primary sources are: incidents or situations, themes, settings, and characters. Although the original spark of a dramatic idea may originate from any one or a combination of these sources, the writer still must explore, expand and focus that source, relate it to other dramatic elements, and completely and consistently integrate the various elements into a strong and versatile premise for further dramatic development. Otherwise, the drama will fail to provide heightened and suspended reality for an audience.

The best ideas for dramas are those drawn from your personal experiences, observations, and consciousness. Ideas come from what you see, hear, read, observe, and experience. It might be an emotion you feel. It could be a word or phrase or even a piece of music that continues to ring with meaning long after it is heard. It could be a facial expression, a gesture, or even a mood that lingers in your consciousness.

Explore your curiosities, creative inclinations, and intuitions. Cultivate a sensitivity to the routine and mundane incidents of life so that you are able to recognize and then extract the essence of an important human moment. Filter these experiences and observations creatively to provide the germ of a story idea. The prolific playwright Neil Simon indicates that story ideas "come from your own experiences, the sum total of who you are. Your brain, your personality is used as a filter so there is a little bit of you in everything you write."[1]

The more knowledgeable a writer is about the subject matter, the more enlightening and engaging is the story. The writer's extra efforts in researching an unfamiliar subject and becoming engrossed in the mood and feelings of the settings, theme and characters will pay dividends when the script is being written. The reality and authenticity of each scene will shine through.

The story ideas (no matter what their source) are only the beginning of the dramatic writing process. Eventually, these ideas must be expanded and crystallized so that the reality they reflect is compressed and rearranged to provide heightened drama and intense audience involvement. A dramatist should devote more time and energy to the planning and writing of the drama than to an analysis of how or why an idea was selected and developed.

PRINCIPLE ELEMENTS OF DRAMA

It is important to recognize and know how to use the principle elements or components of a drama. Each element fulfills a unique function, which, when combined with the other dramatic elements, produces a unity and cohesiveness that is a mark of dramatic excellence. The elements within a drama must relate thoroughly and completely to each other to achieve a unity of action and impression for the audience.

Theme

The theme is the central idea of the drama, the moral of the story, the word or phrase that best describes the central issue or problem posed by the dramatist. It is the underlying message, truth, conclusion, or thesis expressed by the writer in the specific terms of the script through the story and characters. The theme is the audience's intellectual conclusions about the drama based on the emotions displayed in the characters, dialogue, setting, plot, and story line.

An unlimited number of themes can be explored through a drama. Some dramatists reflect a wide range of themes in their work while others explore the intricacies of a central theme in practically all of the dramas they write. The late Eleanor Perry is perhaps most noted for dealing with the subjects of human disintegration and mental illness as explored in her screenplays *David and Lisa* and *Diary of a Mad Housewife*. As a film writer, the late Carl Foreman concerned himself primarily with one major theme: the struggle of the individual against the often hostile pressures of his or her environment. This theme is reflected in many of his screenplays—*Champion, The Men, High Noon, Guns of Navarone* and *Bridge over the River Kwai*. The themes expressed through dramas can range from the social and cultural to the personal and interpersonal to the philosophical and even the metaphysical. The late Paddy Chayefsky's teleplay and later screenplay entitled *Marty* explores the theme of self-image and self-realization through the character of a New York City butcher who comes to realize that he is not as ugly and undesirable as he had imagined or had been told by his friends and relatives. Other examples of theme-generated dramas include: *Absence of Malice* (power of the press); *Kramer vs. Kramer* (divorce); *Taps* (a sense of honor); *Carnal Knowledge* (sexual hangups of men); and *Making Love* (homosexuality).

Themes are best expressed as an inseparable part of the fabric of the drama rather than as blatant messages which the writer imposes on the script. The theme should be implicit in the characters and actions created by the dramatist. The theme should be expressed through the story rather than the other way around. If the story intrigues the audience, the theme will emerge—naturally, effectively, and memorably. The theme may serve as a point of departure, a guidepost for the writer, but the story and its structure must dominate, providing bits of insight about the theme as the story progresses and as characters develop. The theme should emerge and take shape for the audience through thoughtful and insightful reflection on the actions the central characters take to resolve their problems.

Some dramatists devise the theme before beginning the writing process. Others prefer to concentrate on constructing the drama and to allow the theme to evolve and take shape as the writing process continues. Once the theme is clearly focused, however, the writer must make certain that all dramatic elements contribute to the effective revelation of the theme. Nothing should remain in the drama that is extraneous to, inconsistent with, or detractive from the theme.

Taking the time to focus and limit the nature and scope of the theme helps the dramatist construct a plot involving strong emotional concerns that are important to the audience. The higher this level of emotional involvement, the more easily the audience will understand the theme, embrace its meanings, and individually act upon its implications.

Setting

Setting indicates environment, backdrop, time, place, or locale. This dramatic concept can be broadly applied. Setting can be a particular country, region of a country, culture, era, lifestyle, neighborhood, socioeconomic group, time of day, holiday, time of year, and even type of physical environment (e.g., dusty, sandy, rainy, snowy, wet, dry, etc.).

The setting helps establish mood, tone, and atmosphere for the drama. By identifying the particular surroundings in a drama, the writer can refine script details and ultimately provide those extra insights that are inobtrusive but still important for total emotional involvement by the audience. Judicious selection and use of a dramatic setting help reinforce the theme, advance the action or plot of the story, and reveal characterizations convincingly and naturally.

A distinctive setting is an integral part of such television drama and comedy series as *Trapper John, M.D., Alice, M*A*S*H, Taxi, Love Boat, Cagney & Lacey, St. Elsewhere, Hill Street Blues* and *Dallas.* Motion pictures that exemplify this dramatic element include: *Rollover* (the business world); *An Officer and a Gentleman* (military training); *Rocky* (boxing); and *Urban Cowboy* (country disco lifestyle). Some dramas indicate by their titles the backdrop used (e.g., *Hotel* and *The Hospital).*

Premise

The construction and eventual writing of a good drama begins with a good story; however, not all stories make good dramas. A worthwhile drama must actively involve the audience, which needs to become emotionally absorbed in the action and reaction of identifiable characters to a set of progressively extenuating crises that test the characters' emotions and motivations. Each component must be present if a story is to be considered worthwhile as an engaging drama. When creating a drama or comedy, the writer begins with a broad overview of the story and then progressively elaborates or fleshes in details with each succeeding step in the writing process until the story has blossomed into a finished script. The first step in the dramatic writing process is the formulation of the premise.

The premise is the basic story idea told in the fewest possible words from beginning to end. It tells what the story is about. A complete premise statement describes who the central character or protagonist is, the main goal or motivation of the protagonist, the conflict that develops between the protagonist and an opposing force, the principal complications or problems that provide actions, reactions, and progressive involvement, and how the main conflict will be resolved. The premise eventually might be reduced to one or two short sentences, as in the description of programs found in your local television listings, called a *log line.* The premise has also been labeled the synopsis, concept and story line.

Here's how the premise statement for the award-winning television mini-series *The Thorn Birds* might be written: A priest, torn between his love for a woman and his devotion to his church, tries to resolve his inner conflict as he rises to a position of power in the church. His pride and ambition compel him to remain a priest even after a brief, but intense, love affair with the woman. His life is turned upside down when he learns that he has a son whom he has unknowingly fostered in the priesthood and who has died. Obviously, much of the color and flavor of this outstanding adaptation have been left out, but essentially that is the story placed into the proper dramatic terms of a premise.

It is important to formulate a precise but complete premise statement. By doing so, the writer constructs the basic dramatic conflict-development-resolution structure and points the way to later story development through the script. Only after the writer has identified the major conflict of the main character can the direction and tone of the story be developed. The premise helps shape the "spine" of the drama that unifies and integrates all of the story elements. Each moment, each scene, each sequence, each act, each piece of dialogue and action in the script must be a part of this basic spine. Once formed, the premise provides the basis for constructing the story into effective dramatic form, eliminating extraneous elements, and developing those elements that will enlarge the premise. Unless the writer gets everything set up at this early stage, unnecessary complications and confusion will develop later when the script is written.

Dramatists use various techniques to devise the premise. Some search for even a tentative or working title for the drama that helps capture the spirit and meaning of the story. Others select a vital moment from reality based on a simple incident, theme, background, or character and then expand and refine it through creative rearrangement. Alfred Hitchcock's *The Birds* evolved out of a startling incident. In this classic movie, a small northern California town is suddenly invaded by birds of all descriptions. As the townspeople struggle for survival against the birds, the drama builds in intensity through Hitchcock's unique style of character and plot development and sense of the macabre. Other dramas that have featured unusual or startling incidents or situations as a basis for an engaging story include: *The Poseidon Adventure, Airport* and *Quest for Fire*. Many writers use a variation of the "What would happen if..." approach. For example, what would happen if a sense of honor and duty were carried to an extreme as in *Taps* or what would happen if a woman pretended to be a man pretending to be a woman as in *Victor/Victoria*. Use this or a similar brainstorming technique if it helps to mold a basic story into a concise premise that displays solid dramatic development potential.

Plot

With the premise firmly established, the dramatist is in a better position to construct the plot. Experienced writers often formulate both premise and plot simultaneously. Until the principles of dramatic writing are firmly in hand, however, it is best to separate the two steps.

There is a difference between premise and plot. A premise tells *what* happens. A plot tells *why* it happens. A premise tells the sequence of events, the chronological order of the story. A plot arranges the events of a story into a pattern that shows their relationships. A plot connects the events of a story to create a progressive intensity and involvement for the audience through action instigated by characters in a predetermined structure or plot.

Plot is story construction, the blueprint on which the story is built. It constructs the protagonist's plan of action to reach a certain objective. It organizes the premise or story so that the central character confronts a problem that develops into an inevitable conflict with a strong opposing force. This force complicates the situation and presses the conflict into a major crisis that must be resolved by the protagonist in a final, climactic scene. As the protagonist struggles to achieve a predetermined goal, problems or complications develop. The protagonist must make decisions. Each decision produces a change in the situation that causes even more urgent decisions or choices to be made. This involves the protagonist even more deeply as the struggle gets progressively worse. This is the kind of plot progression that produces conflict, suspense, intrigue, emotional involvement, and meaningful action. All are important components of strong dramatic structure.

The plot serves as the framework from which characters, events, and circumstances emerge and join in a conflict. It helps the audience to participate mentally and emotionally in the drama as they anticipate events and developments. Devising a plot means building a structure, constructing a story. It means planning. This is the heart of the dramatist's work. Dramatic writing must evolve from this sense of structure and unity.

Approaches. Several approaches can be recommended for constructing the plot. Each approach works better for some dramatists than for others. Many writers use a combination of approaches or vary their approaches depending on the nature of the writing project and the premise.

One approach is to list the major problems to be faced by the protagonist and increase the frequency and intensity of these crisis points as the drama progresses until they culminate in the final confrontation and climax. Another approach is to identify the climax to be reached and then work backwards to ensure that each character's motivations and actions are completely logical and build progressively along the spine of the premise. Other writers prefer to set up the principal characters, the major problems they will face, and the crucial conflict that develops, and then let the various dramatic elements interact to form the climax in a unique and creative manner. Playwright Neil Simon outlines the story in his mind using only a few lines to describe the characters or setting. Then, he lets the story take on a life of its own under his loose control. He has a basic plan when he writes, but he likes to be as surprised as the audience about what finally happens.[2]

Plot Structure. The plot must be divided into three separate but related parts or acts. This structure may not coincide with the unique commercial requirements of the electronic media, especially television. To accommodate the multiple commercial breaks needed within an hour the writer must provide a dramatic highpoint and a natural pause in the progression of the plot. These commercial breaks may have to be artificially induced in the plot structure, but should always be an outgrowth of the basic three-part or three-act plot framework.

Here is how the standard plot is structured into three acts:

Act I. The central character (protagonist) is introduced, establishes an objective or goal, and faces a problem that develops into a conflict with some kind of opposing force. The conflict intensifies as the protagonist attempts to solve the problem but fails.

Act II. The conflict deepens as the protagonist struggles to overcome the opposing force. Unexpected complications cause the problem to worsen, the protagonist's decisions to become more difficult, and the consequences to become more foreboding. A crisis is reached when the protagonist realizes that unless the problem and conflict are resolved, disaster will result.

Act III. Extreme steps are taken by the protagonist to alleviate the problem and the conflict, but instead they become even more insoluble. The protagonist makes one, final decisive choice that causes the problem and conflict to come to a head and require final resolution in the climax.

The plot must be organized into this basic framework. Each dramatic unit or element must be a vital link in the plot chain, forming a definite pattern or structure for the entire screenplay or teleplay. Each element must serve a specific function. Each scene must advance the plot, reveal character traits, develop conflict, and present a specific crisis that grows naturally out of the plot. The scenes within a sequence must provide even larger parts of the plot puzzle. The sequences within each act must provide a sense of unity and cohesiveness that heightens the audience's successful involvement in the plot and story line.

Plot Patterns. The dramatist may utilize various plot patterns within the basic framework of the plot structure. These patterns help arrange or construct a story to heighten dramatic action, intensity, emotional impact, continuity, unity, and credibility. How the dramatist decides to present the story determines which pattern to use.

The most common plot pattern is a simple, direct, chronological arrangement. If the story is complex, however, or traces intricate biographical details, it could begin as the climax is forming and then, through the flashback technique, jump back in time to show earlier complications that led up to the forming of the climax and then move on to the resolution of the main conflict. A multiple or simultaneous plot pattern presents different characters involved in separate plots, all linked to an underlying story line that is resolved at the end of the drama. It is difficult to sustain interest and continuity as the presentation alternates between the various story lines. The multiple or simultaneous plot pattern is evident in the motion pictures *Hotel* and *Airport* and in the television series *Love Boat* and *Fantasy Island*. Under certain circumstances, the dramatist may use a combination of patterns to help develop the main plot.

Point of Departure. The dramatist must determine the point of departure, the point at which the story and the plot begin. This starting point is not arbitrary. It is determined by the nature of the story and how the writer wants to unravel the plot. A story may be told in any number of ways. The plot pattern and the point of departure chosen determine *the* way in which a particular story will be told.

The point of departure could be a startling or intense action that upsets or alters an established balance of forces as in *Raiders of the Lost Ark*. It could show a character already embroiled in a critical situation as in *Star Wars*. It could present an unusual, perhaps confusing, setting or character as in science fiction dramas (e.g., *Quest for Fire*).

Whatever the point of departure selected, it must capture an important and critical moment in the drama. It must quickly establish characters, story line, and the emerging conflict. It should lay the foundation for the rest of the drama, signal the plot pattern to be used, and begin to establish the mood, tone, and pace of the plot.

Conflict. A primary component of compelling dramatic action is conflict which is an opposition between two strong, mutually incompatible forces. Conflict initiates the plot and develops the basic premise. Conflict is formed as the goals of the protagonist are thwarted by an opposing force who places obstacles in the path. The conflict between the protagonist and the opposing force must be drawn clearly, sharply, and deeply for the audience if the dramatist is to justify the eventual resolution of the conflict in the climax.

The intensity of the conflict is determined by the nature and strength of the opposing forces. The audience must perceive that the main conflict involves crucial life and death issues and situations and believable characters struggling to survive. The more significant and threatening the conflict, the more the drama engages the attention, interest, and involvement of the audience. Although one kind of conflict will dominate the plot, the protagonist will face and have to resolve any number of combined or related conflicts or confrontations that increase in intensity as the plot progresses.

In simplified form, dramatic conflicts can be categorized as:

- *Individual versus individual.* Variations of this type of conflict are individual versus group and group versus group. Examples include the struggle between opposing athletes as they approach a crucial contest as in *Chariots of Fire* and *Rocky*, the conflict between a spoiled playboy and a Kansas wheat harvester as in the television drama *Amber Waves*, a senator's fight against organized labor as in *Blood Feud*, and the struggle for power and control between two crime syndicates as in *The Godfather*.
- *Individual versus self.* Two or more opposing courses of action force a central character to make a final choice. Examples include a character's struggle to overcome dependence on valium as in *I'm Dancing as Fast as I Can*, the triumph of an individual over a physical handicap as in *The Terry Fox Story*, and the dilemma faced by a superhuman character who must choose between the love of a woman and the pledge to protect Earth from intergalactic arch-criminals as in *Superman II*.
- *Individual versus fate.* This kind of conflict could force a central character to face

the wrath of nature or some unknown entity as in *Condominium, Alien, Dragonslayer,* and *Brian's Song.*

Several techniques can be suggested for developing strong and meaningful conflict in a drama:

1. Clearly delineate characters who have recognizable goals and the capacity to overcome the complications presented.
2. Place these characters into situations that are emotionally charged and that generate suspense, intrigue and life-threatening danger.
3. Create in the audience a sense of urgent anticipation, concern, and curiosity about the problems faced by characters.
4. Heighten the conflict as the plot moves closer to the climax. Make the audience emotionally cry out for the final resolution of the conflict.

Climax. The climax is the final part of the drama, in which the conflict presented at the beginning of the story is finally resolved. The protagonist resolves the main conflict that has progressively worsened throughout the story and in the process makes a new discovery about himself or herself or about life in general. Both plot and character development culminate in the climax. They should reach their peak at the same time. As they come together, the theme should emerge since it is this new discovery by the protagonist that best reveals the central idea or theme of the story. The nature of the eventual resolution of the conflict in the climax must interrelate with the nature and capacity of the protagonist. This is revealed through characterization, which is discussed later in this chapter.

Exposition. Another important component of plot development is exposition or backstory, which helps the audience understand and appreciate the protagonist's situation and the impact of current developments. It brings in other story details that fill in the gaps so the emotional involvement of the audience can be intensified. Exposition helps give the plot greater significance and depth and makes events and characters more vivid and compelling.

Exposition should be woven into the fabric of the plot and revealed as a natural part of the actions and dialogue of the characters. Exposition is needed at the beginning of the story, but should not be given all at once. It should be imparted briefly, interestingly, and without undue distraction throughout the drama. It should fit naturally into the action of the plot and story line. Make the character giving this background information want to give it to a particular character who needs to receive it at that particular point in the plot. Make the audience need to have this background information to be temporarily satisfied emotionally. In effect, motivate exposition. Make it part of the protagonist's immediate problem.

Various devices can be used for dramatic exposition. Most often dialogue is used. On occasion, a reflective monologue might be effective. Exposition could be given by a narrator or by titles on the screen. A flashback sequence is another alternative; there is the danger, however, that, if prolonged, the flashback might temporarily slow down the momentum of the plot and thus diminish emotional involvement. In most dramatic and comedic television series, initial exposition is accomplished through a montage review of important characters and past developments during the opening credits, or even through the lyrics of the series theme song. Select the method in which exposition is presented based upon the nature of the dramatic situation.

Preparation. An important tool for plot development is preparation. It involves the technique of "planting," or foreshadowing, later story and character developments so that they are believable and acceptable to the audience. Foreshadowing subtly prepares the audience through action or dialogue for what is to come so that in retrospect the audience can realize that the outcome was inevitable, that it could not have been otherwise given the characters and circumstances established in the plot.

The subtle techniques of foreshadowing are often overlooked. It might be a brief, leering glance by a character that hints at a future romantic indiscretion. The twinge of a leg muscle during training could signal the eventual defeat of an athlete in a climactic marathon race. Foreshadowing is done throughout the progression of the plot so that the climax seems logical and thus acceptable to the audience.

Subplots. A subplot is a story line related to the main plot. It contains the same components as the main plot (i.e., conflict-development-resolution) but involves characters and situations in a different kind of conflict on a different level. Subplots add variety and interest as well as reinforcement to the main plot. The number and use of subplots increase as a larger, more complex dramatic framework is formulated. Subplots should be identified and developed as part of the main story line; however, it should be possible to remove all subplot elements from a drama without disturbing the fabric of the main plot.

Characters

The dramatist needs to recognize the importance and function of characters in a drama. For many in the audience, characters are the most interesting and memorable dramatic element. We are easily attracted to characters because of a natural desire to share their victories and defeats, to love and to hate them, to embrace and to reject them. Character development helps shape and reveal the story and the plot and vice versa. In effect, they become fused, each influencing the other.

Each dramatic character must be shaped by a unique set of values and beliefs which determines what each character feels, thinks, says, and does. This uniform set of traits, revealed best in response to critical situations, determines identifiable goals that must be made clear to the audience. The goals or objectives of each character heighten the conflict that moves the plot to its predetermined climax.

Components. The dramatist must be alert to create and develop characters so that they fulfill the necessary dramatic functions. The following several components of character delineation should be kept in mind:

1. They must be *based on reality*. Each character, especially central characters, should have a full, rich, and complete background and dimension. Nevertheless, only the essential portion of each character's background should be revealed in the dramatic script. All characters, to be accepted by the audience, must be credible. Thus, there should be a certain degree of vulnerability and uncertainty built into each character. "Real" characters does not imply stereotyped characters. If turned upside down, a stereotype can be an interesting dramatic vehicle. Otherwise, it should be avoided.

2. They must be *consistent*. Based upon both revealed and concealed past experiences as well as the exigencies of the plot, each character must display traits that motivate actions that are logical and natural throughout the course of the drama. A character must act a certain way at a given point in the plot because of who or what that character is or is destined to become.

3. They must *progressively develop and change*. Consistency should not mean stagnation. The dynamics of the plot require that each character develop or change and that this development be motivated by a unique set of traits and characteristics that has been logically and firmly established. Without progressive development in the plot and characters, the dramatist cannot hope to continually involve the audience.

4. They must be *distinguishable,* one from the other. Each character must be an individual, clearly identifiable by the audience. Although characters may be similar, they cannot be identical. To do otherwise would be cheating the audience, who expect a rich, full, and varied set of characters.

5. They must *attract interest and involvement*. This is crucial to the potential success of the drama. Interest and involvement lead to meaningful caring about characters, wondering how they will cope with other characters and the constraints of the conflict. The audience will not necessarily like each character, but should be interested and involved in their plight.

6. They must *have enough depth and dimension* to sustain the impact of the conflict, convincingly struggle to resolve the conflict, and move the plot and story line along to its appropriate resolution. Each character, especially central characters, must be multidimensional, flexible, versatile, able to reflect a rich array of emotions and attitudes. There should be enough complexity and dimension to allow the audience to project its own interpretations of each character and to engender a certain measure of mystery and intrigue about each character. It is important to let the characters grow and expand to fill the void created by the plot's major problem and the resultant conflict.

7. They must *interrelate dynamically*. Interrelationships reveal how characters feel about themselves and about others, what they want, what they know and don't know, their emotions, their values, and their motives. It is this kind of information

that brings a character to life and provides the proper environment and motivation for plot and character development.

8. They must be *goal centered*. Each character, especially the protagonist, must have a clear sense of direction throughout the drama. Each must have an identifiable goal or objective based on the attitudes and motivations displayed through the plot and story line.

   Techniques. The writer can make use of several techniques to create and develop effective characters for a drama or comedy and to achieve the goals or components of character delineation just discussed:

1. *Determine character goals and motivations.* Carefully analyze and critically examine each major character. Ask questions or briefly sketch fictional biographies of principal characters to get a better feel for the emotional dimensions and motivations of each character. Determine predominant goals, values, attitudes, interests, and priorities. Determine how each character thinks, feels, acts, and reacts in each kind of scripted situation. In effect, get to know your characters well.

2. *Emphasize key characteristics.* Select two or three primary characteristics for each character that are important and appropriate for the plot and story line. Emphasize and expand these dominant traits throughout the drama by revealing various dimensions in a number of situations.

3. *Place characters within the plot.* Characters are the primary movers of the plot. Their actions cause the plot to move to a predetermined climax. Plot and characterization must fuse together to form a unified impression for the audience.

4. *Provide characterization through action.* The values and motivations of a character are best revealed by the instinctive and spontaneous manner in which that character reacts to emergency situations that impinge upon that character's very existence. Action is crucial to plot development. It is through action, reaction, and interrelationships that each character is brought to life for the audience and plays an important role in reaching the climax of the drama. Continually ask yourself, what would this character *do* in this situation? Explore the possibilities and then select an action that is based on predetermined traits, that fulfills the needs of the plot and that keeps the characters interesting for the audience.

Many dramatists evolve a central character and then let the plot or action develop out of the nature of this character. Examples of dramas in which the story, theme, dialogue, plot, and situations are formed more strongly by the characters than by any other dramatic element include: *The Boston Strangler, Patton, Bonnie and Clyde, Butch Cassidy and the Sundance Kid, Mommie Dearest, Ghandi,* and *Tootsie.*

Creation and development of characters are interesting aspects of the dramatist's craft. Once the plot has been constructed, the writer paints in color and dimension, and adds meaning and impact to the drama through rich, vivid characterizations. For many writers, the characters in a drama become very real people. They become close, personal friends. In many cases, the writer struggles, along with the characters, to find the appropriate solution to the perplexing conflict that must be resolved. In the process, the characters, and the writer, make intriguing discoveries about themselves.

Dialogue

Dialogue provides the words spoken by characters in a drama or comedy. It is an important dramatic element since dialogue must be coordinated with the visual actions and movements of characters. Since screenplays and teleplays tend to emphasize visual elements, appropriate dialogue functions and techniques often are neglected or overlooked.

Functions. Dialogue serves several important functions in a drama. It

• provides insight into the scope and nature of the character speaking—what a character says reveals motivations, intentions, goals, priorities, feelings, emotions, and concerns; dialogue also reflects personality nuances as well as a character's education, lifestyle, and social standing
• differentiates one character from another
• indicates a character's relationships with other characters
• provides the information necessary for the audience to understand and become progressively involved emotionally in the plot and story line
• links the words spoken by each character to the action and forward movement of the plot—dialogue helps reveal the subtle shifts in a character's perceptions and attitudes that evolve as the plot develops; effective dialogue makes these changes believable in the audience's mind; plot is structure and movement realized through action, what characters do and say
• unveils the theme—each piece of dialogue, if written effectively, provides extra insight into the nuances of the theme
• creates the rhythm, tempo, pace, and flow desired by the dramatist—dialogue is an essential tool for creating and controlling the audience's perception of the mood and atmosphere of the drama
• presents more refined language usage (e.g., unspoken implications, innuendoes, suggested meanings, double entendres, and opposite meanings); a convenient term for such a dialogue usage is "subtext"

Techniques. To achieve these and other functions, several techniques and approaches are recommended:

1. Provide dialogue that compresses, concentrates, and distills the essence of real life conversation. Dialogue should reflect reality in an efficient, direct, and economical manner by providing words that address directly those matters that are important to the plot and story line.

2. Use natural pauses, hesitations, restatements, interruptions, incomplete phrases, and sentences to reflect natural conversation. Write dialogue for the ear, not the eye, of the reader.

3. Create dialogue that matches the nature and intensity of the situation. Some situations require more dialogue than others. Determine the goal of each character at every point in the plot and use this determination as a springboard to write appropriate dialogue.

4. Make certain the dialogue is consistent with already established character traits. Dialogue can help the audience begin to accept subtle changes in a character's attitudes and motivations, but this must be based on traits already revealed through previous action and dialogue.

5. Listen to your characters. Get in touch with them. Notice their distinctive speech patterns, vocabulary, word choices, sentence construction patterns, idiomatic expressions, and accents. Close familiarity with the characters in a drama often allows the dramatist to let the characters seem to write their own dialogue, naturally and almost effortlessly.

6. Take proper steps to reflect accurately the speech patterns of certain occupations, geographic regions, or periods of time. It is best to immerse yourself in the environment of a particular kind of character that requires special treatment and then to have someone familiar with this kind of character review and test your dialogue for authenticity, believability, and acceptability by the audience.

7. Write leanly. Use only enough words to advance the dramatic development of the story, plot, and characters. Five or six lines of dialogue (written within the space of the standard dialogue column width) should be sufficient at one time. The use of more than six lines of dialogue, uninterrupted, should be reserved for special situations.

8. Avoid providing too many dialogue interpretation notations in the script. The motivated interaction between distinctive characters in a particular scripted situation should be sufficient for performer interpretation. An intelligent performer, under creative and sensitive direction, will provide proper interpretation of dialogue lines in most situations. Such notations should be used only when necessary.

9. Control pace and rhythm through dialogue. Short, almost staccato, dialogue tends to increase the tempo of a scene and the involvement of the audience. But vary the length and frequency of the dialogue to provide variety and to sustain interest.

10. Substitute, whenever possible, strong visualization for dialogue. Powerful, meaningful pictures are better than distracting, ambiguous dialogue. Pictures provide more intense and lasting images.

11. Choose words carefully to provide both the explicit and the more important implicit meanings.

12. Read the dialogue aloud. Listen critically to the content, meanings, and implications of what each character says.

Sunshine's On the Way

W. W. Lewis received a Writers Guild of America award for his moving television drama entitled *Sunshine's On the Way*. The 1-hour program aired on the NBC-TV

Network and later on Cinemax, a pay-TV subscription service. The script is an excellent example of an interesting story line and vivid characterizations. It illustrates many of the dramatic principles discussed in this chapter.

The central characters in the drama are from the South and speak with distinctive Southern accents. The story centers around Bobba June Strong, a rather plain and irrepressible teenager, who wants to be a professional jazz trombonist. Her mother operates a small beauty salon in her home and wants Bobba to be more realistic in her goals. Bobba works as a nurse's aide at the Sugar Hill Nursing Home. She is permitted to start a band among the elderly residents. All of the band members were working musicians at some time in their long and colorful lives. All defend their musicianship and look forward to any engagement as the "oldest" jazz band in America. Often the music they play is a bitter-sweet parody of sounds made in greener years.

Bobba's idol, trombonist Theodore "TP" Jackson, is admitted to the nursing home after a stroke. Bobba coaxes him into critiquing the residents' band. TP is bitter and crotchety and considers the group beneath his performance level. Bobba persists in trying to get TP to give her trombone lessons. Finally, TP decides to help her. Eventually, TP joins the group and rehearses intently for a hastily arranged appearance on *The Tonight Show Starring Johnny Carson.* The nursing home administrator refuses to allow them to go to California for the television appearance, but they go anyway. Figure 12-1 shows the script for the next few scenes just before the group's TV appearance.

The old musicians play as they did thirty years ago—bright, sharp, supper club jazz. Bobba June becomes an attractive, radiant, mature, self-confident woman. In many ways, this is a story of a young girl reaching for her dream and, in the process, discovering her adulthood. But it is also a tender, sensitive story about a unique lifestyle exemplified by a group of lovable, intelligent, and talented octogenarian musicians.

PRINCIPLE ELEMENTS OF COMEDY

Humor and laughter are intensely personal experiences. The forms of humor are so diverse and the art of writing creative comedy so complex and intricate that it is difficult to provide universal concepts and techniques for all possible writing situations. The writer of comic material must develop an innate sense of timing and humor and must cultivate and nurture special kinds of skills to provide a unique perspective on the human condition. Successful comedy writers are grounded in sound dramatic principles and display a special instinct for exaggeration and caricature of everyday human values, traits, mannerisms, and situations. No matter how well one understands the process involved in creating humor, it is the skill, insight, experience, and comic instinct of the individual writer that determines the ultimate success of the comedy seen and heard in situation comedies, comic monologues and the comedy sketches used as part of variety programs.

Nature of Comedy

Wit, comedy, and humor, terms used interchangeably by most writers, refer to forms of comedy that generally produce laughter and enduring pleasure for most audiences.

ACT IV

38. INT. HOTEL HALLWAY - LATER THAT NIGHT
Hallway is quiet. The sound of snoring can be heard coming from the rooms.

39. INT. HOTEL ROOM - VERY EARLY IN THE MORNING

Emma is waking Bobba from a sound sleep.

> **EMMA**
> (very gently) Wake up, child.

> **BOBBA**
> (half asleep) Huh? Is it showtime?

> **EMMA**
> Not that kind of time, honey.
> Come on with me.

40. INT. HOTEL HALLWAY - SAME TIME

Emma and Bobba walk down hall towards TP's room.

> **EMMA**
> He's been askin for you. (pause)
> It's gonna be alright, child.
> Guaranteed! Jist indigestion from
> that airplane food. Doctor's on
> the way.

> **BOBBA**
> I was supposed to take care of
> him.

> **EMMA**
> You ain't a 24-hour nurse.
> (She smooths her hair)
> Go on. Gonna be a long day.

41. INT. TP's HOTEL ROOM - SAME TIME

TP is quite ill. Bobba comes over to the bed.

Figure 12-1 Excerpt from the television drama entitled *Sunshine's On the Way. (Courtesy of W. W. Lewis, Linda Gottlieb [Highgate Pictures], and the National Broadcasting Company)*

                    BOBBA
            What's the matter?

                    TP
            (very low) I let you down,
            shortcake.

                    BOBBA
            Got a temperature?

                    TP
            Wish I did. (Pause) You know --
            Bible says -- time to plant and
            time to sow --

                    BOBBA
            TP, why you talking so funny.

                    TP
            -- and they's a time to be a girl --
            time to be a woman. Tonight --
            your time. Comin on strong. I
            feel it. You gonna be TP.

                    BOBBA
            Oh, no. There's only one TP --
            that's you.

                    TP
            Who's the teacher -- you the
            teacher, or'm I the teacher?

                    BOBBA
            But I -- ah -- can't do it, TP

                    TP
            Got to. They gonna need a
            trombone.

                    BOBBA
            You'll be there: I know you will.
            You jist got a little indigestion.

Fig. 12-1 *(Continued)*

                         TP
        No, little slip. This is your night.
        "Here she is folks -- the Georgia
        dazzler --"

Reaction shot of Bobba, her eyes filled with tears.

                    TP (cont'd)
        "B. J. Strang -- and the Georgia
        Wildcats." When you lift that
        horn out there -- you gonna be
        more than B. J. Strang -- you
        gonna play like old Sachmo did --
        breathin' life into brass -- you
        gonna be somethin!

                       BOBBA
        Way you talk, TP, think you
        gonna expire or something. You
        ain't afraid -- ?

                         TP
        Naw. 50 or 60 afraid, maybe --
        'fraid you gonna miss something
        big and fine. 70 you shift gears --
        coast a while. 80, gits to be
        slowdown time. A sadness, the
        memories get hazy.

                       BOBBA
                    -- and then?

                         TP
        Some mornin you jist forget to
        wake up. And He says, "tol you
        TP. You forgot to wake up."

                       BOBBA
                And what will you say?

                         TP
        Tell him to look after my bes'
        friend. The lady of jazz: B. J.
        Strang! (He brings her closer to
        him) (confidential) They's $10 in
        my pants. Get some gardenias
        for the ladies tonight!

Fig. 12-1 *(Continued)*

BOBBA
Sure, TP, sure.

42. INT. DAY. TV STUDIO CORRIDOR

Camera follows Bobba, alone and in a hurry, laden with corsages, as she moves along a busy corridor, nervous and dwarfed by TV equipment and unfamiliar surroundings. She makes her way across a set area to a dressing room.

43. INT. DAY. DRESSING ROOM

Bobba enters, closes the door, and the buzz of studio activity is silenced.

It is a large cast dressing room, mirros on the wall, changing cubicles, etc. The band is here, dressed in travel clothes, bags packed; they are seated, waiting, the vacant look again.

Bobba is alert to the somber mood. Her friends seem lost, out of place in the harsh light.

BOBBA
What's the matter? Why's everybody sitting around instead --

HETTY
He's gone, Sunshine.

Bobba moves toward Hetty's open arms; now crying -- a flood of tears.

BOBBA (sobbing)
Shoulda tol him -- not to forget
to wake up. It's my fault. Should
never have let him come.

EMMA
Wouldn't have stopped him; just
gettin here was half the fun.

A grievous silence, punctuated by Bobba's sobs.

HETTY
(handing her the trombone)
Left his horn for you, Bobba
June. Said there was notes in
there hasn't been touched yet.

Fig. 12-1 *(Continued)*

Bobba wipes a tear from her eye.

                    ROXANNE
          Come on, child. Help us get
          underway. Wouldn't be proper
          now to play in public.

Bobba opens the trombone case, then turns to the group, <u>a woman of</u>
<u>maturity and resolve.</u>

                    BOBBA
          Bushwa!

                    HETTY
          What's that?

                    BOBBA
          (bristling with activity)
          I said, "Bushwa." Suds. Get
          them slippers off and dress for
          the show. Hetty, Emma -- get the
          gowns on. We ain't goin' home;
          not yet. I'm gonna play TP's
          horn. I got the lip -- I got the
          heart -- and the seeds are in full
          bloom. And if you all don't swing
          tonight, I'm goin back and say
          you're jes too old to cut the
          mustard.

                    EMMA
          Now, don't start with us, child.

                    ROXANNE
          And bottle the mustard. It has
          nothing to do with age.

                    HETTY
          The girl is right. Now -- are we
          gonna shuffle or deal cards?

44. INSERT: TONIGHT SHOW - COMMERCIAL BREAK LOGO

                    ANNOUNCER (VO)
          ...and now back to the Tonight
          Show.

Fig. 12-1 *(Continued)*

CUT TO THE BAND ON STAGE, WAITING FOR THEIR NUMBER TO
BEGIN.

          ANNOUNCER (VO) (cont'd)
          Tonight we've got a special group
          with us. Ladies and gentlemen,
          from Atlanta, Georgia, the
          Georgia Wildcats.

MUSIC: "HELLO, SAD AND LONELY"

Fig. 12-1   *(Continued)*

What is funny? How does a writer know what will work in a given situation? The
answer lies in the development of an intuitive sixth sense about the nature of comedy
and the kind of stimuli that will compel an audience to respond in a certain way.
The desired result could be a subtle, knowing, satirical response or a broad, obvious,
raucous spurt of laughter. The writer must know the kind of response needed in a
given situation and then create material to elicit that response in the audience.

Comedy implies different things to different people. Most agree that it reveals our
basic human pretensions and absurdities in a pleasant, although often exaggerated,
way. Comedy unveils our common foibles and sensitivities. It is often impolite and
even sacrilegious to established mores and traditions. It provides vicarious release from
traditional restraints and constrictions (e.g., religion, authority figures, patriotic representations, etc.). It allows us to share a few moments with a fellow human being who
struggles, as we do, with life's daily problems. In the process of enjoying comedy,
if it is successful, we learn something about ourselves, our priorities, and our problems.

Experienced writers who create comedy material regularly trust their instincts rather
than abstract knowledge about the nature of comedy. They know what works in a
given situation because of past experience. They have searched and probed, failed
and succeeded enough in previous writing assignments to project the kind of comedic mood necessary for a given time and situation. Trying to dissect the nature of
comedy only to determine what makes us laugh results in a clinical approach that
produces a mechanical, almost "plastic," form of humor. Memorable and creative
comedy evolves naturally out of a potentially humorous situation featuring recognizable
comedic characters.

Principles of Comedy Writing

Effective comedy writing must be based on the principal dramatic elements described
earlier (i.e., theme, setting, premise, plot, characters, and dialogue). These elements
are universal although their application varies for serious drama and for light comedy.

The writer must establish the comic mood early to avoid confusing the audience.
The audience must be prepared for the humor that unfolds. Occasionally, the comedy

writer, using delicacy and sensitivity, is capable of mixing humor with serious drama.

Humor must evolve naturally and spontaneously from situations and characters. Add fullness, richness, and meaning to each situation by analyzing each element available and determining what can be manipulated to interject humor as a natural and spontaneous outgrowth of a recognizable situation. If comedy is written naturally and realistically, the laughter will follow.

The spontaneous nature of comedy must be tempered with exaggeration or understatement. To provide the incongruity, contrast, and often absurdity that forms the basis for much humor, characters and events need to be creatively exaggerated or understated. Comedy has a special meaning and impact when the audience suspends reality and accepts, even momentarily, the exaggeration or understatement of characters and situations.

Much of the success of humor rests with the audience's sense of superiority over the comedy and comedy characters. Audiences tend to savor the misfortunes that overcome others. There is a certain amount of sadistic satisfaction watching a comic character struggle to overcome slightly exaggerated circumstances. We tend to empathize with characters who face our problems in a unique, humorous, way. There is a fine line between providing only sadistic relief for an audience and providing an opportunity to see ourselves through the actions and words of others and to learn an important life lesson from that experience.

Just as in serious drama, comedy must build to a climax. The punch line (which may be verbal, visual, or both) often includes a surprise twist that fits the comedic situation, but also provides a new and unexpected resolution of the situation. The laughter is a result of changing the audience's expectations and meanings. The humor may be enhanced by topping the punch line with yet another, more humorous, punch line.

Delaying the punch line or climax is an effective technique. Just when the audience thinks it has accurately anticipated the next action or line of dialogue, the climax can be delayed to produce an even richer comic moment. For example, in the motion picture *What's Up, Doc?* during the climactic chase scene, workers are carrying an oversized piece of glass across the street. Suddenly, they must precariously balance their precious cargo as they dodge the rapidly approaching vehicles. The audience expects the glass to break, eventually, but they don't know when or how. The obvious does not happen. The speeding vehicles do not crash through the sheet of glass (as the audience would expect). Instead, just when it appears that the large piece of glass is safe, the last possible vehicle roars by and hits a ladder that supports a worker hanging a sign over the street. It is this innocent worker who crashes through the glass, producing a hearty delayed response from the audience. The inevitable happens, but in a fresh, creative way, enriching the comic moment for the audience.

Comic plots utilize any number of devices. For example, a running gag can be used to repeat a visual or verbal comic bit any number of times with predictable results. This becomes a kind of comic shorthand for the writer and the audience. Examples include the bigotry of Archie Bunker, the fastidiousness of Charles Winchester III in *M*A*S*H,* and the pseudomacho attitude of Herb Tarlick in *WKRP in Cincinnati.*

Another device is the use of mistaken identity as in the baffling exchange of suitcases in *What's Up, Doc?* Any number of devices can be used to heighten and pace comic plots. These are discovered through study, observation, and experience.

One of the most successful television comedy series was *Barney Miller*. This long-running, award-winning series offered a unique blend of comedy and drama placed against the somber backdrop of a busy New York City police precinct squad room. The series is an excellent example of careful scripting, solid plot and character development, clever and insightful dialogue, creative humor, and many fine talented performances.

Figure 12-2 shows the opening scene from one program in the *Barney Miller* series. Notice the fine blend of comedy and drama as characters reestablish their identities and personalities through clever but meaningful dialogue and how the viewer can begin to sense the principal outlines of the story that is about to unfold.

ELECTRONIC MEDIA APPLICATIONS

Radio

Although now very few radio drama and comedy scripts are written regularly, the young dramatist should not neglect this medium. Radio rightly has been called the "theater of the imagination" since the writer is limited only by the listener's engaging imagination and willingness to creatively accept enhanced and suspended reality. Radio drama and comedy offer an interesting challenge to the writer in that there are virtually no time and place unity restrictions and radio programs can be produced relatively quickly and inexpensively.

The basic dramaturgical concepts and principles apply to radio as well as to the other dramatic and comedic media; however, in radio, for the most part, subplots are avoided. Characters and the central plot are established quickly and early. The plot may have to be artificially enhanced to incorporate all of the necessary dramatic components and to accommodate time and commercial constraints. Characters must be vividly created in the listener's mind and imagination. The number of characters in each scene and throughout the drama or comedy should be limited to help the listener differentiate between the various voices. Characters should speak each other's names often to reinforce identification. Dialogue is especially important; it should delineate characters and should reveal changes and progressions in locales and plot development. Narration, along with music and sound effects, are basic tools for the radio dramatist to use to mark transitions, entrances and exits, and beginnings and endings of scenes and acts, and to punctuate special dramatic moments or developments. Narration is an effective tool for providing exposition. The narrator could be one of the characters or an informed source separated from the characters and action of the story.

Since only sound is used in radio dramas and comedies, the writer can more easily focus the attention of the listener and thus control the various dramatic elements and

FADE IN:

INT. SQUADROOM

(A LITTLE LATER, HARRIS, WOJO ARE OUT. DIETRICH IS WITH MISS
MARKHAM AT HIS DESK, WHICH HE HAS MOVED AS FAR AWAY
FROM HARRIS AS POSSIBLE AND POSITIONED SO THAT HIS BACK
WILL BE TO HARRIS)

> DIETRICH
> So, about the woman who moved
> into the building next to you -- ?

> MARKHAM
> Meg Scott.

> DIETRICH
> Right. Is there anything beyond
> her being --

(READS FROM STATEMENT)

> "a big-busted, bleach blonde,
> two-bit harlot" -- that leads you
> to believe she's involved in
> prostitution?

> MARKHAM
> She had her face lifted.

> DIETRICH
> That follows.

> MARKHAM
> All I know is what I see from my
> window.

> (MORE)

Figure 12-2 Sample pages from a one-column four-camera full-script for the television comedy series *Barney Miller. (Courtesy of Four D Productions)*

ACT ONE

                    MARKHAM (CONT'D)
            Ever since she moved in, it's
            been nothing but violent
            arguments, wild parties with
            strange men traipsing in and out
            of the apartment -- drugs -- !

                    DIETRICH
            Drugs? Are you certain?

                    MARKHAM
            They all have those little spoons.

                    DIETRICH
            Maybe they're for the guacamole.

(MARKHAM JUST STARES)

                    Avocado humor -- kills on the
                    West Coast.

(BARNEY ENTERS FROM HIS OFFICE. AS DIETRICH RISES FROM HIS
DESK, BARNEY GLANCES AT THE NEW ARRANGEMENT AS DIETRICH
CROSSES TO HIM.)

                    BARNEY
            You moved.

                    DIETRICH

(NODS)

                    That's why you're Captain.

                    BARNEY
            What brought this about?

                    DIETRICH
            Harris suggested it.

Fig. 12-2   *(Continued)*

309

their impact. Other media tend almost to bombard the senses and scatter the intensity and focus of each dramatic element. Television and motion pictures do exercise some control over audience focus, but using both picture and sound. In radio, the sound dominates and projects the whole impact of the drama or comedy.

Television

When applying dramaturgical concepts to the television medium, certain special considerations must be observed. Stories must be structured into 30-, 60-, and 120-minute lengths with the end of each multiple act providing a dramatic high point and a natural pause in the story line just prior to each commercial break. The television dramatist works under severe production, budget, and time constraints. The nature of television viewing precludes audience interaction in a meaningful and shared experience as in a stage play. The number of different characters and settings is limited (especially in regular series) because of the smaller screen size, the more intimate nature of the medium, and time and financial constraints that require concentration on a limited number of dramatic elements.

Despite these limitations, the television medium allows the dramatist to reveal the inner nature and intimate details of vital, human characters, to explore sensitive, personal, and contemporary themes and issues, and to create visual effects and impressions that would be impossible or difficult to execute in any other medium.

Regular Series. Regular or continuing television series feature the same central characters in separate and complete stories or episodes. Since viewers already know the primary settings and background of central characters, limited exposition is necessary. The writer can focus on character and plot development. There are some limits on the nature of the plots and crises featured. And the identity and individuality of the series must be sustained through each script generated.

Regular series are presented in 30- or 60-minute episodes. A 30-minute program is written in two acts of approximately equal length with a total story time of approximately 24 minutes. There may be a short prologue or teaser before the first act begins and a short epilogue or tag after the second act concludes. Commercial breaks are inserted between each script segment—Prologue, Act I, Act II, Epilogue. One-hour programs are written in four acts with a total story time of about 52 minutes. While there are no strict lengths for each act, in most cases Act I is 12 to 14 minutes, Act II 10 minutes, Act III 12 minutes, and Act IV about 16 minutes. Prologue and epilogue segments may also be used with approximately 1 to 3 minutes allocated for each. It should be emphasized that the standard three-act plot structure described earlier remains intact no matter how many breaks are required because of commercial considerations.

Preparing script material for a regular television series is a special kind of writing experience. The series idea must be accepted by the network or distribution company, a pilot program produced and reviewed, and a limited number of episodes ordered for production (not more than twenty-two, often as few as six episodes). There is a complex organization established within the production company that produces the series with various supervisory positions created for reviewing script material (e.g., story editor, executive story consultant, creative consultant, script supervisor, etc.). Most of these people will write scripts for the series. After a series has been approved for a season's run (generally in late spring), this small group of people consult each other for a concentrated period of time (eight to fifteen days) to determine the various story lines or premises for the season's episodes. Then, they scatter and write the individual scripts. They reassemble, polish each other's scripts, and make final decisions about other tentative premises for the few remaining episodes.

The free-lance writer has limited opportunities to write for regular series. If the writer is known to series coordinators, a first draft, full-script may be ordered after the initial idea is verbally pitched and accepted. An unknown writer may be permitted to submit a treatment, but then will not write the full-script even if the story idea is accepted. Time and budget constraints allow a narrow margin for error. Thus, producers and script coordinators tend to use writers who are known to them and who have a proven record of writing experience.

Serials. A serial features a complex array of characters involved in larger-than-life emotional entanglements and situations that continue to embroil them in a never-ending plot and story line. It is the type of drama that works well in daytime or nighttime (e.g., *Dallas, Dynasty, Knots Landing,* and *Falcon Crest*) program schedules, on open-circuit as well as on cable systems. The serial resembles the novel in its dramatic form, style, and approach.

The serial, a durable dramatic form, continues to attract large and loyal followings. Loyal viewers read about their favorite serials and serial characters in various national publications. People use home videocassette recorders to tape the daily episodes they miss, and arrange their lunch hours around the broadcast of a favorite serial.

A number of reasons have been advanced for the continued success of serials: they provide an emotional catharsis or release for the audience which seeks escape from the cares and problems of everyday life; they fulfill a natural human curiosity and interest in the problems of other people; and they are an acceptable way to consider such vital issues and concerns as abortion, alcoholism, child abuse, narcotics, marital infidelity, political intrigue, and so on. The characters and situations in serials often become a very real part of the viewers' daily lives.

The characters in a serial must be the kind with whom the audience can identify. They should have backgrounds and experiences that audience members would envy. How the characters earn their livings and where they reside are not as important to these viewers as the problems they confront and the personalities they encounter. The problems encountered must be of an infinite variety. Characters must face obstacles of the most difficult sort in a strong, emotional manner. Interesting characters produce good stories.

Because of the number and complexity of the characters involved, and because of the emphasis that should be placed on characters in a serial, it might be helpful to formulate a family tree, displaying the genealogy of the characters along with brief descriptions of each one and essential interrelationships between them. This should help develop the serial and keep the various characters separate and distinguishable.

In a serial, the writer must create a clever web of interlocking relationships. One character's actions, motivations, and complications should affect the lives and activities of other central characters. A number of stories and plots must be presented simultaneously to sustain audience interest and suspense. Just when a climax appears imminent, when a perplexing problem is about to be resolved, the writer moves to another character and another situation and leaves the audience to wonder what finally happens. At a later time, this first story can be resumed (often at a later point of development) and further complicated, but never resolved completely. And so the construction of an effective serial continues.

The plots in a serial require special attention. Because a serial is a continuing dramatic series, many subplots and main plots must be developed simultaneously. Plots for daytime serials should be outlined, divided, and subdivided into the installments for each day and each week. Plots should unfold slowly with careful repetition, without making the events seem insignificant. There should never be a final climax to any plot, but rather continuing complications that approach the crisis point at the end of each day's episode and especially at the end of each week. "Lead-in" and "lead-out" techniques help establish these sometimes artificial crisis points. A lead-in can be used at the beginning of a day's episode to recap or summarize the basic situation currently existing in the serial. A lead-out provides a suspenseful preview of the next episode. To accomplish the purposes of either the lead-in or lead-out, an off-screen narrator or serial character can be used while excerpts from the appropriate serial episode are shown.

The dialogue in a serial must be slower, more deliberate, and more repetitious than in real life. More emphasis is placed on the spoken word than on the visual image so that the viewer need not be riveted to the television screen to follow plot and character development. The "viewer" should be able to "hear" the serial while performing personal or household tasks.

The locale in a serial often is a small, unrecognizable town or some generic urban area. Because of the professional backgrounds and occupations of a majority of the characters, the settings generally are doctors' or lawyers' offices as well as hospitals, courtrooms, restaurants, and socially acceptable rooms in a typical home. Many serials now use outdoor as well as indoor settings.

The continuing nature of a serial, featuring a relatively large group of central characters, requires that the writer: accommodate tight time and production schedules by working from established, predetermined plot and character patterns; anticipate real-life situations like illnesses, contract disputes, death or introduction of characters; and write honest, human dialogue and strong emotional scenes to create intriguing and suspenseful plots and characters. Special skills and abilities are needed by the serial writer, who generally works in a writing team to provide the necessary script material for 30- and 60-minute programs each weekday. Writing for a dramatic serial requires a lot of talent. It requires planning and foresight and the ability to write material consistently and rapidly under often severe time limitations.

Long Forms. A made-for-TV movie is not unlike a theatrical motion picture release. Both are produced by independent production companies or studios. Most made-for-TV movies are 2 hours long and require seven acts written in approximately 105 full-script pages.

A mini-series presents a complete story in several installments broadcast over several hours and spread over several days or even weeks. Mini-series generally are adaptations of novels or plays or special material written on a grand scale for television use. They are considered solid audience builders during crucial rating periods, or "sweeps." Notable mini-series include *Roots, Holocaust, Shogun, Masada, The Winds of War,* and *The Thorn Birds*.

Even though these long-form dramas provide a broader "canvas" for the dramatist, basic dramatic concepts and standard scripting processes must be followed. There still must be a solid story premise forged into the framework of a tightly structured plot that features opposing forces engaged in a strong conflict that is resolved in a climax. These long-form dramas call for the scripting process outlined in chapter 3 (proposal, treatment, teleplay or screenplay, production or shooting script).

Adaptations. Made-for-TV movies and mini-series often are adaptations of dramatic material from other media (primarily novels and stage plays, but also magazine and newspaper articles, short stories, and even cartoons and comic strips). One of the attractions of an adaptation is that the audience is already presold on the quality of the original work. A major consideration for the adapter must be how closely the adaptation should be based on the original work's characters, theme, mood, tone, plot, and settings.

The challenge for the adapter is to transpose the original work to the new medium with as much fidelity, sensitivity, and skill as possible, making adjustments to accommodate special requirements. The unique characteristics of the new medium must be utilized to the fullest. It is best to retain the key elements and to capture the creative and artistic spark of the original work, and then skillfully transpose these elements to the new medium, allowing additional creative dimensions to emerge and be explored. Try to maintain the dramatic integrity of the original work. This becomes more difficult when long narrative passages must be transposed into engaging action and dialogue, or when a major character or event must be eliminated or formed into a composite because of time or production requirements.

Here are the steps recommended for writing adaptations:

1. Select an original work that, after creative development, will retain its original "personality" but still enjoy an enhanced sense of unity, meaning, and dramatic power because of the transposition to the new medium.

2. Secure copyright clearance to use the original work.
3. Become thoroughly familiar with the original work as though it were your own. Clearly identify and critically analyze plot, characters, dialogue, settings, theme, conflicts, exposition, and the other major dramatic elements. Determine what will have to be done to transpose the original work effectively to the new medium. Carefully outline the story by scenes and sequences, and then combine, change, eliminate, or add dramatic elements as needed to make the adaptation interesting, effective and viable. Plan your changes and modifications as fastidiously as though you were developing an original drama.
4. Follow the standard scripting development process outlined earlier to focus and plan the adaptation.
5. Write the first and subsequent draft of the adaptation script.
6. Evaluate the impact and effectiveness of the adaptation to the new medium.

If the original work needs to be lengthened (as in adaptations of a one-act play or a short story), the adapter must carefully expand the number and type of characters and situations. While the central conflict should be retained, the adapter must add new crises and new complications to further heighten the plot and story line. In effect, the original work must be expanded, but always in keeping with the essential spirit, style and quality of the original work and always with the purpose of increasing the audience's emotional involvement in the story, the conflict and the characters.

If the original work needs to be shortened (as in adaptations of a three-act stage play or a novel), the adapter faces a different kind of challenge. Each time a character is eliminated or a scene is dropped, the story line and plot are affected. The adapter must determine what realistically can be eliminated from the original work and still provide an effective presentation in the new medium. The cutting process can begin by: eliminating all or most of the subplots, condensing crucial scenes and eliminating extraneous scenes, forming composite characters to represent various supporting characters, beginning the story at a later point of departure, and providing dialogue or strong visual sequences to replace lengthy narration or character introspections in the original work. Understanding the essential feeling and emotion of the original work will guide the writer when deciding what to eliminate and how to shorten the drama or comedy. If, after all reasonable efforts have been made to condense the original work, the writer determines that a disjointed, almost patchwork, adaptation will result, then it is time to re-think the process and consider using the flavor and emotion of the original work, but create an entirely new plot and story line. This decision places the writer outside the realm of adaptations and back into the creation of an original drama or comedy.

Docudramas. Docudramas dramatize factual material. They present dramatized versions of real events and persons based on reenactment and fictional reconstructions. They are a hybrid presentation form that combines the background and content of the traditional documentary with the often more attractive and startling presentation form of the drama. The docudrama presents the audience with the sense of real events and persons reappearing in a contrived and manipulated presentation.

The docudrama offers several interesting challenges to the writer. Original events and persons must be presented in a believable way. Additional material may have to be created to fulfill dramatic requirements and to present a full and interesting story. There is the extra burden of creating and sustaining a certain degree of suspense and intrigue since the audience usually knows the final outcome of the story. If based on well-known characters and events, the writer does not have the luxury of surprising the audience as in an original drama. The writer's greatest challenge is to interpret reality in a creative and believable way, and to provide a simple, direct, interesting, and dramatically sound story line.

Television has been the primary medium for a number of memorable docudramas, among them: *Pueblo, The Missiles of October, The Execution of Private Slovak, Eleanor and Franklin, Blind Ambition, The Jesse Owens Story, The Executioner's Song* (concerning the execution of Gary Gilmore), and *Grace Kelly*. Although there are ethical questions raised by the presentation of factual or real-life events and persons in a fictional format such as a docudrama, audiences continue to be drawn to these presentations. The ethical writer must ensure that dramatic license is taken only when necessary and that events and persons included in a docudrama have been verified through extensive research. The best dramas are those drawn from real life, without the need for contrived events and characters.

SCRIPTING DEVELOPMENT CHECKLIST

For dramatic and comedy writing, the writing process begins with a story idea or premise. This is expanded upon in various kinds of written or verbal presentations—proposals, treatments, first and subsequent drafts of the teleplay or screenplay, and finally a shooting or production script.

Following this scripting development process allows the novice dramatist to progressively examine key elements of the drama or comedy and to make adjustments at various preliminary stages rather than as the final draft script pages are written, when changes usually are more difficult to accomplish. Experienced writers may combine or bypass one or more of these creative stages.

As the writer prepares the script material for a drama or comedy in progressively more specific forms, he or she should ask a series of questions to test the value and quality of the work. The questions posed summarize the dramatic principles discussed in this chapter. These and other questions can be asked at each stage of scripting development:

GENERAL

Is there justification for everything that happens in the drama or comedy?

What elements should be added or subtracted to heighten and intensify plot and character development?

THEME AND SETTING

Does the theme emerge clearly and naturally through the actions of established characters?

Are the settings clearly established, dramatically relevant and helpful?

PLOT

Is the "spine" of the story, or premise, reflected in the effective development and progression of the plot?

To heighten dramatic impact, are there scenes that could be eliminated, shortened, or that should be added? What are these "soft" spots? How can they be improved?

Does each scene (sequence) (act) have a beginning, middle, and end or climax, reveal character, join the conflict, and move the plot forward?

Does each scene build upon the previous scene and lead logically, naturally, and effectively into the next scene?

POINT OF DEPARTURE

Does the story begin at the ideal point to engage the audience and heighten emotional involvement?

Does it begin at a crucial emotional moment that is clearly established as important to the protagonist and other central characters?

CONFLICT

Are the protagonist's goals clear and meaningful?

Are the protagonist's opposing forces clearly identified, sufficiently strong, and meaningfully important to frustrate the protagonist's goals?

Does the central conflict emerge clearly, progressively, and early enough to create anticipation and intrigue for the audience?

Does the conflict worsen and deepen as the plot develops?

Can you identify the crucial scene in which the conflict reaches its ultimate intensity and in which the protagonist is forced finally to resolve the conflict? How can the dramatic value of this scene be improved?

CLIMAX

Is the climax reached at the end of the plot and not prematurely?

Is the climax clearly, logically, and naturally related to the crises and complications presented earlier? Is it on the "spine" of the story, or premise?

How can you sharpen or intensify the climax, make it more compelling?

EXPOSITION AND PREPARATION

Is the backstory creatively and unobtrusively woven into the main fabric of the story line?

Is there too little or too much exposition?

Has there been sufficient and appropriate preparation early in the drama or comedy that permits the audience to clearly connect what is revealed later with what was presented earlier?

Is the exposition and preparation that is presented crucial to the progressive development of the plot and essential to forming and resolving the central conflict?

SUBPLOTS

How many subsplots are there? Do they relate to the central plot?

Could the subplots be removed from the drama or comedy without serious loss to or deterioration of the "spine" of the story, or premise?

Are the subplots resolved effectively as the main plot is resolved?

CHARACTERS

Is each character unique, believable, clearly differentiated, and consistently developed?

Is there meaningful motivation for the major actions of each character?

Are character interrelationships clearly and compellingly drawn?

Do all of the characters concern themselves in some way with the central conflict and its resolution?

DIALOGUE

Is the individuality of each character expressed through the dialogue?

Is the dialogue based on conversational speech and does it reflect unique dialogue characteristics?

Would it be impossible to transfer the lines given to one character and to give them to another character?

Is dialogue used effectively to present exposition and preparation and to move the plot along to the climax?

AUDIENCE

Why will the audience be attracted to this drama or comedy within the first five minutes?

What specific dramatic elements and techniques have you used to progressively sustain and heighten emotional involvement?

What specifically can be done to increase audience anxiety, anticipation, suspense, and intrigue?

UNITY AND CHANGE

Are changes in mood, flow, pace, and tempo logically motivated and effectively executed?

Does the plot display structural unity?

What are the high and the low points in the plot development?

Track the intensity level of the plot. Does it continually increase?

Are there scenes that need more evident conflict and action?

Are there too many intense moments that strain credibility and exhaust audience participation and involvement?

PRACTICAL MECHANICS

Is the script material in proper professional form?

Is the script visually dynamic and descriptive?

Have only essential visual and aural elements been included to provide a meaningful perception of the drama or comedy?

Is the script realistically producible for the intended market (television series, made-for-TV movie, theatrical motion picture, etc.)?

SUGGESTED EXERCISES AND PROJECTS

1. From your own background and experience, list three items or ideas for each source of dramas and comedies: situations or incidents; themes; settings; characters. Explain why you believe each item is the starting point for an effective drama or comedy script.

2. Prepare a treatment for a 1-hour radio or television drama based on one of the following themes or backgrounds:

   a. World War II   b. England in the 1920s
   c. Colonial America   d. courage and pride
   e. fear   f. self-preservation

3. Watch one of the following and then prepare a written critique in which you analyze and evaluate theme, setting, story premise, plot, characters, and dialogue based on the discussion in this chapter and the script development checklist presented: a television situation comedy series episode; a television drama series episode; a made-for-TV movie; a television mini-series episode; or a theatrical motion picture.

4. In a one- or two-page narrative, describe the principal character traits of one of the following and indicate how you would reveal these traits in a dramatic or comedy script:

   a. Rocky Balboa   b. Winnie the Pooh
   c. Spiderman   d. Charlie Chaplin
   e. E.T. (the extraterrestrial)   f. Mary Poppins
   g. Dagwood Bumstead   h. Napoleon

5. Write the full-script for a few scenes in which the traits described in exercise 4 are revealed.

6. Evaluate the dialogue given to two different kinds of characters in the *same* drama or comedy program in terms of content, word choice, length, structure, rhythm, and pacing. Concentrate on the dialogue and not necessarily on the performance of the actor or actress.

7. Observe, and, if possible, record (after receiving prior permission) a conversa-

tion in a natural social setting or situation. Write the full-script for a dramatic or comedy scene based on this conversation in which you heighten the conversation by using meaningful and purposeful dialogue.

8. Write a treatment for an episode for a current regular television network drama or comedy series.
9. Write the full-script for the first few scenes in the episode outlined in exercise 8.
10. Watch all episodes of one daytime television serial for one week. Describe the plot and character developments during this week's programs. Follow the same process, but four weeks later. Compare each week's plot and character developments.
11. Prepare a treatment for an original made-for-TV movie. Write the full-script for the first three to five scenes for this movie.
12. Write the full-script for a 30-minute radio or television drama or comedy program adapted from a short story or one act play.
13. Prepare the treatment for the adaptation of a novel to a television mini-series consisting of three 2-hour episodes seen on consecutive nights. Accommodate 12 minutes of commercials each hour plus teasers, transitions, and tags as you outline each episode. Include descriptions of theme, setting, story line, plots, subplots, characters, and dialogue development.
14. Prepare a treatment for a 1-hour radio or television docudrama based on a significant and recent news event. Include in the treatment: sources of research, chronology of events, and the principal people involved.

NOTES

1. Neil Simon, quoted from the PBS television series *Screenwriters/Word into Image*, 1982.
2. Neil Simon, comments from the PBS television series *Screenwriters/Word into Image*, 1982.

ADDITIONAL READING

Adler, Richard P. *All in the Family: A Critical Appraisal*. New York: Praeger, 1979.

Andrews, Bart. *Lucy & Ricky & Fred & Ethel: The Story of I Love Lucy*. New York: E. P. Dutton, 1976.

Brady, Ben. *The Keys to Writing for Television and Film*. 4th ed. Dubuque: Kendall/Hunt, 1982.

Brenner, Alfred. *The TV Scriptwriter's Handbook*. Cincinnati: Writer's Digest Books, 1980.

Brooks, Tim, and Marsh, Earle. *The Complete Dictionary of Prime Time Network TV Shows: 1946–Present*. New York: Ballantine Books, 1981.

Cantor, Muriel G., and Pingree, Suzanne. *The Soap Opera*. Beverly Hills: Sage, 1983.

Cassata, Mary, and Skill, Thomas. *Life on Daytime Television: Tuning in American Serial Drama*. Norwood, N.J.: Ablex, 1983.

Cousin, Michelle. *Writing a Television Play.* Boston: The Writer, Inc., 1975.

Egri, Lajos. *The Art of Dramatic Writing.* New York: Simon and Schuster, 1960.

Field, Syd. *Screenplay: The Foundations of Screenwriting.* Rev. ed. New York: Dell Publishing Co., 1982.

Gerrold, David. *The Trouble with Tribbles.* New York: Ballantine Books, 1973.

_____. *The World of Star Trek.* New York: Ballantine Books, 1973.

Gianakos, Larry James. *Television Drama Series Programming: A Comprehensive Chronicle, 1980-1982.* Metuchen, N.J.: Scarecrow Press, 1983. (Note: Three earlier volumes trace television drama programming since its beginnings: *1947-1959; 1959-1975;* and *1975-1980.*

Greenberg, Bradley S. *Life on Television: Content Analysis of U.S. TV Drama.* Norwood, N.J.: Ablex, 1980.

Gruner, Charles R. *Understanding Laughter: The Workings of Wit and Humor.* Chicago: Nelson-Hall, 1978.

LaGuardia, Robert. *The Wonderful World of TV Soap Operas.* New York: Ballantine Books, 1974.

The Making of James Clavell's Shogun. New York: Dell/Delta, 1980.

Miller, William. *Screenwriting for Narrative Film and Television.* New York: Hastings House, 1980.

Rose, Reginald. *Six Television Plays.* New York: Simon and Schuster, 1956.

Stedman, Raymond W. *The Serials: Suspense and Drama by Installment.* 2d ed. Norman, Okla.: University of Oklahoma Press, 1977.

Straczynski, J. Michael. *The Complete Book of Scriptwriting.* Cincinnati: Writer's Digest Books, 1982.

Swain, Dwight V. *Film Scriptwriting.* New York: Hastings House, 1976.

Trapnell, Coles. *Teleplay: An Introduction to Television Writing.* New York: Hawthorn Books, 1974.

Vale, Eugene. *The Technique of Screen and Television Writing.* Rev. ed. Englewood Cliffs, N.J.: Prentice-Hall, 1983.

Wertheim, Arthur Frank. *Radio Comedy.* New York: Oxford University Press, 1979.

Whitfield, Stephen E., and Roddenberry, Gene. *The Making of Star Trek.* New York: Ballantine Books, 1979.

Wolper, David L., and Troupe, Quincy. *The Inside Story of TV's 'Roots.'* New York: Warner Books, 1978.

Chapter Thirteen

PROFESSIONAL BROADCAST WRITING OPPORTUNITIES

The telecommunications industry continues to expand and develop beyond even the most optimistic projections. This rapid technological development creates an even greater demand for writers who can meet or exceed the expectations and challenges of this burgeoning industry. No matter what technological changes occur in the future, writers with talent, initiative, commitment, and flexibility will always be in demand.

This chapter provides an overview of professional writing opportunities. The writing marketplace will be examined to identify the kinds of employment available as well as the areas of specialization and the potential for income and advancement. Emphasis will be placed on how to market your writing talent—setting realistic and challenging goals, developing contacts, preparing effective resumes and script samples, handling personal job interviews and script conferences, working with agents who help market the writer's creative efforts, and guilds and unions that enhance the writer's professional development. The business aspects of writing will be examined with particular attention to protecting the writer's material and avoiding common legal problems associated with a writing career. This discussion provides essential information on writing career development. The books listed at the end of this chapter contain more complete discussions of various aspects of professional writing opportunities.

THE WRITING MARKETPLACE

Categories of Employment

There are three categories of employment for the broadcast writer:

• *Staff writers.* These work for weekly or monthly wages on projects assigned by a studio, broadcast facility, or production company.

• *Free-lance writers.* These submit script material on speculation without assurance of pay, prior acceptance, or continued employment. Free-lancers must line up clients in advance and overlap projects to maintain their reputations, livelihoods, and sanity. Productive work habits and sound business practices are the hallmark of a successful free-lance writer.

• *Contract or commissioned writers.* These receive prior approval and guaranteed pay for work done on a specific project. While the contract writer does not enjoy the economic and employment stability of the staff writer, he or she is on more solid ground than the free-lancer since signed contracts assure that the commissioned writer receives payment for the work done, even if the script material is never used.

Many writers have abandoned the more restrictive "writer" classification in favor of increasingly common hyphenated designations—writer-director, writer-producer, or even writer-producer-director. There are several reasons for this development. Writers who combine their primary function with another generally make more money; they can also exercise more control over the production of the scripts that they write. Writers have often expressed frustration because once their scripts are finished and turned over for production, the writer's basic concepts can be altered considerably without any recourse by the writer. The writer serving in two or more functions, however, can make certain that the original ideas and emotions expressed in his or her script are brought to life just as he or she visualized. A writer can assume a combination of responsibilities only after many years of experience as a writer and only after there is some assurance that the writer is ready.

Areas of Specialization

There are many professional opportunities for the broadcast writer. Some require minimal writing experience while others necessitate an extensive background in a very narrow writing specialty. These opportunities exist in various kinds of facilities and systems—local broadcast stations, production and program syndication companies, networks, cable systems, advertising agencies, private businesses and corporations, charitable and service enterprises, and governmental agencies.

What follows is a brief profile of the employment opportunities the young writer should consider.

Advertising Copy. If you are interested in creating copy for commercials and public service announcements (PSAs), prospective employers include advertising agencies, broadcast stations, charitable and public service organizations, and governmental agencies. Advertising agency work is difficult, if not impossible, to find as a young writer. You will have a better chance if your background includes both print and broadcast copy work. As a young writer, it is more productive to work for a commercial retail client, a non-profit organization, a newspaper, or a radio or television station before attempting to land a job at an advertising agency.

Promotion and Public Relations Work. Practically all of the prospective employers listed earlier require writers for various kinds of promotion and public relations material. Again, a solid background in writing for the print media is helpful since it demonstrates flexibility and diversity to a prospective employer. In a broadcast station or network, the writer could generate promotional announcements for on-air programs but also would be expected to be able to handle news releases, design handbills or billboards, prepare sales presentations, conduct facility tours, plus many other jobs. This kind of work requires someone who has a wide-ranging background and diverse professional interests.

News-Sports-Information Related Specialties. There are numerous subspecialties within this classification. These include general news and sports writers as well as specialists in business, consumerism, agriculture, health, meterology, and documentary and investigative reporting work. Each requires a unique and specialized educational background as well as extensive writing experience before work in these special writing areas can be considered. One way for the young writer to acquire the necessary experience is to work full- or part-time in a small commercial or non-commercial broadcast station or facility. Perhaps there is a job as a reporter or intern, on a paid or unpaid basis. Networks or production companies often need temporary assistants for special broadcast projects; however, the competition for these jobs is fierce.

Industrial and Corporate Presentations. Many private companies and businesses now maintain a staff of writers and production personnel to handle in-house sales presentations, training programs, promotional campaigns, and corporate communications. The writer often serves a variety of functions because of the shortage of staff and the diverse responsibilities involved. A business background is helpful but certainly not required for such positions. Some prior writing experience usually is necessary. This kind of staff job offers the writer interesting and challenging work that could lead to even more responsible positions in middle and upper management within a company.

Educational and Instructional Opportunities. School systems, public radio and television stations and networks, production companies, governmental agencies, and other kinds of facilities need writers for educational and instructional material. While some staff writing positions are available, much of this kind of work is done on a free-lance or contract basis. Combined responsibilities are common in this specialty.

Drama and Comedy Writing. This is not a specialty the young writer should contemplate before acquiring considerable writing experience, background and training. Prospects for employment for a young, novice writer are slim. It is a tough, demanding job because of the kinds of pressures faced by the writer and the special kinds of writing skills required to succeed (see chapter 12). Because of the nature of the work, the writer eventually will have to obtain representation by a literary agent and join a guild or union, and consider relocating to a major production center, especially southern California.

Scripts for ongoing television series are written by experienced staff, free-lance, and contract writers. Most series scripts are staff written. Submitting unsolicited scripts on speculation is not the best route for the beginning writer to follow. The material will not be read because of time pressures and legal constraints, but also because similar story ideas may have been developed by writers whose talents are known by the series producer and who are available for the crucial phone calls, story conferences and memos which are all part of this kind of writing work.

Instead of writing a speculative script for a series that may or may not be renewed next season, it would be best for the young writer to generate an original comedy or drama, perhaps for made-for-TV or mini-series development or for a pilot program. This kind of script allows the young writer creative flexibility to demonstrate his or her ability to produce quality material without the requirement that the writer incorporate a cast of continuing characters or predetermined locations or situations in a tightly written, easily marketable script.

A small percentage of writers work on serials, generally on a contractual basis for a designated period of time. The writing team consists of one or two highly experienced head writers and four to ten dialogue writers. This is a very specialized writing area. It requires extensive dramatic writing experience and a firm grounding in dramatic techniques in order to withstand the pressures of daily deadlines. It is unlikely that a young writer will be involved in writing a serial until substantial experience has been acquired and significant contacts within the writing community have been cultivated.

Other Opportunities. There are many other kinds of writing opportunities to consider. These require unique writing skills and combined function responsibilities. Some of these opportunities include: writing music and variety programs for radio or television stations, networks, production and syndication companies; developing game shows for network or syndication use; preparing news or sports related special events coverage; writing treatments and scripts for animation projects such as cartoons, theatrical motion picture features, television series and commercials; and working as a writer-producer-host for a talk or magazine program produced by a local station, network or independent production company. Positions of combined responsibilities generally require sound writing as well as performance skills.

Each professional writing opportunity must be considered carefully. The writer should determine what is available and then pursue the kind of work which interests him or her most and which will lead, in some way, to his or her predetermined writing goal or objective. Each job taken by the writer should sharpen his or her skills and perceptions and enhance and deepen his or her writing craft.

Income and Management

It is difficult to make generalizations about income and advancement potential. Much of it depends on the talent and initiative of the individual writer. A bright, talented writer can earn a lucrative wage and advance quickly to more prestigious and complex writing work. Other young writers struggle to remain in their first writing job.

How much you earn and how quickly you advance to larger, more challenging writing projects depends on your personal and professional goals as well as the kind of writing you do (your specialty), your title and responsibilities, your geographic location and willingness to relocate, the reputation of the facilities that employ you, the reputation of your previous work, and many other factors. In general, the smaller the market or facility in which you work, the lower the wages and the more limited the chances for advancement. But at a small station you get more opportunities to write a much wider range of material and, thus, to acquire a much broader writing experience. Generally, television and motion picture work pays more than radio work, although there are notable exceptions.

MARKETING YOUR WRITING TALENT

Writing quality, marketable script material is important, but only the first step on the road to becoming a professional writer. No matter how good your writing, others still must see your work and become convinced that you have the necessary skills and background to work as a professional writer. It is advisable to develop a strategy to market your writing talent. This strategy should involve setting realistic goals, making professional contacts, preparing sample script material and often writing a resume, and surviving job interviews and later script conferences. For some writers, the services of an agent, guild or union may be needed. Developing a marketing strategy for your writing talent requires thoughtful planning and persistent execution.

Goals and Timetables

The writer's professional goals should be in writing and should include decisions on such matters as geographic preferences and requirements, writing specialties and interests, and personal writing ambitions. These goals should be reevaluated periodically to reflect changes in interests and employment patterns.

A realistic timetable should be devised to accomplish each goal. How long do you plan to remain in the first writing job you have identified? How long in the second and third jobs? What kinds of professional developments would alter your timetable? What are your two-, five-, and ten-year career plans? How long will it take to reach your ultimate goal? These and other questions should be thoughtfully considered before a professional writing timetable is developed.

Contacts

It is important to cultivate and maintain personal contacts within the telecommunications industry. Who you know and the kind of work you have done for someone in the past often will determine whether you get the assignment for that special program or whether you are added to the writing staff of a broadcast station or production company.

There are several ways to establish contacts within the industry. There are various kinds of media directories available that list the names of individuals and companies in various geographic areas that may be interested in your work if professional contact is made; ask a reference librarian for assistance in locating and using such reference works as *Standard Directory of Advertising Agencies* (the Agency Red Book) and *Broadcasting/Cablecasting Yearbook.* Many organizations listed in Appendix A offer placement services that often prove beneficial to the young writer. Appendix B lists periodicals and trade publications that can provide potential job contacts for broadcast writers. Subscribe to the publications that best match your writing objectives and respond to the job opportunities offered. Stay in touch with those with whom you have worked in the past; often they move to new, more responsible positions, and could be of assistance. You might have friends or relatives who know influential people you need to contact. Literary agents are essential for some kinds of writing work.

Resumes

A discussion of the steps involved in preparing a professional resume is beyond the scope of this book. When applying for many beginning writing jobs (especially at broadcast stations, networks, and production houses) a resume is just as much a part of the application process as the presentation of writing samples. There are numerous books and pamphlets available that provide the basic information needed to prepare an effective professional resume. Consult your local library or a professional employment agency.

Script Samples

The best way to get work as a writer is to write something to present to a prospective employer. If you have identified a specific writing career objective, prepare several samples of your creative work in this area. Samples could be drawn from previous work in writing classes, but retype the script material in proper form and do not include the comments made on the original scripts. You could create scripts for existing products, services, programs, or personalities or you could invent your own within realistic limits. You might volunteer to write script material for a public service agency, a non-profit group, or a local or state governmental agency. Work with them as a client, as though you are already a full-fledged, professional writer. Do it on a speculation, non-paying basis, if necessary. Whatever script material you do prepare, make certain it represents only your best work. Your scripts present you and your standards of professionalism to the employer. The important thing is to demonstrate to a prospective employer that you have the ability and resourcefulness to produce quality creative script material.

You may want to consider compiling script material into a portfolio with recent samples of your work. This is a common practice for writers of commercials, public service announcements, promotional copy, editorials, commentaries, and news and sports copy. You could use acetate-covered black pages to display your work, or place each script in a separate file folder, clearly labeled and briefly explained.

Interviews

Many staff writing positions require a personal interview before employment can be secured. Other kinds of writing jobs bypass this step until the new writer is already hired. In either case, knowing what employment interviews are supposed to accomplish and how to conduct yourself in such situations are important considerations for the young writer. A more complete discussion of this subject is available from career counselors and various career planning books and pamphlets.

Employment interviews serve two primary purposes, each equally important: (1) to convey information about your qualifications that will convince the prospective employer to hire you for a specific job; and (2) to uncover as much information as possible about the job opening and the person you will be working with so that you can determine whether this is the job for you and if the interviewer represents the type of person for whom you can work happily, creatively, and productively.

Set up a specific, person-to-person interview with the individual responsible for hiring. Learn as much as possible about your prospective employer's needs, problems, interests, and concerns. Give some thought to how you would respond to specific questions that could be asked. Prepare to discuss your professional attitudes and standards.

Make the interview situation as pleasant and productive as possible. Once the interview begins, be alert for opportunities to discuss your professional background and interests. Talk about the quality and diversity of your writing. Indicate that you are interested in becoming an active part of a creative and challenging experience, that you have the qualifications needed to produce solid, professional script material. Diplomatically convince the interviewer that you can think creatively, that you can put these creative ideas in proper form on paper, that your scripts are commercially viable, that you are aware of the demands and pressures placed on the writer, and that you work well under these conditions. Respond to questions briefly and directly, but always fortify your answers with all of the positive information about yourself and your work that you can muster. Cite specific examples of successful performance in the past to illustrate your points. Try to use each question as a springboard to uncover more information about you and your writing experience. Remember not to oversell yourself or to talk too much. Your goal should be to have a friendly discussion that provides a full understanding of your qualifications and of the duties included in the job offered. Be certain to ask specific questions about the job—duties, wages, standards, and so on.

After the interview, leave something behind—your business card (if you have one), resume, writing sample—anything that can remind the employer about your visit and how to contact you. As you leave, express your appreciation for the interview. Follow up with a short note thanking the interviewer for his or her time and consideration.

Maintain contact with the prospective employer. If a decision on an opening is still pending, phone or write the employer and provide additional information or comments that may have been overlooked or inadequately discussed in the interview. At the same time, stress your strong interest in the job and confidence in your ability to produce the caliber of script material needed. When looking for work, especially as a writer, persistence and tenacity are important to achieve success—a job!

Script Conferences

Another kind of personal meeting is the script conference. Script conferences are sessions in which an attempt is made to improve the quality of a writer's work. They are a part of the marketing effort by writers of dramas, comedies, advertising copy, and animation projects as well as editorials, commentaries, industrial, educational, instructional, and corporate presentations. Ideally, the person coordinating such sessions thoroughly understands the writing and production process, clearly knows what is needed and desirable, expresses views freely, clearly, and persuasively, and makes the necessary decisions about script changes within a reasonable amount of time. Unfortunately, this ideal person is not always in attendance.

At a script conference, the writer should follow these suggestions:

1. *Come prepared.* Know the script well. Anticipate questions and problems. Evaluate the material from as many perspectives as possible.
2. *Be ready to* talk *about the script.* People prefer to hear rather than read about a script idea or concept. Develop your improvisational skills. Rehearse yourself. Practice with a tape recorder or a friend. Make your narrative vivid, colorful, interesting, memorable. Make the idea come alive in the listeners' minds. Explain your scripting approach and style as clearly and persuasively as possible. Match your style of oral presentation to the audience's expectations.
3. *Answer questions simply and directly.*
4. *Be a professional at all times,* no matter how inane the comments or questions.
5. *Keep the mood of the session light but productive.*
6. *Know when to stop.* Determine when major ideas and suggestions have been made and then make an obvious move to exit. Many writers have successfully developed what has been called the "door knob" technique—one final, fleeting, loosely constructed idea tossed out as the writer reaches the door to leave the room. Often, these vaguely formed ideas are readily accepted, then enthusiastically developed and eventually produced.

Agents

An agent is a middleman between the writer and prospective buyers of the script material. He or she markets a writer's scripts or services and negotiates prices and contract terms. An agent relies on personal contacts, experience, and a thorough knowledge of current marketplace demands and trends to service writer clients. For the effort, an agent receives 10 percent of a writer's earnings. Literary agents, who should be bonded and licensed, are needed by writers of dramas and comedies as well as major productions mounted by large broadcast facilities, networks, and syndication companies.

If you need the services of an agent, write to a few agents whose names and addresses can be supplied by the Writers Guild of America. Agents willing to consider representation of young writers are indicated by an asterisk on the WGA list. If you know a professional writer who is willing to recommend you, obtain this endorsement and have this writer contact the prospective agent on your behalf. When writing to an unknown agent, introduce yourself. Briefly explain your writing interests and goals and stress that you are serious about writing as a professional career. In a few sentences, describe the script material you have prepared and request that a program material release form be sent so you can send your treatments, proposals, story ideas, or scripts. Include a self-addressed stamped envelope (SASE) for the agent's response. If no response is received in about four weeks, write again and remind the agent about your previous correspondence. If there is still no response after a few months, try other agents. Be persistent!

Agents are looking for promising writing talent as well as marketable script material written in proper form. Agents tend to favor clients who will regularly provide solid money-makers. High-quality, productive writing clients enhance the agent's reputation and income.

Guilds and Unions

As your work in the broadcast media takes you into larger production facilities and markets, you will find it necessary to consider union or guild membership if you wish regular employment. While some criticize these organizations because of various regulations and restrictions, others welcome the specialization and protection afforded by such membership.

If you hope to write network or syndicated programs, an integral part of your work will involve submitting prospective script material for review, acceptance, and ultimate production. Information on how, when, and where to submit this material is provided through literary agents who could represent your interests, through informal associations with other writers, and through membership in a guild or union.

The acceptance of your script material may depend upon your membership status in the appropriate guild or union. Essentially, these groups are associations of individuals with similar interests and pursuits. Usually, it is possible to have your script material reviewed by a potential employer even though you are not a member of a particular guild or union at the time of your initial submission. Use of the program material release form is recommended. Should your initial work prove meritorious, you would be expected to join the appropriate guild or union. Once a member, you may be expected not to submit material to those who do not abide by the rules or regulations promulgated by your guild or union membership. Adherence to this membership restriction allows the organization to protect its members and to provide a unified front when negotiating specific issues and concerns of the membership.

The largest radio-television-motion picture writers' guild in this country is the Writers Guild of America, Inc. (WGA) with offices in Los Angeles and in New York City. Among the *primary functions of the WGA* are:

•to represent writers for the purpose of collective bargaining in the motion picture, television, and radio industries
•to verify and administer individual writing contracts
•to prepare market lists and other informational material and to provide services to assist members in writing for specific series or projects
•to organize craft meetings and workshops to improve members' writing skills
•to study and report on copyright, censorship, taxation, and other matters affecting Guild members
•to undertake special projects for Guild members, such as maintenance of a pension fund, a credit union, and a group insurance plan

The *minimum requirement for WGA membership* is that you have had employment as a writer for screen, television, or radio, or that you have sold original material to one of these media. The initiation fee is $500. Your membership application must be supported with a copy of your contract or other acceptable evidence of such employment or sale.

The WGA requires members and contracting companies to adhere to strict contract standards. In 1981, there was an extensive revision of the WGA's Theatrical and Television Basic Agreement. This document provides specific information on: compensation rates (including those for pay-TV, videocassetes or videodiscs); pension and health contributions; minority employment; extended rights of Guild members; screen credits; and many other concerns.

Specific information about the WGA is available from either Writers Guild of America, West, Inc., 8955 Beverly Boulevard, Los Angeles, CA 90048 or from Writers Guild of America, East, Inc., 22 West 48th Street, New York, NY 10036. The Guild will send information about membership requirements, functions of the WGA, the manuscript registration service, the Television Market List (listing contact and submission information on current weekly primetime television program series) published in the Guild's monthly *Newsletter*, standard contract forms, minimum contract fees for WGA members, and a current list of agents subscribing to the Guild regulations. Some of this information requires payment of nominal fees.

THE BUSINESS OF WRITING

A successful writer must also be effective in business. Many writers have their agents handle these business details and thus free themselves to concentrate only on their writing. Others handle the business details themselves. They maintain tax and script submission records, check contract terms (even though agents are responsible for this), and take steps to protect their work. Legal and financial protection has become an increasingly important part of the writer's world.

A minimal amount of record keeping is needed. If you work as a free-lance or contract writer, keep track of your script submissions by noting the name or nature of the project, to whom the script material was sent, when a response was received, and what (if any) follow-up was done. For tax purposes, maintain a separate account to handle earnings and expenses. Financial record keeping should be accurate and complete and backed up with receipts, cancelled checks, deposit slips, sales tickets, and other documents. Check with an accountant or tax consultant about other financial information related to the writing profession.

Before you sign a contract, read it carefully. These written agreements specify what services you will provide, with what compensation, and within what period of time. Writers are often involved in step-deal contracts which specify what payment is to be made at each script development stage. Generally, there are provisions for stopping development at each stage if the script does not proceed according to expectations.

Take steps to protect your work. Your scripts are precious commodities. As a professional writer, they are your source of income, the results of your creative efforts. Make certain that what you write is copied, dated, clearly identified as your work, and (if appropriate) registered with either the WGA or with the copyright office *before* you send it out for review.

The WGA registration service is available to members as well as nonmembers. Registering your formats, outlines, synopses, story lines, and scripts with the WGA does not confer statutory protection, but merely provides evidence of a writer's claim to authorship of the literary material involved and of the date of its completion. To register script material with the WGA, write to either of the WGA addresses provided earlier. Request the appropriate form to be sent and ask to know the cost of registration before sending one copy of the script material prepared in standard copy form and accompanied by a check or money order for the registration fee.

More secure protection is obtained through formal copyright registration. Application for copyright registration is made on one of four forms corresponding to the nature of the work. The four classifications are:

Class TX: Nondramatic Literary Works (includes advertising copy or scripts)
Class PA: Works of the Performing Arts (includes dramatic works, motion pictures, and other audiovisual works)
Class VA: Works of the Visual Arts (includes logos and photographs)
Class SR: Sound Recordings

The proper application form plus additional information on copyright regulations as applied to broadcast-related writing may be obtained from: Register of Copyright, Copyright Office, Library of Congress, Washington, DC 20559.

Another option available to the writer interested in protecting his or her creative work is to mail back to oneself by registered mail a copy of the script material. The postmark on the envelope verifies that the material was sent through the mails on the date indicated. To reap the benefits of this process, it is important that the writer not open the registered envelope unless or until legal questions arise concerning the script material.

CONCLUSION

There are many exciting and challenging opportunities available to the writer who has creative talent and who recognizes the need to market that talent. Take the steps necessary to create a demand for your creative services. Evaluate your background and skills and then determine where you want to be as a writer. Then, go for it!

Write because you are enthusiastic about what you are doing and not because of the wages or prestige your writing might bring. Develop a commitment to yourself and to your audience that is reflected in the quality of the scripts you write. There are no short cuts. It may be a difficult journey, but one that will provide a great deal of personal satisfaction, one that will contribute significantly to the improvement of the human condition.

SUGGESTED EXERCISES AND PROJECTS

1. Identify five specific writing opportunities in the electronic media in your area or locale. Contact one of these potential employers and determine the qualifications necessary for an entry-level job. Report your findings.
2. Consult appropriate career literature and employment agencies to determine the recommended contents for a professional resume. Prepare your typed resume stressing electronic media writing experience and goals.
3. Prepare a portfolio which contains three to five samples of your writing. Write a generic cover letter (which would accompany your resume and portfolio) that explains the purpose and contents of each writing sample and that briefly outlines your goals as a writer.
4. Team up with another person in a role-playing exercise. You are a writer applying for an entry-level job. The other person interviews you for the position. Agree on the type of job under consideration. Stress your positive writing abilities and potential. If possible, record the short interview. Critique your abilities as a job interview subject.

ADDITIONAL READING

Berlyn, David W. *Your Future in Television Careers.* 2d ed. New York: Richards Rosen Press, 1980.

Brohaugh, William, ed. *The Writer's Resource Guide.* Cincinnati: Writer's Digest Books, 1982.

Caldwell, S. Carlton, and Niven, Harold. *Broadcast Programs in American Colleges and Universities.* 15th Report. Washington, D.C.: Broadcast Education Association, 1981.

Denny, Jon S. *Careers in Cable TV.* New York: Harper & Row, 1983.

Ellis, Elmo I. *Opportunities in Broadcasting.* 2d ed. Skokie, Ill.: National Textbook Co., 1981.

Froug, William, ed. *The Screenwriter Looks at the Screenwriter.* New York: Dell Publishing, 1972.

Gross, Lynne Schafer. *The Internship Experience.* Belmont, Calif.: Wadsworth, 1981.

Hallstead, William F. *Broadcasting Careers for You.* New York: E. P. Dutton, Inc., 1983.

Nash, Constance, and Oakey, Virginia. *The Television Writer's Handbook: What to Write, How to Write It, Where to Sell It.* New York: Harper & Row, 1978.

Reed, Maxine K., and Reed, Robert M. *Career Opportunities in Television and Video.* New York: Facts on File, Inc., 1982.

Schemenaur, P. J., and Brady, John, eds. *Writer's Market.* Cincinnati: Writer's Digest Books. Annual.

Shanks, Bob. *The Cool Fire: How to Make It in Television.* New York: Random, 1977.

SELECTED LIST OF PROFESSIONAL ASSOCIATIONS

Review the discussion in chapter 1 concerning the importance and benefits derived from professional organizations. Significant national and international groups, which offer individual rather than only station or company membership categories, are listed below. Many offer student or associate memberships at reduced rates. You are encouraged to communicate with groups appropriate to your interests. Some of those listed provide a broad perspective and interest in the communications field, while others offer more specialized viewpoints. Telephone numbers are listed if known. Brief descriptions are provided for some listings if the organization's name did not appear to encompass current membership characteristics and interests. The latest edition of *Broadcasting/Cablecasting Yearbook*, published by Broadcasting Publications, Inc., 1735 DeSales Street, N.W., Washington, DC 20036, provides an annual update of listings for many of these national associations and professional societies.

Alpha Epsilon Rho (national honorary broad-
casting society)
College of Journalism
University of South Carolina
Columbia, SC 29208   (803) 777-6783

American Meteorological Society
45 Beacon Street
Boston, MA 02108   (617) 227-2425

American Women in Radio and Television
Inc.
1321 Connecticut Avenue, N.W.
Washington, DC 20036   (202) 296-0009

Association of Black Broadcasters
3 East 4th Street
Cincinnati, OH 45202

Association for Educational Communications
and Technology
1126 Sixteenth Street, N.W.
Washington, DC 20036   (202) 466-4780

Association of Independent Video and Film-
makers, Inc.
625 Broadway, 9th Floor
New York, NY 10012

Broadcast Promotion and Management
Executives
248 West Orange Street
Lancaster, PA 17603   (717) 397-5727

Economics News Broadcasters Association
1629 K Street
Washington, DC 20006   (202) 296-5689

Information Film Producers of America
750 East Colorado Boulevard
Pasadena, CA 91101   (213) 795-7866

International Association of Business
Communicators
870 Market Street, Suite 940
San Francisco, CA 94102   (415) 433-3400

International Television Association (non-
profit organization for professional video
communicators)
136 Sherman Avenue
Berkeley Heights, NJ 07922   (201) 464-6747

National Association of Farm Broadcasters
Box 119
Topeka, KS 66601   (913) 272-3456

National Association of Spanish Broadcasters
2550 M Street, N.W.
Washington, DC 20037   (202) 293-3873

National Audio-Visual Association
3150 Spring Street
Fairfax, VA 22031   (703) 273-7200

National Broadcast Editorial Association
c/o WTMJ-TV
720 East Capital Drive
Milwaukee, WI 53201   (414) 332-9611
(Note: Mailing address changes to reflect
yearly elections.)

Public Relations Society of America
845 Third Avenue
New York, NY 10022   (212) 826-1750

Radio Television News Directors Association
1735 DeSales Street, N.W.
Washington, DC 20036   (202) 737-8657

Society of Professional Journalists, Sigma
Delta Chi
840 North Lake Shore Drive, Suite 801W
Chicago, IL 60601   (312) 236-6577

Writers Guild of America, East, Inc.
22 West 48th Street
New York, NY 10036   (212) 245-6180

Writers Guild of America, West, Inc.
8955 Beverly Boulevard
Los Angeles, CA 90048   (213) 550-1000

SELECTED LIST OF PERIODICALS AND TRADE PUBLICATIONS FOR BROADCAST WRITERS AND COMMUNICATORS

The function and value of periodicals and trade publications for the broadcast writer is discussed in chapter 1. Significant national publications (both general and specialized) are listed below. Publications provided as part of professional association memberships also are listed. It is recommended that you identify the publication(s) which are appropriate for your interests and then write for subscription information available from the circulation department at the addresses provided. The brief description for each listing, provided by the author, may not coincide with other contemporary evaluations of publication content.

Advertising Age
Crain Communications Inc.
740 Rush Street
Chicago, IL 60611
  Advertising industry newspaper. Weekly.

Audio-Visual Communications
United Business Publications, Inc.
475 Park Avenue South
New York, NY 10016
  Magazine for A-V managers, producers and business executives using audio-visual media. Monthly.

Backstage
Backstage Publications Inc.
330 West 42d Street
New York, NY 10036
  Entertainment industry newspaper. Weekly.

Billboard
Billboard Publications, Inc.
One Astor Plaza
1515 Broadway
New York, NY 10036
  Music and recording industry news magazine. Weekly.

Biomedical Communications
United Business Publications, Inc.
475 Park Avenue South
New York, NY 10016
  Journal for media professionals in medical education and health care delivery systems. Bimonthly.

Broadcasting
Broadcasting Publications, Inc.
1735 DeSales Street, N.W.
Washington, DC 20036

A primary news magazine of the broadcasting industry covering regulation, programming, news, sales, and management systems. Weekly.

CableAge
Rockefeller Center
1270 Avenue of the Americas
New York, NY 10020
   Reports on the issues, developments, and trends in the cable industry. Biweekly.

Cash Box
1775 Broadway
New York, NY 10019
   Popular music industry trade publication. Weekly.

Channels of Communications
Box 2001
Mahopac, NY 10541
   Magazine featuring discussion of contemporary issues in advertising, news, language, programming, and management systems pertinent to broadcast and related delivery systems. Bimonthly.

Columbia Journalism Review
200 Alton Place
Marion, OH 43302
   Publication featuring critical review of the media and subjects covered by the media. Bimonthly.

Coming Attractions
133 Christopher Street
New York, NY 10014
   Contains information on writers and others who participate in the creative process of making motion pictures. Bimonthly.

Daily Variety
Daily Variety Ltd.
1400 North Cahuenga Boulevard
Hollywood, CA 90028
   Entertainment industry newspaper. Daily, Monday through Friday. See listing for weekly Variety publication elsewhere in this appendix.

The Hollywood Reporter
6715 Sunset Boulevard
Hollywood, CA 90028
   Entertainment industry newspaper. Daily, Monday through Friday.

Hollywood Scriptletter
1626 N. Wilcox, #385W
Hollywood, CA 90028
   Newsletter for television and film writers. Monthly.

Journal of Broadcasting
   & Electronic Media
School of Speech Communication
Kent State University
Kent, OH 44242
   Research journal providing contemporary perspectives on criticism, regulation, effects, programming, and other aspects of the broadcasting industry. Editorial offices periodically change with editor adjustments. Quarterly.

Journal of Communications
P.O. Box 13358
Philadelphia, PA 19101-9916
   Research journal providing contemporary perspectives on telecommunications, new technology, popular culture, children, education, social issues, and other areas in the broad communications field. Quarterly.

The Quill
840 North Lake Shore Drive, Suite 801W
Chicago, IL 60611
   Publication of the Society of Professional Journalists, Sigma Delta Chi. Features articles on ethical questions related to the practice of print and broadcast journalism. Eleven issues each year.

Radio & Records
1930 Century Park West
Los Angeles, CA 90067
   Popular radio music industry publication featuring research, formats, national programming, and industry news. Weekly.

Religious Broadcasting
c/o National Religious Broadcasters
Box 2254R
Morristown, NJ 07960
   Publication of the NRB organization. Presents contemporary issues relevant to religious broadcasters. Bimonthly.

RTNDA Communicator
c/o Radio Television News Directors
   Association
1735 DeSales St., N.W.
Washington, DC 20036
   Publication of the RTNDA. Emphasizes freedom of information and broadcast news management issues. Monthly.

Shooting Commercials
101 Crossways Park West
Woodbury, NY 11797
   Magazine for creators and producers of television commercials. Monthly.

Sightlines
43 West 61 Street
New York, NY 10023
   Journal of the Educational Film Library Association. Timely resource articles and interviews. Quarterly.

Television/Broadcast Communications
P.O. Box 12268
Overland Park, KS 66212
   International journal of broadcast technology devoted entirely to the needs and interests of the television industry. Monthly.

Television/Radio Age
Rockefeller Center
1270 Avenue of the Americas
New York, NY 10020
   Covers all aspects of radio and television industry. Biweekly.

Variety
154 West 46th Street
New York, NY 10036
   Entertainment industry newspaper. Weekly.

Videography
United Business Publications, Inc.
475 Park Avenue South
New York, NY 10016
   Magazine for video users in business, education, cable, broadcasting, retail, production, and the arts. Monthly.

Video Systems
P.O. Box 12901
Overland Park, KS 66212-9981
   Publication for professionals engaged in various applications of video and audio production and communications. Monthly.

Washington Journalism Review (WJR)
2233 Wisconsin Avenue, N.W.
Washington, DC 20007
   Features profiles, legal considerations, and issues related to print and broadcast news coverage and management. Ten issues each year.

WGA Newsletter
c/o Writers Guild of America, West, Inc.
8955 Beverly Boulevard
Los Angeles, CA 90048
   Publication for Writers Guild of America members. Features activities of the Guild and Its members plus the Television Market List (contact and submission information on current primetime television program series). Ten issues each year.

Writer's Digest
9933 Alliance Road
Cincinnati, OH 45242
   Magazine featuring writing and marketing articles for writers in all media. Monthly.

Appendix C

SELF-REGULATION EFFORTS: PROGRAM STANDARDS AND PRACTICES AND CODES OF ETHICS

Pages excerpted from a document entitled *NBC Broadcast Standards for Television* are presented here to give the broadcast writer some notion of the nature, scope, and concerns of self-regulation efforts by major commercial television networks. These selected pages are not meant to represent the entire statement of current NBC television broadcast standards.

The two statements from the Public Broadcasting Service—*Statement of Policy on Program Standards* and *Document of Journalism Standards and Guidelines*—represent the collective judgment of the public television system with regard to standards and practices in its nationally distributed programming. They were recommended to the full station membership of PBS by its board of directors, were adopted by overwhelming majorities, and were subsequently endorsed by the Board of the Corporation for Public Broadcasting.

Standards for gathering, writing, and presenting news are provided in two codes from two national news organizations: Radio Television News Directors Association and The Society of Professional Journalists, Sigma Delta Chi. Both codes stress the need for accuracy, objectivity, responsibility, and fair play when writing news and information scripts.

NBC BROADCAST STANDARDS FOR TELEVISION*

Introduction

NBC is mindful that television is a home medium designed to appeal to audiences of diverse tastes and interests. Consequently, the

*Courtesy of the National Broadcasting Company.

Company recognizes its obligation to maintain the highest standards of taste and integrity in all its programming. In general, programs should reflect a wide range of roles for all people and should endeavor to depict men, women and children in a positive manner, keeping in mind always the importance of dignity to every human being.

In 1934, NBC became the first broadcasting organization to adopt a Code of Broadcast Standards. This Code has been revised periodically to meet the changing interests and expectations of a nationwide audience and to express NBC's own concern that its program service acknowledge the needs of the millions of homes we enter every day of the year.

The standards set forth in this Code must, of necessity, be expressed as general principles to be applied with sensitivity and intelligence on a case-by-case basis. The responsibility of interpreting and implementing those principles and proposing new or modified standards, rests with NBC's Broadcast Standards Department.

The general provisions of this Code apply in principle to the NBC Radio Division although the Radio Networks and the owned Radio Stations administer them independently.

Each NBC owned television station has its individual Broadcast Standards unit, which applies these standards to locally originated broadcasts in terms of community needs and interests.

News and information programs produced by NBC News are supervised by that Division which has its own set of policies and procedures.

Entertainment Review Procedures

Scripted Programs All network programs are reviewed by the Broadcast Standards Department throughout the production process, from story outline through script and rough-cut to final film, tape or live telecast. Typically, the Broadcast Standards editor receives a story outline or synopsis, notes potential problem areas and brings them to the attention of the Program Department and program producer. Subsequently, the editor reviews the script, specifies cautions about subject matter, scenes or language, or requests changes or deletions. When the film or tape is in rough-cut stage, the editor exercises still another opportunity to effect further revisions or deletions. Approval for broadcast is given only after editors and their supervisors are

satisfied that the program meets generally accepted standards of taste and propriety.

Unrehearsed Programs NBC seeks to exercise all control possible over programs for which complete written or recorded scripts cannot be submitted in advance. Where deemed necessary, participants in these programs are briefed on the applicable NBC policies and the necessity to comply with them. The program standards described in this manual also apply to such programs.

Broadcast Standards' editors attend tapings of unscripted programs. Programs acquired after completion are screened in advance of broadcast and edited as necessary. When circumstances warrant, editors attend productions shot on location to assure compliance with this Code.

Motion Pictures Films produced for theatrical release are subjected to careful review by NBC. In considering a film's suitability for purchase, the Broadcast Standards' editors, as a preliminary procedure, usually consult the findings of various rating services, examine critical reviews and ascertain a film's popular acceptance through box office returns.

After appropriate screenings, analysis and discussion, the editors and their supervisors determine whether a film is acceptable for broadcast and whether editing is required.

If a theatrical film is edited for any reason prior to broadcast, this fact is acknowledged by a statement at the beginning of the telecast.

Game Programs Quiz, game and similar programs that are presented as contests of knowledge, skill or luck are reviewed for taste and propriety by the Broadcast Standards Department and are supervised by the Compliance and Practices Department and are subject to the requirements set forth in the Compliance and Practices Manual.

Variety Programs These programs are scrutinized by the Broadcast Standards

Department through every phase of production.

Service Programs Programs not under the auspices of NBC News which are devoted to service features, such as shopping guides, fashion shows or consumer reports, are supervised by the Broadcast Standards and Compliance and Practices Departments.

Sports Programs The content of commentary and the selection of coverage at sporting events is the responsibility of the Sports Department. All sports programs must comply with the requirements of NBC's Sports Policy Guidelines.

Religious Programs NBC cooperates with recognized organizations within each of the three major faith groups—Catholic, Jewish and Protestant—in presenting religious programming.

Solicitation of funds is not permitted in these programs. Offers of printed material may be made on such programs, subject to NBC approval.

Nature Documentaries The special provisions governing non-fiction nature programs are set forth in the Compliance and Practices Manual.

General Entertainment Program Standards

Animals The use of animals shall be in conformity with accepted standards of humane treatment.

Disadvantaged Special precautions must be taken to avoid demeaning or ridiculing members of the audience who suffer from physical or mental afflictions or deformities.

Dramatizations Dramatizations which would give the false impression that the dramatized material constitutes an actual event occurring at the time of presentation are not permitted. Such introductory terms as "Flash" or "Bulletin" and statements such as "We interrupt this program to bring you..." are reserved exclusively for news broadcasting.

Drugs Narcotic addiction shall be presented only as a destructive habit. The use of illegal drugs or the abuse of legal drugs shall not be encouraged or shown as socially acceptable.

Gambling The use of gambling devices or scenes involving gambling that are necessary to the development of plot, theme or character must be presented with discretion and in a manner that would not promote illegal gambling, or offer instruction in gambling techniques.

Hypnosis The creation of a state of hypnosis by act or detailed demonstration on camera is prohibited. Actual hypnosis as a form of "parlor game," or to create humorous situations, is forbidden.

Impersonations NBC does not permit impersonations in radio and television presentations that would lead the public to believe that it had heard or seen someone who, in fact, did not personally appear on the program. When a living character is impersonated, NBC reserves the right to require that person's consent and written authorization for the impersonation.

Language Speech should be consistent with the standards that prevail throughout a substantial portion of the television audience. Language generally considered to be coarse or offensive should never be used for shock effect or as the basis for humor.

Liquor The use of alcoholic beverages should be deemphasized and restricted to situations and circumstances necessary to plot and/or character delineation.

Minorities The representation of ethnic and

social minorities in dramatic material proposed for television will be carefully reviewed to avoid portrayals that incite prejudice, promote stereotyping or offend legitimate sensitivities.

Obscenity and Profanity Obscene, indecent or profane material is prohibited.

Prizes Identification of merchandise and its donors on game shows shall conform to all applicable laws and regulations as well as with the NBC Compliance and Practices Manual.

Professions Professional behavior, advice, diagnosis and treatment will comply with law and recognized professional standards.

Pseudo-Sciences Program material promoting belief in the efficacy of fortune-telling, occultism, astrology, phrenology, palm-reading, numerology, mind-reading, character-reading, and the like is unacceptable.

Sponsor References Sponsor references other than previously reviewed and accepted commercial announcements, billboards, program titles and the like, are unacceptable unless approved by the NBC Compliance and Practices Department.

Sexual Themes Explicit, graphic or excessive presentations of sexual matters and activities will be avoided. Sexual themes may not be gratuitously injected into story lines. When such themes contribute to plot or characterization, they must be presented with intelligent regard for commonly accepted standards of taste and propriety and not in a manner that would appeal to prurient interests.

Stimulation No program shall be presented that will mislead the audience as to any material fact. Reasonable judgment must determine whether a particular method of presentation would constitute a material deception or be accepted by the audience as recognized theatrical illusion.

Stereotyping Special sensitivity is necessary in presenting material relating to sex, age, race, color, creed, religion or national or ethnic derivation to avoid contributing to damaging or demeaning stereotypes.

Violence NBC recognizes its responsibility to the public with respect to the depiction of violence—the intentional infliction of physical harm by one person upon another. In all cases, such depictions must be necessary to the development of theme, plot or characterization. They may not be used to stimulate the audience or to invite imitation. Violence may not be shown or offered as an acceptable solution to human problems.

Scenes showing excessive gore, pain or physical suffering are not permitted. Scenes depicting abnormal or morbid acts of violence or the use of cruel and unusual weapons are not permitted. Scenes containing extensive and detailed instructions in the use of harmful devices and weapons or describing imitable techniques for the commission of crime or the evasion of apprehension will be avoided.

Exceptional care must be taken in stories where children are victims of, or are threatened by, acts of violence.

These considerations also apply to advertising and promotion material.

Children NBC recognizes its special responsibility to young people. The NBC Program Department and the Broadcast Standards Department require that producers be sensitive to their special needs. There is an obligation to present positive and prosocial material and to avoid material that would have an adverse effect on a child's behavior and intellectual and emotional development.

Producers of programs designed for children are directed to avoid:

a. placing children in situations that provoke excessive or prolonged anxiety;
b. content that may give children a false and derogatory image of any ethnic, social or religious group, including their own;
c. depictions of unlawful activities or acts of violence that glamorize such acts or make them appear to be an acceptable solution to human problems;
d. depicting violence in a manner that invites imitation.

Producers of programs designed for children are encouraged to portray unlawful and anti-social activities as undesirable.

NBC is aware that children may watch television programs that are primarily designed for adult audiences in other time periods. Accordingly, as set forth in Program Section, Page 11, NBC will, where appropriate, present advisories to alert parents and other adults that they should exercise discretion in what they permit children in their homes to view.

Within programs designed primarily for children under 12 years of age, appropriate separator devices shall be used to clearly delineate the program material from commercial material.

PUBLIC BROADCASTING SERVICE
STATEMENT OF POLICY ON PROGRAM STANDARDS*

Adopted by the Board of Directors, PBS, April 13, 1971
Adopted by the Members, PBS, April 15, 1971

Introduction

The American public television system is an experiment in mass communications. It is designed to combine programming from a variety of separate, independent production agencies into a single, balanced national program service. These "production agencies" are themselves, with rare exceptions, public television stations. The service is then distributed to more than two hundred local stations fully responsible to their communities for their programming. They are under no requirement to broadcast any national program they receive and, within the limitations of rights, they may schedule programs to fit their local situation. Designed to articulate the diversity and complexity of American experience, this system has no parallel, commercial or noncommercial, among the major broadcast systems in the world. It is

designed to assure considerable autonomy both to producer and to local stations in the development and transmission of programs for the audiences of the service.

The Public Broadcasting Service is charged with the development and distribution of the national program service to the local stations which are its corporate members. In furtherance of this charge, the PBS Board of Directors undertook a study of the problems of national program standards for public television and of the development of effective procedures for implementation of any statement of those standards.

In this system without a model, PBS found wide diversity in the programming standards operating at the various stations which are its members and producing agencies. Moreover, in a period of great uncertainty in all mass communications and in the society they serve and reflect, these varieties are sharpened.

Nevertheless, the Board, upon review of the complex problem of standards, developed a general statement of program

---

*Courtesy of the Public Broadcasting Service.

policy for the Service and the system it serves. In this process, it was aided by information from a variety of member stations. Diverse as the membership itself, it came in the form of statements of station policy, letters and lengthy personal discussion during the development of the draft statement on standards, and in over forty formal responses to the circulation for comment of that draft. In addition, every station was polled on the draft and on the interim procedures used to implement it by PBS.

The response was a solid support of the draft. A variety of modifications were proposed, and some have been included in this revised version. There was clearly expressed by the stations the feeling that the draft, if sometimes imprecise, covered the major areas at issue. Overwhelmingly, there was support for an active role for PBS in working with the producing agencies to implement the policies with enough lead time to make them really effective.

The statement of policy was considered and adopted without dissent at a special meeting of the members on April 15, 1971.

As public experience and technology change, so do tastes and needs. No formal statement on programming policy can stand long without review and revision as needed. The commercial broadcasters have discovered this and public television will likely prove no exception to their experience. As public television develops in the next few years, there must continue an effective interaction between all the parties whom the standards and procedures are to serve. Part of that interaction must be a periodic review of procedures to establish and implement program standards and practices, and a revision of the statement as required. Toward that end, the Board of Directors has charged its Operations Committee with the responsibility of reviewing the policy prior to each annual meeting of the Board, and of making such recommendations to the Board as it deems appropriate.

Background

In the course of the investigation of standards, PBS staff talked with other broadcasters about the techniques they use, including American commercial broadcasters and national broadcasters in other countries. Of particular interest were the formal codes to which the broadcasters subscribe.

People involved in the writing and enforcement of codes joined network practices executives in affirming that the most serious and controversial areas of programming usually fall outside the formal stipulations of the codes. The NAB Code of Good Practices in effect admits this.* Such phrases as "A due regard for the composition of the audience," "integrity of such programs," and "good faith on the basis of true instructional and entertainment values" return judgment on controversial programs to a process of assessment of community needs, tastes, and tolerances. This is the same challenge which we in public broadcasting have so long confronted.

In light of these difficulties, the Board decided that a formal code was not the answer to the standards problem. Like any other statement, a code can be only as good as the procedures used to implement it and the faith of those abiding by it.

The PBS Board of Directors turned instead to an effort to describe a framework or process through which the various agencies within the public broadcasting system can develop procedures and generate faith in them. Such a policy will serve three functions:

---

*The Fourteenth Edition of the NAB Television Code (September 1969) states (Section I, Paragraph 7) that: "It is in the public interest of television as a vital medium to encourage and promote the broadcast of programs presenting genuine artistic or literary material, valid moral and social issues, significant controversial and challenging concepts and other

(1) As guidance for the PBS staff in their regular operation of the network;

(2) As guidance to the producing agencies in their production procedures and as to network practices;

(3) As guidance to the member stations on procedures used nationally, and for assistance in coordinating their own efforts with those of other agencies in the system.

The Board was equally concerned lest PBS become no more than a censor for the programming of the producing agencies. Several factors militate against such a role:

(1) The response of public broadcasting to its charge to be innovative, and to present a broad range of opinion on controversial issues, might be weakened;

(2) The recruiting of bold and creative people to the field might be limited by the presence of a formal censoring agency;

(3) The variety of audience needs can best be met by a system which reduces to a minimum the filters of ideas between the producing agency

---

subject matter involving adult themes. Accordingly, none of the provisions of this Code, including those relating to the responsibility toward children, should be construed to prevent or impede their broadcast. All such programs, however, should be broadcast with due regard to the composition of the audience. The highest degree of care should be exercised to preserve the integrity of such programs and to insure that the selection of themes, their treatment and presentation are made in good faith on the basis of true instructional and entertainment values, and not for the purposes of sensationalism, to shock or exploit the audience or to appeal to prurient interests or morbid curiosity.'' [Note: The NAB Code of Good Practices is no longer in effect.]

and the audiences who will see the program;

(4) Formal censoring would diminish the station's options to deal with programming in terms of its local community. A national censor would usurp the right and responsibility of the licensee, a responsibility which is the keystone of the entire public broadcasting system;

(5) Censorship is a purely negative role. In acting on behalf of the stations, PBS should play a more positive and creative role than this.

(6) The passive role of censor, occurring at the conclusion of the program production process, would inevitably lead to the waste of time, money and energy in the production of programs. Sound stewardship of our resources requires instead that a cooperative interplay between PBS and the producers be worked out earlier in the process.

It was determined, then, that PBS' role with the producing agencies must be cooperative. It must be to work with them to meet station needs and to reduce station problems, to develop programming concepts and techniques which will broaden the utility of the medium, rather than reduce it in disputes about the interpretation and enforcement of a detailed code.

1. PRIMARY RESPONSIBILITY FOR THE CONTENT OF PROGRAMMING DISTRIBUTED BY PBS RESTS WITH THE PRODUCING AGENCY.

The very concept of our multiple-input system demands that the primary control over the creative content of national programs remain with the various production agencies. Nevertheless, PBS does have a responsibility to its member stations to assure a high level of program quality and an efficient use of the distribution system. PBS can not abdicate that responsibility and must work with the producers to resolve questions on programs likely to cause problems within the system.

The development of a detailed code of national program standards will not, as the commercial broadcasters understand, of itself resolve the issues involved in controversial programs. Even with a code, many of the most difficult decisions fall back upon a process of judgment as to the program's content, its significance, and the audience for which it is intended.

The challenge remains the development by PBS and the producing agencies of a cooperative process which recognizes the problems inherent in developing and distributing a national program schedule for responsible stations serving audiences of a great diversity. That process depends on the producing agencies' supplying full information to PBS about any possible problems in its programming in ample time for a review of the material in light of the procedures outlined in this paper.

The producing agencies' responsibility for content in no way diminishes the responsibility of PBS to determine, under the terms of this procedure, its course of action in accepting for distribution a program or series offered by a producing agency.

2. IN THOSE AREAS OF CONTENT LIKELY TO CREATE PROBLEMS, PBS AND THE PRODUCING AGENCY SHOULD COOPERATE TO MINIMIZE THE PROBLEMS AND TO ASSURE THE QUALITY OF PROGRAMMING TO BE DISTRIBUTED.

In those controversial and often ill-defined areas either of taste or of law where problems might develop, the production agency should understand that PBS necessarily acts as agent for the stations in working out the problems. PBS should not take lightly its responsibility in this field. It is the network to which the local stations look for leadership in determining the needs of the system and of the stations within it. In this role, the network is responsible for coordinating the development with the production agencies of standards of quality which its member stations as a whole can accept and themselves maintain.

No role in the practices area will be more difficult to perform than this. PBS should become involved with the development at all producing agencies of programming practices which will minimize the need for its own activity in this area, and which will be satisfactory to its members.

A statement of program standards must not become an excuse for avoiding controversy. Public television should not and must not shrink from controversy in an exaggerated exercise of self-restraint. It must have the courage to seek what the Carnegie Commission called the fulfillment of its promise: "to help us look ... at the far reach of our possibilities." It must at the same time assure that this effort maintains the highest standards of integrity and quality. The stations demand of PBS that it play an active role in offering a program service combining comprehensiveness of scope with responsibility of content.

3. PUBLIC BROADCASTING HAS A RESPONSIBILITY FOR STRICT ADHERENCE TO THE CRITERIA OF THE COMMUNICATIONS ACT AND THE PUBLIC BROADCASTING ACT FOR FAIRNESS IN THE TREATMENT OF CONTROVERSIAL ISSUES, AND TO THE HIGHEST STANDARDS OF JOURNALISTIC INTEGRITY.

The station as licensee is ultimately responsible under the law for assuring that its programming is in accordance with Federal statute and regulation. This responsibility neither can nor should be delegated to any other authority. As a practical matter, however, the licensee must rely very heavily on others: on the producer, who alone can exercise detailed review of programming progress; and on PBS, as the "agent in fact" for all the stations in the development of the national program schedule. The licensee needs assurance that it will have their assistance and cooperation in the exercise of its responsibility. PBS should coordinate the efforts of the producers of national programs in the development of a program schedule which will support rather than limit or complicate that local exercise of responsibility. To this end, a satisfactory set of procedures for implementing the highest standards of journalistic integrity in public broadcasting should be developed. Public television's credibility to its audience is as essential as its need to deal with the complex and controversial.

4. PRODUCING AGENCIES MUST AVOID THE IN-CLUSION IN PROGRAMS OF MATERIAL WHICH IS OF QUESTIONABLE TASTE AND WHICH IS NOT REQUIRED BY THE VALID PURPOSE OF THE PROGRAM.

The producing agencies have a clear mandate to deal in an intelligent and mature manner with the controversial and adult themes of the day. Care must be exercised, however, to assure that programs dealing with such themes be produced with an integrity of purpose which avoids both the slipshod and the sensational. Honesty of subject in this age will inevitably raise issues of theme and taste. Such issues must not be raised lightly nor such content be capriciously included in any programming designed for national distribution. All too often, such content weakens a program by distracting the audience from what is journalistically or artistically important in the program.

5. PBS REAFFIRMS ITS RECOGNITION THAT IN-DIVIDUAL TASTE AND LEVELS OF TOLERANCE VARY AND THAT IT MUST PROVIDE SERVICE TO THAT SPECTRUM OF AUDIENCES.

PBS must construct its national schedule to serve the many audiences of public television, including those which the Carnegie Commission referred to as "those that may otherwise be unheard." It must not become entangled in attempts only to gain large instantaneous audiences; yet it must offer programs to increase total audience awareness

and interest in the medium. In developing its schedule, PBS must constantly consider the diverse nature of the audiences of its various stations. It must play its role in full cognizance of the difficulty of seeking single or simple answers to questions of taste.

Varieties in taste and differences in perception must never become an excuse to include unnecessarily questionable material. Recognition of the open nature of the television audience must be exercised by the producer, just as a proper regard for the probable composition of the audience should dictate the times of scheduling by PBS or the stations of material dealing with adult or controversial themes.

6. IN DEALING WITH CONTROVERSIAL AREAS OF TASTE, THE PRODUCING AGENCY MUST BE AWARE OF THE VARIATIONS IN COMMUNITY STANDARDS AND TOLERANCES, AND MAKE EVERY EFFORT TO ELIMINATE LOSS OF CARRIAGE OF PROGRAMMING OF VALUE BY STATIONS WHICH MAY FIND PARTS UNSUITABLE TO THEIR COMMUNITIES.

The goal of the producing agency is to offer programming of quality worth being seen as broadly as possible. The producing agency must understand that taste and tolerances do vary, and that controversial content in a program may color the entire response to that program in some areas. Wherever contractually possible, the producing agency should help the stations to work out problems so that they can carry the programming.

The best solution, in the context of a limited national schedule, would be for the producer to provide alternative versions of a program. The local station could then choose between the original program containing problem material and an edited version. This option allows the local station the fullest choice in evaluating the program against its own community standards. Economics often makes this solution impossible, however. When this is true other choices should be offered the station who may see a problem in the content of a program.

In the case of problems of language, the producing agency, upon prior request by local stations and if its contractual obligations allow, should consider authorizing specified audio-track editing at local stations.

As its own resources or those of the producing agencies permit, PBS should seek to distribute programs suitable for use by the stations as alternatives to those programs included by PBS as part of the regular scheduled service. Provision of such alternative or "shelf" programs is not directly keyed to controversial programs in the schedule; rather, if provided sufficiently in advance, it permits the station to schedule an alternative when and as it deems necessary.

When none of these options is possible, full notification of any problem material should be given in ample time by the producer to PBS, and by PBS to the local stations, and a preview arranged. The local staion can then decide whether or when to schedule the program. When a significant number of stations conclude that they can not carry the scheduled program consistent with local standards, PBS should consider the feasibility of making a substitute program available, either in advance of or instead of the transmission of the scheduled program. PBS should not, however, deny to the stations on grounds of taste the option to broadcast any given program. If a program is removed from the scheduled service on grounds of taste, it should be made available by tape or pre-feed distribution to stations which wish to receive it, subject only to the availability of facilities and an assessment as to the most economic means of distribution.

In every case, ample lead time is necessary for the local station to exercise its options judiciously. The producing agency must provide the network with programs and program information in ample time to assure that these procedures can operate effectively. In no case should the prior release of publicity limit the operation of these procedures or the implementation of them by PBS or the local stations.

7. FRAMING BY MEANS OF NOTIFICATION OF ADULT CONTENT MAY BE DONE AS DEEMED DESIRABLE EITHER BY THE PRODUCING AGENCY OR BY THE LOCAL STATION, IF IT SO CHOOSES AFTER REVIEWING PROGRAM INFORMATION AND CONTENT.

Many stations have found that "framing" a program with a notice of its adult theme or content is often the most useful device for informing the audience of its nature. Those who wish to do so will be supported by ample and accurate program information and preview. Framing should be coupled with proper regard for times of play, nature of likely audience, and the other factors ordinarily considered in the scheduling of programs for mature audiences.

Summary

Precision in the area of standards is difficult, particularly in public television. No model exists for the system which has evolved, and its complexity compounds the difficulty of dealing with an already complicated subject. The level of actual responsibility demanded of the local station in public broadcasting requires an approach flexible enough to leave options open to stations which serve a wide range of communities with differing individual standards. To meet the problems, cooperation and mutual trust are required. The key to working out a satisfactory procedure must remain the good judgment and willingness to cooperate of all the agencies in public broadcasting.

The station must remain the final point of decision in programming as in other ways. This responsibility can not be abdicated, but PBS must work on behalf of the stations to make the exercise of that responsibility as rational and as satisfactory as difficult times allow.

A sensitivity to the stations' responsibilities and circumstances must guide the agencies which produce and distribute the national public television programming. The normal process of production includes a responsibility for advance consultation and cooperation with PBS, and for an ability to meet the disciplines of a schedule of delivery which will allow stations to perform their judgmental function responsibly. The decision to leave primary responsibility for the content of programming with the producing agency assumes an obligation on its part to work with the other agencies in the system to develop the most effective and satisfactory service possible.

In order for the system to work, it is absolutely essential that there be developed and maintained a clear, rapid and full flow of information among the agencies concerned. Such a flow of information, specific and regular, will assure that refinement of the system of program development, production, and delivery can continue toward the goal of satisfying all parties to the programming process.

Finally, for public broadcasting to succeed, it must have as its cornerstone a general confidence in its journalistic quality and artistic integrity. We work in a system of unusual mutual accountability and cooperative involvement. Unless we can maintain a faith in one another and a trust in our willingness to meet the needs of our ill-defined "public," which includes all people in that range of audiences we so often discuss, our system can not continue to grow in service.

PUBLIC BROADCASTING SERVICE
DOCUMENT OF JOURNALISM STANDARDS AND GUIDELINES*

Recommended by the Journalism Advisory Board, November 15, 1971
Adopted by the Board of Directors, PBS, March 6, 1972
Adopted (with amendments) by the Members, PBS, April 6, 1972

Preamble

Public television is an independent system, mandated to serve many diverse audiences, both local and national. To win and hold their confidence, its programming must reflect the highest standards of courage, responsibility, integrity and fairness.

Television has emerged as the most immediate and emotionally compelling source of news and information for American society. This confers upon public broadcasting a special responsibility together with a positive advantage. Unlike its commercial counterparts, public broadcasting does not sell time for profit; it is free of the cost-per-thousand tyranny that forces commercial broadcasting to pursue audience mass.

In consequence of this advantage, public broadcasting has the unending obligation to experiment and innovate. It can devote the time—and must develop the formats—to overcome certain built-in failings of lowest-common-denominator programming: the tendency to oversimplify and thereby to distort complicated matters; or to fall back upon the conventional wisdom because it is safe.

There is no single American public. There are many. Public broadcasting has both the opportunity and the responsibility of letting those many voices be heard across the land. Because it draws on public funds and uses the public airways, the system cannot turn a deaf ear to any segment of the American audience. Accordingly, public broadcasting must:

*Courtesy of the Public Broadcasting Service.

—Find ways, through increasingly sophisticated programming procedures, to increase the access to the airways for the many publics in its audience as they seek an increasing participation in the broadcast process.

—Explore significant subjects, including those of comparatively little appeal to the mass audience.

—Be bold and strong enough to treat sensitive and complex issues, even at the risk of occasional failures.

—Honestly reflect the controversies and concerns of the society it serves.

Television generally has entered a period of intense introspection. Our audiences have grown more keenly aware of television's power, more concerned with its impact, more questioning of its contents and techniques. As class, race, and political conflicts have sharpened, broadcasters have felt impelled to explore thorny subjects and their work has increasingly provoked resentment or skepticism among viewers.

In this new critical climate, public broadcasting must rise to the challenge of the times. Courageous and responsible treatment of public affairs is a prime responsibility of every individual and producing organization within the public broadcasting system. Complicated, confused issues demand clarification, not evasion. Broadcasting—be it public or commercial—has no responsible choice but to report the tensions, disagreements and divisions of our American society today.

To provide less than the most energetic, responsible investigative journalism would in these times shrivel public broadcasting's spirit and ultimately erode its reason for existence.

Standards

Truth is an elusive target. The journalist does not deal in absolutes, neither absolute truth nor absolute objectivity. Because news is by nature fragmentary, the broadcast journalist must in all humility recognize that at any given moment he is bound to possess something less than the whole truth. He works within the limitations imposed by time, talent, energy and perception. Yet the search for truth must go on in full awareness that— like the perfect vacuum—it will remain beyond his grasp. This unending search calls for an open mind, conscious efforts to correct for one's own prejudices, and continuous adherence to the highest standards of journalism.

Therefore:

—WE RECOGNIZE THE OBLIGATION TO BE FAIR. Our first duty is to the viewer. For him, we must neither oversimplify complex situations, nor camouflage straightforward truths. We will not misrepresent or distort the facts.

The men and women who are the subjects of our programs equally deserve fair treatment. Their participation will only be won through a widespread belief that people appearing on public broadcasting are treated with respect and with appreciation for their points of view.

Finally, we must be fair to our colleagues. Those who do the research, interviewing and reporting are entitled to know that their original work will not be distorted to produce the finished program.

—WE PLEDGE TO STRIVE FOR BALANCED PROGRAMMING. Even in public broadcasting, the constraint of time and the complexity of subject matter conspire against balance within one news segment or program. The broadcaster must aim to achieve balance over the full range of programming. No simple, precise formula, such as "equal time," can guarantee this. In fact, heavy reliance on the stopwatch concept of balance can do disservice to the viewer by distorting complex relationships and undermining the role of intelligent journalism—to make sense out of confused and complicated issues. Most serious issues pose many "sides," not just two starkly opposed views that can be accommodated by a neat, even treatment.

Balance requires the honest, unceasing effort to recognize and represent this full range of views. It demands that the broadcaster direct his attention not only to internal treatment of subject matter, but also to the broad sweep of programming. He must ask himself if he has made an honest effort to apply both of these tests: Has he handled the internal content fairly? Is there an imbalance of specific issues or points of view? The answers to these questions represent the most subjective of judgments, but honest recognition of the problem is the best, indeed the only, solution.

—WE RECOGNIZE THE OBLIGATION TO STRIVE FOR OBJECTIVITY. Complete objectivity, like balance, is an evasive, unattainable ideal, limited by human emotion. But the quest for objectivity also sharpens our intelligence and gives meaning to our work. Reporters and production teams can naturally and legitimately start with a hypothesis; they abandon their professionalism when they refuse to revise that hypothesis in the light of contrary evidence. Such a commitment freezes the interchange of ideas, inhibiting thorough and thoughtful investigation. Objectivity demands an unconditional allegiance to accuracy; it permits no room for distortion by conscious manipulation of selected facts. But objective, honest reporting is more than a mechanical process of collecting raw data. If it requires conscientious attention to detail and honest commitment to inquiry, objectivity also imposes on the journalist the obligation to indicate trends and to identify conclusions that may naturally emerge from his work.

—WE ACKNOWLEDGE THE OBLIGATION NOT TO LET TECHNIQUE BECOME THE MASTER OF SUBSTANCE. Television, the most expressive of the public media, is especially vulnerable to abuse. Neither people nor ideas deserve to be victimized by technical trickery. For broadcasters, this approach can only be self-defeating, diverting attention—as it inevitably will—from central issues to peripheral detail. Like the admonition to achieve balance, awareness of the danger remains the best defense against its practice.

—WE RECOGNIZE THE OBLIGATION TO REFLECT VOICES BOTH INSIDE AND OUTSIDE SOCIETY'S EXISTING CONSENSUS. The surest road to intellectual stagnation and social isolation is to stifle the expression of uncommon ideas. Today's dissent may be tomorrow's orthodoxy. The broadcaster should never ridicule an idea or belief in the guise of objective reporting. To examine these ideas critically is part of the broadcaster's role; he cannot fulfill it if he does not conscientiously attempt to understand those ideas—and the forces that created them.

Recommended Guidelines

There is no simple formula for translating these standards into practice. Any set of guidelines, no matter how elaborately conceived, would fall short of anticipating even a fraction of the actual situations with which broadcasters must contend daily; any list of detailed restrictions would probably stifle creativity and imagination.

Nor could any list hope to fit the needs of the dozens of production centers and stations that comprise the public broadcasting system. Local tastes vary; wide differences in program subjects and constant developments in broadcasting techniques further compound the difficulty of drafting comprehensive guidelines. Local stations and production centers should develop their own manuals of guidelines, constantly reviewing their current practices to assure that past lessons do not go unheeded. Public broadcasting, if it is to achieve its potential, must participate in a constant process of self-education.

Nevertheless, certain areas present dangers so frequently that they merit explicit warning:

1. Television is an extraordinarily powerful instrument, and the mere presence of television cameras can change, or influence, events. Broadcasters must minimize and, to the extent possible, eliminate this interference. In crowd situations or demonstrations, camera crews and production teams should attempt to remain inconspicuous;

when their presence excites an extreme reaction, they should consider withdrawing or capping their lenses. Even in less dramatic circumstances, broadcasters will be the constant target of manipulative attempts by outsiders. In no circumstances must broadcasters encourage this manipulation by deliberately staging events or suggesting that others stage events for the sake of broadcast coverage. There may be instances when recreations or simulations are necessary and desirable; in fairness to the viewer, whenever these situations raise the possibility of misrepresentation, they must be clearly identified.

2. All journalists face the necessity of selection—which material is to be left in, which is to be edited out. No journalist could possibly aspire to high standards of objective and balanced reporting without amassing far more information—written, oral, or visual—than limitations of time or space allow him to present his audience. Reducing and organizing this information is the journalist's craft.

The broadcaster's problem is especially difficult, because his edited material is likely to give the impression of continuous reality. The broadcaster's standard in editing interview or film sequences is to remain faithful in both tone and substance to the original. In interviews, questions and answers must not be edited or transposed to distort the full meaning of a subject's remarks. In splicing film segments, broadcasters must never sensationalize events or create a misleading version of what actually occurred; when relevant interruptions of time or changes of setting occur, they should be unambiguously identified to the viewer.

3. The credibility of the broadcasting process is jeopardized whenever the viewer or the news subject is duped—or feels duped. Candor and common courtesy must govern broadcasters' behavior. For the viewer, broadcasters must distinguish clearly between news and commentary.

4. Our legal system presumes that criminal defendants are innocent until proven guilty. Broadcasters should act to reinforce this precept. They should remain cautious about devoting excessive amounts of air time to pretrial publicity, remembering that the media can create an atmosphere that may endanger the defendant's constitutional right to a fair trial. Broadcasters should be wary of self-serving statements from both prosecutors and defense attorneys; the use of alleged evidence on pretrial broadcasts also demands constant review.

* * * *

Broadcasting is not a science. The honesty of a broadcast, accordingly, can never be measured by precise and mathematical standards. Even when broadcasters can agree on guiding principles, disagreements over what those principles mean—and whether they are being met—will persist. The elusiveness of these goals should inspire a sense of humility and high purpose. In the end, the quality of programming must depend on the broadcaster's professionalism—his independence, his integrity, his sound judgment, and his common sense.

CODE OF BROADCAST NEWS ETHICS
RADIO TELEVISION NEWS DIRECTORS ASSOCIATION*

The members of the Radio Television News Directors Association agree that their prime responsibility as journalists—and that of the broadcasting industry as the collective sponsor of news broadcasting—is to provide to the public they serve a news service as accurate, full and prompt as human integrity

---

*Courtesy of the Radio Television News Directors Association.

and devotion can devise. To that end, they declare their acceptance of the standards of practice here set forth, and their solemn intent to honor them to the limits of their ability.

Article One

The primary purpose of broadcast journalists—to inform the public of events of importance and appropriate interest in a manner that is accurate and comprehensive—shall override all other purposes.

Article Two

Broadcast news presentations shall be designed not only to offer timely and accurate information, but also to present it in the light of relevant circumstances that give it meaning and perspective.

This standard means that news reports, when clarity demands it, will be laid against pertinent factual background; that factors such as race, creed, nationality or prior status will be reported only when they are relevant; that comment or subjective content will be properly identified; and that errors in fact will be promptly acknowledged and corrected.

Article Three

Broadcast journalists shall seek to select material for newscast solely on their evaluation of its merits as news.

This standard means that news will be selected on the criteria of significance, community and regional relevance, appropriate human interest, service to defined audiences. It excludes sensationalism or misleading emphasis in any form; subservience to external or "interested" efforts to influence news selection and presentation, whether from within the broadcasting industry or from without. It requires that such terms as "bulletin" and "flash" be used only when the character of the news justifies them; that bombastic or misleading descriptions of newsroom facilities and personnel be rejected, along with undue use of sound and visual effects; and that promotional or publicity material be sharply scrutinized before use and identified by source or otherwise when broadcast.

Article Four

Broadcast journalists shall at all times display humane respect for the dignity, privacy and the well-being of persons with whom the news deals.

Article Five

Broadcast journalists shall govern their personal lives and such nonprofessional associations as may impinge on their professional activities in a manner that will protect them from conflict of interest, real or apparent.

Article Six

Broadcast journalists shall seek actively to present all news the knowledge of which will serve the public interest, no matter what selfish, uninformed or corrupt efforts attempt to color it, withhold it or prevent its presentation. They shall make constant effort to open doors closed to the reporting of public proceedings with tools appropriate to broadcasting (including cameras and recorders), consistent with the public interest. They acknowledge the journalist's ethic of protection of confidential information and sources, and urge unswerving observation of it except in instances in which it would clearly and unmistakably defy the public interest.

Article Seven

Broadcast journalists recognize the responsibility borne by broadcasting for informed analysis, comment and editorial opinion on public events and issues. They accept the obligation of broadcasters, for the presentation of such matters by individuals whose competence, experience and judgment qualify them for it.

Article Eight

In court, broadcast journalists shall conduct themselves with dignity, whether the court is in or out of session. They shall keep broadcast equipment as unobtrusive and silent as possible. Where court facilities are inadequate, pool broadcasts should be arranged.

Article Nine

In reporting matters that are or may be litigated, the journalist shall avoid practices which would tend to interfere with the right of an individual to a fair trial.

Article Ten

Broadcast journalists shall not misrepresent the source of any broadcast news material.

Article Eleven

Broadcast journalists shall actively censure and seek to prevent violations of these standards, and shall actively encourage their observance by all journalists, whether of the Radio Television News Directors Association or not.

CODE OF ETHICS*

THE SOCIETY of Professional Journalists, Sigma Delta Chi, believes the duty of journalists is to serve the truth.

WE BELIEVE the agencies of mass communication are carriers of public discussion and information, acting on their Constitutional mandate and freedom to learn and report the facts.

WE BELIEVE in public enlightenment as the forerunner of justice, and in our Constitutional role to seek the truth as part of the public's right to know the truth.

WE BELIEVE those responsibilities carry obligations that require journalists to perform with intelligence, objectivity, accuracy and fairness.

To these ends, we declare acceptance of the standards of practice here set forth:

Responsibility:

The public's right to know of events of public importance and interest is the overriding mission of the mass media. The purpose of distributing news and enlightened opinion is to serve the general welfare. Journalists who use their professional status as representatives of the public for selfish or other unworthy motives violate a high trust.

Freedom of the Press

Freedom of the press is to be guarded as an inalienable right of people in a free society. It carries with it the freedom and the responsibility to discuss, question and challenge actions and utterances of our government and of our public and private institutions. Journalists uphold the right to speak unpopular opinions and the privilege to agree with the majority.

---

*Courtesy of the Society of Professional Journalists, Sigma Delta Chi.

Ethics:

Journalists must be free of obligation to any interest other than the public's right to know the truth.

1. Gifts, favors, free travel, special treatment or privileges can compromise the integrity of journalists and their employers. Nothing of value should be accepted.

2. Secondary employment, political involvement, holding public office and service in community organizations should be avoided if it compromises the integrity of journalists and their employers. Journalists and their employers should conduct their personal lives in a manner which protects them from conflict of interest, real or apparent. Their responsibilities to the public are paramount. This is the nature of their profession.

3. So-called news communications from private sources should not be published or broadcast without substantiation of their claims to news value.

4. Journalists will seek news that serves the public interest, despite the obstacles. They will make constant efforts to assure that the public's business is conducted in public and that public records are open to public inspection.

5. Journalists acknowledge the newsman's ethic of protecting confidential sources of information.

Accuracy and Objectivity:

Good faith with the public is the foundation of all worthy journalism.

1. Truth is our ultimate goal.

2. Objectivity in reporting the news is another goal which serves as the mark of an experienced professional. It is a standard of performance toward which we strive. We honor those who achieve it.

3. There is no excuse for inaccuracies or lack of thoroughness.

4. Newspaper headlines should be fully warranted by the contents of the articles they accompany. Photographs and telecasts should give an accurate picture of an event and not highlight a minor incident out of context.

5. Sound practice makes clear distinction between news reports and expressions of opinion. News reports should be free of opinion or bias and represent all sides of an issue.

6. Partisanship in editorial comment which knowingly departs from the truth violates the spirit of American journalism.

7. Journalists recognize their responsibility for offering informed analysis, comment and editorial opinion on public events and issues. They accept the obligation to present such material by individuals whose competence, experience and judgment qualify them for it.

8. Special articles or presentations devoted to advocacy or the writer's own conclusions and interpretations should be labeled as such.

Fair Play:

Journalists at all times will show respect for the dignity, privacy, rights and well-being of people encountered in the course of gathering and presenting the news.

1. The news media should not communicate unofficial charges affecting reputation or moral character without giving the accused a chance to reply.

2. The news media must guard against invading a person's right to privacy.

3. The media should not pander to morbid curiosity about details of vice and crime.

4. It is the duty of news media to make prompt and complete correction of their errors.

5. Journalists should be accountable to the public for their reports and the public should be encouraged to voice its grievances against the media. Open dialogue with our readers, viewers and listeners should be fostered.

Pledge:

Journalists should actively censure and try to prevent violations of these standards, and they should encourage their observance by all newspeople. Adherence to this code of ethics is intended to preserve the bond of mutual trust and respect between American journalists and the American people.

Adopted 1926, revised 1973.

INDEX